k for yourself"
Prenti ll – Philosophy

Prentice Hall's *Basic Ethics in Action* series includes both wide-ranging anthologies and brief texts that focus on a particular theme or topic.

Anchor volume
Michael Boylan, *Basic Ethics*, 2000

Business Ethics

Michael Boylan, ed., *Business Ethics*, 2001

Patrick Murphy, Gene R. Laczniak, Norman E. Bowie, & Thomas A. Klein, *Ethical Marketing*, 2005

Dale Jacquette, *Journalistic Ethics: Moral Responsibility in the Media*, 2007

Joseph R. DesJardins, *Business, Ethics, and the Environment*, 2007

Environmental Ethics

Michael Boylan, ed., *Environmental Ethics*, 2001

Lisa H. Newton, *Ethics and Sustainability: Sustainable Development and the Moral Life*, 2003

J. Baird Callicott & Michael Nelson, *American Indian Environmental Ethics: An Ojibwa Case Study*, 2004

Medical Ethics

Michael Boylan, ed., *Medical Ethics*, 2000

Michael Boylan & Kevin Brown, *Genetic Engineering: Science and Ethics on the New Frontier*, 2002

Rosemarie Tong, *New Perspectives in Healthcare Ethics*, 2007

Social and Political Philosophy

Seumas Miller, Peter Roberts, & Edward Spence, *Corruption and Anti-Corruption: An Applied Philosophical Approach*, 2005

Journalistic Ethics

Moral Responsibility in the Media

DALE JACQUETTE
The Pennsylvania State University

PEARSON
Prentice
Hall

Upper Saddle River, New Jersey 07458

Library of Congress Cataloging-in-Publication Data

Jacquette, Dale.
  Journalistic ethics : moral responsibility in the media / Dale Jacquette.
     p. cm. — (Basic ethics in action)
  Includes index.
  ISBN-13: 978-0-13-182539-0
  ISBN-10: 0-13-182539-9
  1. Journalistic ethics. I. Title.
  PN4756.J33 2007
  174'.907—dc22

2006032461

Editorial Director: Charlyce Jones-Owen
Editor-in-Chief: Sarah Touborg
Senior Acquisitions Editor: Mical
  Moser
Editorial Assistant: Carla Worner
Director of Marketing: Brandy Dawson
Assistant Marketing Manager: Andrea
  Messineo
Marketing Assistant: Bekim Perolli

Managing Editor: Joanne Riker
Production Liaison: Joanne Hakim
Manufacturing Buyer: Christina Amato
Cover Art Director: Jayne Conte
Full-Service Project Management:
  Suganya Karuppasamy/GGS Book
  Services
Printer/Binder: RR Donnelley & Sons
  Company

Credits and acknowledgments borrowed from other sources and reproduced, with
permission, in this textbook appear on appropriate page within text.

Pearson Education LTD., London
Pearson Education Singapore, Pte. Ltd
Pearson Education, Canada, Ltd
Pearson Education–Japan
Pearson Education Australia
  PTY, Limited

Pearson Education North Asia Ltd
Pearson Educación de Mexico, S.A. de C.V.
Pearson Education Malaysia, Pte. Ltd
Pearson Education, Upper Saddle River,
  New Jersey

10 9 8 7 6 5 4 3 2 1
ISBN 0-13-182539-9

for Tina

Contents

Chapter Nine

Afterword

Appendices

Preface

Journalism is merely history's first draft.
—Geoffrey C. Ward

This book offers a critical exploration of key concepts and typical moral decision-making scenarios in journalistic ethics. It is intended for college students in applied ethics courses, for journalism students at all levels, and for anyone interested in the moral problems encountered by professional news reporting and the moral standards to which we can reasonably expect professional journalism to aspire.

The chapters introduce moral concepts and discuss moral problems arising for professional journalists. Illustrated throughout with contemporary journalistic case studies and historical background information, each topic is approached from a dual practical standpoint. The book considers moral choices facing working journalists at the production end of the news and its impact on news consumers at the receiving end. We assume that the moral responsibility of professional journalists is primarily to their readership or audience whose vital interests are potentially affected by the quality of daily news reporting. Journalists are morally responsible to the public whose informed decision-making and other aspects of their welfare can depend essentially on the relevant truth content of news reports. It is in terms of the news audience that journalistic ethics must primarily speak, for the sake of those whom the reporting of news events is ultimately meant to serve and on whose lives its content can exert a profound influence for good or bad.

We begin by identifying basic ideals for a journalistic ethics. We ask why it is that journalistic ethics is needed and how it could be of help to practicing journalists and the public they serve. Where does the right to gather the information journalists deem as newsworthy come from? What other rights, sometimes thought to include freedom from censorship and political interference and protection of confidential news informants, are implied by the most basic of journalistic rights to discover and disseminate information? From what fundamental moral values or concepts do journalistic responsibilities derive? How, exactly, are journalistic rights and responsibilities related? How can we be sure that there are good reasons standing behind the kinds of activities that journalists are asked to carry out or that they are forbidden from doing on pain of violating professional moral standards? The lists of what professional journalists should try to do and what they should try to avoid that appear in journalistic ethics codes, such as the representative samples attached as Appendices near the end of this book, turn up at best only at the end of a philosophical inquiry into the obligations that are relevant to the profession. It is only after we have looked critically into the questions posed in this book and satisfied ourselves that we understand whether and why journalists have certain moral rights and responsibilities that we will be in a good position to judge for ourselves the appropriateness of the rules of behavior for members of the press that professional journalists have devised and whether or not journalists can have defensible reasons for accepting any of their codes of professional conduct.

That principles of professional journalistic ethics of one sort or another are essential should be obvious enough. For the truth is that journalists wield enormous power. They are regarded internationally as a source of accurate information that begins with intelligent, aggressive investigative reporting. What they say in relatively free press societies is supposed to be capable of being credibly relied upon from the lowest to the highest level of decision-making across a vast clientele. If we consider the implications of making important decisions on the deliberately false report of a rogue journalist, then we begin to get a sense of the reasons why professional ethical standards are needed. Accordingly, we must consider the reasons that have persuaded journalists of the need for a professional ethics code. This, in turn, requires a carefully thought-through journalistic ethics code in a more searching philosophical sense.

When journalists exercise their professional rights they incur professional responsibilities. This book invites the reader to ask how these various aspects of a journalist's professional work are interrelated. The subject before us, as a result, is part business ethics, part personal virtue ethics, and part philosophical theories of knowledge. We shall make use of at least as much common sense as any exploration of practical affairs might require, without dodging important theoretical questions that ought to be of interest to everyone affected by how the news is reported. We must ask many questions and be persistent in trying to find the right answers. Among other things, we must ask whether the standard of truth we require of journalists is realistically attainable. We must inquire about the concept of freedom of the press and its scope and limits if journalism, as traditionally understood, is to be defined as truth telling about current events in the public interest. We must ask about the scope and limits of censorship, protection of confidential sources, objectivity, perspective and bias, editorial license, and the moral role of news editing. We must inquire about the special ethical problems that are posed for journalists who are also committed to the functioning of a for-profit business or at least a nonprofit but still cost-conscious news organization. In the process, we shall present a positive moral ideal for journalism as a force for social good.

If truth telling with appropriate qualifications is a realistic moral aspiration for professional journalists, as in the end we shall argue, then striving to satisfy the requirements of journalistic integrity is to fulfill the profession's noblest expectations at the same time that it continues to provide the most reliable route to lasting recognition of genuine journalistic talent.

I am grateful to Michael Boylan for inviting me to contribute this volume on journalistic ethics to his applied ethics series at Prentice Hall. I thank the following societies and associations for permission to reprint current formulations of their ethics codes or statements or governing principles of professional journalistic conduct in whole or in part, as indicated in the appendices: The Society of Professional Journalists, the International Federation of Journalists, the Associated Press Managing Editors, and the Radio-Television News Directors Association. I would like to thank Christopher Hanson, University of Maryland, for reviewing this manuscript. I also wish to thank Suganya Karuppasamy for overseeing the typesetting and production of the book and guiding it to publication. My wife Tina, who on general principles deserves as much praise as I can decently commit to print, earns special thanks this time for lending her formidable research skills to locating background information for many of the journalistic case studies included in the chapters. The Netherlands Institute for Advanced Study in the Humanities and Social Sciences (NIAS), Royal Netherlands Academy of Arts and Sciences (KNAW), generously provided a resident research fellowship in support of this among other projects during the academic year 2005–2006.

Journalistic Ethics

Introduction

What Journalists Do

NEWS INFORMATION

If we ask why there are journalists, the obvious answer is that journalists provide an essential news information service. We make decisions in many areas of our lives on the basis of information that we do not have the resources and expertise to collect on our own, for which we depend daily on professional journalists. Journalists gather and report the news for us to use. Like any precious and potentially dangerous substance, purity of information is a primary concern. We see in the first part of this book that all journalistic ethics can be summed up in the injunction for journalists to provide *maximally relevant truth telling in the public interest.*

What journalists primarily do is to discover and report the facts of the world. Such an innocent seeming description already raises important philosophical issues that are directly relevant to the world of professional journalism. If we propose to hold journalists morally responsible for the truth content of their reporting, then we must make sure that we are not asking journalists to do something that they cannot do. The general principle, first articulated by the philosopher Immanuel Kant in the late eighteenth century, is that "ought" implies "can."[1] The principle entails that persons cannot be held morally responsible for failing to do something that was not in their power. According to Kant's principle, we are only morally obligated with respect to things we can actually do. Intuitively, this restriction seems right. I should not be held morally responsible for not stopping a devastating earthquake because it is not in my ability to control such powerful natural forces. In order to know whether we can hold journalists morally responsible for telling the truth, we similarly need to ask philosophical questions about whether truth is something attainable, or in what exact sense of the word we can expect journalists to try always to tell the truth.

Truth telling in the public interest is a noble ideal. Like other abstract ideals, it risks conflict with real-life pressures. There are moral issues for

---

[1]Kant, "The Metaphysics of Morals" in Kant, *Practical Philosophy*, p. 513.

1

professional journalists that arise in particular from the fact that news publishing or broadcasting in most instances is also a business. Unfortunately, we cannot simply point to a well-received theory of business ethics and apply it directly to the special problems of journalism. The difference between journalism and other kinds of business has to do with the specific kind of product or service that professional journalism provides. Journalism fulfills its responsibility to deliver true information in the public interest only to the extent that there is respect and protection for a free press. This means that for the most part a free press society expects the government not to interfere in reporting the news, but to be as cooperative with journalists as their other conceivably more vital obligations permit. There are many ways in which this type of journalistic freedom, like any kind of freedom, can be abused in the effort to turn a profit. Bringing the news to readers and viewers takes money and makes some people, especially investors, advertisers, and certain producers and reporters, an enormous amount of money. It is a big business with business ethics issues of its own that are not immediately relevant to the news industry in its dealings with conditions outside the newsroom. We must nevertheless not lose sight of the fact that journalism can be as much a dog-eat-dog business as a conscientious vocation. The fact that news information is bought and sold as a commodity within the news industry by itself does not mean that it is automatically suspect. This book is intended to help interested readers think carefully about what we as news consumers want from the news and about how we think news investigators and reporters should conduct themselves in bringing us the news. If we are sensible throughout this inquiry, however, then we should not expect the news to be altogether detached from the sorts of financial pressures prevailing generally throughout the culture.

We pay for the news in many ways, whether we know it or not. We do so when we subscribe to a cable network that includes news programming as much as if we subscribe in the old-fashioned way to the local newspaper or newsmagazines. We do so even if we get our news online and are simply exposed to advertising on a web page or in pop-ups. One way or another, as consumers of news while it *is* news, we pay for the information we receive. That, moreover, is probably how it should be in a market-regulated exchange of value for value. The problem of whether news reporting is best pursued as a business is not at issue here, particularly if we answer the question about why there are journalists as we have above. Nor are we here to question the root or fruit of journalism in the context of modern capitalism as a topic for journalistic ethics. The questions we want to raise in this book concern the morality of practicing professional journalists within prevailing political and economic realities, rather than in the dream world of a moral utopia. The point of establishing a moral ideal, even one with sufficient grit to apply more or less directly to the real world, is nevertheless that if an attainable ideal were actually to be adopted by the journalistic community, then a beneficial moral order would begin to prevail in the field that could set a powerful example for others. A good moral principle, if it makes sense to enough people and is followed in practice as a standard of professional conduct, can contribute to progressive change in the world. If it cannot bring about a moral utopia, it can at least help to make things better.

MORAL RIGHTS AND RESPONSIBILITIES

Journalists have special moral rights and correspondingly special moral responsibilities. The same is true, with respect to a different but related set of rights and responsibilities, of news consumers. The picture of journalistic ethics that this book paints is one in which the work of professional journalists provides a unique service in discovering and communicating useful facts to all who might responsibly profit from the information. The moral imperative of professional journalism, its purpose, and what it requires of its practitioners, we shall argue, is to provide relevant truth telling in the public interest. All journalistic rights and responsibilities, every moral principle that we shall discuss in this book, derive from this single statement of the journalist's professional calling.

When professional ethics is examined from a philosophical perspective, the point is never simply to present a list of dos and don'ts for specialists to follow if they want their professional conduct to be considered morally correct. There are in fact codes of ethics consisting of just such guidelines for what professional journalists consider to be ethically proper professional journalistic behavior, each prepared by a different professional journalistic society and reflecting their perspective on moral values relating to the news. Professional journalistic ethics codes fulfill an important function, by helping to spell out and reminding journalists about the moral choices they are likely to face in reporting the news and by providing them with a sense of their responsibilities and what is expected of them in the pursuit of their duties. They are generally required by such codes to report the news accurately, after which they are typically cautioned about specific kinds of temptations to steer clear of in order to avoid being guilty of professional misconduct. Codes of ethics provide valuable insight into what journalists perceive as the limits within which they think it is necessary to try to regulate the ways news is gathered, edited, and reported. In glancing at the lists of moral advice in professional journalistic ethics codes in the Appendices, we see that they represent high ideals for news reporting and warn journalists about some of the moral hazards they might confront; in effect, as we have said, they amount to a list of what journalists are to do and not to do. Merely presenting practicing and prospective journalists with a list of dos and don'ts is nevertheless not enough to provide what we shall mean here by *journalistic ethics*. Moral instruction in the form of a professional ten commandments, however valuable a touchstone it might be for a journalist pursuing his or her career, does not begin to explain or justify *why* any given set of rules is appropriate. Why should a journalist entering the profession agree that these are good principles? Why should a journalist choose to honor these particular professional moral guidelines, even if we assume they are right, especially if they conflict with another desired object?

To address these kinds of questions we must first clarify the aim and purpose of journalism and uncover the philosophical basis of journalistic moral rights and responsibilities. What exactly is it that journalists as journalists are supposed to do? If proper journalistic practice has something to do with discovering and reporting facts, in the sense of truths expressed by true sentences, then we must ask probing questions about the nature and existence of truths, true facts or sentences, and whether truth is something attainable by human beings. In this effort, we are in a way doing the same kinds of things that professional journalists do in order to discover the facts they report in the news, although our topic is not current events but moral concepts and advice for practicing journalists.

Journalism as a knowledge-seeking endeavor obliges philosophers in particular to ask about the *epistemology* or *knowledge theory* status of news reporting. Approaching these problems for the first time, it is an open question for philosophy as to whether there are attainable standards of truth and knowledge in what is supposed to be truthful reporting of the news. The news community and its respective audiences, as far as their members can usually tell, seem to proceed in their business with perfect confidence, as though the concepts of fact, truth, and knowledge were well understood and generally accepted. Nor need we, in examining problems of journalistic ethics philosophically, feel compelled to dispute this implicit assumption. We merely want to know: What are the rules of journalistic truth telling, and do they stand up to philosophical scrutiny? Presumably, we cannot morally require journalists to report the news truthfully if there is no philosophically intelligible concept of knowledge or truth. How then should we proceed? Should we simply accept whatever passes for journalistic truth among professional journalists and adopt the same conditions as a basis for judging whether or not a given journalist is fulfilling or violating a trusted principle of journalistic ethics? What about the effect of individual perceptual and cultural perspective or bias as obstacles to journalistic objectivity? If there is no such thing as genuinely objective truthful reportage of news events, how can we possibly hold particular journalists morally responsible for falling short of what is at best for them, as it would be for anyone else, an impossible unattainable standard? What are professional journalists morally responsible for doing in that case in reporting the news? We do as a matter of fact frequently hold journalists morally responsible for the truth content of their news reporting. In developing a philosophical investigation of the main problems of journalistic ethics, we now want to ask whether we are right to do so. If the answer is yes, then we must further inquire to what standard of truth we expect to be able to hold journalists as public truth tellers responsible. What, if anything, can a philosopher, drawing on key ideas of theoretical epistemology, say to help clarify a journalist's practical intellectual and moral situation?

In due course we shall address all of these among many other questions. We shall try to present sound philosophical reasons to accept a standard of truth that journalists in practice can reasonably attain and to a high degree actually succeed in attaining. We shall also find ourselves substantially in agreement with the spirit of the ethics codes that societies and institutes of professional journalists have developed. We shall then be in a strong position from which to conclude that journalists have a moral responsibility to collect newsworthy facts about world events and report them accurately and in a timely way to whoever desires to know. We all crucially depend on such knowledge; we rely on the truth content of news reports in the course of our daily lives. Since knowledge is also power, as Francis Bacon observed already in the seventeenth century, information provided by journalists is also potentially dangerous to individuals and societies. Accordingly, we expect and demand, as a humanly attainable moral objective, that the press report the news both truthfully and expeditiously in the public interest. This fact alone makes it mandatory to ask whether truth is a mysterious concept, something so elusive that we can never hope to touch it in our desire for knowledge, or whether it is what any news consumer on the street would say marks the difference between true and false news, simply on the basis of whether or not what the reports convey actually happened.

We should try to project ourselves into the perspective of practicing professional journalists in order to understand the moral dilemmas with which they must cope. This will be easy if we are already working as journalists embarked on a professional career or studying to become professional journalists. Other readers will need to imagine that they are news investigators, reporters, or editors, working in the field. What, then, shall we take as our moral standards for professional conduct as journalists? If as journalists we hope not only to earn our bread or have a satisfying career but to contribute to the social good, then what kinds of actions are morally supportable as contributing to benefit the world? What kinds of actions would be morally objectionable? We can maintain moral ideals, if we are strong, and try energetically to live up to them, even in circumstances that do not clearly encourage or reward virtue. The extent to which we are able under difficult conditions to approximate a moral ideal provides a standard by which our professional journalistic conduct can be evaluated. We must therefore consider carefully what a moral ideal for journalism should look like and set a practical target of compliance with the minimal moral

requirements for responsible news reporting. It is important to establish a
well-demarcated division between what is morally justified and what is
morally unjustified for journalists to do in gathering and reporting news
information. A working journalist wants to proceed with confidence within a
set of clear-cut moral boundaries, if they are judged acceptable, and try his or
her best thereafter not to stray beyond professional moral limits. Journalists,
in short, would like to know in concrete terms that it would be okay to do
this, but morally wrong to do that. So would we all. The answers, interestingly but also somewhat frustratingly, are not always that easy. Moral problems of real life unfortunately are often more resistant to untangling than
anything to be found in a book. Written explorations of ideas with all their
limitations can nevertheless also play an important role in charting a life of
moral progress by challenging us to think about hypothetical situations that
are sufficiently similar to the problems we are likely to encounter in actual
circumstances.

We typify for explanatory purposes when we try to articulate
an abstract theory. This is true not only in philosophy, including ethics, but
in physics, chemistry, biology, psychology, and the social sciences. There is a
danger of oversimplifying our reactions to what can actually happen
to a person caught in a moral dilemma or involved in a serious moral
transgression. Thinking about the problems that might be encountered in
practice, and what moral quandaries can mean with respect to the credibility of the profession and its potential effects on the interests of other
persons, can help prepare journalists to avoid a host of similar kinds of situations that might be morally compromising or blameworthy. Generally, we
avoid such embarrassments by trying our best to do the morally right thing,
depending on what we recognize as moral responsibilities. Often, we may
believe we know by gut instinct or proper upbringing what it is right or
wrong to do. All the same, we improve our chances of arriving at sound
moral judgments if we try to understand our moral compulsions to do or
refrain from doing something by codifying these principles in language and
considering their implications. It is very much in our interests for all of
these reasons to begin thinking rigorously about what is and what is not the
morally right or wrong thing for professional journalists to do. By reflecting
on some of the obvious moral lessons of selected case studies we sharpen
our sensitivity to the moral nuances and implications of real-world moral
decision-making.

MORAL PROBLEMS FOR JOURNALISTIC ETHICS

Whether we are journalists ourselves, aspire to become journalists, or are
simply glued to the tube whenever the news comes on, as informed citizens
we need to be alert to the moral problems confronting news investigators
and reporters. We all have a vital stake in truthful, accurate, timely, and

socially responsible news. What are these responsibilities, and how should they be thought of as a particular chapter of professional ethics?

Anyone who follows the news regularly may come to recognize that moral issues arise for practicing journalists every day. There are problems about what stories to report and how to report them, conflicts and moral dilemmas about the public's right to know versus individual privacy, national security or related social pressures for withholding information, protection of confidential sources, holding the line against censorship, and many other difficulties. A theory of journalistic ethics should explain where journalistic rights and responsibilities come from and how they are related to the proper moral conduct of professional journalists. At the same time, a useful philosophical discussion of journalistic ethics should offer clear-cut examples of ethical and unethical conduct to serve as exemplars for practical reasoning about the morality of some of the choices professional journalists face.

Journalists on the whole are conscientious investigators and reporters with a sense of mission. They want to discover and transmit the truth, to share what is of importance happening in the world today while still respecting people's rights and balancing the insatiable demand for news against other public and private concerns. By doing so, informing a population about important events and acting as watchdogs in the public interest, they can indirectly bring about positive change for the social good. This is undoubtedly why many persons choose to become professional journalists, aiming to emulate the best examples of how journalism can serve the public interest and make things better in the world. Even with the best intentions, competent journalists can do their valuable work better and more confidently if they are made aware of the kinds of moral problems that can arise within their profession. If journalists are encouraged to think about hazardous matters of ethical choice in reporting the news, then they can provide themselves with a practical moral philosophical framework within which to consider the many shades of difference between morally permissible and morally objectionable journalistic conduct. Those of us who are not journalists but news consumers can in turn better appreciate what goes into the tasks of collecting and disseminating news information and the interesting moral situations that professional journalists sometimes find themselves in, by attuning ourselves to the ethical debates surrounding problems of news reporting.

This book came about as a result of the desire to clarify the central problems of journalistic ethics. I have sought throughout to provide a handbook of practical moral reasoning for working journalists. The ideas presented here offer a systematic theory of journalistic moral rights and responsibilities, together with a collection of problems to consider in ongoing disputes about journalistic ethics. We have already indicated that while professional codes of ethics can provide food for philosophical thought, they cannot be regarded as the final word on the subject. Philosophers, who themselves are seldom journalists, are prepared in other

ways to analyze the principles by which journalists propose to govern themselves and to establish the bounds of morally proper and improper conduct
in reporting the news. The arguments we shall consider are not intended
only for journalists, as a consequence, but for everyone who enjoys or
depends on their important work.

If you open the pages of a newspaper or magazine or listen to a news
report on the radio or television, then you have made yourself part of a vast
interactive network by which information from around the world is discovered, documented, and edited to be made available to satisfy curiosity and
provide important data for individual and organizational decision-making.
The philosophical issues associated with journalistic ethics are interesting in
their own right and because of their practical implications, but for other reasons as well. The problems of bias and perspective in news reporting have
general implications for truth-seeking methodologies in knowledge theory
as they apply also to science, history, and our general grasp of the facts of the
world. Questions of privacy and obligations concerning the rights of journalists when they conflict with those of the general public are not only issues of
individual morality, but have important consequences for political philosophy, philosophy of law, and the concept of the social good.

The ethics of any profession, journalism included, provides a miniature
model of moral value for everyone. Insofar as the principles by which each
profession tries to regulate the conduct of its members reflect values inherent
in the larger community, they constitute a microcosm of all moral rights and
responsibilities. The study of the particular ethical rules of a discipline such
as journalism offers a close-up view of how specific problems confronting a
professional guild as a moral sub-culture within the larger community can
have wider and more far-reaching implications for the ethics of society as a
whole. Where journalistic ethics is concerned, this is especially true, because
we are all to a greater or less extent involved in activities of learning things
about the world and sharing the information we uncover with others, even if
we do not do so as a profession. We must all learn how to receive and
process news information, and we must decide how to use the content of
news reporting responsibly in our lives. In this limited sense we are all journalists, and accordingly we must all try to attain some insight into the work-
ings of journalism and the moral dimensions of news making. The present
book was written for this reason also, to promote an awareness of journalistic ethics and the importance of news information in our daily lives and to
help advance open discussion of the cognitive, moral, and political values
that converge dramatically within the profession.

News reporting on a mass scale through modern telecommunications
technology in newsprint, radio, television, video, satellite, and computer
Internet Web sites can be a force for enormous good or evil, depending,
like all technologies, on how it is used. An example of the potential for
journalism to make positive moral contributions is the accurate reporting of

an impending natural disaster, of health, travel, environmental risks, or the like, all of which can be important factors in protecting lives and property. In contrast, irresponsible news reporting can create panic or complacency in such a way as to create or aggravate existing social problems by spreading false information or, for example, by presenting correct information in an emotionally inflammatory way. These are extreme cases, about which many reflective persons can probably agree. Beginning with obvious examples helps us to get started thinking about the principles that ought to govern professional journalism. The problems that need to be addressed in a complete treatment of the subject nonetheless are often much more subtle, complicated, and consequently less amenable to off-the-cuff moral reaction as to the types of professional journalistic conduct that are morally justified or unjustified.

CRITERIA OF PROFESSIONAL ETHICS

We begin again to sharpen our sense of what is required of a theory of journalistic ethics by asking what is special about professional ethics and journalistic ethics in particular, as contrasted with the general ethical principles that we might suppose apply to every responsible person. The distinction between professional and general ethical standards is well illustrated in the case of journalistic ethics.

Let us first draw some basic distinctions. There are moral issues that journalists must try to resolve that are not questions of journalistic ethics. Should two journalists who find themselves thrown together on an assignment consider having an affair? Would that be a violation of professional journalistic ethics? I should think it would not be, although it might be a violation of other more general moral principles that are not specific to professional journalism. We can say the same with respect to off-topic questions about whether it is morally right or wrong for journalists to pay their income taxes, to take drugs for recreational purposes, or to have an abortion. Even the most complete theory of journalistic ethics is not going to answer moral questions that must also be considered by non-journalists.

Journalistic ethics needs to be as specialized in corresponding ways as professional journalism. The point is made by recognizing that while everyone generally, journalists and non-journalists alike, has an obligation to be truthful, journalists are often considered to have a special responsibility, within the limits of their ability, always to report only the truth to a much larger audience. We are all morally required not to deliberately distort or misrepresent the facts in communicating with others or to lie to others about what we believe to be the case. Journalists, in contrast, because of the potential consequences for their telling or not telling the truth, the mass uptake of the information they distribute, the amount of respect they command as authorities about the state of the world, and the far-reaching ways in which people rely on the kind of information they report for their own decision-making, gives them a higher degree of responsibility for honesty in their professional work than applies to the general public. If I falsely tell a friend that war has been declared in some part of the world, not as a lie, perhaps, but because of a rumor the accuracy of which I have not bothered to check, then the misapprehension and decisions based on it are likely to have at most a limited impact on the course of human events. As an ordinary citizen, I simply do not reach enough people in my casual conversation to make much difference. If a respected journalist reports the same falsehood in a world-wide broadcast on the evening news, the effect and the potential for harm is obviously much greater and thereby implies for the journalist a higher standard of fact-checking and accuracy in describing the state of the world for news consumers.

The relation between general moral obligations and special responsibilities incurred by individuals practicing a particular profession, abstracting from this single case, can be taken as the hallmark of what for present purposes we shall consider to be *professional ethics*. It is relatively easy to see how the criterion can be adapted to account for professional ethical responsibilities in business ethics, medical ethics, legal ethics, and the like. In the case of journalistic ethics, there are many aspects of the activities that go into gathering and reporting the news that apply equally to all persons, but for which journalists, because of the specific type of work in which they are professionally engaged and its potential implications for society, bear an appropriately enhanced degree of professional moral responsibility.

We are accustomed to thinking of news as always available whenever we want it. It is, in most places in the world where this book is likely to be read, like flipping a switch to fill a room with electric light or turning on a water faucet. There are many different newspapers and newsmagazines, and there are television programs on the news that are broadcast at regularly scheduled times or as twenty-four-hour news services. The convenience of access to news encourages us to take its existence for granted. It is always there for us, and we can choose to spend our time following the events it reports or in other ways. We can watch sports instead, if we prefer, or sitcoms, or turn off the television or put down the newspaper altogether and become more physically active in our lives. Sometimes the news is so engrossing that we cannot get enough of it, and sometimes it is so boring or depressing that we may prefer to escape. Regardless of our changing attitude to the news, we cannot overlook its importance in our daily experience. If we stop to reflect about where the news comes from, we cannot fail to notice that the news consists of information that is gathered and presented by persons who have received a certain professional training and are engaged in a certain sort of professional career. On further consideration, we may also come to recognize that journalists are subject to all the same types of strengths and weaknesses of moral character as other persons and that these factors can have a direct effect on the way in which the news is reported, thus potentially affecting the lives of millions of news-dependent consumers. Additionally, journalists face many kinds of ethical choices that are unique to the profession.

The ethics of journalism as such constitutes a special topic area in the general field of applied professional ethics. Journalists are professionals of a specific sort, and the work they do, because it is undertaken by fallible persons who must decide how they will pursue their work in light of its impact on others, is subject to specific moral considerations involving a specific set of moral principles or rules of conduct. Nor in this context should we ignore the fact that for many readers and viewers news has become a form of entertainment or is often accompanied in its reporting by presentations intended primarily for their entertainment value. The entertainment component in reporting the news brings additional moral issues to bear on the manner in which news is collected and presented. It is an element of news reporting that dovetails in important ways with the fact that journalism is usually a way of making money; yet it is often something more. The value of entertainment pieces, even in serious journalism, is that they can help knit together a social community, enable us to understand current events in a different way, sometimes through comic relief, and thereby provide a perspective on various aspects, especially of popular culture, that can often be justified as communication in the public interest.

chapter one

Truth Telling in the Public Interest

We have already considered the importance for journalists of truthful reporting. False "information," as we have suggested, is not really information; hence it is not really news, even if it is offered in the context of a news report. We are not informed about the state of things in the world if someone tells us it is raining when in fact it is not raining. Journalists accordingly do not fulfill their fundamental professional responsibility to discover and communicate information when they do not report the truth.

TRUTH AND ITS CONSEQUENCES

Commitment to truth and accuracy in news reporting is recognized as a fundamental obligation of journalistic ethics. The requirement is emphasized by Tunis Wortman in his now classic 1801 work, *A Treatise Concerning Political Enquiry and the Liberty of the Press*. Wortman offers one of the earliest efforts to articulate the obligations of media always to tell the truth:

> Every departure from truth is pernicious. Impartiality should be a perpetual attribute of the press. Neither fear on the one side, nor the hope of reward on the other, should intimidate or influence its enquiries. It should neither be bribed to lavish unmerited applause, nor menaced into silence. The usefulness of periodical publications depends upon their steady and inflexible adherence to rectitude. The moment that corrupt or foreign considerations are suffered to bias, or to stain their pages, they become injurious to the genuine interests of society.[1]

Some commentators on the rights and responsibilities of the news profession similarly contrast the freedom of the press with the requirement to avoid false or inaccurate misinformation. The 1947 Robert M. Hutchins Commission on Freedom of the Press similarly finds the following important qualification whereby freedom to report the news is carefully distinguished from the wanton license of journalists to say whatever they want regardless of its truth or falsehood:

---

[1]Quoted in Knowlton and Parsons, *The Journalist's Moral Compass*, p. 64.

The right of free public expression does include the right to be in error. Liberty is experimental. Debate itself could not exist unless wrong opinions could be rightfully offered by those who suppose them to be right. But the assumption that the man in error is actually trying for truth is of the essence of his claim for freedom. What the moral right does not cover is the right to be deliberately or irresponsibly in error.[2]

The point is that news information has the potential to be used, and its use carries implications for the welfare and happiness of others. In extreme cases, the true or false content of a news report can make a difference between life and death for those who choose to act on what they believe to be the information the news contains. It is the consequences of presenting persons with what purport to be facts, information, and truths about the world, knowing that such persons may well make decisions that can affect many aspects of their lives, that is an important source of the professional moral responsibility journalists have in reporting the news. It is the basis for the moral requirement of professional journalistic ethics that investigators and reporters hold themselves to a high standard of truth telling.

DELIBERATE AND INADVERTENT FALSEHOODS

Falsehoods can enter into news reporting in at least two ways: deliberately or inadvertently. Let us consider a typical worst-case scenario of deliberately false news content, in order to better understand why such behavior is professionally unethical. Then we will be in a good position to evaluate the ethics of journalistic truth telling as a moral ideal.

Suppose that a journalist reports on an impending stock market increase in the values of high-tech stocks. The report is complete with graphs and testimony from experts in the field and all the trimmings of a legitimate journalistic analysis of the projected upcoming economic conditions. I watch the report on television and come to believe that the trend described is true. As a result, I withdraw a large amount of my savings to invest in the high-tech market. The report, as it turns out, is a complete fabrication that was intended only to fill air time with something pleasant and uplifting for persons who want to believe that the economy is improving. The graphs are fake, and the interviews are

---

[2]Ibid., p. 213. See also Day, *Ethics in Media Communications*, p. 82: "First, and most obviously, the reporting of a story must be *accurate*. The facts should be verified; that is, they should be based on solid evidence. If there is some doubt or dispute about the facts, it should be revealed to the audience. This is a threshold requirement, because inaccurate information can undermine the credibility of any journalistic enterprise. Quotes should also be checked for accuracy. From the standpoint of ethical practice, the altering of direct quotes to avoid embarrassment to the speaker is questionable. If there is a problem in this respect, indirect quotes or paraphrases should be used. Nevertheless, some reporters believe that 'cleaning up' an interviewee's faulty grammar is justified out of fairness to the person. What is *not* acceptable within the industry and is indeed considered to be a mortal journalistic sin is the fabrication or alteration of the substance of quotes, even when they reflect the essential truth of what was said."

merely arranged with friends to give the impression of the reporter's having consulted with knowledgeable economists.

Now imagine that the stocks are in fact terribly weak and that the rogue reporter knew this, thereby giving a deliberately misleading picture of the stocks' prospects. The result is that I may lose my life's savings or, in any case, suffer a serious loss of money that in turn makes it impossible for me to meet my financial obligations. To be sure, there is a certain amount of inevitable risk in stock market investments. I cannot simply shift the blame for making a bad choice about how to use my money on an unscrupulous news reporter. Still, if the reporter has deliberately misrepresented the facts, then the situation that results is almost as bad as if he or she had assisted in an effort by others to steal my money. We can easily generalize the example to involve, for example, a fisherman's decision to sail on the basis of a maliciously false news report that the weather will be fine or a student's decision to move to a certain neighborhood on the basis of a false news report that the neighborhood is safe.

The problem is greater still if news reporters choose not to report on efforts by government officials to subvert the Constitution or make up false reports of such activities that cause civil liberties to be restricted in order to prevent a coup. It is possible as a result to project a continuum of cases that, through irresponsible journalism, finally threaten the very foundations of a free society. The events need not always be quite so dramatic. The same effects can occur slowly and virtually unnoticeably over time through the creeping erosion of social values brought about by the intentional or incompetent mismanagement of news reporting.

Case Study 1

Newsweek and the Holy Koran at Guantánamo Bay

On Tuesday, September 11, 2001, four airplanes were hijacked by radical Islamic militants supported by the terrorist network Al Qaeda. The first outrage occurred in the late morning as two of the planes were flown by their hijackers into the World Trade Center in New York City. The World Trade Center itself and several surrounding buildings were demolished, in the course of which approximately three thousand persons lost their lives. A third plane hit the Pentagon in Washington, DC, and a fourth, apparently commandeered to strike another target in Washington, possibly the White House, crashed in rural Pennsylvania after angry heroic passengers struggled to gain control of the plane. Following the crackdown on Islamic terrorists worldwide in the aftermath of the Al Qaeda attacks, suspected terrorists arrested in the custody of the United States, many of them combatants captured during subsequent operations against the Taliban in Afghanistan, were detained in what has turned out to be a controversial military prison in Guantánamo Bay, Cuba.

On May 9, 2005, the newsmagazine *Newsweek* published a story by two of its seasoned reporters, Michael Isikoff and John Barry, purporting to describe culturally insensitive interrogation methods by the American military at Guantánamo. In one particularly objectionable instance, *Newsweek* reported that soldiers abused and desecrated copies of the Koran, the Moslem holy book, placing them on toilets and, in one case, flushing a copy down a toilet. On the basis of this story, violent anti-American protests in the international Islamic community followed, which the Associated Press reported on May 17, 2005 left at least fourteen people dead in Afghanistan and inflamed an already tense situation of hostility and distrust between Islamic and non-Islamic nations.

Two weeks later, in its May 23 issue, the magazine retracted its story about Guantánamo. Editor Mark Whitaker recanted the allegation in these words: "Based on what we know now, we are retracting our original story that an internal military investigation had uncovered Koran abuse at Guantánamo Bay." The retraction was in a sense voluntary, but came from the magazine only after severe criticism from American military and other governmental officials demanding that the story be withdrawn. The American Joint Chiefs of Staff on May 16 issued a statement saying "We can't find anything to substantiate the allegations that appeared in *Newsweek.*" Indeed, reportedly, upon a review of 25,000 documents from the prison, investigators were able to identify only one incident in the prison logs involving a copy of the Koran. In the case in question, it was not an American soldier, but an Islamic militant detainee at Guantánamo who had supposedly stuffed pages from a copy of the Koran into a toilet in order to protest conditions at the facility.

The occasion for the false report in the magazine seems to have been a confidential informant who in the past had been a highly reliable source of information. This, by itself, in retrospect, was evidently insufficient to guarantee the story's truth. The effects of the mistaken report have nevertheless had worldwide reverberations, in particular for the credibility of American news reporting, and, needless to say, for the persons killed or injured in the resulting rioting and their families and friends.

QUESTIONS

1. How much damage to individuals and national interests can potentially be indirectly caused by erroneous news reports like the Koran abuse story in *Newsweek*? What repercussions might there be for American international policy, its war effort in Iraq, and the struggle against global terrorism? Does

a news outlet bear any moral responsibility for what others choose to do on the basis of its true or false news reports?

2. What kind of effort does it take to undo the loss of credibility suffered by a news outlet in reporting sensational stories that can lead to loss of life, property, national prestige, and the prosecution of governmental purposes by a false news story once it has been circulated?

3. What precautions would you insist upon if you were the editor overseeing the production of the Guantánamo Koran abuse story? Could the problem have been avoided prior to publication of the story? What general editorial policies should ideally be practiced in order to prevent similar fiascos?

4. How would you answer a critic who might reply that if the story had been true, then it should definitely have been published by the magazine, and that, moreover, if it had, the damage resulting in rioting and loss of life and the effect on American foreign policy and its efforts to contain terrorism worldwide would have occurred anyway? What difference does it make if the story printed by *Newsweek* were true or false in terms of the consequences that ensued? What is so important about truth in news reporting when the effects of a true or false story are comparable?

5. The Associated Press, after discussing several other recent incidents of plagiarism and false news reporting, closed its dispatch of May 17 with cautionary words: "The Pew Research Center recently released findings that 45 percent of Americans believe little or nothing they read in daily newspapers. In the past six months, U.S. newspaper circulation has dropped 1.9 percent on weekdays and 2.5 percent on Sundays, the largest drop for newspapers in more than a decade, the Audit Bureau of Circulations reported on May 2." What can be done to restore reader confidence in the content of newspapers and newsmagazines in the wake of publishing scandals? What would you do as managing editor of a news outlet in order to improve reader confidence after disclosure of a harmful mistaken report?

The same kind of responsibility, to a different degree, attaches to anyone who conveys information to another person. This is why we all have a moral obligation to tell the truth, at least when our audience can reasonably be assumed to know that we are not spinning yarns, telling jokes, writing fiction, rehearsing the lines of a play, or the like. The difference for professional journalists is that they have a special institutional role to play in the dissemination of information. They are thought to have a special authority as dispensers of truth, and they reach many more people than the average person conveying information to a small circle of friends and acquaintances. The kinds of information journalists generally report, moreover, is often of a more serious and potentially consequential sort than that to which ordinary individuals are expected to have access. Hence, journalists once again bear a special moral responsibility, above and beyond the injunction for all persons to tell the truth to the best of their ability. They have an exceptional moral duty to avoid falsehood in their reporting, to correct errors that may have occurred inadvertently in their accounts of facts and current events, and most definitely not to engage in deliberate falsehood. Here is another remarkable case study:

Case Study 2

Staged Incidents in *Dateline NBC* Investigative Reporting

"On November 17, 1992, *Dateline NBC* ran a fifteen-minute segment, 'Waiting to Explode.' Its focus was the safety of General Motors' full-size pickup trucks in model years 1973–1987. These trucks were designed with gas tanks mounted outside the frame.

The *Dateline* report began with the story of Shannon Moseley, a teenager killed in a pickup given to him by his parents. A law officer described Shannon's screams as he died in the fire. Another segment showed a tearful twenty-two-year-old mother whose two infant daughters died in a similar crash. She could hear their screams as fire engulfed the cab. In this episode, *Dateline* also showed an empty pickup being hit from the side and bursting into flames. NBC called it 'an unscientific demonstration' of how the gas would ignite if the tank were punctured on impact or fuel forced out of the cap.

NBC did not tell viewers that the tank had been filled to the brim and an improper gas cap used to seal it. *Dateline NBC* did not inform viewers that toy rocket engines had been taped under the truck to ensure a fire even if the tank did not explode or gas did not leak out during the crash test. The incendiary devices were connected to a remote control and activated just before impact. NBC claimed a faulty headlight wire on the old car sent crashing into the pickup had actually sparked the fire, in effect making the flares unnecessary; therefore, they were not mentioned in the program.

And NBC did not tell viewers that its estimates of crash speeds were underplayed for both crashes. All these facts would come to light through the careful investigative work of—not the media—but the corporation whose reputation *Dateline* had impugned."[3]

QUESTIONS

1.   Why might *Dateline NBC* be believed to have followed unethical practice in presenting its exposé of alleged safety hazards involving GM trucks? What,

---

[3]Christians, Fackler, Rotzoll, and McKee, *Media Ethics*, pp. 41–42.

exactly, are they supposed to have done that is morally wrong or offensive? What is the problem posed by this case study for professional journalism?

2. Is staging an event or "re-creation" for the benefit of the camera necessarily morally wrong, if the reporters and producers sincerely believe that a problem exists? What if they are only trying to provide dramatic accompanying footage to illustrate the kind of thing that can happen if appropriate safeguards are not introduced? If this is the rationale for staging an event like the explosion of the GM truck, what accompanying messages, disclosures, or disclaimers should a journalist make in order to avoid misleading viewers and perhaps thereby prevent themselves from being guilty of professional misconduct?

3. To what extent, if any, can the visual medium of television be blamed for encouraging news reporters to contrive incidents in order to re-create or demonstrate previously verified conclusions that they have independently reached? Is it any moral excuse to say that an audience expects and demands dramatic video, such as a truck blowing up on screen, in order to believe that vehicles of a certain type might be dangerous to own and operate? If you find the *Dateline NBC* program to be morally at fault in this incident, does it make any difference in your judgment, whether or not it is true as a matter of fact, that the vehicles in question are actually dangerous and that what the report showed is something that *could* happen to them under the wrong conditions?

4. What rules should news investigators, reporters, and producers follow in order to avoid any hint of moral compromise in their reporting of news stories like the example in this case study? How can journalistic integrity be preserved from a news management perspective in order to prevent consequent allegations of professional ethical impropriety? What would you do and what do you think you should do if you were a colleague of a reporter who suggested that an explosion of a truck be staged on camera in order to illustrate the problems that can occur? Why? What would you do and what do you think you should do as a news editor or producer if you became aware that such an event had been staged as part of the exciting video presentation of a news report?

5. What can a journalist or news outlet do to compensate a victim of staged reporting? Is it always enough to explain the circumstances of the staging or re-creation later as an afterthought? Or should journalists be morally responsible for punitive damages to those affected by staged events in reporting? Does it make any difference in that case whether or not the allegations accompanying the story are true or false? Where shall we try to draw the line between journalistic fraud and creative news investigation, documentation, and reporting?

Ordinarily, journalists have good intentions with respect to reporting all and only the relevant truths that pertain to a particular story they are covering. There is the greatest difference between trying sincerely to report on an occurrence truthfully and simply making honest mistakes along the way that unknowingly result in a false account, as opposed to deliberately choosing to misrepresent the truth or, as we might also say more simply and directly, lying. Even with the best intentions we can make mistakes and get things wrong as we strive to relate what we genuinely believe to be the facts. This happens to scientists and philosophers as well as journalists and to each of us in everyday transactions. We try to tell the truth, as best we know it and to the best of our abilities, but for a variety of reasons we sometimes fall into error. What, then, should we take to be the proper moral attitude of professional journalists toward the truth content of news reports?

FUNDAMENTAL PRINCIPLE OF JOURNALISTIC ETHICS

We now present and then elaborate and further defend what we shall call the *fundamental justificatory principle and moral mandate for professional journalism*. The principle spells out professional journalism's raison d'être, its reason for being or its obligation, in the following formulation of its most basic statement of every journalist's moral mandate:

FUNDAMENTAL JUSTIFICATORY PRINCIPLE AND MORAL MANDATE FOR PROFESSIONAL JOURNALISM

Journalists are morally committed to maximally relevant truth telling in the public interest.

We will make frequent appeal to this principle in addressing the moral problems confronting professional journalists. We argue, for example, that the right of a free press, of journalists to freely discover and communicate the contents of news stories, derives from the above principle, and in effect from the public's need and right to know. Without this assumption, journalists would have no obligation to maximize relevant truth telling in the public interest and for the public good. The connections between some problems in journalistic ethics are more obvious than others, and in certain instances we shall need greater effort to explain how concepts beyond cases like politically motivated censorship, including protection of confidential sources, respecting the privacy of individuals, among others, relate directly or indirectly to the fundamental principle of professional journalistic ethics.

TRUTH TELLING JOURNALISTIC IMPERATIVES

We now proceed to explain, defend, and examine some of the main consequences of the fundamental principle of journalistic ethics. These provide a good starting place to initiate discussion about the problems of truth telling in journalistic ethics.

We have not tried to *deduce* the fundamental principle. That, indeed, is part of what makes it fundamental. Like the axioms of a system of mathematics, we do not try to prove anything so basic. Rather, we propose the principle as the best way of understanding and systematizing the moral obligations that are most often attributed to professional journalists. The method is also analogous to that of the natural sciences. In science, a hypothesis is advanced to explain complex phenomena that is suggested but not yet confirmed by the scientist's pre-theoretical expectations of what is likely to be true.

The task for journalistic ethics is similarly to try to clarify whatever might be implied by the above principle as reflecting the minimum of what we expect from the conduct of professional journalists. The exercise in turn is intended only as a first step in trying to decide whether or not the implications of the principle are true, and ultimately whether or not the principle itself from which the implications follow is correct. We begin with these consequences of the fundamental truth telling moral precept of professional journalistic ethics. We must ask whether or not the following items describe reasonable moral obligations for journalists:

TRUTH TELLING IMPERATIVES

- It is morally obligatory for journalists to the best of their abilities to tell the truth in reporting the news and to avoid both deliberate, and, to whatever extent possible, inadvertent falsehoods.

- It is morally obligatory for journalists to the best of their abilities to counteract the effects of bias and consider the impact of perspective, predisposition, and other factors that can affect truth telling in reporting the news, and, again, to the best of their abilities, to overcome these and other frequently encountered obstacles to truth telling in journalism. Journalists are morally responsible for being aware of the extent to which any and all such factors can affect the truthfulness of their reporting and taking steps to identify and counteract them.

- Journalists are responsible not to plagiarize the reporting of other journalists, thinkers, or writers, not merely because to do so represents a violation and theft of the intellectual property rights of those persons, but because to plagiarize without due attributions of original authorship constitutes a form of deliberate inaccuracy and misrepresentation of the contents of a news story as though it had been independently discovered and verified for its factual content by the journalist whose name it fraudulently bears.

- Journalists are further responsible when and where it is appropriate for checking on the truth of one another's reports, and in this way for providing a mutual self-regulation on the professional conduct of news reporting, acting in good faith to find and correct deliberate or accidental errors.

- Finally, when errors in reporting are discovered, journalists are morally obligated to correct them publicly, to set the record straight, and to mitigate to whatever extent possible the misleading impressions their false reports may have created.

We should emphasize once again that the above are not the only moral obligations bearing on professional journalistic ethics. They are special principles applying to journalism with respect to the particular problems of truth telling. Truth telling, in turn, is only one aspect of journalistic ethics, yet it is obviously an important one, given journalism's mission of discovering and communicating information for the society it serves, whether understood as a particular local community, nation, or the world.

TRUTH AS CORRESPONDENCE WITH FACTS

We are at once besieged by philosophical questions that impinge on journalists with respect to their moral obligations for truthful reporting, but that affect every branch of knowledge and have troubled philosophers from its beginnings. What is truth? How can we recognize truth, and how can we communicate it? Do we not inevitably distort the truth when we try to represent it for others? Must we not oversimplify the facts in condensing them for purposes of expression, especially in crisp newspaper columns and in brief moments of precious air time on the radio or television? How can we avoid the pitfalls of unnoticed bias and inherent limitations of perspective in trying with the best intentions always to tell the truth? What is an error, a falsehood, and how can it be corrected? Even if it should turn out to be not exactly *the truth* that journalists can be expected to seek, it might still be at least something true-*ish* (or the-*ish*). We should nevertheless have a better sense of exactly what we are talking about as the proper goal of professional journalism only after we have looked into these matters more thoroughly and thought about the possibilities with some care. Only then can we have a solid basis from which to discuss the ways in which journalists might try to attain their objectives, as we consider morally justifiable journalistic pursuits.

Deeper philosophical problems about the nature of truth do not necessarily need to be settled once and for all in order to arrive at workable guidelines for truth telling in the news. We can say that the same standards apply to journalism as to other areas of everyday life. We know what it means for a child to tell the truth or to lie about whether it has been in the cookie jar, and we know roughly as well what it means for a news reporter to tell the truth or to convey something false. It will nevertheless be worthwhile to say something more concrete and definite about these intuitive ideas, by clarifying the journalist's moral obligations toward the truth. We can say as a first approximation and in general terms that it is *declarative sentences*, also known as *propositions*, that are true or false. There are sentences such as questions, commands, or requests that are not propositions because they do not propose that a particular state of affairs exists. We see this clearly in a comparison of the sentences: "The door is closed." "Is the door closed?" "Please close the door." Only the first of these is true or false, depending on whether or not in fact the door is closed. We cannot make sense of the question, "Is the door closed?" as either true or false, and similarly for the request, Please close the door. A true proposition in turn is a proposition that corresponds positively to the facts that the sentence expresses or represents. It declares a certain state of affairs to exist, and if in fact the state of affairs actually exists, then the proposition is true. A false proposition on this conception is one that does not correspond positively to the facts it purports to represent. We can think of a false proposition as a proposition that is not or that fails to be true.

Some everyday examples should help to make the concept clearer. If a news reporter says that the president of the United States has signed a bill making it illegal to skateboard, when the president has only considered the matter but not yet put pen to paper creating a law, then what the reporter has said is false. If a news reporter reports that the president has slipped in the bathtub and injured his neck, and in fact these events have occurred, then what the reporter has said is true. As a general characterization, we can say that a proposition is true if and only if the state of affairs it is intended to express or represent positively corresponds to a state of affairs actually occurring in the world. This, with certain refinements and qualifications, is what is sometimes known as the *correspondence theory of truth*. A standard example is to say that the proposition "Snow is white" is true if and only if snow is white. This means that the sentence is true just in case the state of affairs the sentence expresses actually exists. The formula " 'Snow is white' is true if and only if snow is white," from a syntactical standpoint, merely removes the quotation marks from around the proposition expressed in language in order to represent the fact or state of affairs that establishes the proposition's truth conditions. It is accordingly sometimes called a *redundancy* or *disquotational theory of truth*.

It might be wondered what all the fuss is about. "Snow is white" is true if and only if snow is white; "The president slipped in the bathtub" is true if and only if the president slipped in the bathtub; and so on. Such a formula does not give us anything solid to go by in trying to decide which propositions are true and which are false. In a way, however, that is just the point. The correspondence or disquotational theory of truth is a *formal* theory; it provides only the form and not the content or substance of truth. It certainly does not try to go beyond these matters of form by telling us what we must do to set about learning whether or not a given proposition is true. What the theory says is nevertheless theoretically useful, within the limits for which it is intended. Applications of the definition presuppose that we have a direct way of knowing what fact or state of affairs a proposition is intended to express or represent and knowing whether or not the corresponding fact or state of affairs actually exists in the real world. Although philosophers, in trying to test the conceptual limits of these definitions and of our ideas of truth and knowledge, have contrived ingenious thought experiments that push the ordinary meaning of the analysis to extremes, for practical purposes in trying to understand the moral requirements of truth telling in journalism, and even in science, mathematics, and everyday affairs, the definition is perfectly correct.

PRACTICAL TRUTH CRITERIA AND CROSS-CHECKING NEWS CONTENTS

We have already seen, as a kind of baseline for thinking about the nature of truth telling in journalism, that journalists tell the truth when they offer propositions that positively correspond to the facts. The facts or state of affairs that actually obtain in the world are generally something public that other persons can investigate for themselves. They are truths in particular that other journalists or interested nonprofessionals occasionally learn about in their own interactions with practical matters. Their experience often serves as an external check to verify or disconfirm what other journalists have reported.

For the most part, in the vast majority of instances in which journalists report on events, they are communicating information about things they have observed or that are reported by what other reliable witnesses have perceived. They are therefore the kinds of facts that other persons could also discover or fail to discover in confirming or disproving the content of a journalist's reportage. In a later chapter, we shall maintain that in a free society no public official should believe that his or her actions cannot be scrutinized and reported on to the general public, for the good of the free functioning of society. Providing this kind of watchdog service for news consumers on the integrity of public officials is one of the important functions of a free press. In the same way, and ultimately for the same reason, no journalist should believe that his or her reporting will not be carefully scrutinized and checked for truth or falsehood by other journalists or members of the public. In principle, the putative facts that journalists report are subject to the same investigative reporting as any other occurrence of interest, for the betterment of journalism in all its activities and, ultimately, for the betterment of society.

We should expect that most journalists, if they are in tune with the moral obligations of truth telling in the profession, are always aware that there are external checks on the truth or falsehood of their reporting. They should therefore welcome the fact that their work must constantly stand the test of truth, of positive correspondence with the facts, in the same way that any scientist should expect his or her theories and experimental results to be evaluated for truth by repeated peer review. It is standard policy in many newsrooms for journalists to confirm the truth of any assertion in their reports by means of two or more independent sources. If truth is the game, the purpose of journalism and its justification, then whatever contributes to perfecting the truth content of journalistic reportage is an essential part of the ethos of professional journalistic practice. As in science or history, the goal in journalism is the discovery and communication of relevant truths, not the egos or career advancement of individual journalists. What is most important, the keystone of professional journalistic ethics and the guiding star from which journalists must take their bearings, is the search for truth and the desire to the best of their ability to report all the relevant facts of newsworthy events.

PLAGIARISM

The use of another person's thinking or writing without explicit acknowledgment or its original source is known as *plagiarism*. We know about the problem of plagiarism in classroom situations, where students sometimes copy other people's work and present it to satisfy a course assignment as though the ideas or their expression were their own. This, we rightly assume, is wrong; it is morally objectionable behavior. It makes no difference whether plagiarism is committed by a student cheating on an exam, turning in someone else's essay or homework answers; or by a scientist, historian, or philosopher falsely claiming another person's work as their own; or by a journalist pretending to report the results of an original news investigation that have actually been produced by another reporter or team of reporters.

Why is it morally objectionable to plagiarize? There are two reasons. The first is that plagiarism amounts to a violation of the intellectual property rights of others, which in the case of plagiarism effectively constitutes theft. It is taking public credit for someone else's ideas and someone else's work. The plagiarist illegally appropriates another person's efforts without the original author's consent and without compensating the original author for his or her efforts. The second reason, which is more germane to the present discussion of truth telling in journalism, is that plagiarism constitutes a deliberate inaccuracy and misrepresentation of facts. This is the result even when the content of the plagiarized news report itself happens to be 100 percent truthful. If a journalist signs an article or presents a news story on the air as though it were the fruit of his or her labor, as something he or she has researched and whose facts he or she has personally verified, when in fact the content of the material has been plagiarized from another author, then the reader or audience is misled as to the source, originality, and credibility of the information that is conveyed. A plagiarist lies, consequently, to the public about the authority of a news item, even when the item itself contains no falsehoods. It does not matter in this regard, from the standpoint of a journalist's primary professional moral obligation to maximize relevant truth telling, whether the plagiarist happens to plagiarize true information or false misinformation. An obvious effect of the profession tolerating or turning a blind eye to plagiarism is a corrosion of the credibility of the news, first, of a particular offending news outlet, but also more generally of the news in any of its forms. Journalists as a result are professionally ethically obligated to avoid plagiarism in their own news reporting and to uncover and impose meaningful sanctions against journalists who knowingly plagiarize the work of others.

What then are we to say about most of the news reported on radio, television, and in many newspapers? It is widely recognized in journalistic circles that the lion's share of original investigative reporting, at least in the United States, is undertaken by a relatively small number of newspapers and news agencies.[4] Investigative reporters work often under difficult circumstances and scant operating budgets in order to unearth the facts that appear replicated in many other news sources, especially on radio, television, and the Internet. It happens for a variety of socioeconomic reasons that the burden of journalistic investigations falls on newspaper reporters in particular. What they discover is picked up by other news reporters and repeated in many different news venues. There are international news services, like the Associated Press (AP) and Reuters News Agency that provide news reportage that is purchased by many broadcast news programs and even by other newspapers for publication. Is this plagiarism? Ordinarily, it is not. The reason is that responsible news reports always include a reference to the original source of information. These can include information prepared by news services for other news outlets. At the beginning or end of the first or last column of a news story in a newspaper or somewhere in the reading of a news report on the radio or television, Internet source, or the like, there is generally a reference to the wire news service or other original source of the information the story contains. If you listen carefully to news reports on radio and television, for example, somewhere during the retelling of a news item, or at the beginning or end of the broadcast, or in the broadcast acknowledgments and disclaimers that are scrolled by, usually at the end of a broadcast or broadcast day, you will find the original sources credited. The stock phrases in a broadcast report are often contained in such formulas as "According to X," "Based on a recent report in the X City Tribune," and the like. Where this practice is observed there is no question of plagiarism having occurred. The original source is properly credited, those who labored to uncover the facts have presumably been appropriately compensated in some way for the information they

[4]See Downie, Jr. and Kaiser, *The News About the News: American Journalism in Peril*, esp. 64: "We live in the television age, surrounded by other, old and new forms of electronic journalism, but newspapers still do most of the original reporting. In America's towns and cities, the local newspaper sets the news agenda. A few major newspapers do the same for the national news media. Of all the participants in the news business, none is remotely as committed to covering news as the country's daily papers.... The news organizations maintained by newspapers are what make America's free press meaningful."

provide, and no one who pays close attention to the facts as reported is misinformed or otherwise harmed.

MORAL INTEGRITY AND JOURNALISM'S RAISON D'ÊTRE

These are perhaps obvious enough observations. Later we will see just how important it is to make sure of our first steps and the direction in which they lead. We must have a sound basis from which standpoint we can judge the merits of related issues in journalistic ethics. We shall see that most questions about the proper conduct of journalism can be addressed by making appropriate reference to the fundamental purpose of journalism in the discovery and communication of relevant truth.

We have not thus far fully analyzed this concept. We are limiting the methodology of truth seeking in journalism for the most part to ordinary perception and the interpretation of events in public space that any person with normal perceptual abilities and competence in grappling with the everyday challenges of life could in principle attain. We have yet to broach the philosophically more difficult topics of relevance in news reporting and of the interpretation of occurrences that are presupposed by more complicated kinds of journalistic activities. Even so, we have not yet exhausted all that is of philosophical interest in considering major pitfalls for conscientious journalists who want to report truthfully on world events.

There are hazards even for honest journalists who are concerned to the best of their abilities to report only the truth. Most false news reporting probably comes about through accident rather than intentionally, since most journalists understand and make every effort conscientiously to avoid misrepresenting the facts. If this were not the case, then journalism would not enjoy the high esteem and reputation for reliability that on the whole it does. An interesting range of examples concerns problems of accuracy in the use of quotations. In general, quotations are only to be used in news reporting when the exact words used by the person being quoted can be independently documented. Electronic recordings or stenographic records are one obvious method. It is not good enough for reporters to quote someone as having said something that is close to what they may have said or even identical in meaning. There are many subtle differences of nuance that are lost even by slight misquotations, and to alert readers or an audience that a person of note is being quoted conveys to them the impression that the report of their speech act to follow is a word-for-word repetition of what they said. If this is actually not the case, then a falsehood is perpetrated by the reporter that is inimical to the fundamental moral principle of journalistic ethics always to maximize relevant truth telling in the public interest. Thus, if a congresswoman says, "I support the Strategic Defense Initiative," and a reporter misquotes her as saying instead "I support Star Wars technology," then a falsehood has entered into the journalist's report, even if "Star Wars technology" is just another more popular term for "Strategic Defense Initiative." That is *not* what we are supposing the congresswoman actually said, so that to quote her as saying something else is to introduce a falsehood that could potentially have serious ramifications.

There are regrettably also some outstanding scandalous incidents of journalists fabricating false stories out of laziness or for ulterior purposes. Sometimes irresponsible rogue journalists have acted from a perverse wish to challenge themselves to see whether and to what extent they can get away with making things up, even going so far as to invent sources and believable but completely substance-less faux evidence, deceiving the public and their editors, as proof of what they may assume to be their own cleverness. These instances are fortunately the exception in an otherwise morally upright truth-honoring profession. We shall not dwell excessively on these pathological examples except to emphasize them as an extreme. Journalists as a rule are outraged at these blatant violations of professional ethics, which cast doubt on the integrity of their own work and on that of all news reporters within the industry even when they are not themselves directly involved in any wrongdoing.

Case Study 3

Jayson Blair at the *New York Times*

A recent notorious instance of sheer fabrication of news content is that of Jayson Blair, who was forced to resign from the *New York Times* on May 1, 2003, after working there for four years.

Blair was accused of committing multiple acts of journalistic fraud, submitting dispatches for publication ostensibly from Maryland, Texas, and other locations, when in fact he had never left New York City. He invented comments and quotations and concocted scenarios that never took place. He engaged heavily in plagiarism, lifting details from other newspapers and wire services, creating the false impression that he had traveled to cover the news and met with persons involved in news stories.

Blair's made-up interviews included those in stories related to what at the time was a series of vicious sniper attacks in the suburban Washington DC area and northern Virginia and Maryland. Ultimately, this was part of Blair's undoing, as those who had supposedly been interviewed by him and quoted in his stories came forward afterward to complain that they had never spoken with him and that the content of what he had reported was untrue.

Problematic journalistic content was discovered by the *New York Times'* internal investigation of Blair's professionally unethical behavior in at least thirty-six of the seventy-three stories he reported for the newspaper since he began receiving national news reporting assignments in October 2002. Blair, of course, was fired for this professional misconduct. The newspaper also adopted the unusual decision to open up a hotline for readers to report additional reportorial errors and misinformation directly to the paper's fraud investigator.

QUESTIONS

1. What is the importance of truth in news reporting?
2. Why should Jayson Blair be criticized for making up news stories, manufacturing nonexistent information sources, and the like, when this is what novelists do all the time? If news reporting has come to involve entertainment as well as fact, analysis, and editorial opinion, what difference does it make if news stories are true or at least partly fictional?
3. How would you as an editor have dealt with the revelation that a reporter on your news staff had deliberately falsified the content of news reportage? What actions would you find it appropriate to take, and, more important, why would you think such actions justified? What reaction should a colleague reporter have upon discovering that another reporter has been manufacturing false news reports for publication or broadcast?
4. How can news organizations prevent journalistic misconduct like that encountered at the *New York Times*? What values should be instilled in every member of a news team, and how should they be explained, justified, promoted, and enforced?
5. Many people believe that once you are lied to by another person thereafter you can never trust what that person says again. Is this true? Why or why not? Should we consider the situation of news outlets and agencies to be any different? If so, why? If not, why not? What can be done by responsible reporters and the news outlets they serve to correct the damage done by rogue reporters publishing inaccurate and in some cases deliberately fabricated falsehoods in their pages or during their broadcast time? Should Blair have been fired from his job, or should the editorial hierarchy have found a way to reform his bad journalistic practice in order to prevent him from repeating the offense?

Such practices, when they occur, according to the truth telling requirements for journalistic ethics, are without a doubt professionally unethical. They are as immoral as it would be to lie to a friend about something important. Because of the larger scale of the lies told by rogue journalists, however, and because of their potential to affect many more people through the wide public dissemination of their falsehoods through the media, deliberate communication of falsehoods by journalists are proportionately that much greater moral offenses. The profession in its self-regulation is obligated to try its best to root out such offenders, to publicize the wrong they have done, to try to correct whatever damage may have occurred by making the public generally aware of the specific falsehoods or unsupported content of bogus reporting. Those in authority within the profession may also be justified in taking further punitive actions within their power, such as ostracizing rogue reporters, refusing them further employment or recommendations for employment, and, in some cases, depending on the severity of the offense and the applicable laws, having them remanded for criminal prosecution. These instances, fortunately, are outstanding exceptions among what for the most part are persons of exceptional integrity who want to tell the truth about the events on which they report.[5]

RELEVANCE AND THE CONCEPT OF RELEVANT TRUTH

We have said that journalists not only have an obligation to report the news, but to maximize the truthful reporting of *relevant* information. What is relevance, and what is relevant information?

Like the problems of perspective and interpretation, these are questions that philosophers have investigated in-depth and in some cases to a greater degree than may be strictly necessary for the practical purposes of news reporting. We begin by taking stock of basic facts about relevance as the concept is ordinarily understood and as it seems to be applied in practical matters. We turn first to the ways in which we ordinarily think and talk about relevance in other practical affairs. Relevance is itself a relative matter of interest, context, and judgment. What may seem relevant to you may not seem relevant to me, just as what I believe to be true is under no obligation to cohere with what you believe to be true, and conversely. Still, most of the time we agree on these things, so that in principle we should mostly be prepared to acknowledge a relevant sense of relevance to apply in evaluating journalistic performance.

---

[5]Nor, unfortunately, is Jayson Blair's case unique. Stephen Glass, a likeable young reporter at *The New Republic*, was exposed as having committed extensive journalistic fraud in 2003, fabricating the content and sources for over half of his articles. Other well-known and widely discussed recent examples include Janet Cooke at the *Washington Post* and Patricia Smith at the *Boston Globe*. Glass's case is extraordinary in the sense that he went to unusual lengths to fabricate sources, including Internet Web sites, in order to support some of his allegations, thereby circumventing the two-independent-sources rule for cross-checking accuracy of information in journalistic reportage that is intended to guarantee truth and accuracy in news stories. Glass's conduct was the subject of a scathing *60 Minutes* documentary. A movie, *Shattered Glass* (2003), was also made criticizing Glass's journalistic misbehavior, and Glass has since published a novel about a character who does what he himself was discovered as having done at *The New Republic*, titled *The Fabulist* (Simon & Schuster, 2003). The world of fiction is arguably the only proper home for these kinds of creative writing exercises that have no legitimate place in professional journalism.

The fundamental principle and moral mandate for journalistic ethics refers for good reason explicitly to the concept of maximizing *relevant* truth (in the public interest). This qualification reflects the fact that we do not expect reporters to describe absolutely everything about the news events they are asked to cover. They must be selective. The editorial process does not begin when a reporter turns over copy to an editor. Every reporter edits his or her own news stories right from the beginning, in deciding, often under managerial editorial guidance, what aspects of an event to include and what to exclude.

Here are some extreme cases to prime the pump in thinking about the concept of relevance in news reporting. If a reporter is sent to cover a jury trial of a person accused of mass murder, it would not be relevant, we would ordinarily say, for the reporter then to devote the whole of the news coverage of the event to a description of the clothes and hairstyles of the jury members. The jury members' apparel and coiffures make no difference to the question that is reasonably assumed to be of interest in the case, concerning the force of evidence and arguments put before the jury in trying to decide the guilt or innocence of the accused. If a journalist is sent to report on a fashion show, on the other hand, it would presumably not be relevant to turn in copy or footage with sound track and voice-over ignoring the styles on display in deference to a discussion of the political affiliations and criminal backgrounds if any of the models and designers.

We similarly would not regard a news reporter as fulfilling a professional ethical obligation by reporting on the shoe size of a Supreme Court nominee, *unless it should turn out to be* (surprisingly) *relevant* to understanding the events being reported. Not all facts are worth reporting, and professional journalists must pick and choose what to report and what to ignore based on professional standards and their own commonsense judgment and experience. Reporters are supposed to identify only information that is pertinent to a news event, which they then convey to their readers or audience in a way that helps make sense of what has occurred. Obviously, such distinctions to some extent are matters of subjective judgment that can vary from reporter to reporter. What, then, is meant by the concept of relevance, and how can news reporters decide what is relevant and what is not in the journalistic domain?

There is no pat answer to the question of what constitutes relevance. It is a concept that is relative to many different kinds of factors. These include the interests of an audience and the inherent explanatory importance of a given fact or set of facts in trying to understand another occurrence. The shoe size of the Supreme Court nominee would ordinarily not be relevant to news about the individual being nominated, although with a little imagination one can conjure up circumstances in which such a fact could be relevant. What we mean thereby is that the fact that an individual has a certain shoe size does not help to explain the things in which as a practical matter we are ordinarily interested. We will want to know why the person was nominated, what qualifications they have for the office, and what the person would be likely to do if confirmed for the appointment. We may want to know, for example, about the person's stand on the death penalty and other issues of the day or looming in the future. Unless shoe size somehow bears on the question of performance in office, we are inclined to suppose that facts about shoe size do not matter in contemplating this individual rather than another who has been nominated. All of the reasons that enter into our being interested in knowing that a certain person has been nominated to this judicial office in the ordinary course of things are completely unaffected by shoe size. The fact, assuming it is a fact, does not affect whether the person will make a good Supreme Court justice, and this is ordinarily the kind of thing in which we are most interested. If the person has a highly unusual shoe size or if having such a shoe size has somehow affected the individual's development of character, then there might be interesting implications connecting shoe size with judicial outlook and likely judgments if confirmed for the nation's highest court. The fact, if sufficiently odd, might deserve journalistic comment as a human interest item. In comparison with the print space or air time that might be devoted to more interesting aspects of the nominee's career and attitudes toward the law, however, it is easy to see that a news reporter that devoted even so much as a single sentence to the nominee's shoe size would be exposed to ridicule as wasting an opportunity to inform readers or an audience of other matters that might make a difference with respect to important aspects of their lives if the nominee in question is approved. The factors that make a difference to assumed interests, like the nominee's stand on the death penalty, are deemed relevant, while factors that make no difference to the individual's expected performance in office if confirmed in the appointment are judged irrelevant. It follows that the same fact reported by a journalist might be relevant in one news story context and irrelevant in another.

What is relevant to a particular task depends generally on its purpose. In the case of journalism, relevance depends on whether, when, and how an investigator or reporter may try to address the interests of a particular readership or audience by choosing to emphasize some rather than some other aspects of a news story. In journalism, what is relevant truth telling depends on what we as journalists are trying to do and what we rightly believe we are supposed to be doing in covering a particular sort of news story. As news consumers, a group that incidentally also includes all journalists, what we find relevant in news reporting generally and very specifically depends on our interests as reflected in the amount of time and effort we are willing to devote to scanning it for content. Someone might read only national and international news in that order, and only glance at the local news; or the opposite. Another reader might consult only the comics and completely ignore the business section, sports section, and all human interest material. There is no moral obligation that has ever been argued for patrons who pick up a newspaper or tune in a news program to pay attention to anything that does not address their interests. We may all stand in need of being better educated about our true interests, and the media can also help in this regard. However, it appears contrary to insist that news consumers have any particular moral obligation to favor any part of what passes for the news in the absence of good reasons implying that we should have a particular set of interests. We may then as responsible citizens have a general moral obligation to keep ourselves informed of current events, according to our interests, and yet have no obligation to read every square inch of the paper or listen or watch every part of a news broadcast. As individuals, accordingly, we bear moral responsibility for what we choose to give our time and attention from the extraordinary media menu available today.

The remote control device on a modern television is a behavioral analyst's dream come true. We can see what interests viewers and what does not simply by keeping track of the number of times they change channels at the touch of a button and the length of time they watch programming with one type of content rather than another. A viewer might be following environmental programming intensely, almost to the point of exclusivity, while another has predominant interests in political developments in Africa. If a newspaper or news program contains mostly sports and we have no interest in following the teams and players, then we will probably vote with our feet by choosing another news source, one that better addresses our interests, whatever we rightly or wrongly consider them to be. It is a journalist's responsibility to provide news deemed relevant to a particular part of a population in the sense of addressing its interests. The news addresses a particular set of interests in turn by providing information to satisfy the consumer's curiosity about a matter of interest.

News as a commodity succeeds in the marketplace when it satisfies a sufficient public to support its operating costs. It succeeds as news on the other hand, regardless of its ledger book bottom line, only to the extent that it satisfies the legitimate demand for information associated with a specific set of interests. The investigators, reporters, and other producers of news, if this characterization of their moral situation is correct, are not, as journalists, professionally responsible for the nature or intensity of their customers' interests. The customers must look to themselves for these, and the arguments that would make it morally obligatory to know what is happening in the world at large, but not to know what sports records have been broken, or the reverse, are not topics of journalistic ethics but of a less specialized social-political ethics. What this means is that in theory we ourselves, rather than the journalists whose information services on which we rely, are responsible for our interests. Journalists can nevertheless play a role in cultivating their news customers' interests. This is the exception mentioned above. They do so when they responsibly publicize something that in their judgment deserves to be but have not yet been widely adopted as a focus of interest, thereby in effect creating an interest in a news subject that did not previously exist. This is what exposé journalists typically do, although their methods are only one of many ways that news reporting symbiotically creates at least part of the interest in particular kinds of information it serves. This type of journalism has sometimes been called "muckraking" by both its detractors and admirers. The image is one of investigative reporters stirring up trouble by uncovering facts that powerful persons would prefer to remain unknown. In less colorful terms, it often amounts to a print or electronic media campaign or crusade to arouse public interest in what a news outlet considers to be a vital but initially underappreciated issue.

Finally, we should recognize that journalists are not morally off the hook by virtue of catering to any and every interest their customers might happen to have. They would be wrong to try to satisfy what they themselves would deem as morally objectionable interests, which we need not excessively tax our imaginations to consider. Confidential medical information about otherwise unnoteworthy persons in a community is one obvious example, and we can easily think up many others. While journalists are not morally responsible for their clients' interests, except insofar as they have been instrumental in helping to shape them, they are morally responsible for those of its clients' interests they choose to address, as well, of course, for exactly how they choose to address them. Journalism at its best projects its news reporting to a sense of its clients' interests as members of a common community. It may seem dangerous to put things in quite this way, but good journalism aims at the interests a customer base realistically should have or what ideally can be thought to represent its best and most enlightened rational interests. The strategy of pitching news to this ideal is generally successful, not only in serving the fundamental principle of professional journalistic ethics and its moral mandate, so to speak, in the marketplace of ideas, but also in the economic marketplace. Wisely identifying their customers' best or ideal interests, that which they should be interested in, is not patronizing or condescending, but on the contrary represents respect for customers as intelligent rational agents. It has proven itself time and again also from an effective business standpoint in which professional journalism succeeds by best fulfilling its acknowledged purpose.

The guidance needed for making correct relevance judgments is common sense. It concerns the sort of information it is reasonable to expect consumers of the coverage will need and want to receive. Needless to say, the obvious cases with which we might begin do not settle questions of more fine-grained difficulty. We nevertheless assume that the same general principle applies in every case, even when the application itself is more complicated. Relevant information is always relevant relative to an assumed purpose or goal, directed toward a particular set of interests. In most cases, the purpose for which information is sought can be taken for granted by any reporter with experience. In other instances, the relevance of information that a reporter might choose to include or exclude may be more difficult to determine than the issue of whether or not to mention a jury member's fashion sense, or a Supreme Court nominee's shoe size.

Consider the former case again. How do we decide whether it is relevant to reporting on a murder trial whether or not the defendant frequently took notes and frowned during the proceedings? Is that something a reader or audience for a televised news story should be told? What about whether the judge decides to call for an early lunch prior to the defense attorney's summation? Whether or not such facts should be included in a news report are all matters of good journalistic judgment, and different reporters with different sensibilities and different perspectives are likely to decide these questions differently. What we can offer journalists by way of a moral signpost in professional journalistic ethics is the reminder that their fundamental obligation is to tell the truth and that the choice of what information is relevant or irrelevant to a given news story has a direct impact on whether or not they are adequately addressing their customers' legitimate interest-driven desire for information.

As in other contentious choices in reporting the news, journalists can make mistakes in reaching judgments of relevance. They can overlook essential aspects of a story by focusing on things that in retrospect may turn out to have been beside the point. What we generally require of journalists is that they make sincere energetic efforts to report what they genuinely consider to be the relevant facts and details of facts in reporting the news, together, as we shall now see, with something more. It is not enough for journalists merely to communicate whatever relevant truths they deem newsworthy, but, as in subsequent chapters we shall begin to explore, to do so to the best of their abilities more specifically *in the public interest*.

Summary

We require journalists to write and speak the truth. This is not an exaggerated, unattainable ideal, but one that, within the limits of practical affairs to which news reporting belongs, journalists can responsibly try to respect and observe. What we mean by truth is not something mysterious or impossible. It entails difficulties, to be sure, for the truth is not always easy to discover or communicate to others.

The standard of truth to which it makes the most sense to hold journalists professionally ethically responsible is that there be a positive correspondence between the facts as reported in a news item and the actual state of affairs that the report purports to describe. When a reporter says that it is raining and it is in fact raining, then the reporter has told the truth; otherwise, the report is false.

Falsehood can enter into news reporting in any of a variety of ways, through careless use of unreliable sources and in countless deliberate and inadvertent ways. Deliberate falsehoods in news reporting are the work of rogue reporters whose professional misconduct is morally intolerable. We should expose journalistic fraud wherever it occurs and impose appropriate professional sanctions against the deliberate purveying of falsehoods in the press and all news media.

Inadvertent falsehoods can also creep into the news in many different ways, all of which in our analysis amounts to saying that something has happened that did not in fact happen. Whether and how the inadvertent occurrence of false reporting can be discovered and how it should then be revealed is another question. News organizations should nevertheless make every attempt to root out mistakes and inaccuracies in their reporting and take action thereafter by reporting the mistake and acting to correct the damage its erroneous reporting may have caused by setting the record straight. Moral censure can still be justified even in such cases when news organizations do not act quickly enough on their own initiative or with insufficient publicity for mistakes in the reporting for which they are responsible.

The general professional ethical principle to which we appeal in considering all such cases of truthfulness in news reporting goes back to what we have here proposed as the fundamental justificatory principle and moral mandate for professional journalism, that journalists are morally obligated to provide maximally relevant truth telling in the public interest. The implications of this principle, and hence the question of whether it is finally correct or not, we have only begun to explore. We nevertheless see already at this early stage that the reactions on the part of ordinary news readers and audiences and by members of the profession to journalistic fraud strongly supports at least the component of the principle that emphasizes the importance of truth and accuracy in the news.

Anyone, journalists included, can make honest mistakes in sincerely trying to tell the truth. Journalists by avocation and professional training may have special motivations and skills to help them minimize the extent of their inadvertent inaccuracies. These include but are not limited to the independent checking of facts and inferences by sources and colleagues. Journalists nevertheless are by no means exceptions to the general rule that human beings are epistemically fallible. Professional journalistic ethical responsibility in such cases includes a provision to try to avoid all error in the first place, to actively seek out errors in the news and expose and correct them, and to take appropriate action to mitigate the damage caused by inadvertent falsehoods. The importance of correct, reliable, and accurate information content means that we as news consumers should expect no less of all members of the profession, on whose actions we daily depend for informed decision-making that for good or ill can vitally affect our lives.

chapter two

Journalistic Rights and Responsibilities

We expect of professional journalistic conduct not merely useful truth telling, but truth telling in the public interest. This adds a social element to journalistic ethics, which in this chapter we explicate as an interconnected network of journalistic moral rights and responsibilities.

RIGHTS AND RESPONSIBILITIES

We are told throughout life that rights and responsibilities go together. Something like this is probably true. A right gives us an opportunity to do something that no one else has the right to prevent us from doing. If we choose to exercise the right and actually do what we are entitled to do, then we incur responsibilities for the way we choose to act and the consequences of our decisions for ourselves and others. Hence the linking of rights and responsibilities. What, more specifically, does this mean for professional journalists? What are the ideal moral professional rights and ideal moral professional responsibilities? Where do moral professional rights, ideal or otherwise, come from, and how exactly are they related to moral professional responsibilities? Our task is first to understand the concepts of journalistic rights and journalistic responsibilities and to get a sense of what kinds of rights and responsibilities professional journalists in the politically most liberal progressive societies are typically said to have. Then we must ask about the origins of journalistic rights and responsibilities and try to understand how they are related. Along the way we consider ethical questions about specific presumed journalistic rights and responsibilities in recent journalistic practice.

LEGAL AND MORAL RIGHTS

The formula according to which rights entail responsibilities already stands in need of refinement. We must distinguish between *legal* and *moral rights*. Then we can say, for example, that a legal right gives us an opportunity under the law to do something that no one can legally prevent us from doing. We can also argue on the basis of this distinction that a moral right gives us an opportunity as far as a given principle of ethics is concerned to do something that no one can morally prevent us from doing.

The concept of a right, whether legal or moral, entitles us to do something. Whenever we have a right, other persons have no right to prevent us from doing it. Thus, if you have a right to express an opinion, then I have no right to obstruct you from doing so. If I have a right to vote in an election, then no one has a right to obstruct me when I try to vote. Rights confer a certain status on our conduct, both in private and public. We exercise our rights when we do what we are permitted to do or what as we ordinarily say we have the right to do. Lawmakers and philosophers sometimes speak of and argue about whether there is a right to life, a right to self-determination, a right to the pursuit of happiness, and so on. In every case, attributions of rights imply that an individual or social entity can do a certain kind of thing if they choose in the sense that no one has a right to prevent them. We do not speak of rights where persons are required to do something or are forced against their will. In such instances, the appropriate concept is rather that of having an obligation or duty or simply of being compelled regardless of rights and obligations. A right is something that is open to an individual or group to exercise or not. This is true even in the case of a right to life, if we suppose that it is up to each morally responsible person, especially at times of extreme crisis, to decide whether or not to choose life.

We have many legal and moral rights. Sometimes the two coincide, but our legal and moral obligations can also sometimes diverge. When this happens, we can be legally entitled to do something that is not approved by correct moral principles; or, in the contrary case, we can be morally entitled to do something that is not legally permitted. There are conflicts that sometimes arise between what we believe we ought morally to do and what the social institutions of law in a particular place and time permit or require us to do. We have the legal right to drive a car if we have met all the requirements to have a driver's license and a license has been issued to us. Then we can do certain things that we could not otherwise do. We can drive a car, other things being equal, virtually wherever we want and can afford to go. A critic of this assertion might object that driving is not a right, but a privilege. What this frequently heard slogan maintains is perfectly correct, but it embodies a kind of confusion. Although some people speak of there being a privilege rather than a right in these cases, generally what they mean is that there is no *inalienable right* concerning the activity in question, a right that holds no matter what or that cannot be taken away by others. We do have a legal *right* to drive when we are duly licensed to do so, even though our having the right is not inalienable or unconditional. Driving a car is in this sense a privilege granted to qualified persons by the state. It is also a right that can be taken away, contingent in particular on the driver's conduct. Driving is not only a conditional legal right for those who have been licensed to drive, but also truly a responsibility. We are legally responsible for our actions if we choose to exercise the legal right to drive. The law exists in part to protect persons from the irresponsible actions of others, so there is naturally a strong motivation for the law to inflict serious penalties on reckless driving, holding motorists legally responsible for the proper use of an automobile. Laws, after all, exist in theory primarily to protect society at large from the potentially harmful conduct of individuals.

Moral rights and responsibilities are precisely parallel to the distinction between legal rights and responsibilities. We expect in both cases that moral rights give us the right morally rather than legally to do something and that if we choose to exercise a moral right then we thereby incur corresponding moral responsibilities. Thus, suppose we have a moral right to care for our bodies. If we choose to exercise this right, which to some minimal degree we must if we are to live at all, then we are morally responsible for what we do to or with our bodies, allowing or restraining ourselves from getting too much sun or having too many sweets, or for having a sensible program of physical activity, good diet and exercise. A moral right in the end is only a moral opportunity. What we do with such an opportunity expresses and defines our moral character and gives us an opportunity in turn to behave in a morally praiseworthy or blameworthy way. Rights offer an open door, and we must choose whether and how to enter and how to behave with respect to the opportunities each right presents if we choose to act as the right permits.

What then are the rights and responsibilities of journalists? Is a newspaper or television program even partly morally responsible for a terrorist incident if the terrorists wanted to use the sensational news coverage for its own political gain? Are there limits beyond which no morally responsible journalist should stray in reporting the news? Does it matter how journalists get their stories or the social circumstances in which they publish their findings? What does it mean for journalists to be purveyors of truth about current events specifically in the public interest?

We consider these questions more pointedly in connection with the following recent case study.

Case Study 4

Right to Publish and Responsibility for News Content

The *Sunday World*, an Irish newspaper, in an article written by Paul Williams, contained an inflammatory report concerning an alleged Irish criminal, Martin Foley, notoriously known as The Viper. The four-page article appeared under the heading, "Foley's a Dead Man Walking." The article was an extract from a new book on the criminal underworld in Dublin by Williams, a crime journalist.

The *Irish Tribune*, a New York newspaper specializing in news for the Irish and Irish-American community (January 19–25, 2005, volume 19, issue 3, p. 4) reported that Foley's attorney subsequently described the article as "among the most profoundly irresponsible journalism and editorship of a widely circulating national newspaper that I could conceive of." The article in particular revealed the reporter's discovery or perhaps only an expression of opinion that Foley has been a police informant, hence, the significance of the article's title. Foley through his attorney appealed to the High Court in Dublin to stop publication of such stories as endangering his life by informing other criminals of his providing the police with information. Foley, aka The Viper, according to the *Irish Tribune*, has forty-five criminal convictions and has already survived three assassination attempts by Dublin's criminal gangs. Williams himself has since been subjected to intimidation and is under twenty-four-hour protection after a hoax bomb was planted under his car outside his home in November 2003, of which police sources believe Foley may have been guilty.

The *Sunday World* in the meantime has defended its decision to publish the article on grounds of its journalistic rights and responsibilities to keep the public informed of criminal activities.

QUESTIONS

1. Did Williams have a moral right as a journalist to publish his claim that Foley was a police informant? Does he bear any moral responsibility if harm should come to Foley as a result from other criminals?

2. What moral responsibility does the *Sunday World* have for printing Williams's story? Is there a special problem connected with the fact that Williams or an editor at the newspaper chose to title the article, "Foley's a Dead Man Walking"? Can this be regarded as especially inflammatory or as inciting criminals to take action against Foley on the belief that he has been a police informant? Or is the title, sensationalistic as it might be regarded, irrelevant to the question of the author's and paper's moral responsibility in the matter?

3. Does a convicted criminal have rights to privacy and protection from what might be said about them in the press? Does it make a difference with respect to the moral responsibility of the author and paper for printing the allegation whether the allegation is true or false?

4. Having hypothetically uncovered the fact that Foley had been a police informant and knowing that publishing this information might endanger his life, would Williams have been acting morally responsible as a journalist if he had not written his article and published this supposed fact?

5. Is it important for the public to know that a certain person has been a police informant? Is this the kind of information that should ever be published by a morally responsible news outlet if the person in question is likely as a result to suffer retribution? What are the lengths and limits of moral rights and responsibilities on the part of professional journalists in this case? What would you do, what do you think you should do in this situation, and, most important, why?

CONSEQUENCES FOR ABUSING RIGHTS

What happens when we act morally irresponsibly or even reprehensibly? What, if anything, happens if we act immorally? Why should we care if an action that gives us satisfaction is labeled by others as "moral" or "immoral"?

There are, as we should reasonably expect, all kinds of penalties that attach to immoral as well as illegal behavior, although the enforcement mechanisms for violations of an ethics code are often different from that of the law. We should remember first of all that many moral rights and responsibilities are also recognized and enforced by law. Ideally, the law should always be in step with good moral reasoning so that the provisions of social statutes match up positively with the most enlightened thinking about what it is morally right or wrong to do. Thus, legal penalties can also apply to violations of moral rights and responsibilities. Additionally, moral infractions are punished by earning a bad opinion among persons who accept and try more willfully to follow the prescriptions of what they take to be the moral obligations of a particular walk of life. In a professional context, earning the bad opinion of a sufficient number of one's peers can have a significant negative impact on the success or failure of a moral wrongdoer's chosen career. Of course, one can acquire a bad reputation through no fault of one's own, and many persons who act morally wrongly or irresponsibly completely escape acquiring a bad moral reputation. The usual situation, however, is rather one in which sooner or later persons earn the moral reputations they deserve, and those who are concerned to uphold moral standards can have second thoughts about entering into professional relations with persons who are known to behave improperly. The social enforcement of a professional moral code can thus become a meaningful deterrent to professionally unethical conduct, even for persons who are not otherwise prepared to act rightly if left entirely to their own judgment.

The question of moral sanctions for infractions of an ethical code is the subject of lengthy philosophical debate. We can say, as John Stuart Mill does in his 1863 moral-political philosophy essay *Utilitarianism*, that sanctions are of two kinds, internal and external.[1] The internal sanctions are by far the most powerful. They involve our wanting to do what we know to be right

---

[1]Mill, *Utilitarianism*, Chapter 3, Of the Ultimate Sanction of the Principle of Utility.

for the sake of our own peace of mind or if for no other reason then simply because we recognize it to be the right thing to do. What makes internal sanctions so powerful is that they are more natural, unforced, and they command greater voluntary energy of a moral agent acting rightly—in the present case, on the part of a morally responsible professional journalist. Internal motivations for morally responsible action are nevertheless of such a nature that some persons will feel and act upon their call, thinking that no other course is possible, while others will be altogether unmotivated to bring their own actions within the limits of morally proper decision-making.

Internal sanctions are typically found in the behavior of persons who regard themselves as under an obligation or sense of duty to do what is right, provided they can assure themselves that they are in acting rightly. They want to do what they believe they are morally obligated to do or even to go beyond the call of duty by doing morally approved things that are not strictly required. Such actions are said to be *supererogatory*, and they include acts that help others to whom we are strictly under no moral obligation to help. Why do people act morally? It is in large part because they seek to maintain a self-image of themselves as guiding their actions in accord with moral principles. Most people desire to do the right thing without having external pressures exerted against them. They prefer to act from a sense of their own good character rather than being forced by threat of law or external social sanction of any kind to do what they can satisfy themselves is morally right.

It is primarily to persons in this category that a book like this one on professional ethics is addressed. It would be naive to suppose that in the course of a few hundred pages we could persuade persons by argument, who are otherwise inclined toward abusing their rights and shirking their responsibilities, to suddenly turn their lives around and act as they should. Rather, we assume that the reader already has an internal self-motivated desire to act morally within whatever professional ethical guidelines it seems appropriate to adopt, once they are informed about them and persuaded of their legitimacy. These morally self-motivated individuals are naturally invited to join in discussion as to what the proper understanding of moral rights and responsibilities for professional journalists should be thought to consist. It is only worth knowing as an interesting sideline that persons who make themselves egregious violators of moral principles can find themselves on the wrong end of a bad reputation that can affect how others freely choose to interact with or avoid them both personally and professionally. This is certainly not a sufficient motive in and of itself to curb moral wrongdoing generally or in the particular professions, but it is something almost as predictable as thunder after lightning that follows immoral behavior in a social context, given enough time and a community of persons who are trying themselves to conduct their lives and their careers within the limitations of a moral code.

For similar reasons, we should recognize that moral principles can at best only be imperfectly enforced by statutory law. A corrupt individual who knows that it is morally obligatory to do a certain thing can always contrive ingenious excuses as to why the principle does not apply in a particular case where it is advantageous to act immorally. They may also convince themselves that they will not be discovered, as some of the bad actors in recent instances of journalistic plagiarism mentioned in the previous chapter may have believed. Or they think that if they are caught they will be able to avoid punishment through luck, lack of prosecutorial commitment, or by having a good attorney. Some individuals will always feel the need personally to push the boundaries of what they know to be legal and of moral limitations on their actions by trying to see how much they can get away with in violating conventional moral principles, in order to challenge themselves and the social system in which they live.

As an exercise, try to list some of the things that you believe you are morally obligated to do, for which the law has no provisions. Then list some of the things you believe you are legally obligated to do, for which moral principles as you intuitively understand them have nothing whatsoever to say. Here are a few examples to help you get started. We are morally obligated not to tell lies, but the law has no mechanism for requiring that we always speak the truth except in special circumstances, as when we are on a witness stand in court and offering testimony under oath, or when we are advertising a product and making claims about what it can do for persons who spend their money on it, and the like. We may also be morally obligated to help other persons in distress, for example, by donating part of our income to charities. Certainly, however, the law has no stipulations for making sure that the citizens under its governance act charitably toward others. On the other side of the equation, we may be legally required to register for the military in a certain country, if that is what the law requires, but it is controversial at best to suppose that we are therefore also morally obligated to do so. We may be legally required for similar reasons not to drink alcohol before we have attained a certain age, but we may wonder whether there is any deeper moral reason not to drink until a particular birthday has been reached.

When morality and the law agree, we can refer to the same sets of rights and responsibilities indifferently as moral or legal. Ideally, then, as we have said, the law is judged to be correct because it reflects a set of morally correct principles, and the moral principles in turn ideally have inspired and guided the drafting and enforcement of laws. This, remarkably, is not always the case. The law does not consider various moral rights and obligations as any part of its concern, and ethics typically is understood as both the foundation of law and, given the imperfection of human lawmaking, as sometimes at odds with the legal tenets that happen to prevail. The most conspicuous cases of divergence between morality and the law occur in societies whose moral principles seem far removed from our own, as in dictatorships where the morality of law has been subordinated to political interests. The general conclusion to be reached in these considerations is that while law and morality, legal and moral rights and responsibilities, can sometimes coincide, they need not always be consistent. Often we find it important to question the morality of the law or of a proposed law, which in itself indicates the extent to which we are prepared to consider ethics and the law as distinct.

When we consider the part played by journalists in reporting the news and meeting their professional moral obligation to provide relevant truth telling in the public interest, special moral problems can arise. The following case study illustrates the moral responsibilities journalists can encounter in fulfilling their obligation to publicize potentially sensitive information that they perceive to be in the public interest.

Case Study 5

Role of News Reporters as Responsible Citizens in Criminal Investigations

The recent court trial of pop singer Michael Jackson raises an interesting problem about the potentially conflicting moral rights and responsibilities of news investigators. News investigators as a general rule are expected to distance themselves from the events on which they report. We study this aspect of journalistic ethics later in another chapter in more detail. A case can nevertheless be made on moral grounds for journalists to provide relevant information to legal authorities in prosecuting accused criminals.

A question has been raised as to whether Court TV's reporter Diane Dimond may have helped prosecutors gather evidence in prosecuting Jackson on a variety of charges connected with incidents involving minors at his so-called Neverland Ranch in California, and, if in fact she did so, whether she acted rightly or wrongly from the standpoint of journalistic ethics.

The details of the accusation concern Dimond's discovery of a soiled item of clothing that may have belonged to Jackson in the possession of a New Jersey businessman named Henry Vaccaro Sr.'s collection of Jackson family memorabilia in a warehouse in Asbury Park. Dimond, upon making the discovery, reportedly declared that she would reveal the facts she had uncovered to prosecuting Santa Barbara District Attorney Tom Sneddon.

A New York newspaper, the *Daily News,* reported on March 15, 2005 that the morning after Dimond's visit to the Vaccaro warehouse Sneddon telephoned Vaccaro to ask permission to borrow the items housed in his collection for possible use in the district attorney's office criminal investigation of Jackson. Dimond, however, through a Court TV spokesperson, commented that she had simply sought a reaction from Sneddon's office concerning "some evidence that might be of interest to the prosecution."

Dimond was indeed shown in a Court TV broadcast carefully lifting items of clothing that reportedly belonged to Jackson in Vaccaro's collection and speculating that they might contain DNA evidence useful to the prosecution of the Jackson case. Vaccaro recalled, as the *Daily News* reported, that when the camera was turned off, Dimond supposedly said to Vaccaro that, in Vaccaro's words, "she told me she was going to call the prosecutor about this." In a letter of January 13, 2005, Vaccaro reportedly told Sneddon: "I was contacted by your office after Diane Dimond of Court TV informed you that there were various items of potential interest to you among the contents of a warehouse in Asbury Park, N.J."

QUESTIONS

1. If we suppose for the sake of argument that the information represented above is true, did Dimond act wrongly in contacting the district attorney's office with potential evidence for their ongoing investigation of Michael Jackson? If so, why; if not, why not?

2. How can we begin to understand the Dimond case in terms of journalistic moral rights and responsibilities? Does a news investigator have a moral right or a moral responsibility to alert authorities to evidence that might be helpful to their prosecutions of individuals accused of crimes?

3. A news reporter, like any other citizen, presumably has a responsibility not to conceal evidence connected with a criminal prosecution. Even if it is not part of a news investigator's moral responsibility to reveal possible sources of evidence to legal authorities, would it be an adequate defense of Dimond's hypothetical actions to argue that she did so not as a news investigator but as a concerned citizen, even if she made her discovery while acting in a journalistic capacity?

4. Is there an analogy to be drawn between a journalist's rights and responsibilities with respect to discoveries of evidence relevant to alleged criminal behavior and a priest's or doctor's presumed obligation to preserve the confidentiality of the confessional or examination room?

5. Would Dimond have been acting morally responsibly as either a journalist or citizen if she had discovered evidence that might be relevant to an ongoing criminal investigation or prosecution and failed to report it to the relevant authorities? How shall we try to understand the potential for conflicting moral obligations arising from the kinds of information that

journalists sometimes uncover in the course of preparing news stories? What if a reporter discovers evidence of a planned murder or terrorist attack or of significance to the legal process for such an event after it has occurred? What kind of line can then be drawn between categories of evidence that should and those that should not be communicated to the appropriate authorities?

RELATION OF RIGHTS AND RESPONSIBILITIES

How exactly, then, do legal or moral rights incur legal or moral responsibilities? How are rights and responsibilities related?

If we think about the legal right to drive a car once the licensing privilege has been granted to a driver, it is clear that there is some kind of exchange of value. The driver is given an extraordinary opportunity, as far as the law is concerned, to take under his or her control a powerful and potentially dangerous piece of machinery to use at will within prescribed limits. The driver in turn agrees to accept and as much as possible to drive responsibly within the provisions of the traffic law, and, in general, to drive with consideration for the damage against life and property it would be possible to perpetrate with an automobile. The exchange is one of a new and intrinsically as well as instrumentally valuable opportunity for an agreement to conduct one's behavior in accord with a set of rationally established rules for the minimization of danger to the driver and others with whom the driver might come into contact in the course of exercising the conditional right to drive.

Why are rights and responsibilities interrelated in this way? Why, in order to enjoy the opportunity for action that a right affords, should we be burdened with a certain set of responsibilities? Why can we not simply do what we want without thinking about the consequences of our actions? How does a rights-responsibilities dynamic in ethics or the law get established in the first place?

The link between rights and responsibilities, legal and moral, seems to lie in the fact that the opportunities for action that a right confers upon a moral agent by their very nature create situations of potential loss of something of value by other persons. Those persons may also have the right to do the same kinds of things. By choosing to exercise a moral right themselves in the meantime, they presumably do not thereby relinquish any of their right to be protected from the irresponsible exercise of the same rights by others. Imagine that the citizens of a community gather in a public building and an official there has been designated to hand out moral rights to do this or that. You are given an envelope explaining the particular rights you are about to receive. Some of the rights that are being distributed to persons at the meeting can cause various harms if exercised carelessly. Driving a car is one obvious example, and we have already encountered many more kinds of consequences for the practice of journalistic rights. We can think of countless kinds of similar applications for all of the kinds of rights we know are often made available to persons in a modern community. With the right qualifications and credentials, for example, one has the right to practice medicine or law. We need only reflect for a moment to appreciate the fact that exercising the conditional right to practice medicine or the law can have enormous implications for the welfare of other persons affected by the exercise of such a right. The same kind of thing is true for other kinds of rights that the individuals in a social group might delegate to one another under certain circumstances in the public interest. We see this clearly in the case of persons who exercise rights of government and leadership, police and fire and other kinds of emergency workers, hunters and other gun owners, architects who design the buildings we must trust not to collapse while we are in them, the growers and distributors of food and food products, teachers and artists, and all other members of a community. The community itself in one sense exists in order to oversee and protect the rights and responsibilities of its members.

The reasoning is the same in every application. The community benefits from having rights as opportunities for certain kinds of actions extended to certain of its qualifying members, who in turn thereby accept the responsibility to exercise their rights in a way that causes no undue harm to other members of the community. It is the community in a certain sense that makes moral rights available to its members, in the scenario we have described, in order for the community as a whole to benefit. The community in effect says that this person based on his or her qualifications can be a dentist and another person cannot, that this person can be a horse breeder or an electrician or a journalist, and this other person cannot. The community takes an interest in such questions and invests its time and energy in extending these rights to qualified citizens for the good of the community as a whole. It is therefore morally obligated, because of its responsibility to the community whose interests it represents, to exercise control also over what happens within the community as a result of the exercise of the rights it grants.

It would never do to have a community extend the right of practicing medicine to a given member and then wash its hands of whatever the person choosing to exercise such a right thereafter happens to do. Suppose the individual turned out to be completely incompetent and was ruining the health and even losing the lives of numerous patients. That kind of behavior is obviously not in the interest of the community and is controlled in the main by most persons' internal sense of wanting to do the right thing in a personal or professional moral context. It is also controlled by external enforcement of the community's expectations of moral responsibility when internal sanctions are not enough to maintain the community's interests.

If we were to answer the philosophical question as to where rights and responsibilities come from, as a result, we could say the following. Rights generally are opportunities to act in certain ways for which impediments that would otherwise hinder action have been legally or morally removed. Such obstacles are removed conditionally, assuming that a person is qualified to exercise the right in question and with the proviso that the exercise of the right shall be in accordance with certain expectations related to the community's interests in advancing its values. These are the responsibilities associated with and incurred by the voluntary exercise of rights. The same is true whether the rights and responsibilities in question are legal or moral, between which there exists a strong positive analogy. The principal difference between legal and moral rights and responsibilities is the source and institution from which the rights and responsibilities are thought to derive.

We can often identify the source of legal rights and responsibilities. They are codified in the form of statutes and precedents. There is usually a particular piece of legislation to which we can point as the origin of, say, the right to drive if you have passed the requisite examinations and met all the other legal requirements for becoming a driver. Similarly for the rights and responsibilities of dentists, physicians, architects, journalists, and the like. The source of moral rights and responsibilities is typically less obvious and more open to question. Thus, we should not be surprised to find philosophers debating with some heat the problem of where morality comes from and how it relates moral rights to moral responsibilities outside the jurisdiction of law books and court decisions. Several answers to the question of how moral rights are related to moral responsibilities can be found by understanding their anthropology or origin in human affairs.

We should therefore try to answer this question, as it is vital to the topic of professional journalistic ethics insofar as we try to explain its principles as a matter of professional moral rights and professional moral responsibilities. We are not going to try to resolve long-standing disputes in ethical philosophy in a heavy-handed way by bringing to bear a complex ethical theory. Nor is the following list intended to be exhaustive. We merely take note of some of the most interesting possibilities for identifying a plausible connection between moral rights and moral responsibilities. The point is that we require a minimal theoretical foundation for discussing the nature of journalistic moral rights and responsibilities before we can turn to developments in the philosophical literature that might help guide us in the right direction as we continue to explore the principles of journalistic ethics. Let us therefore consider these options:

- To every (legal or moral) right there corresponds by definition a (legal or moral) responsibility or set of responsibilities; a right on this account is as much associated with a corresponding responsibility as a mountain with a valley.
- Some but not all rights imply corresponding responsibilities; there are exceptions to the interrelation of rights and responsibilities. This raises the question

as to whether or not journalistic rights in particular are associated with journalistic responsibilities.

- Rights as such do not imply corresponding responsibilities, although the exercise
  of certain rights under certain circumstances can imply certain responsibilities.
- Most rights happen to be associated with responsibilities because exercising a right
  construed as an opportunity for action is generally connected as a matter of contingent fact with the potential for abuse and the possibility of inadvertently harming
  others by violating their rights if the right is practiced recklessly or irresponsibly.

It is only because virtually anything we undertake to do potentially
risks harming other persons that responsibilities on the present proposal
arise in the first place. This fact is seen most clearly in circumstances when we
act in full possession of the right to act, when we attribute certain kinds of
responsibilities to the exercise of certain kinds of rights. Its purpose is to urge
caution in the exercise of rights and to put those on notice who choose to act
according to their perception of their rights that they can expect to be held
accountable for the way in which their exercise of rights and its consequences
can affect the welfare of others.

For example, under normal circumstances I may have the right as a
journalist to publish a certain story in a newspaper or on the airwaves.
If doing so offends against the rights of others, however, then my professional moral obligation to act responsibly as a journalist might obligate me to
withhold the story. I have no right to do things that violate the rights of
others, and similarly they cannot engage in activities that would violate my
rights. This means that I can only legitimately exercise my rights within a set
of constraints established by the principle that I must do my utmost not to
infringe upon another individual's rights. The obvious reason is that my
rights to do what I want are never morally more important than those of any
other person. If I have the right to do something, a person potentially
affected by my exercising my rights has the right in turn to be protected from
any damaging effects that result from my actions.

ORIGIN OF JOURNALISTIC RIGHTS

Where do rights, including journalistic rights, come from? The final alternative outlined above, protecting persons from the abuse of rights by others,
offers an important clue. Rights on this view are not brought down from
mountaintops engraved on stone tablets. They exist only insofar as they are
recognized by a society as protected forms of action that are extended to anyone who chooses to exercise them, provided the actions are undertaken
responsibly. In this sense, the set of inalienable or unconditional rights may
shrink to none or perhaps only a very few.

We are accustomed to speaking of the right to life as inalienable, but
even this is philosophically controversial. The verdict is still out on questions

about the morality or immorality of abortion, euthanasia, capital punishment, and certain types of war that are sometimes thought to be morally justified. If any of these practices is morally defensible, then they entail limitations on the right to life. Consider the case of capital punishment, for example. I may have a right to life, but my right need not be absolute, unconditional, or inalienable if I sacrifice my right by committing a capital offense such as murder. In that event, by breaking the moral and social pledge not to deprive others unjustly of their rights, I may morally deserve to lose my own right to life. We need not enter further into the ethics of capital punishment, which is a difficult moral issue in many respects. The general point should nevertheless be clear, for there are other imaginable examples that point to the same conclusion. Suppose that I have a right to life, but that I have contracted an infectious plague that cannot be contained as long as I remain alive. If my right to life is respected, then the result is certain to be the loss of life of many millions of persons. It would be a kind of contradiction to maintain that I have an absolute, unconditional, or inalienable right to life but that for the good of all the right to life I ordinarily enjoy from a moral point of view ought to be rescinded. It is difficult as a consequence to make a strong case for there being any absolute, unconditional, or inalienable rights. The problem of negotiating rights and responsibilities has led to unresolved moral philosophical controversies that have in turn exerted an impact on the law and its social implications.

A person who chooses to exercise a right does so ultimately on the assumption that society benefits from persons being allowed to engage in a permitted course of action. The same is true with respect to rights of religious freedom, enfranchisement or the right to vote, and the right of peaceable assembly, among others. All of these rights prescribe kinds of actions, often in the most general terms, which individuals can choose to practice. Since each of these courses of action can potentially harm others, and hence indirectly harm society, they all come packaged with at least an implicit and sometimes explicit agreement as to their responsible exercise. Society would have no interest and would be remiss in its own duties if it were to extend rights to citizens the exercise of which could weaken or even destroy itself. This is why there are always strings attached where rights are concerned. As the very nature of a right implies that as a course of action the right might be used to harm others, it must be exercised only responsibly with respect to the way in which it is pursued and the consequences that result. If I have the right to freedom of religious expression, I must act responsibly in exercising the right, among other ways, by not acting in such a way as to violate the rights of others, say, by practicing human sacrifice or, less drastically but still offensively, by broadcasting sermons so loudly at night that no one can get to sleep. If rights ultimately derive from society, from the imaginary or documented social contract that binds us to one another in a system of moral rules and expectations, then society has not only the right but the responsibility to expect only the responsible exercise of the rights it bestows on citizens. Society does not give license to individuals to engage in activities that will harm itself; that would not be rational. If we are looking for a reason why responsibilities are so often associated with rights, then we must naturally expect the explanation of how rights and responsibilities are interrelated to be built on rational assumptions.

The implication is that all rights may turn out to be conditional. Rights are seldom if ever unqualified in the sense that they give us free turn to do whatever we like in the particular area of behavior to which the right applies. If I lend you my car to drive, then I will have extended to you a right that we may suppose is in my capacity to bestow. You are now entitled to drive my car. Naturally, since I value my car, I will want to attach certain qualifications, asking you to drive responsibly within the law and perhaps to obey a few rules about when the car is to be returned, in what condition, and with what amount of gasoline in the tank. If our reasoning has been correct, then rights, although extended *to* individuals derive *from* a combination of individual and public interests. The exercise of such rights must therefore ultimately be justified by the extent to which they satisfy individual desires but also by their contribution to the public interest.

This, in any case, is the sort of thing we ordinarily say about social or legal rights. Does the same reasoning apply to moral rights? Moral rights, like legal rights, are not completely inalienable. They are not inviolable in the sense that they can never justifiably be taken away under any circumstances. Moral rights are never unconditional in the sense of being responsibility-free. We might say, by way of posing a counterexample to this thesis, that we have an unconditional responsibility-free moral right to scratch our heads right now if we choose. If we do have such a moral right, it is not the most important one precisely because it does not require much in the way of corresponding responsibility. To admit this is nevertheless not to say that the right is truly unconditional or entirely responsibility-free. For if we owe other responsibilities toward ourselves with respect to the protection and maintenance of our bodies and their good health, then we must presumably not scratch our heads in such a way as to do ourselves a pointless bodily injury, by scratching too hard or too long or by using a dangerous implement, such as a spinning power tool. Nor are we freely permitted to scratch our heads if we know that in doing so we are sure to cause another occurrence that is contrary to a morally preferred purpose. I should not scratch my head, although I have in another sense a moral right to do so, if I have good reason to believe that my scratching will, let us say, alert an enemy to the presence of an innocent intended victim. Then, although I have a moral right to scratch my itch, I am morally obligated to refrain from doing so because my right is overridden by a more highly valued moral responsibility involving the moral rights of others. The fact that I am morally obligated not to exercise my moral right to scratch does not detract from the fact that I have a moral right to scratch, but only from the false expectation that I may have an unconditional or unqualified moral right to scratch. In any plausible real-life scenario, there is no moral obstacle whatsoever to scratching one's head. We have to reach pretty far in our imaginations to find a possible reason to morally restrain persons from scratching their heads. The point is only that even where the most petty of actions is concerned, by virtue of its causal potential or even its symbolic meaning in a social context, there could be reasons to morally override the exercise of a moral right and to cancel the freedom it otherwise affords at that particular time and place.

The exercise of any moral right accordingly entails moral responsibilities. To live is to exercise moral rights of many overlapping and occasionally conflicting kinds with corresponding moral responsibilities. It is the theoretical basis for the concept of persons trying to live morally responsible lives. This is not just a homily, but a fact about the nature of moral rights that derives from their social origin. What it means in practical terms for the moral rights associated with a particular profession, such as journalism, is that journalistic moral rights, like any other rights, are not morally absolute, unconditional, or unqualified, or, in the strict sense, inalienable.

What, then, is the origin of journalistic rights and responsibilities? Where do they come from, and what can we learn from their derivation about the proper exercise of journalistic rights by professional journalists?

If we turn our attention from the most trivial of moral rights, as in the head-scratching example, to what might be called the moral right to life, then we see that to exercise a moral right to life, if there is such a thing, immediately entails that one act in a morally responsible way in all one's doings, minimally, avoiding committing injustices against others. Whether we are also to help others with their problems in addition to doing them no harm is a separate topic for theoretical ethics, one centering on the role of compassion in our moral lives, or on other social contract foundations, or another source of moral obligation, for acting, often at considerable risk to oneself, on behalf of others.

Journalists are sometimes called upon to do this kind of thing as part of their job. They often travel in unconventional ways to dangerous places endangering life and limb in order to bring news to their readership or audience for the public good. If they are the kind of journalists who need to be close to where events are taking place in order to report the news, then in war and natural disaster, among other live events, while still acting prudently to protect themselves, journalists can be killed or seriously injured in fulfilling their duties. They take such risks for the sake of doing their assignments in compliance with their own work ethic, advancing themselves professionally, and making a living at something they enjoy and think is important. If they endanger themselves thereby, it should ultimately be for the sake not of thrill-seeking and living dangerously on the edge, but of bringing valuable information to the public in the public interest. This should constitute an important part of their sense of every journalist's professional responsibility.

Let us consider the matter in more detail by investigating another case study. The following example and questions for philosophical reflection concern a particular journalist's sense of moral responsibility to make "full disclosure" to newspaper readers of background incidents involving a personal incident with a political personality that might be related to the reporter's ability to provide objective reportage about the individual. Here we ask whether the reporter, Daniel Schorr, might not only be fulfilling a journalistic responsibility, but also taking the occasion to reveal some damaging facts about the person involved.

Case Study 6

Journalistic Responsibility Versus Detachment

Distinguished correspondent Daniel Schorr, in an article in the *Christian Science Monitor* for November 12, 1999, page 11, had the following to say about then American presidential candidate Patrick J. Buchanan, who as it happens is also a sometime author and journalist:

> "I have always prided myself on being able to maintain journalistic detachment about politicians, even Richard Nixon. But when my involvement with a politician is such that it could color my views, I count it my journalistic obligation to make full disclosure. The politician in question is Patrick Buchanan. My problem with him—or may be his problem with me—goes beyond his much criticized defense of Hitler as 'an individual of great courage . . . a soldier's soldier . . . a genius' [no source provided]. It goes back to 1971, when Mr. Buchanan was a speechwriter for President Nixon. He drafted a speech in which Nixon promised a Roman Catholic Knights of Columbus audience to rescue the parochial schools in the face of Supreme Court decisions barring federal aid to religious institutions. Asked to report on the CBS Evening News how he would do that, I checked with education officials and Catholic school lobbyists, and I reported that the speech seemed to be little more than political rhetoric. Buchanan expressed his resentment to Nixon, and Nixon had J. Edgar Hoover investigate me in the hope of digging up some dirt on me. When the *Washington Post* broke the story of the investigation with a front-page headline, 'FBI Probes Newsman Critical of

President,' the White House, in a hasty damage-control session, devised a cover story that my background was being checked because I was under consideration for a White House appointment. The story was that, through an oversight, I had not been apprised of the job. . . . What Buchanan would have done with the dirt on me, if the FBI had found any, I would not venture to say. Anyway, nothing bad happened to me. And the misuse of the FBI became one item in the bill of impeachment against Nixon (under Article II, 'Abuse of Power'). So, I'm not mad at Buchanan. But it is interesting to know that at least when he was young and brash, he wouldn't hesitate to use the FBI against someone who got in his way".

QUESTIONS

1. Schorr maintains that he has a journalistic obligation, which is to say responsibility, to disclose circumstances that could "color" his views on a politician. What does he mean by this? Is he right to say that he has a moral responsibility as a journalist to reveal such facts to his readers? Why or why not?

2. From what might Schorr's sense of journalistic obligation derive? What is its source? What would be the consequence if Schorr had reported on Buchanan, then a candidate for president, if he had not made this disclosure about an incident in which he and Buchanan were involved? How does it help or hurt his credibility as a "detached" journalistic reporter to have made such disclosure? Why do you think he felt compelled to report these facts?

3. Can fulfillment of ostensible journalistic responsibilities also be used to disguise ulterior motives, such as the desire to charge another person with such wrongdoing as abuse of power? If so, does this in any way detract from the positive moral value we generally associate with satisfying one's professional ethical responsibilities?

4. The quotation from Schorr presented above appears in the "Opinion" section of the *Christian Science Monitor*. What is the relevance in that context of mentioning Buchanan's past words of praise for Adolf Hitler? Does this also constitute part of Schorr's moral obligation as a journalist, or does it represent another purpose that might in principle be compatible or incompatible with journalistic responsibility to disclose a past possible personal conflict with an individual about whom the reporter is engaged in writing news stories?

5. If Schorr has a moral responsibility as a journalist to reveal a fact about Buchanan as potentially affecting his objectivity as a reporter or opinion editorialist, would it not be better, in the sense of better meeting his professional journalistic responsibilities, for him to decline to write anything at all about Buchanan? Why, if he needs to alert the reader about the incident, does he not simply excuse himself from having any comment about Buchanan's personality or public conduct? Would that be more or less journalistically responsible under the circumstances?

Summary

The moral rights of journalists can be articulated and defended in several ways. What do journalists, morally speaking, have the right to do? We can say, and we shall later explain more fully, that journalists have the right to discover and publish or broadcast newsworthy information in the public interest. This means in effect that journalists would then morally have the right to dig up and publicize information on any other person they choose or their plans and projects.

Why would we agree to accept such snooping in our lives? We might think that we personally will never be affected, because our lives are not interesting or important enough to attract the interest or attention of professional journalists. There are nevertheless countless circumstances in which we can imagine ourselves the subject of a journalistic investigation. We might wonder then why we should ever have allowed journalists to have the political freedom, let alone to grant them theoretically the moral liberty, to investigate any and every subject they choose. Now that we have explored the distinction between legal and moral rights and responsibilities, we are prepared in greater depth in sequel chapters to consider journalistic rights and responsibilities.

These factors are in one sense moral, but are sometimes also legally specified and protected, as we find in the provisions of the law. They are conspicuously represented in other places, explicitly in the provisions of the U.S. Constitution that establish the nation's freedom of the press. The Constitution in turn has served as a model for other nations seeking to establish progressive policies with respect to freedom of the press.

Moral and legal rights and responsibilities can also sometimes conflict. We need to be aware of the kinds of situations in which such conflicts can occur, partly so that we can avoid them if we choose, but also because they illustrate some of the interesting ways in which our practical decision-making can become legally and morally complicated. In the discussion to follow we shall accordingly take time to reconsider what it means to say that journalists ought to have the moral freedom to discover and disseminate news information about whatever topics they deem to be sufficiently newsworthy.

Are journalists morally responsible for the crimes and acts of terror that might be committed in order to generate publicity and notoriety? We have already covered enough territory in this chapter to have the answer. Journalists are responsible for reporting news events in a timely fashion, and, as we have formulated their professional obligations, to provide relevant truth telling in the public interest. Although many subtle variations of the problem are imaginable, each potentially with a different verdict about whether or not journalists have stepped over the line dividing responsible reporting from becoming a propaganda vehicle for dangerous forces that want to disrupt society, it should be clear that journalists are not morally responsible for the criminal acts of persons on which they report. Journalists are nevertheless morally responsible for reporting such occurrences in a responsible way that serves the public interest. If they glorify or vilify persons involved without adequate facts to back up their allegations, or if by the tone or content of reporting they instigate further acts of violence, then we would naturally consider them to have strayed beyond their obligation to report the news responsibly. Merely by reporting the facts about incidents caused by terrorists or other criminals, however, or existing as a news service that is prepared to make such reports, journalists, other things being equal, do nothing morally objectionable. It is the persons who commit such actions that are morally responsible for what they do, even and especially if their purpose is to capitalize on the availability of news coverage to publicize their cause.

In this chapter we have touched on, but have not entered in depth into, questions about what specific professional moral responsibilities journalists can reasonably be thought to have or of exactly how these responsibilities might be related to journalistic rights. Instead, we have concentrated on central topics in the theory connecting moral rights to responsibilities. We have further tried to explain how a society's extending journalistic rights to the members of a profession like journalism is accompanied by expectations that these rights will be responsibly exercised for the good of all. The remaining parts of the book in a variety of ways explore the exact nature of journalistic responsibilities. We shall continue to examine these in ever greater and more specific detail, with an eye to resolving the kinds of moral conflicts of moral rights and responsibilities that can arise in a journalist's daily work.

chapter three

Moral Ideals and Workaday Journalistic Realities

To this point we have projected an ideal of professional journalistic ethics that emphasizes relevant truth telling in the public interest. The relation between journalistic rights and responsibilities entails that journalists have both the right and the responsibility to discover and publish the truth about current events of interest to their readers. This chapter examines the very idea of projecting an ideal for journalistic ethics when journalists must find work in a less-than-ideal world of egos, gritty commercial pressures, and other contra-utopian realities. We offer concrete reasons why even a hard-boiled practicing journalist should care about the philosophical foundations of an abstract moral ideal for professional journalistic conduct.

MORAL IDEALS

Why should anyone care about an abstract moral ideal when we have to live in a real world of harsh realities? Sometimes this question is raised as a way of challenging the applicability of an ethical principle, and sometimes it expresses a moral skepticism that gives in to whatever pressures impinge against our desires to do what we believe to be right. The discrepancy between ideals and the real world can be used to suggest that there may be no point in thinking about moral rights and responsibilities. The argument is that whatever ethical theory tries to tell us about how we should try to live, we will learn soon enough in the real world that moral principles are liabilities rather than assets in almost all aspects of working life, especially in professions like journalism.

Trying to do without an ethics for professional practices like journalism, however, is simply not an option. Just as no society can hope to survive without a social ethics guiding the actions of its citizens and institutions, so no profession within society can expect to fulfill its function in the absence of a professional ethics. The only question is what kind of ethics and what kind of ethical principles a professional journalistic ethics should try to develop. We have already proposed an abstract moral ideal for professional journalism. It is flexible as it stands, but sufficiently specific in its statement to avoid ambiguity in most applications. We should usually be able to decide with enough facts at our disposal whether or not a given journalistic action did or did not contribute to relevant truth telling in the public interest. There is nothing morally ambiguous about a clear-cut case of plagiarism or news source fabrications, nor about accepting a bribe not to publish a story about a politician's son's or daughter's drug arrest. We should recognize at the same time that the real world for practicing journalists is not a moral utopia, but a complicated business environment with many different kinds of personal and professional pressures on those who would otherwise prefer to pursue their work according to appropriate moral standards. In light of these factors, it can seem naive, even laughable, to suppose that a practicing journalist would always adhere to an abstract moral principle instead of acting only to promote his or her interests leading to recognition, promotion, better work conditions, and financial rewards.

CONFLICTS OF MORAL IDEALS AND MARKETPLACE REALITIES

The same thing could nevertheless be said with respect to any moral principle whatsoever. It is easy to portray a morally principled person as a chump when other persons are bending or breaking the rules and apparently getting away with it. We need to ask why the morally justified choice should be made even if to do so does not promote our other desires. The real world will always be more complicated and place greater demands on an individual's moral strength than are fully anticipated in the abstract realm of philosophical reflection on the problems and principles of ethics. If the implication is that we must give up on ethics altogether, then we are in serious trouble as a society. The quality of life would be adversely affected for every one of us if there were suddenly no moral principles or persons willing to follow them. The conclusion that ethics is pointless because of the complexity of prevailing social conditions, fortunately, is not entailed by the fact that other persons do not always act morally or that the principles of ethics are sometimes formulated as abstract idealizations.

Here is an analogy. Suppose that you are training for an athletic competition. You know that your physical limits prevent you from running or swimming a course within a certain time, but you also believe that by holding out the goal of reaching a particular realistically unattainable distance or time, you can improve your skill, endurance, and competitiveness to a much greater degree than if you simply shrugged your shoulders and admitted defeat, telling yourself that you will never be as great as Mark Spitz, Carl Lewis, Crystal Cox, or whoever your sports hero happens to be. The same is true in living a moral life. We need not be assured at the outset that we will be able to surmount every difficulty standing in the way of making ethical decisions about how to conduct ourselves, particularly within a specialized profession like journalism. We would also be incautious, however, simply to follow the behavior of other professionals already working in the field unless we think they are behaving morally as well as succeeding commercially. For this we must approach the daily workplace in journalism with a different set of questions than merely how to solve the immediate crises in the writing and technical production of news reports. We must ask whether the successes scored by professionals are done in the right way, for the right reasons, and with a reflective sense of what should be permitted and what should be prohibited in journalistic conduct.

The picture in any case is not all gloomy, like a Dickensonian workhouse, in 'real life' journalism. We should avoid oversimplifying the problem by imagining that reporters are always in moral conflict with their superiors, beginning with their assignment editors and proceeding all the way to the owners or board of directors. First of all, most journalists want to live and work in a moral environment, whatever that means to them individually. They all have a stake within the profession to play by certain rules, and the nature of the news business as a rapid posting and exchange of information means that trust in other professional colleagues is at a premium even for persons in competition. The rules as they continue to evolve are partly picked up during one's apprenticeship and are otherwise codified in professional ethical principles like those collected in the Appendices near the end of the book. Most journalists, we are told, are in any event too busy getting the news out to get themselves into too many moral dilemmas. They marvel, for example, at colleagues working in the field who have the time for plagiarism, let alone fabrication. Staying on top of the job does not permit a lot of time for moral shenanigans in good journalism assignments, and working one's way up from the ground at almost any busy newspaper or news program should reinforce a journalist's moral common sense about what it would be right and what it would be wrong to do on the job. Journalism houses in turn have a responsibility to cultivate a moral work ethic that rewards employees only when, in addition to being outstanding journalists, their work embodies positive values like respect for the truth and for other persons' moral rights. If we are correct in thinking that the journalist's primary moral right and responsibility is to provide relevant truth telling in the public interest, even when that conflicts with such extraneous factors as the profit motive, then we are projecting an ideal standard of professional journalistic ethics. It is an abstract guide, and, as such, a standard that admits of interpretation in every application. A journalist must decide, often very quickly and in complicated circumstances, what is the truth of the matter, what is or is not in the public interest to tell about the facts, and how they should be published and presented. These are questions that in the workaday reality of the job are not immediately answered by appealing to the formula "Truth telling in the public interest." Perhaps that is the noble ideal to which journalism ought to aspire. Yet it does not by itself answer such questions as what is the truth, in case we are in doubt, or how should it be told, or whether it is in the public interest in this or that instance for it to be told at all. What is truth? What is public interest? and What is in the public interest?

The journalist who wants to act in accord with a morally acceptable code of conduct is likely to feel distant from an abstract ideal moral principle. For it may seem to be of no immediate help in deciding what to do in this or that individual case. There are nonetheless good reasons for accepting the concept of an abstract moral ideal in our ethical thinking generally and in journalistic ethics in particular. The following include some of the most important benefits of adopting an abstract moral ideal:

- Abstract moral ideals provide a cognitive and evaluative foundation for moral decision-making in particular cases.
- Abstract moral ideals systematize our reasoning about what we may believe it is morally right or wrong to do.
- Abstract moral ideals give us a target at which to aim in perfecting our conduct so that it more closely approximates the values to which we aspire.
- When suitably formulated, abstract moral ideals can be as attainable as anything else we may try to do in life. It is only necessary that our principles set a goal that is sufficiently clear and unambiguous in formulating what it is that persons engaged in a certain kind of activity should be trying to accomplish. If in practice we can agree cognitively about what is true, what the facts of a newsworthy event are, and what is or is not in the public interest, then we should have no special problem, at least none that threatens the concept of abstract moral ideals, about actually fulfilling what we have identified as the fundamental principle of journalistic ethics to report whatever truths are in the public interest.
- Finally, by holding forth an abstract moral ideal, we make it easier to explain and justify our actions as moral agents. If we are journalists, then we can appeal to the fundamental principle of journalistic ethics as a way of accounting for our professional conduct in terms of more generally accepted values to which individuals outside the profession can also positively relate.

Needless to say, merely accepting an abstract moral ideal with lip service does not change one's behavior or make it ethical. By identifying a moral principle, we may make it easier for persons who want to do what they believe to be right to focus on a more or less definite articulation of value. We cannot make bad persons good citizens by having them recite the Pledge of Allegiance or the Ten Commandments or the Fundamental Justificatory Principle and Moral Mandate for Professional Journalism or any of the codes of professional journalistic conduct that are collected in the appendices. The understanding of a moral principle must also be accompanied by a determined moral will to act as the principle prescribes if the ideal is to have any impact on the lives and professional behavior of morally responsible individuals.

To spell out what is morally expected of persons and take note of the sanctions that exist to enforce the relevant principles is no more than any ethics can hope to do. An ethical code tells you what we ought to do, but by itself it cannot make us do it unless we choose to act in accord with its principles. For this, in turn, we might as individuals have many different reasons for deciding that the code describes the right way to act so that we choose to follow it in our private lives and professional careers. When we stray and if we are caught, as is almost certain eventually to happen, then there are measures in place to provide penalties for our actions. Such external sanctions are typically never as powerful as our own internal desire to do what we believe to be right, if we do in fact have such a desire and if we truly do believe that a certain course of action or abstract moral ideal is justified. If as a journalist you should ever find yourself in circumstances in which you feel that you are violating a duty to provide relevant truth telling in the public interest, especially, perhaps, under economic and internal administrative pressures, then you might after all choose to violate the duty purely as an expediency to keep a particular journalistic boat afloat. Would you then be acting wrongly? It is hard to imagine circumstances in which you could be morally justified for such a decision; so, the answer is probably yes, as a journalist you would then be acting morally wrongly. Nor is this the only category of situation in which journalists can do something morally objectionable from the standpoint of professional journalistic ethics. It is a decision that could at best only be justified from a moral standpoint other than that of being a professional journalist. Every individual wears several hats and plays a number of different kinds of roles in private and social life. Perhaps someone could try to rationalize an action that is inimical to the fundamental justificatory principle of journalistic ethics not as a journalist, but as a stockholder in the company on whose success the retirement policies of all one's friends at work not to mention one's own depend, or perhaps as a concerned friend of journalism who is willing to fight tooth and nail by any means whatsoever to keep another local newspaper from closing. Here we must seriously ask whether it could ever be morally justified to try to save journalism by violating its most basic purpose of promoting truth telling in the public interest. If the answer is no, then we may need to strengthen our resolve to act rightly for the cause of journalism, even if it sometimes means encountering and doing our best to deal with difficulties, obstacles, and contrary pressures; otherwise, we should reconsider our commitment to the profession and what it requires of journalists.

As the analogy with athletic goals suggests, we can always do better than we would otherwise do by striving to do our best in trying to attain a goal that remains practically out of reach. In so doing, we may thereby come much closer to achieving this desired end than if we allow ourselves to give in to negative thinking about the possibility of ever living an absolutely morally perfect life. There are always setbacks and impediments to accomplishing any worthwhile purpose. The history of journalism nevertheless offers sterling examples of persons who have met the moral challenge in exemplary fashion by doing in commendable ways what we have identified as the fundamental principle of journalistic ethics. If these individuals were to comment on the daily decisions they needed to make in the course of their careers, they would probably report doubts, difficulties, uncertainties, a certain amount of mental anguish, temptations to give in to various sorts of pressures, and many other distractions from doing what they knew it was right as journalists to do. Nevertheless they stayed the course, held fast to their principles, and triumphed against adversities, not only as capable expert journalists from the technical side of the profession, but from a moral standpoint as well. If others have acted rightly in fulfilling the moral requirements of professional journalism, then so can we. In the case of trying to remain true to a professional standard of relevant truth telling in the public interest, we shall document some of the challenges that can make it difficult to follow what we believe to be the morally right course of action. Doing what is right, especially when it conflicts with what is socially rewarded, is not always easy; but then anything of real value, as we know again from the example of athletic training, is seldom free of effort, determination, and hard work. That is precisely the moral challenge of professional journalism as it is more generally of trying to lead a morally upright life.

Here to help focus attention on the problem of maintaining one's journalistic ideals in the face of workplace realities is an intriguing recent case study.

Case Study 7

The Jessica Lynch Incident

Walter Brasch, professor of journalism at Bloomsburg University, writes in his *Online Journal* article for December 30, 2003, concerning the fate of an American woman soldier captured by the Iraqis in the second Gulf War:

> "The most serious cross-over between news, entertainment, and advertising may have occurred when the media began a bidding war to get the 'exclusive' Jessica Lynch story. The *Washington Post* first broke the story shortly after Lynch was rescued after nine days in a six-story Iraqi hospital in April 2003. Using unnamed sources, the *Post* reported that Lynch, a 19-year-old supply clerk who was driving a water tanker 'fought fiercely and shot several enemy soldiers after Iraqi forces ambushed [a convoy of] the Army's 507th Ordnance Maintenance Company, firing her weapon until she ran out of ammunition.' The unnamed sources also

told the *Post* that Lynch 'continued firing at the Iraqis even after she sustained multiple gunshot wounds and watched several other soldiers in her unit die around her in fighting. . . . She was fighting to the death. . . . She did not want to be taken alive.' The *Post* also reported that Lynch 'was also stabbed when Iraqi forces closed in on her position.'

Other media quickly jumped on the story and reported not only was she shot several times by her Iraqi attackers but was also tortured while in the hospital. A daring Navy SEAL/Army Ranger/Air Force rescue effort, against possible hostile fire, freed her after nine days in the Iraqi hospital. The *Post*, quickly followed by other media, reported, based upon the words of an Iraqi, that 'four guards in civilian clothes stood watch at Lynch's first-floor room armed with Kalashnikov rifles and radios.' The rescue came, according to CBS, when special forces 'ran through a hail of gunfire'. The media gave the story front-page play and top-of-the-news broadcasts for several days.

There was only one problem—most of the story, piped to the media by unnamed sources, some in the Defense Department, and never verified by the media—was wrong. Lynch wasn't driving a water tanker but was a passenger in a Humvee; she never fired a shot, nor was she shot; her injuries were caused by being trapped in the overturned Humvee; the convoy wasn't ambushed—it had gotten lost, then was hit by a rocket-propelled grenade from a small group of Iraqi irregulars; she was treated well by Iraqi physicians; she wasn't beaten while held as a prisoner; there was no military opposition to the Americans' rescue operation; the Iraqis even offered to give the Americans a master key to the hospital.

Lynch herself later said the military exaggerated what happened in the desert. In an interview on ABC-TV, she said the lies and use of unnamed sources by the media 'hurt in a way that people would make up stories that they had no truth about'. Before the war, the American public 'were told lie after lie' by the Bush administration, said Sen. Edward M. Kennedy. Rep. Henry Waxman was more specific: 'They lied to promote public relations, from the Jessica Lynch ordeal to the president's campaign landing on the U.S.S. Abraham Lincoln—and about what war would cost our country' [no reference for these quotations cited by Brasch].

Lynch was quick to praise others who had died in the crash or who fought; one, a young soldier, would eventually receive the Silver Star for heroism—and almost no media coverage. But, the blonde-girl-fights-off-soldiers-and-survives-torture made a good story. So good that a CBS News senior vice-president, trying to get exclusive rights, wrote a letter to the Army that blurred the distinction between news and entertainment. In that letter, Betsy West wrote: 'Attached you will find the outlines of a proposal that includes ideas from CBS News, CBS Entertainment, MTV networks and Simon & Schuster publishers. From the distinguished reporting of CBS News to the youthful reach of MTV, we believe this is a unique combination of projects that will do justice to Jessica's inspiring story.'

Writing in the November 2003 issue of *Quill*, the official publication of the Society of Professional Journalists, Peter Y. Sussman pointed out 'it would be exceedingly difficult for any of CBS's 'distinguished' journalists to question dispassionately an interviewee whom their boss had wooed with intimations of lucrative deals and the assurance that the network found her story 'inspiring'.'"

QUESTIONS

1. What moral difficulties posed by real-world circumstances can be identified in the Jessica Lynch incident? Why did seasoned news reporters mistakenly report false information about her ordeal in Iraq? What role did "unnamed" U.S. Defense Department sources appear to play in the fabrication? What additional pressures existed to induce reporters not to check the real facts in this case before reporting the incident?

2. News reporters are as likely as ordinary citizens to be caught up in nationalistic feelings during the turmoil of war. The first casualty of war, we are often told, is the truth. Do journalists then have a special obligation to resist the pressure to report as dramatic and heroic battlefield events things that never actually occurred? If so, why? What, if anything, is peculiar about war reportage that makes it especially prone to exaggeration, demonizing the enemy, and fabricating "facts"?

3. When a dramatic story like that involving Jessica Lynch is presented to reporters, with a high potential for mass syndication (book and movie deals, interviews, and the like), what kinds of pressures can be exerted on reporters to go with the flow rather than question the truth of a popular account? How can such pressures realistically be resisted in the interests of journalistic ethics and the fundamental journalistic right and responsibility to provide truth telling in the public interest?

4. Why would reporters rely on unnamed sources for such a story in the first place, if the principal witness, Jessica Lynch herself, had survived the incident and would be able to confirm or disconfirm anything contained in the report? What are the pressures on news reporters to be first in the field with exciting reportage, even if the "information" should later turn out to be false, manufactured for political purposes? What are the cognitive as well as moral virtues of skepticism and a journalistic work ethic that requires verification of facts before reporting?

5. How does the desire on the part of professional journalists to boost circulation, ratings, and profits affect the quality of news reporting as illustrated in incidents like that involving Jessica Lynch's capture and rescue? In what ways is the media particularly vulnerable to manipulation by governmental agencies that may have a political agenda in promoting certain falsehoods, especially during time of war or other national crisis? What can be done to safeguard journalistic integrity in such circumstances, particularly where assignment editors for a variety of reasons want a false story to be true? What would you have done if you were an editor or reporter working for the *Washington Post* or CBS when the Jessica Lynch story first broke?

Two Sides of Professional Journalism

We should remind ourselves again about the importance of two obvious but not obviously interrelated facts. Journalism is a noble profession aimed at discovering and communicating information that is also big business. It takes money to investigate news stories and to produce hard copy, audio, or video in which news reports are presented. In market economies we know that most large-scale enterprises are undertaken by entrepreneurs who invest capital to provide a product or service with an eye toward making a profit. Why else, indeed, would they do so, unless they were motivated entirely by a spirit of philanthropy, and how else would such complicated and expensive worldwide activities as news reporting be accomplished?

Proceeding from that rhetorical question, we can begin to raise questions concerning journalistic ethics that arise through conflicts of interest between those who make the news and those who directly or indirectly pay for the news to be produced. Although there are substantial profits to be made in all of the news media, and up to this point we have been discussing journalistic outlets generally, or print and television formats in particular, by far the greatest revenue generating news medium currently marketed is television. The dilemma for professional journalism in all communications technologies of serving the public good in a profitable enterprise without compromising the quality of news content is well-articulated in this statement from the sixth edition of a recent textbook by Clifford G. Christians, Mark Fackler, Kim B. Rotzoll, and Kathy Brittain McKee on *Media Ethics: Cases and Moral Reasoning*:

> Nothing is more difficult in the mass media enterprise than promoting the public good even though the rewards—professionally and financially—are not commensurate with such altruism. In actual practice, it becomes extraordinarily difficult to separate the media's financial interests from the public's legitimate news interests. The Constitution protects the media from government constraint, but the news is under the perpetual risk of corporate control. Granted, a conflict between the public's need for unpolluted information and the stockholders' need for profit is not inevitable. Needing to earn a respectable income and deciding to stop a dead-ended investigation could both be appropriate; moral questions emerge when the two are connected as cause and effect. Without a press pool to help pay expenses for a charter, a minor party candidate could not conduct a modern political campaign. One person serving in two potentially conflicting capacities—for example, as executive for Columbia Broadcasting and board member for Columbia University—may indeed be working ethically. Not every owner or executive is automatically suspect.
>
> Nevertheless, ever since mass communications took on the character of big business at the turn of the twentieth century, there have been built-in commercial pressures.[1]

[1]Christians, Fackler, Rotzoll, and McKee, *Media Ethics*, p. 35.

THE MIDAS TOUCH OF TELEVISION NEWS

There are vast profits to be made in television broadcasting, including television news programs. At first this fact might seem paradoxical. While there are around-the-clock news channels, a few daily hour-long news programs, and documentary and investigative journalism shows that usually air once a week available today on American television and throughout the developed world, one would think that news reporting on television in particular occupies only a tiny part of the broadcasting schedule.

This is true, but the fact is that news remains a major source of income for network television where most of the profits are currently to be made. The reason is that news programming is comparatively less expensive to produce than any other type of programming, with a higher percentage of viewer attraction per program production cost. We need only think of how many people make a point of watching the evening half-hour nightly news programs on television. These are deliberately scheduled to coincide with the time most persons have arrived home from work and are either eating or about to eat their dinner. This is the perfect opportunity to get viewers to tune in and, hence, the perfect time to advertise goods and services. It is, moreover, as we all know, advertisers who finally pay the bills for commercial television production costs, including the news. It is the news, however, where the greatest marketing window allows advertisers to reach more potential buyers than any other single hour of the television broadcasting day for a comparable investment.

As expensive as it is to produce the news, it is far more expensive to produce sporting events, situation comedies, or any other regularly featured television offering. Networks need a studio; a news anchor, who is often a charismatic announcer but not always an investigative journalist; a camera crew, which increasingly is computerized and robotic, thus reducing costs even further; wardrobe and makeup artists; sound engineers; producers who organize the broadcast and coordinate all its components; a handful of administrators; and the like. Then, most importantly, of course, there are the field reporters and video camera personnel with their salaries and travel budgets and the costs of equipment and material supplies. The business end of television broadcasting and news reporting in particular is a fascinating subject for economic study; several interesting books have been written exploring the financial side of things. With these assets in place, network television news is ready to sell airtime at prime rates to advertisers when the greatest numbers of affluent viewers are tuning in to watch. Most of the amenities we have just mentioned are also needed anyway in other kinds of television programming, which are overall more expensive because their costs are magnified many times as a result of the numbers of individuals, the expense of sets, actors' and actresses' comparatively higher salaries, script writers, filming on remote location, technical production, and many other factors—all of which add up.

The fact is that as a result news reporting is one of the most profitable of all types of television broadcasting events. Other kinds of programming (puppet shows?) are less expensive to produce, but for a variety of reasons they do not attract as many viewers who are likely to spend money on advertised products. Other kinds of programming are more expensive, but again do not lure as many desirable consumers to the screen. The combination of comparatively low production costs and a high percentage of viewers likely to be influenced by advertising makes news broadcasting one of the most lucrative categories of programming on television. The fact in turn that news sells advertising space at huge profits for news agencies has important implications for journalistic ethics. There are moral dilemmas that arise because of the profit motive in professional journalism and, ultimately, because journalists are asked to do two things that do not always converge on the same set of values.

Journalists, on the one hand, are supposed to report the news as accurately and objectively as possible. On the other hand, they are supposed to help the companies that employ them turn a profit or at least to minimize expenses. These two goals are not necessarily always in conflict, but the fact that they can sometimes run at cross-purposes to one another raises interesting moral problems in difficult cases that create a dilemma about which master to serve. When journalists in real workaday terms fall upon the horns of a dilemma about whether to honor the fundamental obligation to provide relevant truth telling in the public interest or to do what is financially more profitable, they find themselves in the grip of hard decisions about the abstract moral ideals of their profession and often less tractable marketplace realities.

We have been focusing on television for the moment because it is the format for professional journalism that is currently most profitable and because it gives us a chance to say something about the distinctive character of television as a revolutionary force in communicating the news. The conclusions we shall reach concerning journalism and the profit motive nevertheless apply in general terms to any publishing or broadcasting medium, including newspapers, newsmagazines, radio programming, television programming, and even the Internet to the extent that it supports advertising in conjunction with the presentation of news items.

PROS AND CONS OF THE MASS MEDIA AGE

Television is a wonderful source of information and entertainment. It offers a living window on the world that is hard to match in any other medium. Unlike many recent critics, we need not despise or warn people away from television.[2] It is true that the tube can have a disproportionate influence on

---

[2]An excellent case for limiting our reliance on television is made by Mander, *Four Arguments for the Elimination of Television.*

viewers, that it appears to contribute to shortened attention spans, and that it glues some people to their chairs when they could be outdoors exercising in the fresh air or at least reading a book or making love or learning to paint or doing any number of other more personally productive and rewarding things.

Contemporary television programming in many ways has also betrayed much of its promise, for all the reasons its objectors have often lamented. There are entire cable network channels devoted to science that seem to offer nothing but dinosaurs and Egyptian mummies. These are especially visually interesting, more so than cloud chambers and the principles of particle physics, but they are only a tiny fraction of the world of science. There is so much more that could be done to help the population assimilate the basic principles of a scientific education, of which they are desperately in need, from the comfort of their homes. For the same reason, news reporting often overemphasizes the entertainment values in dramatic visual imagery while avoiding both the complicated historical background and analysis needed to truly understand complex current events.

We explore these themes in the following case study. This time we investigate a fictional compilation of television practices that has undoubtedly been repeated countless times in many television newsrooms.

Case Study 8

Warehouse Fire and Homeless Shelter Closing

News agency A and news agency B have reporters working in the same city. Their staffs must decide during the course of each day what kinds of stories to cover on the evening news. On the same day there are two events that catch the attention of assignment editors. One is the closing of a shelter for the homeless due to lack of funds and the other is a warehouse fire in a remote location.

The agencies do not have enough resources to adequately cover both stories, so they must choose which to feature. The closing of the shelter affects hundreds of people, but the event is visually unspectacular. There is an official to interview and footage of the empty building with cots and a kitchen to show on film, together with a bit of background information on how the shelter had gotten started and why it has now been forced to close. The warehouse fire, on the other hand, does not involve the deaths of any persons or the risk of fire spreading to other buildings or residences and does not directly affect anyone as it has been abandoned for years and is no longer owned by any company. On television, the pictures of the fire blazing through the warehouse nevertheless make a powerful visual impression when filmed from different angles and broadcast in color along with dramatic film footage of the firefighters arriving in trucks and trying to gain control of the fire.

News agency A decides to report on the shelter closing, and news agency B decides to report on the warehouse fire. The result is that, although in principle the closing of the shelter has significantly more effect on the local community than the fire, by reporting on the fire, news agency B attracts many more viewers, who find the pictures of the burning building more exciting and absorbing, and as a result the ratings of news agency B soar above those of news agency A. The further result is that as a consequence more companies choose to advertise their products with news agency B than with news agency A as they have noticed that more persons have tended to watch the news programming on B's news than on A's. This in turn has an impact on the profits of the two news agencies, such that B prospers where A loses revenue. Over the long run, as these trends become more entrenched and more and more viewers and advertisers flock to agency B and away from agency A, a powerful lesson about marketplace realities in the news industry is learned. Agency A responds by changing its news profile. It wants to be just as profitable as agency B. As a result, it no longer chooses to cover social impact news stories like the shelter closing and begins increasingly to cover stories that are more like the warehouse burning, purely as a matter of being able to remain competitive with their business opponents.

It might be said that in some sense it would be morally better for viewers to be informed about local issues like the shelter closing. Yet that is not the kind of news coverage as entertainment that we are supposing a significant percentage of the viewing public prefers. The market is driven precisely by these kinds of pressures, and, as a result of the perception of the entertainment value of news and ways of presenting the news, the sheer numbers of persons who vote with their feet by choosing one media outlet rather than another begins to exert a force on the kind of news that is covered and the ways in which it is presented. If the trend, understandable in itself, continues, then the effect can be that the kinds of news that citizens might be said to need for the responsible decision-making they are required to make can begin to be replaced by more sensational kinds of stories that do not offer the background essential to informed participation in the choices facing the community and society at large.

QUESTIONS

1. Did agency A act rightly originally? How about agency B? Did A act rightly afterward in response to B's success? Why or why not?

2. News today is not only a flat report of events, but a part of the entertainment industry. Indeed, news reporting has always incorporated entertainment as well as information, as we know from such hybrid concepts as "infotainment" and "infomercials" in the case of advertising. Philosophically, what should we make of this situation? Does the combining of news and entertainment necessarily violate the fundamental principle of journalistic ethics to provide relevant truth telling in the public interest? When, where, and how can such conflicts arise?

3. What would you do if you were a journalist confronting such a moral decision-making problem? Would your responsibilities be any different if you were a rank-and-file reporter as opposed to an assignment editor? What do you think you should do in the case study situation? (Note that an honest answer to this question will not always match up positively with an honest answer to the first question.) Finally, why do you think you would respond to each challenge with this or that decision or action, and why do you think that you should? (The latter answer is most important in understanding the philosophical basis for reaching a decision about what we think we morally ought to do. If we are not merely proceeding on gut feeling, then we need to spell out the general philosophical principles that would justify our choice of action.)

4. It is only by personalizing the kinds of problems encountered by journalists practicing their profession in the field and in light of the moral dimensions of the special kinds of decisions they must make daily that we can begin to appreciate the principles for a professional journalistic ethics that are considered in this book. We must make the problems our own, as the previous questions require us to do, and ask realistically how we would and should try to deal with them, and then we must try to identify the appropriate higher-level philosophical principles that would account for what our reasoning suggests is the best course of action in each case and category. What, then, is the potential conflict between the fundamental principle of journalistic ethics to maximize relevant truth telling in the public interest and the pressure to provide exciting coverage of events regardless of their intrinsic importance to viewers for financial reasons?

5. How, if at all, can we uphold a moral ideal for journalistic practice in the face of commercial pressures that can affect editorial decision-making? What do we gain or lose as professional journalists if we simply surrender journalistic integrity to commercial or other financial considerations or to pressures such as political intimidation? What can we do to live in the real world of business realities while still aspiring to professional journalistic moral ideals?

The scenario we have just described, simplified as it is, already exhibits many complexities and controversies. We should not assume that the business struggle between news agencies A and B gestures in any single moral direction. The point is rather to get a sense of the real-life moral dilemmas confronting journalists. The above problem depicts how it is that one perception of the moral responsibility of journalists, controversial in itself, to report on certain types of news can be jeopardized by market forces when we acknowledge that journalism is not only the daily grind of finding and reporting the news, but also of doing so in such a way as to compete with other journalists and other news agencies for viewers and advertisers. We cannot adequately appreciate the difficulties impinging on journalists unless or until we enter the profession ourselves and find out in daily practical experience how things can sometimes work. Only then can we arrive at a truly realistic concept of journalism as a business that frankly and deliberately or by default expresses entertainment, patriotic, and other values as well as the information it conveys.

If the news is supposed to provide the kind of information needed by everyone in a free and democratic society to take part intelligently in the issues of the day, then a news agency that permits itself to be swayed too strongly by market considerations and provides more sensational than importantly informative kinds of news might be said to be neglecting an important aspect of its moral responsibility. The problem is articulated in a recent discussion of the conflicting interests in journalism's choice of issues to cover:

> Press critics have argued that for years now the media, especially television and news magazines, have been preoccupied with the sensational Mode Three stories that have attracted huge audiences and advertising revenue. At such times, serious foreign news is ignored. In retrospect, we can ask: Why have local newspapers and television stations been so indifferent to international news during an era in which ethnic conflicts have killed millions and globalization has touched nearly every American community? Part of the reason Americans were so shocked and disoriented by the terror attacks was that they had become so complacent and uninformed about the threat of foreign terrorism to what is now called the "homeland." They certainly did not learn much from their local media or network television (or from the federal government, either) about the possible dangers of such devastating attacks striking close to home.[3]

What, however, is the alternative? The news cannot be produced free of charge. In a competitive market environment in which news agencies are typically independently privately owned entrepreneurial enterprises, it is the advertisers who pay the bills. The advertisers in turn naturally want to have their products seen by the largest numbers of persons who are likely to buy them, and that means that the news agency that satisfies the desires of the largest numbers of persons in their appetite for news will receive the largest numbers of viewers and, hence, the most advertising funding. Even in the case of publicly funded news reporting, such as National Public Radio (NPR) or any of the affiliated networks of the Public Broadcasting Corporation (PBC), there are economic pressures to stay within budget and to attract viewers,

[3]Hachten and Scotton, *The World News Prism*, pp. 17–18.

despite the fact that for such news agencies some of the more compromising dilemmas involve news coverage and viewer or audience appeal.

What are we then supposed to do instead? Should we turn over all news to a government bureau, as some countries have done, and take it out of the hands of private companies? This possibility has both advantages and disadvantages. One advantage is at least the greater potential to avoid the predicament we have just described, in which news of urgent social relevance is sacrificed for the sake of entertainment. The most obvious of many disadvantages is the difficulty of obtaining objective independent news reporting on what the government itself does or on matters in which the government has a vested interest. This distancing of news reporting from governmental interference is generally considered to be one of the most important hallmarks of journalism in a free and open society. When the news is reported by government employees or by agencies entirely supported and hence ultimately controlled by government officials, we must begin to wonder whether the reporting that takes place is truly objective, particularly when reporting on the government itself. Can we imagine that the Watergate break-in and cover-up scandal would have been reported by news agencies under the direction of the Nixon White House? What has happened in other countries where news was the exclusive monopoly of the government? If past experience is any guide, we know the answer is that when government takes over reporting the news to its citizens then the distinction between objective information and propaganda begins at least to some degree to erode. We can expect at best an uneasy compromise between the principles of journalistic ethics and news reporting as a branch of government.

The same is often true when government unduly influences news content, as the following case study further demonstrates.

Case Study 9

Governmental Pressures on Journalism in Mexico

National Public Radio (NPR) in the United States aired the following report that was excerpted from the transcript of its February 17, 1993 program, "Morning Edition," broadcast from Washington DC:

"NEAL CONAN, Host: The Mexican government says it's going to end its longstanding practice of paying gratuities to journalists. That could be an important step in a country that has almost no tradition of an independent press, but as Bebe Crouse reports from Mexico City, the new policy may be less of a breakthrough than it seems.

BEBE CROUSE, Reporter: The political payoff is well-known around this city's newsrooms. It may be as simple as an evening's drinks and dinner or as grand as an all-expense-paid vacation. For most reporters, bribery comes in the form of an embute—that's a sealed envelope filled with cash and delivered directly to the newsroom once or twice a month. Reporters weren't anxious to talk on tape about the custom, but journalist Irma Rosa Martinez says it is widely accepted.

IRMA ROSA MARTINEZ, Journalist: If you talk to many of the reporters, they say that it's part of the salary. We've become here in Mexico a little bit cynical. It's part of our income, yeah.

CROUSE: Without the payoff, most reporters here earn only about $400 or $500 a month. Martinez says that even those who are critical of the government can't afford to refuse the extra cash. But now the government says no more. In what it calls a move to make its dealings with the press more transparent, there will be no more government-paid press junkets, no more free photocopies and tapes, and, above all, no more under-the-table cash. Any money given to the media must now be made by check and reported to the nation's fiscal controller. The move is aimed at cutting out questionable payments.

GABRIEL GUERRA, [Mexican] Presidential Press Secretary [1993]: With these new rules, there will be no room for speculation whether a newspaper is being objective or not in its coverage. This makes it clearer. It gives a higher degree of credibility both to officials and to the media.

CROUSE: Political columnist Raimundo Riva Palacio isn't convinced. He thinks the whole thing is for show.

RAIMUNDO RIVA PALACIO, Political Columnist: As a political gesture, it is a very important step. In practical terms, it is not that big a step.

CROUSE: That's because even without bribes, the government heavily subsidizes the press through completely legal above-board payments. Besides making the usual public announcements, the government buys space in newspapers and other media to place what is essentially advertising for itself, but disguised in the form of news articles. In most cases, these bogus articles are printed right alongside those of the paper's own reporters without any indication that they were written and paid for by the government, and that kind of spending continues to be allowed under the new regulations.

Editors and publishers have also been on the take, not lining their pockets with cash, but receiving more valuable, political favors. It could be the gift of a normally hard-to-get public permit, or perhaps a wink and a nod at unpaid taxes. Those kinds of favors don't show up on any books, and reporter Martinez believes they affect editorial policy a lot more than bribes to individual reporters.

MS. MARTINEZ: We reporters don't have the power to decide what's going on in the papers. In my paper, the paper I work for, it's in a very close relation with the government. Nothing's going to happen. Nothing's going to change."

QUESTIONS

1. What can we learn about the requirements of a free press from Mexico's experience? The overt payoffs to news reporters described in the story are partly attributed to cultural differences between Mexico and the United States. Is this an adequate explanation?

2. Explain the professional journalistic implications of regular payments being made to Mexican news reporters. What is likely to happen if a reporter were to uncover a substantial scandal in the Mexican government and wanted to publicize it? What pressures might be exerted on such a reporter, particularly one who has a history of having accepted government "subsidies"?

3. How does the Mexican journalism situation dramatize the potential conflict between abstract moral ideals in professional journalistic ethics and the realities of trying to make a living as a journalist in a context of low pay, political corruption, and a prevailing custom among journalists of accepting payments from the government for their work?

4. What would you do as a Mexican reporter under these circumstances? What do you think Mexican reporters should do, and why? Are your expectations realistic? How would you propose to mediate between journalistic abstract moral ideals and the reality of the situation encountered by Mexican journalists? What sort of price would one have to pay in that kind of environment for standing up against the acceptance of government payments to journalists? Would it be worth it even then to preserve one's moral ideals in the brunt of such incentives for corruption?

5. The report filed by Neal Conan for NPR was broadcast in 1993. As an exercise in investigative journalism, look further into the matter of what has happened since 1993 to the current date in the Mexican government's relation to its news media. Have there been any significant developments? Has the ban on overt payoffs made any difference in the quality and especially the objectivity of news reporting in Mexico?

COMMERCIALISM IN THE NEWS

Within its proper limitations, television is an extraordinarily useful way to learn things about the world that we could not discover in any other way. It has an immediacy and range that cannot be duplicated by print or audio. We can only hope that television both as a general format for communication and an outlet for news telejournalism will continue to improve as the medium matures and regain a sense of its ethical mission.

Meanwhile, there are interesting moral questions raised by the fact that television is not only a conduit for news information but a highly profitable enterprise. These potentially negative factors have an impact upon the content at least of major network news broadcasting on television. Neil Postman and Steve Powers, in their widely discussed analysis of the impact of commercial pressures on contemporary media, *How to Watch News*, are impelled to issue the following recommendations for persons who might otherwise be inclined to rely on television as their major source of news information:

> There are things the public must know whether or not they "like" it. To understand what is happening in the world and what it means requires knowledge of historical, political, and social contexts. It is the task of journalists to provide people with such knowledge. News is not entertainment. It is a necessity in a democratic society. Therefore, TV news must give people what they *need*, along with what they *want*. The solution is to present news in a form that will compel the attention of a large audience without subverting the goal of informing the public. But as things stand now, it is essential that any viewer understand the following when turning on a TV news show:
>
> 1. American television is an unsleeping money machine.
> 2. While journalists pursue newsworthy events, business-oriented management often makes decisions based on business considerations.
> 3. Many decisions about the form and content of news programs are made on the basis of information about the viewer, the purpose of which is to keep viewers watching so that they will be exposed to the commercials.[4]

When we think of journalism as a business, journalistic ethics becomes a special episode of business ethics. As such, the moral dilemmas and potential conflicts between news reporting and the profit motive are analogous to the kinds of moral dilemmas encountered in other professions that are also at least partly profit driven, such as medicine, engineering, and the law.

These are also vocations that are expected to make money for their practitioners and businesses. The two sides of professional businesses can ideally walk side by side without conflict or collision. It is the task of journalistic ethics as a chapter of business ethics then to reconcile these two aspects of profitably reporting the news so that neither side suffers unduly at the expense of the other. The profit motive in particular must not be allowed without protest to whittle away at the ability of professional journalists to meet their moral obligations as journalists, citizens, and moral agents generally, insofar as ethical principles obligate them to act independently of their professional affiliations.

If we are able to reach a philosophical understanding of how a professional vocation dedicated to public service can be combined and reconciled with a profitable business practice as in the case of journalism, then the same model might be usefully extended with appropriate adjustments to other professions, such as medicine, engineering, and the law, that are also conducted as businesses. The same types of moral problems

---

[4]Postman and Powers, *How to Watch News*, p. 9.

arise for professional journalists as for physicians who are morally professionally obligated to prevent diseases and heal the sick, and, at the
same time, make money from other peoples illness and death. Or for
attorneys who are morally professionally obligated to serve the law by
prosecuting or defending those who are accused of crimes or involved in
torts, while at the same time turning a profit from other people's legal
misfortunes.

MAKING A PROFIT IN JOURNALISM

It will be helpful to proceed with an example in which a moral dilemma
arises for journalists because of a conflict between the duties of reporting the
news, and in particular of satisfying the fundamental moral obligation of professional journalistic ethics to maximize relevant truth telling in the public
interest, and the desire and need to do so profitably, to make money from the
news. There are, as we shall see, many such situations, each posing interestingly different problems that can enhance our appreciation for the ethical
predicaments in which journalists sometimes find themselves. As Leonard
Downie, Jr. and Robert G. Kaiser argue in their recent authoritative book, *The
News About the News: American Journalism in Peril*, again with reference to the
profits made by television news:

> Because news is the most profitable product of local television, newsroom
> obligations to the station's business can go considerably beyond just winning
> high ratings. At many stations the news is part of the overall marketing effort,
> often in ways that raise ethical questions and undermine the newscasts' credi-
> bility. Some stations sell advertising tie-ins on news programs; others use news
> broadcasts and personalities to promote the station, its programs and its net-
> work's programs.[5]

Many different kinds of pressures are exerted on journalists trying to
discover and report the facts in order to turn a profit. Profits, we know from
elementary economics, are achieved in two ways: by increasing income and
reducing expenses. Both of these strategies must work together in order to
produce maximum profits. What shall it profit a corporation if it increaseth
its revenues but allows expenses to rise far in excess of its income? What further shall it profit the stockholders if the corporation decreaseth its expenses
but still does not produce enough income to pay for its production costs with
something substantially more left over to pay back in the form of dividends?
The fact that good business practices require the coordination of these two
columns of double bookkeeping suggest two corresponding ways in which
journalists can be at risk in trying to maximize relevant truth telling while

---

[5]Downie and Kaiser, *The News About the News: American Journalism in Peril*, p. 176.

contributing to their news company's income and reduction of expenses, of making more money come in or less money go out. We shall accordingly consider moral dilemma or profit motive conflict scenarios in both of these two complementary categories.

INCREASING INCOME FROM NEWS REPORTING

First, let us construct another imaginary case in which professional journalists might be called upon to help increase income for their news agencies in a way that is not obviously compatible or obviously incompatible with their professional moral obligation to maximize relevant truth telling in the public interest.

The situation we propose is one in which a journalist who has uncovered some very prejudicial facts about the misconduct of one of the networks most lucrative advertising sponsors. Perhaps a baby food company has been marketing some of its products that are known to contain trace amounts of dangerous substances in third world countries where the standards for food and drug purity are not as stringent as they are in the company's home country. The reporter discovers these facts and prepares a news story complete with video documentation, interviews with health officials in the affected population, and a scathing conclusion about what the baby food company has done to off-load what it knew to be its tainted merchandise on innocent children in another land that did not happen to have the same legal safeguards as those closer to home.

The editor and producer are impressed with the story. They watch the video, consider the documentary evidence, and acknowledge that the report is superbly done and greatly in excess of the highest standards of journalistic excellence. They further agree that the news item is of considerable importance. It is not absolutely the most important story of the day, but they consider it to be the third or fourth item in the queue they have established for the order in which news items might be presented. The unspoken concern, however, which the station managers understand but is not mentioned explicitly to the reporter, who we may suppose is also well aware of the fact, is that the baby food company is one of the network's three major corporate sponsors and that it would be an embarrassment to the company to have its bad behavior exposed on a television news program that it financially supports.

Now, in an ideal world, we might imagine the network's board of directors sitting down together and declaring that if the baby food company has been up to such misdeeds in marketing inferior and dangerous products abroad then they no longer want them to advertise on their programs and will terminate their contract at once. That this is fantasy, an almost comical way of continuing the melodrama, is testimony to the fact that advertisers for the most part call the shots in the media industry because they are on the giving rather than receiving end of the money flow that is the lifeblood of professional journalism. We would be naive to suppose that this is what would ever happen in practice, except in the most extreme imaginable cases, let us say, where the company in question was nothing but a front for a terrorist organization dedicated to overthrowing the government, or, say, an organized crime affiliate involved in murder, extortion, and racketeering. Then, perhaps, the network would consider severing ties with the advertiser, but otherwise probably not. What we can expect to happen instead is that the network executives, recognizing a threat to their profits, are likely to do something to suppress or at least water down the story. We must ask about the intrinsic morality or immorality of such a decision, and we must try to evaluate the proper stance for a journalist to take in light of such occurrences when trying to accommodate both the journalistic abstract moral ideal of maximizing relevant truth telling in the public interest and working in a business that is also professionally dedicated at least in part to turning a profit.

CONFLICTS WITH ADVERTISERS OVER NEWS CONTENT

Here are several more plausible ways in which the scenario might play out. We consider in due course the implications for journalistic ethics in each:

(1) The network calls the reporter into its main office and tells the reporter in no uncertain terms that the story will not be run and orders the reporter to turn over all records of the investigation.

(2) The network takes the reporter out to lunch and praises the story and the reporter's good work. The editors or other executives then mention, almost as an aside, that the story would probably have more impact if it were shortened and generalized to refer to food product companies that over the years have engaged in such practices, without mentioning any particular offenders by name; they indicate incidentally in this connection that they have been considering the reporter for a significant promotion and salary increase.

(3) The network informs the baby food company that some version of the story is going to be broadcast, and the baby food company threatens to withdraw its advertising if the story is actually broadcast.

(4) The network informs the baby food company that some version of the story is going to be broadcast, and the baby food company threatens to withdraw its advertising if the company is mentioned by name or if sufficiently specific information is given whereby the company can be identified by average viewers.

We have simplified the situation for the sake of emphasizing some crucial points. These are nevertheless caricatures of the kinds of things we might reasonably expect to happen in the case we have described. What should be the reaction of the reporter, editor, and other professional journalists, network executives, and the baby food company? What shall we conclude about the apparent conflict between abstract moral ideals for journalistic ethics and the realities of commercial television production?

Again, if we are simply fantasizing about what ideally ought to take place in a morally perfect world, we might imagine the baby food company acknowledging its wrongdoing, apologizing to the public and to the third world countries where it has shipped its inferior contaminated products, refunding the money it wrongfully gained by means of its fraudulent practices, and making reparations to anyone affected, vowing never to repeat the offense. It should happen, and it could happen, but realistically it most probably will not happen. Since journalists in the real world need to deal with advertisers and other factors that affect their profitability who are less than ideally moral, they need to consider what their moral stance will be in confronting corruption. The question is in many ways general, asking how morally upright persons should interact with others who are not morally upright.

MORAL CHOICES IN REACTIONS TO ADVERTISER PRESSURE

What, specifically, are the options for journalists who want to do the right thing? In situation (1), network executives insofar as they are committed to the enterprise of professional journalism, are clearly acting wrongly. Where a conflict between advertisers and the moral obligation of journalists to maximize relevant truth telling in reporting the news, journalists, and the teams of editors, producers, and network executives who support them and are also committed to the goals of professional journalism, are morally obligated not to yield to financial pressure, but to stand firm against efforts by advertisers to dictate the contents of the news.

Network executives ought to have at least an explicit personal if not contractual understanding with advertisers that they are never to have any input to the journalistic content of the news. That, of course, will not prevent them from simply withdrawing their advertising, and they can hint without threatening that they will do so if they are unhappy with what the network does. Advertisers are not journalists and so cannot be held responsible for adhering to the principles of journalistic ethics. Advertisers and manufacturing companies have professional business ethics of their own to consider, and these enter into the overall picture of moral rights and responsibilities in this scenario, but for the present we are only examining the obligations of journalists.

Reporters, editors, and news company executives, if they are going to observe the fundamental principle of journalistic ethics to maximize relevant truth telling in the public interest, accordingly should never bow to pressure from advertisers or other outside financial entities to control news content. In a healthy economy, there should always be other advertisers from whom a news agency can find alternative financial resources for its operations and thereby survive the loss of morally undesirable advertisers. Network executives should consider instead the impact on their long-term profitability of having the general public discover that they have been accepting advertising money from unscrupulous businesses that they knew about because of their own reporter's investigations, but which they suppressed or tried to cover up. Such facts usually have a way of coming out sooner or later, and the damage to the network as a business can be even greater as a result of yielding rather than standing up to advertiser pressure to control news content. This kind of consideration constitutes a *prudential* rather than *moral* reason for not giving in to efforts to manipulate the news for the sake of preserving profits from advertising income. It concerns what it is smart to do rather than what it is morally right to do.

The moral reason for refusing to yield to such pressure is that to do so violates the fundamental moral obligation of professional journalists to publicize important truths. The suppression of a news item for the sake of protecting an advertiser from scandal is not a form of self-regulation or self-censorship consistent with the moral obligation of journalists to tell the truth in the public interest. If the reporter and editor and news executives believe that they have stumbled onto the truth about the baby food company and if they believe the information is vital to their audience and to the welfare of persons in the world at large, then they are morally obligated to report it, even if it means the loss of advertising revenue and even if, in the financially worst-case scenario, it entails such a significant loss of profitability as to cause the news company to fail. What is to be hoped in any case, again from a prudential standpoint, is that by taking a resolute moral stand against corrupt attempts to influence the contents of the news, the news service and the journalists in question who work there will earn the moral respect of other advertisers who will at least supplement, and possibly even increase, the profits otherwise derived from the baby food company. Is this a realistic expectation or unfounded pie-in-the-sky moral idealism?

MORAL OBLIGATIONS FOR JOURNALISTS TO REMAIN PROFITABLE

The same is true in all four scenarios above. In any of these situations journalists are morally obligated to resist whatever external influences threaten to adversely affect their ability to tell the truth, whether by favors or payoffs from the government, wealthy advertisers, or other influence peddlers. To yield to such pressure is unconditionally a violation of journalistic ethics.

We should nevertheless pause to consider a further dilemma that seems to arise for journalists standing tall against advertiser pressure to control news content. If journalists are morally obligated to bring the news to their public, are they not also morally obligated to stay in business in order to continue reporting? If so, are they not morally obligated to satisfy their advertisers, even in matters of journalistic content, if that is what it takes to keep the presses printing and the cameras rolling? Otherwise, are they not also guilty of failing to meet their obligation to report the news? There are several key considerations to take into account in evaluating this dilemma. We do not suppose that journalists are morally obligated to ply their trade under any and all circumstances. We may admire the courage and tenacity of reporters and news agencies that continue to report the news as best they can even under a dangerous political dictatorship in which news is heavily censored and violations are punished by violence, on the grounds that they can then at least do some good and hold out the possibility for the future institution or restoration of a free or comparatively freer press.

This is not quite the same situation that exists in the case of advertisers who try to bully reporters and their employers into manipulating the news for the sake of corporate interests. Advertisers cannot literally force journalists to do anything they do not want to do, but can only exert powerful financial influence. Rather than fail to satisfy the moral obligation of all journalists to provide relevant truth telling in the public interest, news reporters and their editors and business administrators in a free society might choose to accept the loss of profits and if necessary allow themselves to go out of business rather than disgrace their journalistic mandate. As individual journalists, they can always find another way to report the news, to work for another news agency or to start their own, secure at least in the knowledge that they have not violated their commitment to the responsibilities of professional journalism. Otherwise, and this is what is crucial, they are not acting as journalists in the first place in the true sense of the word. If they cannot fulfill the duties of a professional journalist, then they might as well allow themselves to drop out of the business and find another way to make a living. The unfortunate truth is that in some circumstances it is morally better to walk away from corruption than to give into its demands.

INTEREST GROUP INFLUENCE ON NEWS REPORTING

The same is true for efforts on the parts of viewers, sometimes organized into interest groups, to influence the contents of news reporting. Viewers can threaten to boycott certain news outlets if they disapprove of what a network, newspaper, magazine, or radio station has to say. Imagine that a large group of religious fundamentalists decides that it is displeased with the fact that news stories are reporting gay lifestyles or advances in evolutionary biology or other kinds of religious practices around the world. They may threaten to petition the network's advertisers or simply refuse to watch the network, thereby adversely affecting the network's ratings on which its advertising revenues and hence its overall profitability depend.

Journalists, assuming as always that they are committed to the truth of what they are reporting, should stand firm against any such efforts to control the contents of the news *regardless of financial consequences*. They should be brave and firm in their moral conviction not to bow to pressures that would cause them to violate their fundamental moral obligation to maximize relevant truth telling. Otherwise, they are not acting as journalists or doing what journalists are supposed to do. In practical terms, in a pluralistic free society, we do not expect any single corporation, advertising company, or private interest group to be able to shut down a network or news agency or even to cause such financial damage as to make it no longer profitable to continue producing the news. We should assume instead that in a pluralistic society, most citizens, with an intuitive understanding of the importance of journalism in maintaining a society's freedoms, will respect and admire a reporter and news network who stand up against coercive pressure from advertisers or censorship from interest groups and lend the individuals and the news service an even greater share of their moral and material support. Journalists are part of a social community and can take comfort in the fact that if their situation is made known, then right-thinking persons will rally to their cause.

CALL FOR JOURNALISTS TO STAND FIRM AGAINST FINANCIAL INTIMIDATION

The implications of journalistic ethics in all the scenarios are uncompromising. A reporter, editor, or news executive who yields to pressure affecting the contents of news, and in particular eliminating or diluting the truth, is acting wrongly, contrary to the moral obligations by which all journalists are authorized freely to investigate and present the news. Advertisers should understand their moral responsibility as citizens of a free society not to interfere in the production of the news insofar as it reports the truth. They should be encouraged to interpret efforts to control news content as a kind of censorship, and journalists, editors, and news executives at every level should be encouraged to resist whatever efforts are made on the part of advertisers and special interest groups to exert undue influence on the conduct of news reporting. Any attempt to limit or proscribe relevant truth telling is a violation of journalistic ethics and should be resisted by journalists and all citizens committed to the free exercise of a free press for the benefit of all citizens.

We should emphasize in case there is any cause for misunderstanding that advertisers as such are not necessarily corrupt. Most are responsible citizens who recognize the need to maintain a free press by not trying to control what is reported in the news. Advertising informs us of new products and services and thereby also serves a useful purpose in a free economy, providing information of yet another sort. We have been discussing the moral response implied by journalistic ethics under a number of related scenarios involving one imaginable source of pressure on journalists to limit their truth telling and trying to dramatize the potential for abuse on the part of individuals and corporations that supply a major part of the income on which a news agency's profitability and hence their ability to report the news is predicated. Here, as we have seen, the principle at least is clear. Whether in practice there are not actual compromises and even capitulations to funding sources for producing the news and gaining profits for stockholders of companies invested in professional journalism is altogether another matter. We are discussing what *ought* to happen, given the principles of journalistic ethics we have already defended, rather than predicting what news reporters and network executives will actually do in transacting the business of making the news. If they do capitulate to financial pressures of the kind we have described, then they are acting wrongly, contrary to the principles of professional journalistic ethics. It is reasonable to expect that if they are discovered as having yielded to such pressure—and we have emphasized the importance for professional journalists also to serve as watchdogs for other journalists as well as governmental agencies and individuals and businesses outside the profession, so there is always some likelihood of their actions becoming known—then they will be publicly criticized and reprimanded by other journalists. If so, then there is a further indication of the extent to which professional journalists regard it as morally wrong to compromise journalistic standards for the sake of profits, even if at a human level they might feel sympathy for colleagues caught in such a practical moral dilemma.

INCREASING JOURNALISTIC PROFITS BY REDUCING COSTS

Let us turn now in the second instance to a case in which professional journalists are required by the business aspect of their work to reduce expenses in a way that is not obviously compatible or obviously incompatible with their professional moral obligation to maximize relevant truth telling in the public interest when reporting the news. Profitability depends not only on bringing in revenue, but on controlling expenses. The question is always one of choosing what sorts of expenses can reasonably be cut without negatively affecting the quality of the product; in this case, of the journalism that is produced.

There are often ways of cutting costs that do not necessarily reduce the quality of the work. The use of computers to prepare text and video images, to collect information over the Internet without actually traveling to remote locations, and in many other ways, helps not only to save money and thus increase profits, but also improves rather than degrades the quality of news reporting. Many other examples might also be given. Depending on what a news agency has been spending, it can save money by all sorts of internal economic reforms: conserving energy, limiting waste of materials used in the production of news, buying only needed supplies from more competitive merchants, and so on. These are all methods that any business can legitimately adopt to save money and increase its profits that do not reduce the quality of its products or services, but can actually improve them through greater efficiency.

Beyond such standard methods of increasing profits, what should be the attitude of reporters, editors, news producers, and executives when other kinds of cost-cutting measures are suggested or imposed that directly affect the ability of journalists to practice their profession? We shall proceed as before by conjuring up typical cases that illustrate the principles at issue. Suppose that a local news office proposes to cut back on its reporting staff, relying instead increasingly on prepackaged news stories from a national office rather than investigating events for themselves. Or suppose that a national news agency proposes to save money by foregoing some of its usual procedures for checking on the accuracy of a news story, thereby potentially limiting the ability of news reporters and their diminished staffs to confidently report on important events in a timely fashion. We might imagine that without their assistants to check on certain details of their stories, reporters can still determine the truth, but can only do so too slowly to be competitive with other news agencies. Where market forces hold sway, we can easily imagine that a news agency will take whatever decisions are necessary to remain competitive. What, then, if a number of different news agencies choose more or less simultaneously, either in concert or coincidentally, to reduce their staffs correspondingly, so that all are then in the same boat and competitive market forces will have no effect on the news agencies considered collectively? The consumers of news might complain and object, and in some circumstances this might lead to one or more news agencies breaking ranks and trying to gain a competitive edge by increasing their news gathering and verifying capabilities. If they do not do so, however, then the public might have no alternative to which they can turn.

If we make all of these assumptions, then we can see that under the circumstances described the decision to cut back on news production expenses in ways that affect the ability to report the news can be a violation of the fundamental moral obligation of journalistic ethics to maximize relevant truth telling in the public interest. To the extent that increasing a news agency's profitability by reducing expenses also reduces its ability to discover and communicate information to its customers, to that extent the agency is acting contrary to the principles by which professional journalism receives its moral mandate. If we are not simply talking about buying pencils at a bargain rate but making administrative decisions that are known to inhibit the ability of reporters to tell the truth, simply for the sake of increasing profits, then such actions are inconsistent with journalistic ethics and hence professionally unethical. The trouble is that when such changes are made, they are generally done incrementally, a little bit at a time, effectively limiting journalistic truth telling, but in such a way that makes it hard in practice to notice the difference and take a moral stand against the incursions that finally undermine effective news reporting. This does not make the curtailment of a journalist's ability to report the news purely for motives of profit any less morally objectionable from the standpoint of journalistic ethics, but is rather something equally to be resisted and counteracted to whatever extent possible. News agencies and executives on the contrary should be doing the opposite, acting to increase and improve their reporters' abilities to discover and report what is happening in the world that may be of interest and importance to the public they serve. If they do not do so, then they are no longer properly engaged in the business of journalism.

WEAKNESS OF WILL AND THE TEMPTATIONS OF FINANCIAL GAIN

Money, contrary to the popular aphorism, is not always or necessarily the root of all evil. When we think of the clash of professional responsibilities that occur because of the profit motive, it remains hard to assign blame to the opposite side of the equation by suggesting that there is something wrong with the ethics of journalism and, in particular, with the principle that journalists are morally obligated to maximize relevant truth telling.

Thus, it does not begin to ring as true to say, for example, that preventing disease and healing the sick is the root of all evil, or that prosecuting the law and defending the accused is the root of all evil, or that investigating events in the world and reporting information in accord with the principle to maximize relevant truth telling is the root of all evil. If there is a source of moral wrongdoing in the professions, what better place to locate it than in what many persons are willing or find it expedient to do in order to make money? Moral agents not infrequently suffer from *weakness of will*, a limitation that in particular limits the ability of even the best-intentioned persons from actually fulfilling what they recognize as their moral responsibilities.

Ancient Greek philosophers referred to moral weakness of will as *akrasia*, by which they meant the limitations of incontinent persons to actually do what they know to be morally right. Weakness of will is often an indication of a character flaw, but it is one that is especially put to the test where large sums of money or items of comparable value are concerned.

As we know from common experience in the workaday world, people sometimes relax or even abandon their moral principles for the sake of money, and especially for large amounts of easily obtained money. The fact that monetary gain is a powerful incentive that can potentially distract moral agents from their responsibilities makes it all the more necessary for persons interested in maintaining the standards of journalistic ethics to keep a vigilant watch on the activities of advertisers, activist groups, and others who might try to dictate or control the contents of the news through financial means and to provide moral and material assistance to journalists and news executives to resist urges to sacrifice journalistic excellence for the sake of increased profitability.

STEALTH ADVERTISING

There are even more subtle ways in which the moral integrity of journalists can be compromised by the lure of financial gain. Since these raise further classic problems for journalistic ethics, we should consider some of the most important devious methods by which truth telling can be jeopardized by moneyed interests and offer concrete moral guidelines for professional journalists and news executives.

The cost of preparing newscasts makes it attractive for networks to include prepackaged programming, with verified facts of interest to viewers and documentary images prepared for airing on videotape or DVD. Some of these materials are sold to news agencies by independent sources or freelance journalists who do not necessarily work for the news outlets in the sense of being a regular employee on the payroll. This is not inherently a morally questionable practice, and news agencies do this kind of thing all the time, regarding it as a valuable as well as economically attractive source of information for their viewers. Here is an example, however, of how things can sometimes go wrong when these prepackaged news items are uncritically published or broadcast, potentially raising problems of professional ethics for journalists in any of the news media.

Case Study 10

Strangers Bearing Gifts

A salesperson arrives at a newsroom and offers a prepackaged videotape to fill several minutes of airtime, concerning a new medical treatment that will help patients suffering from diabetes. The video is well authenticated, all of its facts are correct, and it includes interviews with recognized, respected health officials who offer their candid opinion of the potential health benefits and risks of the procedure, which has the possibility of helping many persons improve their condition and even to save lives.

This is precisely the kind of thing that viewers of the network are keen to see and learn about. It is a program, moreover, that would otherwise be expensive to produce if the reporters working for the agency were to undertake the work themselves. The story is ready to plug and play, suitable for broadcast without further ado, and at a fraction of what it would otherwise cost. There is only one condition. When the video, which has been prepared at the expense of an international pharmaceutical company, is broadcast, the announcer is supposed to mention that viewers can contact their physicians or local hospital for brochures describing the procedures in more detail. All this sounds innocent enough, except for the fact that the brochures, for anyone who cares to pick one up, contain a significant amount of promotional advertising for the pharmaceutical company that financed and produced the video.

This is indirect marketing on the part of the drug company. It involves the reporters for the network rather obliquely in a trail of information that leads interested viewers to a source in which the company advertises its products. It does not do so immediately by including its name or logo as part of the news broadcast, but it provides useful information in the context of which viewers are directed to obtain product literature, only if they are sufficiently interested, to pursue the matter with their physicians or local hospitals with whom the pharmaceutical company just happens to have a preexistent agreement. It can easily be worthwhile for the sake of attracting a select group of potential clients to their advertising for such a company to spend the money needed to produce the video; it is a smart marketing ploy. The question is whether the reporter or network knowing or even suspecting these facts acts wrongly to air the video as part of its regular news broadcast.

As a legitimate business, in principle there would be nothing wrong with the drug company buying advertising time on the network to market its products. The disincentive for it to do so is that such advertising time is enormously expensive when compared with the costs involved in making a news story for the network to present along with its other coverage. The company then need only pay whatever is additionally required to print the brochures for physicians and hospitals to make available when they receive inquiries about them from persons who have seen the newscast. The company additionally gains an important marketing advantage that it cannot secure by means of ordinary conventional advertising. By being associated in viewer's minds with the scientific news report of an important new development in health treatment, the pharmaceutical company earns the gratitude of its potential customers who as a result may be more likely to use its products or request their physicians to prescribe the drug treatments in conjunction with the new diabetes procedures and perhaps for other unrelated health needs generally. The company thereby receives more bang for its advertising buck by producing a medical news story and only indirectly leading viewers as customers to its explicit advertisements on the brochures that the reporter is supposed to announce as part of the lead-in or follow-up to the story when the video is aired.

QUESTIONS

1. Does the reporter or the network act wrongly in accord with the principles of journalistic ethics by accepting the video and including it among news items in a nightly report? Why or why not?

2. Would it make any difference to the journalistic ethics of the situation if the drug company did not include a reference to the brochures about the treatment available at the doctor's office or hospital? What if they printed such brochures and had them on display in these locations but did not mention the fact in the news story itself? Some patients would then happen upon the pamphlets in the course of their own efforts to get professional advice from their physicians about the procedure described in the report. Would this absolve the reporters or network from any potential professional journalistic wrongdoing?

3. How, exactly, if at all, does the drug company's clever strategy to promote its product without paying ordinary advertising fees conflict with the fundamental principle of journalistic ethics to maximize relevant truth telling in the public interest? Why, exactly, if in fact it is wrong, would it be morally objectionable for a news program to include such a prepackaged medical information program under the guise of reporting the news?

4. A still more devious effort on the part of businesses to advertise their goods on the air or in printed or audio interviews is for a celebrity to casually mention in the context of a conversation with an interviewer that such-and-such a new product has helped them. If the celebrity has been paid by a manufacturer to drop this information on the audience but the interviewer did not expect this or was not informed that it might happen, is there any violation of journalistic ethics in the resulting interview? What if the reporter or the news agency did know this in advance or even participated in the interview by cueing the celebrity with specific questions prepared in advance either by the celebrity or by the company the celebrity surreptitiously represents?

5. If you think there is something morally questionable about the celebrity use of a product name in the course of an interview, where should journalistic ethics try to draw the line? Should celebrities on television be allowed to wear recognizable clothing or jewelry brands? Is there anything wrong in their promoting products visually in this way as opposed to making offhand verbal endorsements? Why or why not?

MORAL QUANDARIES ABOUT "HIDDEN" ADVERTISING

The problem in the final composite case study of this chapter is especially intriguing because it does not obviously violate the prime directive of news reporters to maximize relevant truth telling.

The story by hypothesis does not contain any falsehoods, and the medical information it conveys is immediately relevant to the public, who naturally take an interest in new treatments for serious diseases like diabetes. They will be usefully informed by the video, satisfying the duty of journalists in all media to inform their audience. What is more, the reporter presenting the prepackaged story is not being asked to accept a bribe or any other incentive, except to contribute to the network's profitability by filling several minutes of news airtime with a worthwhile story that will cost the network either nothing to report, if the pharmaceutical company is distributing the video free of charge, or in any case much less than it would cost the network to produce the video on its own using its own personnel and facilities. It is an easy way to reduce costs, and, what is more, it seems to carry no explicit taint of commercial exploitation by the company, because the company's name is not mentioned anywhere in or on the video. Those who merely view the video on television and do not take the further step of requesting the company's brochures from their local hospitals or physicians will never come to know anything about the company as a result and will certainly not associate the company with the production of the news story.

Like most things that seem too good to be true, the example of the pharmaceutical company's production and distribution of the breakthrough in diabetes treatment story is also fraught with unforeseen moral difficulties. We are supposing for simplicity sake in the first place that the reporters and network are not aware that the video is sponsored by the drug company or that it has included advertising on the brochures that viewers are to be advised can be obtained from their local health providers. If the news reporters and executives are unaware of these facts, are they morally culpable for accepting the video and presenting it as a news story? Presumably in that case the pharmaceutical company is guilty of deception, if, for example, as we should probably imagine, the video is misrepresented as having been produced by a freelance journalist of the sort that many newscasters frequently rely on for coverage of special topics, including health, medicine, science, and many other kinds of events. The pharmaceutical company has then perpetrated a kind of fraud by falsely offering as news something that is actually a disguised and indirect effort to advertise its products. A journalist cannot be morally responsible for being omniscient about all of its sources. We might nevertheless maintain that if the truth about the video purveyor's real motives were later to surface, it would be morally incumbent on the network to report the fact to its viewers, explaining the effort to surreptitiously insinuate its advertisements by using the news as an unknowing and unwilling accomplice. We can also say that the reporter and network supervisors in question have a further moral obligation to inquire carefully into the circumstances of such a video's production and sponsorship. It should seem suspicious to any prudent news professional if either the video is offered for free or with the condition that the brochures be mentioned when the video is aired. A freelance journalist produces news reports or research for a living and would not give away his or her efforts for free. Nor would a freelance journalist ordinarily place conditions on the publication of a news item, such as the requirement that the network mention the availability of the brochures.

The reporter or the reporter's editor or other supervisors in the network chain of command should accordingly ask to see one of the brochures to determine whether or not it is free of advertising or whether some further deception is involved. A reporter and a news agency need not be excessively shrewd to engage in this level of further investigation. It is, after all, the kind of thing that investigative news reporters do professionally for a living. If such facts are uncovered in the process, then it is reasonable to conclude that the video should be refused if it can only be aired under those conditions. We do not expect journalists to be so gullible as to fall for the kind of advertising scam we have so far described, although it is conceivable for some to be taken in by much more clever schemes that no one could be expected to recognize, at least at first. Even in the most cunning cases of deception, we require as a part of journalistic ethics that persons associated with news production should take reasonable precautions and try sincerely to discover attempts at fraud, to inquire into the reasons why a prepackaged report has been prepared and why it is being offered. We do not morally require reporters or news agencies to be all-knowing. We do, however, consider them to be morally obligated professional discretion and to exercise ordinary caution in preventing what is actually a disguised attempt at advertising from being presented simply as news.

This, in any case, seems to be the morally right advice. If we ask why, as we should, the answer is surely that, in accord with the fundamental moral obligation of journalistic ethics to maximize relevant truth telling, it is misleading in the extreme to present something as simply a news item when it is not simply a news item but disguised advertising designed to attract interested viewers to a commercial product. It involves a higher level of falsehood that violates the requirement to maximize truth telling in journalism beyond the internal content of a news report itself. In this case, the deception makes it morally objectionable to air the story under false pretenses or to overlook the signs by which a prudent professional working in the field should be able to tell that something is fishy about the proffered news material. If reporters or their supervisors know in advance that this is the intent of the news item, then they have a clear moral obligation not to make use of it under the conditions imposed.

The reason is the same, since in that case they recognize that their audience will regard the story as another item of news when in reality it is something more, something different than what it purports to be. A similar distinction applies, as we have already remarked in discussing the problem of journalistic ethics in light of different types of bias, for a story to be presented purely as a news item when in fact it is something more, a subliminal political or religious comment or attempt to influence opinion rather than to merely inform. Journalists owe it to their readers or viewers to be as forthright as possible about the information they are conveying. They are obligated to look into the circumstances under which it is presented, offering explicit guidance as to the real import of the information they make available, and not allowing such significantly different categories as objective information and advertising to be deliberately confused in their readers' or audiences' minds. To do so is precisely not to advance relevant truth telling, but to fall culpably short of that journalistic goal and professional moral responsibility.

PRODUCT PLACEMENT IN THE NEWS

There are other ways in which news reporting can become mixed up with product endorsement. These also potentially result in a conflict of interest between the obligations of truth telling in journalism and the avarice that drives much of the industry. Suppose that a supervisor reminds a reporter that advertising is itself newsworthy and then recommends that the reporter cover a story about one of the network's major advertisers, whereby its name and products are frequently mentioned in a favorable light as part of the story. The reporter in that case inadvertently manages to include positive references to a corporate sponsor of the news agency under the guise of presenting a legitimate news item that once again is not entirely what it is cracked up to be.

Consider the possibilities of apparently incidental product placement in the news that has become popular in the cinema. Corporations pay movie producers large sums of money to include particular products among the props and background of the set when a film is made as a way of passively advertising their products. We can imagine the same thing happening in the case of news reporting, primarily on television, but in principle also in print media. For example, a network news program airs a story on a criminal investigation, or a new play opening in the theater district, or just about anything else. It offers nothing nonfactual, but includes among its stock footage of a city brightly lit neon billboards advertising the same products that its sponsors otherwise pay for airtime to promote. Thus, a comedy premiering on Broadway can be introduced with a few shots of Times Square in New York City in which flashing signs advertising soft drinks or electronic equipment can easily be seen in the background. If this is done deliberately by journalists producing stories about such events for the sake of some sort of economic benefit on the part of the corporations whose products are featured and, more immediately, to the news companies they serve, then they are in clear violation of the principles of journalistic ethics on truth telling grounds in their reporting, presenting what is meant to be advertising under the guise of informing viewers of the facts. In other imaginable and real-life cases, the moral responsibility for product placement in the news may be more ambiguous in interpretation.

Summary

We have not tried to consider all the possibilities of conflicts of interest between journalistic truth telling and the profit motive. Nor have we touched on all the ways in which abstract moral ideals in journalistic ethics can run into conflict with workplace realities for news professionals. The representative cases we have selected for discussion nevertheless provide a kind of template for evaluating the morality of many if not all potential conflicts.

Journalists as individuals, like everyone else in this vale of tears, need to make money, and their companies need to make money too. If they do not, then they cannot pay the journalists in their employ or provide the essential equipment, materials, and services needed to publish or broadcast the news. These items are expensive, and, except in the case of nonprofit news organizations, of which there are only a few, news agencies are additionally expected by their stockholders and corporate executives to turn a profit, often a rather handsome profit, in producing the news. There is absolutely nothing morally wrong with any of this as far as professional journalistic ethics is concerned. It is only a question of how the profit is made and what journalists and their supervisors are or are not willing to do in order to make money from the investigation and reporting of the news.

We have identified several ways in which things can go wrong from a moral point of view. We have learned to recognize some of the pitfalls and moral dilemmas into which journalists can be led by the desire to make the news profitable as well as informative for the public news reporting serves. The general principle is that anything that subtracts from maximal relevant truth telling in the news is a violation of journalistic ethics, even in those cases where the contents of news items is 100 percent true. The frame and context in which news is presented is an important part of the information a news report conveys, and it can also misrepresent the truth, deceive a reader or viewer, or diminish the total truth content of the report. These potentially morally compromising situations are all to be avoided and carefully scrutinized because they can arise in unexpected ways. A morally responsible journalist who wants to hold to high professional ideals while at the same time living and working in the real, typically less-than-ideal world of journalism, needs to consider the implications of every item of reportage and to have the moral strength of will to resist any journalistic activity that might turn out to be unethical in the sense of violating the fundamental moral principle of journalistic ethics to maximize relevant truth telling in the public interest. With the right sort of attitude there need be no insuperable difficulty in adhering to journalism's abstract moral idea while working in the sometimes morally challenging day-to-day practice of professional news reporting.

The ideal we have proposed is practical in the sense that it can actually be put to use in guiding journalists in their profession. Although the ideal imposes a demanding criterion of professional conduct, it is realizable to the extent that all journalists can make a sincere effort to live up to its requirements and meet its obligations. The moral obligations of journalistic ethics in this regard are no different than those of theoretical ethics of the most general sort or of any other branch of applied or professional ethics. We do not declare a moral system impractical or beyond the ability of real flesh-and-blood moral agents to put into practice merely because it posits an ideal that cannot always be attained. We recognize morality as a matter of degree, and we expect that good efforts and earnest endeavors in the spirit of a moral principle are often the measure of whether or not individuals are acting in accord with appropriate ethical standards, contributing to what a given moral principle requires and intends. It is rather a question in each case of what journalists are trying to accomplish in their work, their honest intent, as well as the extent to which they achieve their purpose. Journalists can always try to make a concerted effort to maximize relevant truth telling in reporting the news, even if they do not always succeed. Journalists working as editors can similarly be expected to editorialize responsibly without confusing value and opinion with the facts of the news, doing so, moreover, in a way that is consistent with whatever other more highly prioritized moral obligations may also impinge on them as morally responsible members of society.

If we ask from a practical point of view whether journalists and news companies can actually resist the demands of the marketplace by emphasizing information over entertainment content in the news, standing up to advertisers when conflicts arise, rooting out bias, refusing to pander to special interests, and doing whatever else is required in order to approach as near as possible the ideal of maximizing relevant truth telling without violating other more important moral obligations, then we encounter another aspect of the practicality of the fundamental moral principle of journalistic ethics. We are then inquiring in effect whether any news agency can realistically go up against current trends and market forces in the wider society when their competitors can probably not be expected to join with them in doing what journalistic ethics seems to require. The answer is surely that news companies and individual journalists, like athletes in training, can indeed strive to fulfill their professional obligations even in the face of powerful opposing factors and even if their competitors do not also comply.

We also considered the extent to which certain commercial interests can and should be overridden by professional moral obligations. It might be true that a news company cannot make as much money if it adheres to the principle of maximizing relevant truth telling in the public interest. We have no reason to think that a news company conscientiously fulfilling its fundamental professional journalistic duty cannot continue to make enough money to stay in operation and might even find itself prospering by comparison with its more ostensibly profit-driven competitors who have lost sight of the main purpose of engaging in the news information business in the first place. To whatever extent possible, individual journalists should also be able, like other professionals under financial pressure, to find the inner strength they need to oppose an excessive profit motive in reporting the news. It is within their abilities, realistically speaking, to establish standards for excellence in news reporting that make as few concessions as possible to commercial interests when the latter threaten to infringe on the accurate impartial reporting of news and the useful dissemination of information for the public good.

Maintaining independence from both government and finance, avoiding censorship and undue influence in journalistic reportage, protecting privileged sources, while respecting the privacy of news subjects, preserving also the proper journalistic distance and objectivity while investigating and gathering the facts of the news, and offering commentary within the parameters of responsible editorializing, are not too much to expect of journalists. Indeed, most practicing journalists admirably satisfy these professional ethical expectations. Comparison with the professional codes of ethics and the guidelines for proper journalistic conduct reproduced from the public domain in the appendices attached to this book indicates the extent to which journalists themselves recognize the same sorts of moral obligations that we have considered, which constitute an important ingredient in professional journalism's moral self-regulation.

The purpose of our investigation of journalistic ethics has not been in any case to try to dictate moral principles to journalists from without. Rather, it has been to help working journalists recognize all that is at stake in their professional conduct as the protectors of the liberty of free people in a free society. We have sought to promote an understanding of how the various moral obligations that are distinctive of journalistic practice can all be related to the special responsibilities of journalists to offer accurate news reporting, or, as we have formulated the principle, maximal relevant truth telling in the public interest. The remarkable way in which journalists' obligations fit together within the framework we have described illustrates the general theme we have also developed and supported as a characterization of professional ethics. It is that journalists in a sense have the same moral duties as anyone outside of journalism, only magnified to a proportionately higher degree because of the extent to which journalists can affect a wider public of individuals who rely on news reports for information through the truthful and accurate reporting of current events.

We have described journalism as a noble profession. The work journalists do in the abstract is indeed noble, and the practitioners of the profession are individually noble to the extent that they live up to its ideals. If journalists strive to their utmost only to tell the truth in the public interest, then, in fulfilling the fundamental moral obligation of professional journalistic ethics, they will satisfy the requirements of their trade. At the same time, they will also make a valuable contribution to the preservation of the freedom of society as a whole by protecting the freedom of the press, in which all members of a free society have a vested interest. The concept of a free press and some of its more noteworthy implications is accordingly the subject of the next and subsequent chapters.[6]

---

[6]We would be hard-pressed to find a better, more compact statement of the attitude concerning the importance and limitations of a free press in a free society than that provided by Walter Lippmann in his (1922) book, *Public Opinion*, quoted in Knowlton and Parsons, *The Journalist's Moral Compass*, p. 111: "The press is no substitute for institutions. It is like the beam of a searchlight that moves restlessly about, bringing one episode and then another out of darkness into vision. Men cannot do the work of the world by this light alone. They cannot govern society by episodes, incidents, and eruptions. It is only when they work by a steady light of their own, that the press, when it is turned upon them, reveals a situation intelligible enough for a popular decision. The trouble lies deeper than the press, and so does a remedy. It lies in social organization based on a system of analysis and record, and in all the corollaries of that principle; in the abandonment of the theory of the omnicompetent citizen, in the decentralization of decision, in the coordination of decision by comparable record and analysis. If at the centers of management there is a running audit, which makes work intelligible to those who do it, and those who superintend it, issues when they arise are not the mere collisions of the blind. Then, too, the news is uncovered for the press by a system of intelligence that is also a check upon the press."

chapter four

Freedom of the Press

We have now considered relevant truth telling in the public interest. We have discussed the moral rights and responsibilities of journalists in theory and to a limited degree in practice, and we have taken into account an important distinction between abstract moral ideals and everyday working realities for professional journalists in the field. This background equips us for approaching a vital presupposition that runs through all of these issues concerning the freedom of the press. We shall argue that if the exercise of morally responsible freedom in any category is a morally good thing, then we should work to protect and maximize all such freedoms. We should do so, moreover, not merely on general principles, but because the value of journalistic reporting is in direct proportion to its degree of socially responsible but otherwise unbounded freedom. Again we turn to case studies to focus analysis on the virtues of a free press within the limits of sound practical judgment involving the greater social interest. Accordingly, we choose this opportunity to understand the importance of the abstract moral right of journalists freely to report facts and express opinions in a practical workaday context of journalistic social responsibilities.

FREE PRESS DILEMMAS

The idea of a free press is another ideal moral abstraction. As such, freedom of the press is subject to all the same ambiguities and qualifications as discussions of freedom generally. This does not mean that the concept of a free press is meaningless, rather only that the idea must be carefully characterized and precisely defined within the circumscribed limits to which it applies if we are to avoid misrepresenting the concept and drawing false inferences from it. The philosophical task for this chapter is thus primarily one of conceptual clarification.

There is no such thing as an absolutely free press, just as there is no such thing as absolutely free human action in any other sphere. To take an extreme example, although we suppose that American journalism enjoys a high degree of freedom of expression in reporting the news, we do not imagine that this freedom includes the license to publish photographs of child pornography or sensitive military secrets or instructions about how to make pipe bombs. There are in fact many categories of information that we do not want and do not expect journalists freely to report. Philosophy seeks to understand the sorts of limitations that rightly apply to freedom of expression in news reporting and, more importantly, perhaps, to explain the value of a free press within these limitations, while exploring the question of whether and why such limitations are ever truly justified. Thus, we find a widely held principle concerning the limitations of a free press in a free society, as expressed by Fred Siebert, Theodore Peterson, and Wilbur Schramm, in their 1963 study, *Four Theories of the Press: The Authoritarian, Libertarian, Social Responsibility and Soviet Communist Concepts of What the Press Should Be and Do*:

> [T]he legal right to free expression under the social responsibility theory is not unconditional. Even libertarian theory imposed certain minimal restraints on free expression such as laws dealing with libel, obscenity, incitement to riot, and sedition. All of those restrictions, the [1947 Robert M. Hutchins] Commission [on Freedom of the Press] has noted, were based on one common principle: "that an utterance or publication invades in a serious, overt, and demonstrable manner recognized private rights or vital social interests" (66: 123). The legal restrictions on press freedom, then, it argued, might be justifiably extended if new abuses fall within this category.
>
> Take for example degradation. If publications deliberately, consistently, systematically pander in and exploit vulgarity, they have sacrificed their moral right to free expression. Having abandoned their moral claim to it, they have undermined their legal claim. True, there might be a better means than the law of correcting such publications. Yet society may decide that degradation is an invasion of its vital interests against which it is justified in protecting itself. Therefore, it might prohibit degrading publications. However, the burden of proof that society's interests were harmed would rest with whoever would extend the law to cover such new areas of abuse.[1]

Different societies that aspire to high degrees of personal freedom have dealt with the problem of qualifying the free dissemination of information in different ways. There are various sorts of compromises that have been attained in practice in different countries and at different times. They have tried to strike an appropriate balance between the public's right to know the facts of news events and other social obligations and goals that may sometimes stand in conflict with the desire to maintain unrestricted access to information.

One solution to the problem is to allow largely unfettered freedom of the press, while holding in reserve the possibility of censuring such items as might be thought dangerous or prejudicial to the safety of the society as a whole. The

[1]Siebert, Peterson, and Schramm, *Four Theories of the Press*, p. 99.

difficulty with such provisions is that they are sometimes threatened with what logicians call a *slippery slope*. By restricting the freedom of the press in this or that case on legitimate grounds of security, a bad precedent can then be set through which the concept of security itself is stretched to accommodate more and more distantly related situations, so that finally there remains no meaningful freedom for the flow of information. The effect of precedents eroding any type of freedom is particularly dangerous when each new case resembles the previous one only in an insignificant way. It does not take long in such a process for liberties to be degraded or even destroyed in ways that could not have easily been anticipated at the outset.

A society is particularly at risk of undermining the freedom of the press when for one reason or another its vital interests are threatened by the availability of certain kinds of information. Then it is natural for responsible leaders to try to take measures that can help to make its citizens more secure by preventing potentially damaging facts from being too freely disseminated. Such information often includes military secrets and economic assets, but, as the descent down the slippery slope begins, the list can quickly evolve to include many other kinds of information. In the worst-case scenario, all or virtually all important kinds of news can eventually become subject to government censorship on every level to the point where the ideal of a free press is completely lost sight of. The importance of free expression versus the qualification of its free exercise in practice is emphasized in another contemporary critical study by Robert Trager and Donna L. Dickerson, *Freedom of Expression in the 21st Century*:

> Freedom of speech is one of the most important components of being a free person and of having a free society. In democratic societies, there is more freedom of expression than under repressive governments. But even in free countries, not all speech is free. In countries with free speech traditions, judges, attorneys, lawmakers, and individual citizens often face decisions about what expression should be protected, what speech may be proscribed or punished, what justifies more or less expansive freedom of expression, and how free speech is to be balanced against other rights. Because the answers implicate political, religious, and cultural considerations, speech protection varies from country to country, differing even among democratic societies. Freedom of expression's importance in self-development, in human interactions, and in relationships between governments and their citizens makes free speech not just an interesting topic, but one that is crucial to people's lives.[2]

There is thus a potential conflict between the interests of the press and media generally to report whatever is deemed newsworthy and the interests and, in certain instances, even the moral obligations of governments, to exercise

[2]Trager and Dickerson, *Freedom of Expression in the 21st Century*, p. 13.

some form of control over what kinds of news is communicated and how and with what emphasis and perspective. The problem is to strike just the right sort of balance between enabling the press to have maximum free coverage of events on the one hand, while restraining the appearance of information that threatens the safety of individuals and the security of society. The trouble is that both extremes of the continuum of possibilities that we have just described are prejudicial to the interests of society. It is a bad thing for too much of the wrong kinds of information to become public if too many persons or the social structure as a whole is endangered thereby. It is equally a bad thing for the social structure as a whole and hence for individuals living in that society if too much governmental control over the news media is exercised. Somewhere in between these extremes we may hope and expect a proper equilibrium to be found. Exactly where and why this should occur turns out to be a surprisingly difficult philosophical question.

AMERICAN CONSTITUTIONAL PROTECTION OF JOURNALISTIC FREEDOMS

Why, in the first place, we must ask, do we value a free press? There is no doubt that freedom of the press is highly prized in free societies. The U.S. Constitution includes as its First Amendment to the Bill of Rights the injunction that:

> Congress shall make no law respecting an establishment of religion, or prohibiting the free exercise thereof; or abridging the freedom of speech, or of the press; or the right of the people peaceably to assemble, and to petition the Government for a redress of grievances.

These are powerful, stirring words. Nor are they merely words. For they are backed up by social convention and the legal machinery of the courts and executive and legislative branches of government in the United States. Freedom of the press and its protection under the law has also attained a special significance in the larger community of nations.

Philosophically, we should nevertheless not assume that the Constitution is the final definitive word on the rights of journalists and consumers of news information to have free expression and free access. We need additionally to ask whether the First Amendment is justified and whether it serves from an independently philosophically defensible moral standpoint as a suitable model for other societies to follow. We want to know whether the part of the First Amendment concerning the "hands off" prohibition of governmental interference in the freedom of the press embodies the sorts of values that are appropriate to journalistic ethics. The legal basis for the guarantee of a free press underwritten by the

American Constitution has enjoyed widespread support in the history of jurisprudence:

[Chief Justice Sir William] Blackstone's statement, widely circulated in the American states, summarizes the eighteenth-century legalistic position:

> The liberty of the press is indeed essential to the nature of a free state, but this consists in laying no previous restraints upon publications, and not in freedom from censure for criminal matter when published. Every free man has an undoubted right to lay what sentiments he pleases before the public; to forbid this, is to destroy the freedom of the press; but if he publishes what is improper, mischievous, or illegal, he must take the consequences of his own temerity . . . thus the will of individuals is still left free; the abuse only of that free-will is the object of legal punishment. Neither is any restraint hereby laid upon freedom of thought or inquiry; liberty of private sentiment is still left; the disseminating, or making public, of bad sentiments, destructive of the ends of society, is the crime which society corrects (34: 1326–27). Both [Thomas] Erskine and [Thomas] Jefferson contended for a broader interpretation of the constitutional protection of the press from government control than either [Jared] Mansfield or Blackstone was willing to accept. The Erskine thesis was that even though the matter published was erroneous and even though it might adversely affect the interests of the state, no penalties should be placed on the publisher who was honest and sincere in his purposes and intent. Jefferson argued that while the press should be subject to punishment for damages to individuals it should not be held liable for injuries to the reputation of the government. Defining the proper limitations on the freedom of the media is the most disturbing problem facing the supporter of libertarian principles. Even today. . . no agreement has been reached in democratic circles on the proper sphere of government control and regulation of the various types of mass media.[3]

If the Constitution is on the right track, then it correctly formulates an ethical ideal for freedom of the press. If we happen to be Americans, which is

---

[3]Ibid., pp. 49–50. See, among others, O'Neil, *The First Amendment and Civil Liability* and Anthony, *Make No Law*. The reader is encouraged to compare the contents of the four appendices with other expressions of journalistic ethics and with the reduction to the simplifying principle advanced in this treatise of maximal relevant truth telling in the public interest and for the public good. See also, for example, the "Canons of Journalism" (1922), issued by the American Society of Newspaper Editors and revised as "Statement of Principles," October 23, 1975, in the following excerpts:

> The First Amendment, protecting freedom of expression from abridgment by any law, guarantees to the people through their press a constitutional right, and thereby places on newspaper people a particular responsibility.

certainly not presupposed of the reader, we should not as philosophers be too impressed by the fact that the First Amendment happens to appear in the American Constitution as a foundation stone of the social contract by and under the protection of which we live. We shall first have to find good arguments in support of the idea that the press should be to any degree free and that the government should not act to restrain the gathering and reporting of news, in order to agree that the First Amendment is morally justified. Then we can take comfort in and point with satisfaction to the fact that these good reasons are embodied in the text of the Constitution's Bill of Rights. In the process of engaging in open philosophical inquiry into the merits of supporting a free press, we may also need to address the more difficult problems of how freedom of the press is to be properly interpreted and how, in particular, its accompanying responsibilities to the society it serves can best be met. For the time being, we take the commitment to a free press expressed in the First Amendment merely as historical evidence, sociological data, of the fact that freedom of the press has been highly cherished by the founders of such societies as the United States.

Thus journalism demands of its practitioners not only industry and knowledge but also the pursuit of a standard of integrity proportionate to the journalist's singular obligation.

To this end the American Society of Newspaper Editors sets forth this Statement of Principles as a standard encouraging the highest ethical and professional performance.

ARTICLE I—Responsibility
The primary purpose of gathering and distributing news and opinion is to serve the general welfare by informing the people and enabling them to make judgments on the issues of the time. Newspapermen and women who abuse the power of their professional role for selfish motives or unworthy purposes are faithless to that public trust.

The American press was made free not just to inform or just to serve as a forum for debate but also to bring an independent scrutiny to bear on the forces of power in the society, including the conduct of official power at all levels of government.

ARTICLE IV—Truth and Accuracy
Good faith with the reader is the foundation of good journalism. Every effort must be made to assure that the news content is accurate, free from bias and in context, and that all sides are presented fairly. Editorials, analytical articles and commentary should be held to the same standards of accuracy with respect to facts as news reports.

Significant errors of fact, as well as errors of omission, should be corrected promptly, and prominently.

ARTICLE V—Fair Play
Journalists should respect the rights of people involved in the news, observe the common standards of decency and stand accountable to the public for the fairness and accuracy of their news reports.

Case Study 11

Thomas Jefferson on the Importance of a Free Press

Here is a selection of quotations from the papers of Thomas Jefferson, author of the American Declaration of Independence and philosophical statesman, collected in the Library of Congress:

> "The most effectual engines for [controlling a people] are the public papers. . . . [A tyrannical] government always [maintains] a kind of standing army of newswriters who, without any regard to truth or to what should be like truth, [invent] and put into the papers whatever might serve the ministers. This suffices with the mass of the people who have no means of distinguishing the false from the true paragraphs of a newspaper."(Letter to G. K. van Hogendorp, Oct. 13, 1785)
>
> "Our liberty cannot be guarded but by the freedom of the press, nor that be limited without danger of losing it."(Letter to John Jay, 1786)
>
> "The basis of our governments being the opinion of the people, the very first object should be to keep that right; and were it left to me to decide whether we should have a government without newspapers or newspapers without a government, I should not hesitate a moment to prefer the latter. But I should mean that every man should receive those papers and be capable of reading them."(Letter to Edward Carrington, 1787)
>
> "Considering the great importance to the public liberty of the freedom of the press, and the difficulty of submitting it to very precise rules, the laws have thought it less mischievous to give greater scope to its freedom than to the restraint of it."(Letter to the Spanish Commissioners, 1793)
>
> "I am . . . for freedom of the press, and against all violations of the Constitution to silence by force and not by reason the complaints or criticisms, just or unjust, of our citizens against the conduct of their agents."(Letter to Elbridge Gerry, 1799)
>
> "The press [is] the only tocsin [alarm bell or warning signal] of a nation. [If it] is completely silenced . . . all means of a general effort [are] taken away."(Letter to Thomas Cooper, Nov. 29, 1802)
>
> "No experiment can be more interesting than that we are now trying, and which we trust will end in establishing the fact, that man may be governed by reason and truth. Our first object should therefore be, to leave open to him all the avenues to truth. The most effectual hitherto found, is the freedom of the press. It is, therefore, the first shut up by those who fear the investigation of their actions."(Letter to John Tyler, 1804)
>
> "The functionaries of every government have propensities to command at will the liberty and property of their constituents. There is no

safe deposit for these but with the people themselves, nor can they be safe with them without information. Where the press is free, and every man able to read, all is safe."(Letter to Charles Yancey, 1816)

"The only security of all is in a free press. The force of public opinion cannot be resisted when permitted freely to be expressed. The agitation it produces must be submitted to. It is necessary, to keep the waters pure."(Letter to the Marquis de Lafayette, 1823)

QUESTIONS

1. Does Jefferson make a good case for the freedom of the press? Why or why not? How would you explain his arguments for a free press in these letters?
2. What role does Jefferson attribute to the independent investigation of news events by journalists in the preservation of a society's liberties? Why, exactly, is the free flow of information supposed to be so important to a free society?
3. Why does Jefferson propose that a free press is a guardian of social freedoms? What does he imagine a free press can do when efforts are made to curtail a people's personal and political freedoms?
4. Is freedom of the press merely an abstract moral ideal to which we can only aspire and approximate in the real world of journalistic and social realities? What makes it such? Or is a free press something that it is within human ability to create and sustain? What kinds of protections does Jefferson suggest might be necessary in order to safeguard a society's freedom of the press?
5. Does it appear from Jefferson's remarks that he would consider any limitations on a free press? Are there reasonable exceptions that might sometimes need to be made in order to preserve a society's interests in areas other than those concerned with information and editorial opinion? If you detect such hints, what are they? If Jefferson does not seem to you to countenance any exceptions to a free press pursuing its business by informing the public, how can he justify potential abuses of news reporters publishing false, libelous, or socially dangerous information? What is the extent and what, if any, are the limits to a free press in a Jeffersonian-style democracy?

PRIORITY OF A FREE PRESS IN THE AMERICAN BILL OF RIGHTS

There are several points of philosophical interest to be discerned in the exact language by which the First Amendment is expressed. What shall we make of the fact that the framers of the Constitution lumped together freedom of religion, freedom of the press, and free assembly and right to petition the government for redress of grievances? Are these just accidentally associated for convenience in the Bill of Rights, or is there a deeper meaning represented by the fact that the authors of the First Amendment chose to join these several kinds of freedom together as inalienable rights for citizens in establishing the nation's rule of law?

We can hypothesize that these liberties being vouchsafed in the First Amendment, rather than somewhere lower down in the list, indicates the importance and high regard in which they were held by the constitutional committee. By including freedom of the press in the First (instead of the Second, Third, or so on) Amendment, the authors seem to have established a definite priority for the value of a free press. What might we reasonably suppose that importance to be? What, further, can we conclude from the fact that freedom of the press appears ranked among these other freedoms, but is listed only after freedom of religion? There are historical and political philosophical conjectures to be considered in investigating these matters, especially if we set aside for the sake of argument the possibility that these are random or purely accidental orderings of rights.

Let us first ask about the significance of appending a Bill of Rights to the Constitution. What does it mean, and why was it done? Why was it thought necessary or worthwhile to add an explicit list of citizens' rights to the law of the land? The answer in part is that the authors of the Constitution recognized that democratic methods of social decision-making by themselves do not guarantee any particular outcome of collective decision-making. Democratic societies in the past have made highly morally regrettable decisions, such as the execution of Socrates in ancient Athens, or the election of Adolf Hitler to be chancellor of Germany at the onset of the Third Reich. There is equally no reason in principle why the citizens of a nation like the United States, through its representatively democratic collective decision-making, might decide to deprive a voting minority of their property or even of their liberty or lives. If we think of democracy merely as a way of converting individual choices to social policy, then there is no intrinsic prohibition against a majority of voters deciding to do horrible things against other citizens, provided that on certain occasions they have enough votes to do so. A democracy is only as morally good in its policies as the individuals that participate in its governance. The fact that abuses by majority rule might be perpetrated against a minority calls for some sort of check against a tyranny of the majority. To protect everyone from potential political harm in a democracy, the authors of the Constitution wisely chose to identify and explicitly prohibit violations of certain kinds of rights, to which they deemed every person falling under the jurisdiction of the law to be entitled. If all individuals have certain rights that are required by law to be respected, then there is no way, insofar as the law is observed, for their interests to be violated by a belligerent majority. This is precisely what it means to have rights and why certain kinds of rights have been recognized and specially protected in the Constitution's Bill of Rights.

Thus far, a Civics 101 lesson. Now we ask more specifically why free-dom of the press might have been regarded as sufficiently important to be included, first of all, in the Bill of Rights, and secondly, if the order once again is not purely accidental, why it was incorporated so conspicuously in the First Amendment. Finally, we want to know why freedom of the press is wedged among these other rights, between freedom of religion and freedom of peaceable assembly and right to petition the government for redress of grievances. What can we determine, logically or philosophically, without consulting the historical record, about the values the framers of the Constitution may have embodied in these compositional choices as they drafted the fundamental legal document of the new American society? What could and what did they likely have in mind in making freedom of the press so primary in the Bill of Rights, while not giving it absolutely the first place among the rights conferred on all citizens? If we can establish the moral right of journalists to collect and report on the news, then we can proceed on firm ground to inquire further into the exact responsibilities required of those who exercise the right to participate in a free press, sustained by philosophi-cal reasoning and explicated and enforced at least in some societies by the highest principles of law.

We should acknowledge from the outset that we cannot expect to answer these questions definitively. The best we can hope for is a plausible explanation that accounts for the most important facts and does not appear to be contradicted by anything else we believe to be true. To proceed with this limited goal in mind is fully in keeping with Aristotle's injunction in *Nicomachean Ethics* 1094b (Book I, section 3) not to expect more precision in an area of discourse than the subject matter permits. What, then, can we say by way of hypothesis about the relative importance of freedom of the press as expressed in the American Constitution and the reasons why it is given only secondary pride of place after freedom of religion? Part of the answer to these questions undoubtedly reflects the concern of the authors of the Constitution, chiefly Robert Morris and James Madison, Jr., about the influence of religious thinking and its potential for affecting the political scene. The founding fathers were North American representatives of the great movement of the European Enlightenment. Many of them had actually been educated in Europe or were influenced by thinkers who had been educated there or were closely following and in some ways imitating intellectual developments of eighteenth-century philosophy. The ideals of the Enlightenment emphasized the new emerging sciences as lighting the path to truth and providing a way of reforming society on the basis of humanitarian principles guided by scien-tific knowledge in place of superstitious authoritarianism. The doctrines of established religion were perceived at the time as reactionary with respect to the advancement of science and the improvement of society. While religious belief was understood as a matter of personal faith, it was not regarded as appropriate in the realm of public politics, especially insofar as experience shows it often tends to impose moral standards that are not always philosophically defensible.

Although the Enlightenment in many ways is almost the exclusive product of European philosophy and science, its social agenda was only slowly and painfully enacted on European soil. Partly this was because of the deep entrenchment of social institutions and a tradition of authoritarian government in established royal houses and aristocratic families over hundreds of years, whose power was in many ways upheld by religious teachings. In America, when the revolution had overthrown British rule, there suddenly existed a relatively open playing field in which to put the political ideals of the Enlightenment into practice on a grand scale. Needless to say, there were many persons in early American society who still equated morality and political authority with religious dogma, and that in a sense was just the problem. The authors of the Constitution, through their direct experience and secondary knowledge of religious conflict in Europe, were keenly aware of the need to attain checks and balances within the law if the ideals with which they were inspired were to be realized. The influence of religious thinking was potentially so powerful, that the founding fathers of the new American nation wanted to limit its impact on the social fabric, just as they wanted to limit the impact of any other single powerful influence. An important measure to assure that the new society would not be burdened with the sorts of religious wars, Inquisitions, "holy" Crusades, and internecine conflicts between different religious sects, was therefore to enforce a legal separation of church and state, which we find reflected in the very first clause of the First Amendment, prohibiting Congress from establishing any religion or prohibiting its free exercise. Religion and government were to be two different aspects of the personal and political lives of American citizens. No one was to be legally bound or forbidden from practicing any religion, and no religion was to be awarded any privileged place under the American Constitution.

The fact that freedom of religion and separation of church and state is made the very first principle in the Bill of Rights is significant. It indicates the extent to which the authors of the Constitution regarded religion as a potential threat to the Enlightenment ideals they proposed to institute. The Bill of Rights authors seem to have believed that religion was among the most personal matters of moral conscience and individuality, an area of the spiritual lives of citizens that each person should be free to follow according to his or her own inclination, without any governmental interference. Religion, accordingly, was not to be a factor in political decision-making in any official capacity, with the understanding that only in this way could the rights of persons generally be protected. If government could have any say in religious practice, then the door would be open to many other kinds of interference, and there would be no area of an individual's personal life in which the government could not also intrude. The influence of religion, moreover, for persons of faith, can be so pervasive as to affect everything they do, thus recommending the attention devoted to it by singling out freedom of religion and the separation of church and state as an important right and hence the first to be mentioned in the Bill of Rights.

Case Study 12

U.S. Supreme Court Decisions Concerning Freedom of the Press (*Pentagon Papers*, Martin Luther King, Jr., and the *Miami Herald*)

The following discussion of U.S. Supreme Court decisions concerning the freedom of the press is taken from *Issues of Democracy*, USIA (United States Information Agency) *Electronic Journal*, Vol. 2, No. 1, February 1997:

> "James C. Goodale served as general counsel to *The New York Times* when the U.S. Supreme Court decided that the *Times* could continue to publish the then-classified *Pentagon Papers*. In the following article, Goodale describes several Supreme Court cases in which First Amendment rights have been upheld, allowing the press to pursue its mission, no matter how odious that mission might seem to those in power. Goodale is an attorney with Debevoise & Plimpton, a New York law firm that specializes in First Amendment and communications law. Craig Bloom, an associate, assisted in the preparation of this article.
>
> The First Amendment to the U.S. Constitution provides that 'Congress shall make no law ... abridging the freedom ... of the press.' Although the First Amendment specifically mentions only the federal Congress, this provision now protects the press from all government, whether local, state or federal.
>
> The founders of the United States enacted the First Amendment to distinguish their new government from that of England, which had long censored the press and prosecuted persons who dared to criticize the British Crown. As Supreme Court Justice Potter Stewart explained in a 1974 speech, the 'primary purpose' of the First Amendment was 'to create a fourth institution outside the government as an additional check on the three official branches' (the executive branch, the legislature and the judiciary).
>
> Justice Stewart cited several landmark cases in which the Supreme Court—the final arbiter of the meaning of the First Amendment—has upheld the right of the press to perform its function as a check on official

power. One of these cases—the 1971 *Pentagon Papers* case—lies especially close to my heart.

Back then I was general counsel to *The New York Times*, which had obtained a leaked copy of the classified *Pentagon Papers*, a top-secret history of the U.S. government's decision making process regarding the war in Vietnam. After a careful review of the documents, we began to publish a series of articles about this often unflattering history, which suggested that the government had misled the American people about the war.

The day after our series began, we received a telegram from the U.S. attorney general warning us that our publication of the information violated the Espionage Law. The attorney general also claimed that further publication would cause 'irreparable injury to the defense interests of the United States.'

The government then took us to court, and convinced a judge to issue a temporary restraining order which prohibited the *Times* from continuing to publish the series. Following a whirlwind series of further hearings and appeals, we ended up before the Supreme Court two weeks later. The court ruled that our publication of the *Pentagon Papers* could continue. The court held that any prior restraint on publication 'bear[s] a heavy presumption against its constitutional validity,' and held that the government had failed to meet its heavy burden of showing a justification for the restraint in *New York Times* Co. v. United States, 403 U.S. 713 (1971). We immediately resumed our publication of the series, and we eventually won a Pulitzer Prize, the profession's highest honor, for the public service we performed by publishing our reports.

Seven years before the *Pentagon Papers* case, the Supreme Court handed *The New York Times* another landmark First Amendment victory, this time in the seminal libel case *New York Times* Co. v. Sullivan, 376 U.S. 254 (1964). This action was brought by an elected official who supervised the Montgomery, Alabama police force during the height of the civil rights movement in the 1960s. The official claimed that he was defamed by a full-page advertisement, published in the *Times*, that accused the police of mistreating non-violent protestors and harassing one of the leading figures in the civil rights movement, the Rev. Martin Luther King.

The Supreme Court found that even though some of the statements in the advertisement were false, the First Amendment nevertheless protected the *Times* from the official's suit. The court considered the case 'against the background of a profound national commitment to the principle that debate on public issues should be uninhibited, robust and wide-open, and that it may well include vehement, caustic and sometimes unpleasantly sharp attacks on government and public officials.' In light of this commitment, the court adopted the rule that a public official may not recover damages for a defamatory falsehood related to his official conduct 'unless he proves that the statement was made with "actual malice"—that is, with knowledge that it was false or with reckless disregard of whether it was false or not.' The court later extended this rule beyond 'public officials' to cover libel suits brought by all 'public figures.' Curtis Publishing Co. v. Butts and Associated Press v. Walker, 388 U.S. 130 (1967).

Although the Sullivan case is best known for the 'actual malice' rule, the Supreme Court's decision included a second holding of great importance to the press. Noting that the challenged advertisement attacked the police generally, but not the official specifically, the court held that an otherwise impersonal attack on governmental operations could not be considered a libel of the official who was responsible for the operations.

The First Amendment also prevents the government from telling the press what it must report. In Miami Herald Publishing Co. v. Tornillo, 418 U.S. 241 (1974), the Supreme Court considered whether a state statute could grant a political candidate a right to equal space to reply to a newspaper's criticism and attacks on his record. The court struck down the law, holding that the First Amendment forbids the compelled publication of material that a newspaper does not want to publish. The court held that the statute would burden the press by diverting its resources away from the publication of material it wished to print, and would impermissibly intrude into the functions of editors.

As the cases discussed above illustrate, over the course of the 20th century the Supreme Court has breathed life into the text of the First Amendment by upholding the right of the press to pursue its mission, no matter how odious that mission might seem to those in power. The courts have imposed some limits on this liberty, and questions remain as to how far this liberty will extend to new media, and to some of the more aggressive efforts employed by journalists to obtain the news. Still, I am confident that the Supreme Court will continue to recognize that, as Justice Stewart wrote in the *Pentagon Papers* case, 'without an informed and free press there cannot be an enlightened people.' "

QUESTIONS

1. What issues of a free press are entailed by the cases Goodale discusses? How, if at all, are they interrelated? Do they have anything in common?

2. Laws are written and then must be interpreted and applied. What significance should be attached to the interpretations of the First Amendment to the American Bill of Rights handed down in these U.S. Supreme Court decisions? How, if at all, have they helped to safeguard the freedom of the press in the United States?

3. What does it mean for workaday journalists in the United States to have these kinds of court decisions and legal precedents standing behind the

practice of their profession? What would it be like to work as a journalist in a society where such freedom of the press is either unacknowledged or in which higher court decisions have tended to erode away the free press and to limit reporting the news?

4. Legal decisions like those reached by the U.S. Supreme Court in the cases Goodale mentions are themselves the result of trying to adjudicate conflicts that arise in the real world between journalists trying to maximize their exercise of the moral right to provide relevant truth telling in the public interest and a variety of individuals and private and public agencies and organizations that in turn have a vested interest in preventing or requiring certain kinds of information from being published in the press or broadcast on the air. There is no higher court of appeal for such decisions in the United States, and the Supreme Court typically demonstrates extreme reluctance to revisit issues it has already settled. What do these facts imply for the preservation of the freedom of the press as guaranteed by the First Amendment to the American Constitution in the Bill of Rights? What would have been the result if the Supreme Court had decided differently in any of these landmark cases? Try to imagine a different outcome for the *Pentagon Papers* case, or another you prefer, and explain how freedom of the press in the United States today would have been changed if the decision you portray had been adopted instead. Would American freedom of the press have been advanced or inhibited by such a court ruling?

5. Does it seem accidental for Goodale to have referred in the final quotation above to the need for a free press among an "enlightened people" and the fact that the American Constitution, like the American Revolution, is a product of the eighteenth-century European Enlightenment? Is there a possible conceptual link between the values of the Enlightenment and the protection of a free press by these U.S. Supreme Court decisions?

FREEDOM'S DEBT TO A FREE PRESS AND THE PURSUIT OF TRUTH

The point of this excursus is not to distract from issues surrounding the freedom of the press. It is rather to prepare the ground for its discussion and to draw general conclusions about the relation between freedom of religion, freedom of the press, and freedom of peaceable assembly and political dissent. The previous reflections on the importance of freedom of religion in a republic that is meant to instantiate Enlightenment ideals now provides a model for considering the significance of freedom of the press.

There is a certain complementarity in these two rights being paired together in the opening items of the Bill of Rights. Whereas freedom of religion goes to the heart of the most personal matters of individual spirituality, freedom of the press concerns the most public events of the nation and the world, the information without which the citizens of a representative democracy cannot responsibly participate in the decision-making processes of self-government. If a society is first protected from what is perceived to be one of the greatest threats to its freedom, the next priority is to assure that the members of the society have maximally unlimited access to whatever information might be needed in order to make informed decisions.

The freedom of the press guaranteed by the Bill of Rights in the American Constitution reflects a number of facts about the press that are relevant to journalistic ethics. These are factors that we can reasonably assume the founding fathers would also have recognized. First, we should acknowledge that there is no telling in advance what sort of information will or will not turn out to be essential to making intelligent decisions. Information, which is to say true or correct information, is the lifeblood of self-government. There is no other way by which the machinery of the body politic can properly work, and there is no way to predetermine the kinds or categories of information that the citizens of a free society will want or need. Purely from the standpoint of keeping democratic institutions in motion, therefore, there can be no justifiable basis for excluding or controlling this or that item or type of information from being made available for public consumption. Second, the only way to guarantee that the information received by citizens in a free society is correct, true, or accurate, to the greatest extent possible, is for the instruments by which information is collected and distributed to be as unrestricted as possible.

The interplay of moral rights and responsibilities is nowhere more clearly demonstrated than in the fine adjustments made within a free society to accommodate as much freedom of the press as is rationally compatible with a society's other vested interests in its own security. We see already at this preliminary stage from whence at least some of the moral responsibility for news content comes as a consequence of the moral right or liberty extended to members of the press. We use the information that journalists provide to make important, sometimes life or death, decisions. Nor does the decision chain end with ordinary consumers of the news but is relied upon as one source of information even by the highest levels of political decision-making in many governments. We individually and collectively make decisions on the basis of what journalists tell us, decisions that affect the welfare not only of ourselves and those immediately around us, but potentially of future generations. Morally, a press must be free in order to fulfill its obligations to uncover and report important information in the public interest. Journalists should be accorded extraordinary freedom in producing news reports. What we require of them morally in exchange is primarily that they report truthfully, that they hold their work as journalists to the standard we have described as relevant truth telling in the public interest.

The only properly useful information is true information. We might even say that only true information is correctly called "information." The truth, in turn, as a practical matter, can only be discovered when there are no artificial hindrances or restrictions placed on its gathering, testing, and correction in a public forum. This process, in turn, can only succeed when inquiry is open, public, and unconstrained by individuals or institutions that might have a contrary interest in trying to prevent others from learning the truth about newsworthy events. It is a cornerstone of the Enlightenment ideal in knowledge-seeking generally that we apply the same open-ended critical methods of scientific investigation to all aspects of life as to the world of nature in order to arrive at the truth of things.

The way science works is by allowing investigators to inquire as freely as possible, subjecting their conclusions to rigorous public scrutiny and criticism, and refining and correcting their results in light of objections and suggestions for improvement. It is not only the best way but ultimately the only way of arriving at the truth. The same, it is reasonable to suppose, holds with respect to any kind of information-gathering interpreted as an extension of scientific method. If we want to discover whether the sun rotates around the earth or the earth around the sun, it will not do to appeal to authority or try to investigate the matter by having nonscientists impose a set of rules on the investigation and regulate the procedure from the standpoint of nonscientific criteria. This is historically what happened when church authorities interfered in the activities of early science, arguing that Scripture provided a higher source of knowledge and believing that science posed a threat to religious faith.

Similarly, if we want to discover whether a certain politician is taking a bribe, or the facts of trade, or the industrial output of a neighboring state, we require information that can only be obtained by free and open inquiry. There needs to be public disclosure of all potentially useful socially relevant information that is uninhibited by political or religious institutions to whatever degree possible. What is thought to be learned in journalistic investigation must then be further checked by the sort of back-and-forth dialogue that occurs between the presentation, criticism, and refinement of ideas that we find alike in modern science and investigative news reporting. That these concepts still seem to hold good after several hundred years testifies to the extent to which Enlightenment concepts continue to exert their positive influence on our thinking to the present time. The great figures of the Enlightenment understood these principles, and part of their legacy is the fact that even today we appreciate the importance of free scientific inquiry. It follows logically that maximal freedom of the press is presupposed by the fundamental principle of journalistic ethics according to which journalists have both the moral right and obligation to provide relevant truth telling in the public interest.

All this is just another way of saying that a free society requires and depends essentially on a free press. The two ideals go together inextricably.

The relationship between a free society and a free press is organic and deeply interconnected, a mutual reliance in which one supports and draws strength from the other. The freedom of a free press can only be sustained by a society that is in other respects free, and a society can remain truly free only to the extent that it upholds the institutions of a free press. We have yet to learn exactly what it means to speak of a free press, but we can already see in rough outline that there is a symbiotic connection, an essential interdependence, between a free society and a free press. If the free society is going to function, it needs truth—true, correct, accurate information—about unlimitedly and unpredeterminedly many different kinds of things, whose relevance cannot be known in advance or controlled in its direction or outcome if truth is the goal. The only way in turn for a free society to obtain the information it needs for informed self-government is by means of a free press.[4]

FREEDOM OF THE PRESS AS THE FOURTH ESTATE OF A LIBERAL DEMOCRACY

In a rational series of steps, we can project a plausible reason why the authors of the American Constitution next added in the third item of the First Amendment in the Bill of Rights, guaranteeing the right of peaceable assembly and petitioning the government for redress of grievances. For it is only if freedom of the press is protected that the citizens of a free society can be relevantly informed about the condition of local and global events, including the state of the union. It is only if citizens have free access to such vital information in turn that they can make informed decisions to meet for purposes of airing objections and organizing themselves for political action.

It is only if the press is free, moreover, that persons in different parts of a society can learn about the activities of others so that grassroots political movements can gain popular momentum. A free press is the only way of protecting individuals assembling peaceably or petitioning the government for redress of grievances through the open reporting of their activities and the government's conduct in reacting to political events. During the Vietnam War,

---

[4]Ibid., p. 1: "The right to speak and publish freely—complaining about the government, criticizing the latest film, arguing about abortion rights—is an essential liberty in democratic countries. Free expression is an inherent part of liberal democracies, a form of government based on self-governance, respect for a multiplicity of views, and the right of individuals to develop their minds and fortunes as they please as long as others are not injured. The United States, many Western European nations, New Zealand, Canada, and Uruguay are examples of liberal democracies, and these countries permit and defend free speech. As law professor Kent Greenawalt (1989) has written, it is an 'important political principle that government should not suppress the communication of ideas. Indeed, this principle is frequently regarded as a cornerstone of liberal democracy' . . ." See also Powe, *The Fourth Estate and the Constitution* and Jeffrey Smith, *Printers and Press Freedom*.

the nation saw clearly the popular response to the U.S. government's efforts to disperse protesters engaged in peaceable assembly. The Ohio National Guard acted to enforce the military's interest in suppressing dissent at the so-called Kent State massacre, where four university students were shot dead and others wounded demonstrating against the hostilities in Southeast Asia. Without a free press to announce the occurrence of peaceful assemblies and to report on the government's responses, the course of the war and of world history might have been very different. In such cases it should be obvious that the government cannot be expected or trusted to withhold efforts in its own interests to suppress the free exchange of information in the press by persons opposed to its policies.

Without a free press as one of the checks and balances by which the actions of the government can become known throughout a society, the government would be unhindered in exerting coercive power over its citizens in a way that the authors of the Constitution wanted to curb and if possible prevent. They were wise enough to know that any government would have police and military power and that the government might try to exercise its power against citizens who opposed its rule. They understood that the only way to assure the government's not exceeding its authority was by extending to citizens the right to peaceable assembly and protest. These rights in turn presuppose and are backed up in practice by a free press. The press is needed, in among countless other ways, to report on the government's posture when citizens exercise their right to peaceable assembly. Just as there is no full participation in collective decision-making in a representative democracy if there is no free dissemination of relevant information, so there is no protection of rights generally if there is no free press to report on the activities of government. It is a key component in the safeguarding of civil liberties for government officials to understand that what they do, except in certain very restricted areas pertaining to national security, is transparently available to every citizen through the watchdog media of a free press. A government that can operate in secrecy, without exposure of its activities, is inherently a dangerous thing in the eyes of the Constitution's authors, who accordingly upheld the freedom of the press as one of the most important rights of all citizens.

This is why in the United States the free press is sometimes referred to by default as constituting "the fourth estate." The existence of a free press scrutinizing the way a government functions complements the official executive, legislative, and judicial branches of government more explicitly established by law. The point is to call attention to the fact that the press and all forms of media are *de facto* a valuable part of what makes self-government in the representative democracy established by the Constitution work effectively. The free press, to pursue an analogy previously mentioned, is the lubricant that makes the machinery of a free democratic society work smoothly. Without a free press, over time other democratic institutions would grind to a halt through lack of reliable information. It is vital to the proper functioning of a free society, if sometimes inconvenient or embarrassing, that every official recognize that their actions are subject to public scrutiny through the constant vigilance of a free press. Every legislator, every executive officer from the police patrolling the streets to the attorney general and president of the United States, every member of Congress, every justice on the Supreme Court, and all officials of the government generally, need to understand that with very few justifiable exceptions what they do in performing their duties or acting outside their authority under the guise of office can in principle be discovered and made public by a free press. The purpose and profession of a corps of dedicated news investigators and reporters in a free society is to discover among other things what the government is doing and plans to do. Its responsibility is to make such information known to citizens for purposes of individual and collective decision-making, in voting to continue or discontinue the terms of office of public servants, or to choose if necessary to gather in peaceable assembly to support or oppose the government's actions. Recalling Thomas Jefferson's praise of the free press for a free society, we may be reminded of his words to James Madison in a letter dated January 30, 1787, with reference to Daniel Shay's rebellion against conditions in Massachusetts that "A little rebellion now and then is a good thing." The value of protest and its role in shaping law and policy, and the importance of journalistic reporting in facilitating peaceable assembly, is a major part of what makes the fourth estate of a free press such a vital force for social good. It is one of the best reasons journalists often have for entering the profession in the first place.

The press, in turn, needs to understand that its reporting must be subject to the same degree of transparency. What the press does needs to be equally subject to public scrutiny through the competitive force of many different news agencies that are privately established, independent rather than exclusively governmentally sponsored, and prepared if need arises to report on one another's infractions of journalistic ethics through false, inaccurate, or malicious reporting, if such infractions should occur. By monitoring the news reporting of other news agencies, journalists also serve, so to speak, to keep one another in check. It is part also of what it means for the press to be free. It must not only be unrestricted as far as possible in gathering and reporting the news, but it must always be possible in practice for new reporters and news agencies to be started up on an entrepreneurial basis when there is thought to be a demand for additional services. To place undue restrictions either on existing news agencies or on the proliferation and innovation of news agencies would not only be an impediment to free trade, but in both forms it would constitute a hampering of the freedom of the press. Healthy competition among different news agencies and different forms of media is an important part of a free press; it is crucial to the discovery and reporting of publicly relevant information.

Case Study 13

Freedom of the Press (or Abridgement Thereof) Worldwide (Second International World Press Freedom Ranking, October 2003)

The following report is offered by Reporters Without Borders. This organization of professional journalists actively defends imprisoned journalists and press freedom throughout the world. The group has nine national sections (Austria, Belgium, Canada, France, Germany, Italy, Spain, Sweden, and Switzerland), with representatives in Abidjan, Bangkok, London, Moscow, New York, Tokyo, and Washington, and more than 120 correspondents worldwide.

"Reporters Without Borders published its second world press freedom ranking on 20 October 2003. As in 2002, the most catastrophic situation is to be found in Asia, especially North Korea, Burma and Laos. Second from last in the ranking, Cuba is today the world's biggest prison for journalists. The United States and Italy were given relatively low rankings.

Like last year, the most catastrophic situation is to be found in Asia, with eight countries in the bottom ten: North Korea, Burma, Laos, China, Iran, Vietnam, Turkmenistan and Bhutan. Independent news media are either non-existent in these countries, or are constantly repressed by the authorities. Journalists there work in extremely difficult conditions, with no freedom and no security. A number of them are imprisoned in Burma, China and Iran.

Cuba is in 165th position, second from last. Twenty-six independent journalists were arrested in the spring of 2003 and sentenced to prison terms ranging from 14 to 27 years, making Cuba the world's biggest prison for journalists. They were accused of writing articles for publication abroad that played into the hands of 'imperialist interests.' Eritrea, in 162nd position, has the worst situation in Africa. Privately-owned news media have been banned there for the past two years and 14 journalists are being held in undisclosed locations.

To compile this ranking, Reporters Without Borders asked journalists, researchers, jurists and human rights activists to fill out a questionnaire evaluating respect for press freedom in a particular country. A total of 166 countries are included in the ranking (as against 139 last year). The other countries were left out because of a lack of reliable, well-supported data.

Wealth and press freedom don't always go together. As in 2002, the ranking shows that a country's respect for press freedom is not solely linked to its economic development. The top 50 include countries that are among the poorest in the world, such as Benin (29th position), Timor-Leste (30th) and Madagascar (46th).

Conversely, the 50 countries that respect press freedom least include such rich nations as Bahrain (117th) and Singapore (144th).

Special situation of the United States and Israel. The ranking distinguishes behavior at home and abroad in the cases of the United States and Israel. They are ranked in 31st and 44th positions respectively as regards respect for freedom of expression on their own territory, but they fall to the 135th and 146th positions as regards behavior beyond their borders.

The Israeli army's repeated abuses against journalists in the occupied territories and the U.S. army's responsibility in the death of several reporters during the war in Iraq constitute unacceptable behavior by two nations that never stop stressing their commitment to freedom of expression.

General deterioration in the Arab world. The war in Iraq played a major role in an increased crackdown on the press by the Arab regimes. Concerned about maintaining their image and facing public opinion largely opposed to the war, they stepped up control of the press and increased pressure on journalists, who are forced to use self-censorship.

Kuwait (102nd) replaced Lebanon (106th) as the Arab world's leader as regards respect for freedom of expression because of cases of censorship in Lebanon, together with abusive judicial proceedings and an attack on the television station Future TV. Saudi Arabia (156th), Syria (155th), Libya (153rd) and Oman (152nd) used all the means at their disposal to prevent the emergence of a free and independent press.

In Morocco (131st), the hopes pinned on Mohammed VI when he became king in July 1999 have been dashed. Independent newspapers are still subject to constant harassment from the authorities. Ali Lmrabet, the publisher and editor of two satirical weeklies, was sentenced in June 2003 to three years in prison for 'insulting the person of the king' because of articles and cartoons touching on taboo subjects.

European Union gets good rankings, except Italy and Spain. Italy received a poor ranking (53rd) compared with the other European Union countries for the second year running. Silvio Berlusconi's conflict of interests as head of government and owner of a media empire is still unresolved. Furthermore, a draft law to reform radio and TV broadcasting, tailored to Berlusconi's interests, is likely to increase the threats to news diversity in Italy.

Spain's relatively low ranking (42nd) is due to difficulties for journalists in the Basque country. The terrorist organization ETA has stepped up its threats against the news media, promising to target journalists whose coverage does not match its view of the situation. Furthermore, the necessary fight against terrorism has affected press freedom, with the forced closure as a 'preventive measure' of the Basque newspaper *Egunkaria*, whose senior staff are suspected of collaborating with ETA.

France is ranked as low as 26th because of its archaic defamation legislation, the increasingly frequent challenges to the principle of confidentiality of sources and the repeated abusive detention of journalists by police.

Former USSR still lags behind. The situation remains worrying in Russia (148th), Ukraine (132nd) and Belarus (151st). A truly independent press exists in Russia, but Russia's poor ranking is justified by the censorship of anything to do with the war in Chechnya, several murders and the recent abduction of the Agence France-Presse correspondent in Ingushetia. Russia continues to be one of the world's deadliest countries for journalists.

Press freedom is virtually non-existent in much of central Asia, especially Turkmenistan (158th) and Uzbekistan (154th). No criticism of the authorities is tolerated.

Non-state violence. Several countries with a democratically-elected government and a free and independent press have poor rankings. This is most notably the case with Bangladesh (143rd), Colombia (147th) and Philippines (118th). Journalists in these countries are the victims of violence that comes not only from the state but also from political parties, criminal gangs or guerrilla groups. In other cases, such as Nepal (150th), the press is caught in the cross fire between security forces and rebels.

Such violence results in considerable self-censorship by the news media, which do not dare to broach such subjects as corruption, collusion between political leaders and organized crime, or sectarian clashes. At the same time, the authorities very often fail to respond to this violence with the appropriate measures, namely protection for journalists and the punishment of those responsible.

News is the victim of war in Africa. Wars and serious political crises have inevitably had an impact on press freedom in Africa. The three countries that have fallen most in the ranking in the past 12 months are Côte d'Ivoire (137th), Liberia (132nd) and Guinea-Bissau (118th). Local and foreign journalists were exposed to the violence of the warring parties in Côte d'Ivoire and Liberia, while the military closed down news media in Guinea-Bissau."

QUESTIONS

1. What is the significance for professional journalists and journalistic ethics of evaluations of the relative freedom of the press in different societies?

2. What do we learn from such comparisons, and why might they be important to sponsor, support, and publicize? Do these reports serve only the interests of practicing journalists, or do they have wider implications for society both within and outside of the countries where journalistic freedom to one degree or another is respected or opposed?

3. Reporters Without Borders emphasizes not only the active opposition by some governments to a free press, but the government's failure in certain instances to do anything to protect its journalists. Is this a legitimate requirement for freedom of the press? Do governments have a moral obligation to

prevent journalists from being hampered and coerced in their work, or does a country's responsibility toward journalists consist entirely of doing nothing to injure or impede what journalists do?

4. Having extolled the virtues of the freedom of the press as guaranteed by the U.S. Constitution in this chapter, it may seem shocking now to discover that the United States is not the forerunner in preserving and protecting journalistic freedoms. Why, according to the Reporters Without Borders report, is this so? What does it signify, and what mitigating factors might be offered to offset the specific objections raised against limitations of a free press in the United States?

5. What does the report suggest about the reforms that might be undertaken in order to assure greater freedom of the press internationally and worldwide? What can individual journalists do to help in the spread of journalistic freedom to all countries and all corners of the globe? What is of interest from the standpoint of abstract moral ideals of journalistic ethics and real-world journalistic practice in recognizing the importance of a free press and the application of its values to all societies by professional journalists?

JUSTIFICATION FOR A FREE PRESS IN A FREE SOCIETY

We, as members of a free society, have an unconditional need for a free press, even if it is not feasible for the press itself to be unconditionally free. We need to know what is happening in the world if we are to vote or participate intelligently in the affairs of state to whatever extent we choose. We cannot personally be on the scene everywhere at once to gather and verify all the information we need; nor, if we have another profession or occupation by which we earn our bread, can we personally invest the time required to investigate all the occurrences in the world involving issues concerning which we might be asked to decide.

We must rely on teams of experts who by vocation are equipped to collect information for our use. Journalists are our eyes and ears on the world. They discover much of what we need to know, even if they also sometimes bombard us with things that we do not really need to know, that we cannot use, or that we may even wish we had never heard about. Without professionals to collect worthwhile information, we would need to make decisions entirely in the dark without adequate knowledge of the facts. In much the same way that we rely on devices such as microscopes and telescopes to learn about aspects of the world that we cannot easily discover only through our natural abilities, so we need to rely on specialized human knowledge gathering by professional journalists. It is only in this way that we can learn about aspects of the world that are too remote, complex, or that require knowledge of cultures and languages or persistent hands-on presence wherever news events are happening for most of us to be able to do the job. As individuals we require the skilled work of journalists, just as we need physicians, jurists, farmers, builders, and engineers. A free society, as we have argued, requires journalists to do their work properly in order to remain free and to function effectively and competitively among other societies in the world.

CHALLENGES TO SUSTAINING A FREE PRESS

What are the specific threats to freedom of the press? They come in many forms. If we look outside the U.S. Constitution to consider the question more generally or in abstract terms, we may recognize that in the world at large a free press encounters many of the same problems in any and every nation.

There is a constant tension of one degree or another between the public's demand for truthful, accurate, and relevant information and a government's interest in controlling, manipulating, and, in some cases, suppressing news or transforming it altogether for its own purposes into propaganda. Knowledge is power, and power is what governments are all about. This basic political fact does not make governments inherently evil, but it does mean that we need to be mindful about how their interests can sometimes differ from those of the public's with respect to the gathering, presentation, and use of information provided by the news.

If we are to be responsible citizens, we must realistically expect there to be occasional conflicts, disputes, and sparring between these opposed interests. People desiring to be politically free, however they may define this concept for themselves, must be especially on the lookout for any systematic degrading of the ability of reporters to practice their profession freely. This means in particular without interference by the government, except in the most urgent circumstances in which the security of the society as a whole is seriously challenged and even only then with appropriate oversight. The important point is that, given the importance of a free press to a free society, any interference in the professional activity of journalists is to be tolerated only under the most extreme circumstances and then only for specified kinds of cases and periods of time. All citizens who aspire to freedom or want their society to remain free should, if this is their goal, be aware of the problems that can result from political and judiciary bodies setting a bad precedent in limiting freedom of the press. For it is in this way that the moral right of a free press can be incrementally degraded step by step in an accelerating slippery slope until the government begins to exert an undue influence over its practices.

A government is not the only source of threat to a free press. In principle, there is a potential risk from any powerful institution with a stake in news reporting. The government shirks an essential moral responsibility if it looks the other way when organized crime, religious fanatics, or other specialized interest groups harass news reporters and make it difficult or even impossible for them to do their jobs. Governments should recognize that it is in their own ultimate rational self-interests to protect journalists whenever the latter encounter hostility from persons who for one reason or another do not want them to discover and publicize certain kinds of facts. The list of concerns related to the institution and maintenance of a free press is open-ended and can include many more kinds of social organizations as society evolves. It is useful nevertheless to mention some of the most obvious of these, taking note especially of religion and big business. Here we must include wealthy individuals with the resources to control a society's information infrastructure, who may desire to exercise their will for interests of their own that are contrary to the free reporting of news. If S is an extremely affluent person who does not want his or her lawbreaking or financial maneuverings to be generally known, then S may try to use that wealth to bribe journalists not to report negative things about him or her or concoct even more elaborate schemes to try to influence the content of news where his or her interests are involved. It might be possible in this way, with the right amount of money, to wage a disinformation campaign, for example, that is favorable to S and that is so carefully contrived that it takes in even the most experienced and skeptical reporters, who thereby become the unwitting dupes of a powerful manipulator. Such reporters, even with the best intentions, might then be induced to report false and misleading misinformation.

We can easily devise parallel scenarios in which religious organizations try to control the media for any number of reasons connected with their special interests. A fascinating albeit presumably fictional case of this kind is suggested by Tom Robbins's novel *Another Roadside Attraction*, in which the body of Christ is discovered in the basement of the Vatican. Since Christ, according to church doctrine, is supposed to have risen from the dead and ascended into heaven, the appearance of what could potentially be confirmed as Christ's mortal remains would be highly embarrassing to Christian religious leaders. Imagine, then, that such a thing occurs and that the church, concerned about the revolutionary impact of this information on its followers, marshalls all of its resources in one way or another in order to suppress the news. As a more down-to-earth example, consider the same kind of thing occurring on a lesser scale. Suppose that church officials try to prevent news reporting of child molestation by priests in a certain community, for fear of the negative impact of bad publicity on its parishioners and, ultimately, on its membership, finances, and moral leadership. The same kind of manipulations of the news can obviously occur through the machinations of big business executives, secret societies, and political activists, to name just a few categories. These persons may not fully share the Enlightenment ideals of a free and open society with a transparently functioning bureaucracy, but want to subvert its purposes. Their ranks could include foreign agents, unscrupulous renegade scientists, or just about anyone else or any group that might benefit from pulling journalists' strings behind the scenes in order to prevent them from correctly reporting whatever news may turn out to be damaging to their interests.

There is an important distinction to observe with respect to these examples. It need not be considered a threat or at least a serious threat to a free press that there occur occasional breaches of the general principle of noninterference in the performance of journalistic duties. A moral problem arises only if and when such infringements become systematic, endemic, or to the extent that they establish a lasting bad precedent from which it is not practically possible to recover, from which it becomes excessively difficult to restore journalistic freedom. How might such a virtually irreducible curtailment of journalistic freedom occur? One conceivable scenario is that in which a large corporation, with many dummy companies under its control that are virtually untraceable to it, begins to buy up newspapers and radio and television stations and other outlets for journalism, and then through its monopoly proceeds to dominate the content of news that is or is not reported, how it is reported, and generally acting on behalf of its own interests and contrary to those of the public's right to know. There are protections within the administration of the American Constitution to try to prevent these kinds of abuses from taking place. Among other safeguards, the law restricts the extent to which a single business or organization can gain control of too many media outlets. Lawmakers and enforcers as a rule have been sensitive to these possibilities and have enacted legislation to minimize the possibility of single-interest control of the news. There may nevertheless be opportunities, through shadow companies and complicated paper trails of ownership, for this kind of threat to the freedom of the press to occur, at least for limited periods of time. The problem represents another respect in which those who value the institution of a free press and its importance to a free society need to stand guard against abuse.

Summary

The concept of a free press presupposes precisely the same conditions as those under which it is possible for scientific inquiry to be free. In good Enlightenment spirit, we can consider the gathering and reporting of news by professional journalists to be a natural extension and continuation of open-minded scientific inquiry by empirical methods. We cannot reasonably expect science to arrive at the truth if we do not allow scientists to pursue their inquiries without overriding supervision or decisive control by nonscientists or by those whose interests might conflict with those of an unfettered discovery of the truth.

It is the same with journalism. If we think of journalism as primarily a search for truth about social facts that are relevant to a society's purposes, then once again we cannot reasonably expect journalism to arrive at the truth if journalists are not allowed freely to pursue their inquiries. This, we have said, from a practical standpoint, means without overbearing supervision or control by non-journalists or by persons whose interests conflict with those of journalism's search for and efforts to share the truth. We consider freedom in this regard in what is often spoken of as a negative concept, in the sense that it involves an absence of constraint.

Constraints on freedom of the press can take many different forms, not all of which we need try to anticipate. Suggestive of the category are efforts to bribe journalists, buy up the tools and outlets of media, unduly influencing the kinds of questions journalists ask or the answers they can give in any of a variety of ways, encouraging the systematic spread of misinformation to be reported as facts, and the like. The use of coercion in any form, especially by the government, religion, or big business, to control the content of news reporting for its own purposes, is the most obvious way in which freedom of the press might be threatened. The risk in most free societies is not that this might be done in one fell swoop with armed soldiers appearing in news offices, but gradually over time, proceeding from precedent to precedent. Public safety can be invoked as an ever-slipperier justification taking us down a slippery slope from full freedom to a few restrictions to a few more restrictions and from a greater perceived threat to a lesser threat and then a lesser threat. With broader and broader interpretations of what counts as a danger to society, it becomes possible for those in authority to exercise increasingly greater control over what the press can or cannot freely report.

These are among the ways in which the freedom of the press can be nibbled away at until there is nothing or next to nothing left. Taking freedom of the press in the negative sense we have proposed, as the maximum absence of restraint on efforts to discover and report facts and recognizing as we did at the outset that there is no such thing as absolutely unrestrained freedom of the press in any responsible society, the greatest risk to freedom of the press is the gradual erosion of its liberty to investigate and report its discoveries in whatever way it deems appropriate. What those who value a free press should require in a free society is that any infringement of its practice be justified as an exception, that exceptions not be allowed to become precedents for ever weaker justifications, and that there be mechanisms in place for restoring freedom of the press to the maximum degree possible whenever the original justification for its curtailment no longer obtains. There should accordingly be a definite process of review for deciding whether or not the reason for restraining the press remains valid. If the danger has passed, and there is no longer a good argument for restricting the press, then, in lieu of another overriding justification, the former liberties of the press should promptly be restored. More long-term reasons for restraining the press in turn should continually be reviewed; they should not be allowed to become entrenched or construed as lowering the bar for the next potential justification for restraining the press in another way or for another reason.

A free press is unrestrained by any interests conflicting with those of journalism's proper aims of discovering and reporting the news. If no press in any responsible free society can be absolutely free, then its freedom should nevertheless be maximized to whatever extent possible. We shall in the following chapter consider the kinds of limits that are reasonably imposed on journalists by discussing the problem of censorship and of voluntarily withholding the publication of certain kinds of information for the greater social good. The reason why a press ought to be maximally free is that a free press is essential to the institution and maintenance of a free society. The two in the long run go intimately together; they cannot survive for long without one another. We are not in a position here to offer a general rationale for the preferability of a free society over those societies in which the social and legal freedom of individuals is sacrificed to increasing degrees up to and including the most extreme forms of totalitarian regimes. We note that truth and freedom generally go together, and we rely on the intuitive, intrinsic value of these interrelated objectives to justify the moral preference for a free society and with it a free press. The alternatives are incompatible with what is generally deemed essential to the full realization of what is most valuable to the human spirit. In the end, this is perhaps all the justification for a free press we may need or can hope to provide.

With freedom, in turn, there comes responsibility. This commonsense implication is as true in the case of individuals and individual freedom as for institutions and societies. A free press as an abstraction of particular journalists and related media professionals accordingly has its own unique responsibilities that go along with its freedom. We have already seen that in a free society journalists play a distinctive role. They are the remote instruments of the information gathering a free society needs to make its decisions and plot its course in the world. They are fourth estate watchdogs that serve to keep elected and appointed officials on their toes, aware that what they do may be discovered and reported to the electorate at large, to hold them accountable for their actions or inaction. What this implies first and foremost is that journalists have a special responsibility to get things right. We are all under obligations to tell the truth to the best of our ability, but we do not bear the particular professional responsibility of journalists to report truthfully and accurately in a timely fashion on all relevant matters of public interest. The fact that so many people depend on correct information from journalists makes them especially responsible for their reportage. Journalists are expected not only to report truthfully whatever it is they choose to report, but, as professionals, journalists are expected to know what is important and worthwhile to report. They must have their thumb on the pulse of what is taking place throughout the world at all levels that might turn out to be pertinent to news consumers. The world, as newspaper reporters used to say, is their beat. We hold journalists morally responsible not only if they give false or inaccurate reports, but also if they neglect to report something that we later believe they should have known to investigate.

The responsibility that journalists bear is largely a function of the importance journalism has in a free society. Journalists are more responsible than ordinary citizens for the news they present. Their choices potentially have an enormous impact on their reading and viewing audiences. They are so closely linked to protecting all the other freedoms that are valued in a free society that they are invested with special professional moral obligations. We rely on journalists, as we do on the three established estates of government, to be one of the most important mechanisms by which the society's freedom is preserved. More generally, we rely on journalists for the information by which we in a free society participate in self-government. We must know in order to judge, and we must judge in order to act, to govern ourselves collectively in a sustainable free society. The moral responsibility of journalists can accordingly be distinguished into two main types. Journalists are morally responsible individually to their news consumers and to society as a whole. We can easily see that journalists bear responsibility for their reportage to individuals who may take the information they provide and make use of it in potentially life-or-death kinds of decisions or in decisions that will minimally affect their welfare and livelihood. The responsibility a journalist bears to society as a whole is not merely the sum of these, but something more. The survival of freedom in a free society, its introduction in a previously unfree part of the world, and, in effect, the survival of the society itself, can depend on the availability of correct, reliable information, of truths pertaining to the society and the outside world, which it is the journalist's charge to provide.

Journalists have a sacred trust to serve the truth and deliver useful knowledge to the public. Having set the stage for a more detailed discussion of the moral responsibilities of journalists from the standpoint of the need in a maximally free society for a maximally free press, we are prepared in the following chapters to consider more specific topics in the ethics of journalism. All questions concerning moral responsibility in the media can be traced back to the important role a free press plays in a free society and whatever is required in order for the press to satisfy its obligations to inform citizens about facts relevant to their decision-making and to a society's self-government. If we value freedom, we must value the freedom of the press. This in turn implies among other things that we must act to preserve the freedom of the press and be constantly vigilant in opposing every unjustified act of journalistic censorship.[5]

[5]The philosophical dimensions of the dilemmas facing freedom of the press we have emphasized in this chapter are powerfully summarized in the 1947 Robert M. Hutchins Commission on Freedom of the Press, in Knowlton and Parsons, ed., *The Journalist's Moral Compass*, when the report concludes, p. 213: "The moral right of free expression achieves a legal status because the conscience of the citizen is the source of the continued vitality of the state. Wholly apart from the traditional ground for a free press that it promotes the 'victory of truth over falsehood' in the public arena—we see that public discussion is a necessary condition of a free society and that freedom of expression is a necessary condition of adequate public discussion. Public discussion elicits mental power and breadth; it is essential to the building of a mentally robust public; and, without something of the kind, a self-governing society could not operate. The original source of supply for this process is the duty of the individual thinker to his thought; here is the primary ground of his right. This does not mean that every citizen has a moral or legal right to own a press or be an editor or have access, as of right, to the audience of any given medium of communication. But it does belong to the intention of the freedom of the press than an idea shall have its chance even if it is not shared by those who own or manage the press. The press is not free if those who operate it behave as though their position conferred on them the privilege of being deaf to ideas which the processes of free speech have brought to public attention. But the moral right of free public expression is not unconditional. Since the claim of the right is based on the duty of a man to the common good and to his thought, the ground of the claim disappears when this duty is ignored or rejected. In the absence of accepted moral duties there are no moral rights. Hence, when the man who claims the moral right of free expression is a liar, a prostitute whose political judgments can be bought, a dishonest inflamer of hatred and suspicion, his claim is unwarranted and groundless. From the moral point of view, at least, freedom of expression does not include the right to lie as a deliberate instrument of policy."

chapter five

Censorship and Withholding Information for the Greater Good

A free press is among the most important moral rights of a free people. Journalists in particular take advantage of this right from which every person ideally benefits. We have already observed that freedom of the press is not an absolute or unconditional freedom. It is exercised within limits established on the basis of a society's other legitimate interests, especially where security and protection of the rights of all its members are concerned. There are real-life situations in which the fundamental principle of journalistic ethics to maximize relevant truth telling must be qualified in the public interest. When news reporting is censored or voluntarily withheld for the greater good, there must always be a sufficiently good reason for the action, and there should always be explicit provision for restoring full journalistic freedoms as expeditiously as possible thereafter.

CENSORSHIP AND JOURNALISM'S MANDATE

We have already touched on the problem of censorship. The moral justification for journalism, its professional mandate, is to provide information for the benefit of persons who, practically speaking, cannot gather the news for themselves. A free press is a necessity for a free society and vice versa. A society cannot function freely unless it has free access to information, because self-government presupposes an informed citizenry acting on the basis of the facts. Freedom of the press in turn exists interdependently in a larger framework of civil liberties that serve to protect the free exchange of information, thereby helping to preserve other freedoms. The only meaningful way to promote the values of a free society is through relevant truth telling. All matters of vital public concern require a free flow of information that is only made possible by the agency of a free press. For a press to be free among other things means most importantly being free from undue censorship.

We begin by defining some of the essential terms required to understand the moral problem of censorship. We shall say that *journalistic censorship* is any action taken to suppress the free discovery and dissemination of news information. Censorship in this sense can thus be *voluntary* or *involuntary*. It can take place as a result of decisions internally reached by journalists or externally by other parties, typically governmental agencies or, historically and in some cases still today, religious authorities. We recognize that censorship is also sometimes directed against artistic expression, fiction and nonfiction books, and many other information sources. Since our concern is primarily with journalistic ethics, we limit discussion for the most part to journalistic censorship and ask about the conditions under which it might sometimes be or might never be morally justified, what meaning it has in a free society, and what limits should be placed on control over news content. We assume that involuntary censorship by definition is always coercive, and we recognize that for this reason, other things being equal, voluntary censorship is inherently preferable to involuntary censorship whenever a good case can be made for any journalistic censorship whatsoever. Finally, we shall for present purposes characterize the *public interest* as any value attached to the preservation and proper functioning of a society. When we require that journalists provide relevant truth telling in the public interest, as indicated previously, we refer to a society's interests in maintaining its own security and well-being, along with promoting whatever other goals are recognized as benefiting the members of the society as a whole. We refine and build on these ideas as we proceed.

HISTORICAL AND PHILOSOPHICAL BACKGROUND

John Milton, in his *Areopagitica* (1644), a paean in praise of free expression and a free press, remarks on the cascading effect of trying to limit the freedom of the press and its ramifications for all aspects of culture, focusing here particularly on music:

> If we think to regulate printing, thereby to rectify manners, we must regulate all recreations and pastimes, all that is delightful to man. No music must be heard, no song be set or sung, but what is grave and Doric. There must be licensing dancers, that no gesture, motion, or deportment be taught our youth but what by their allowance shall be thought honest; for such Plato was provided of. It will ask more than the work of twenty licensers to examine all the lutes, the violins, and the guitars in every house; they must not be suffered to prattle as they do, but must be licensed what they may say. And who shall silence all the airs and madrigals, that whisper softness in chambers?[1]

---

[1] John Milton, *Areopagitica: A Speech of Mr. John Milton for the Liberty of Unlicens'd Printing to the Parliament of England* [London: 1644] (New York: Payson & Clark, Ltd., 1927) (facsimile edition from original copy in the British Museum), paragraph 37.

This same line of reasoning is articulated by Siebert, Peterson, and Schramm in *Four Theories of the Press*, when they explain:

> Under the libertarian concept, the functions of the mass media of communication are to inform and to entertain. A third function was developed as a necessary correlate to the others to provide a basis of economic support and thus to assure financial independence. This was the sales or advertising function. Basically the underlying purpose of the media was to help discover truth, to assist in the process of solving political and social problems by presenting all manner of evidence and opinion as the basis for decisions. The essential characteristic of this process was its freedom from government controls or domination. The government together with its officials was frequently a party with a direct interest in the outcome of a dispute. Therefore, it should not have the additional advantage of exclusive access to the public which ultimately made the decisions. Neither should it have the right or the power to interfere with the presentation of arguments from the opposition. Thus there developed a refinement of the function of the press as a political institution. It was charged with the duty of keeping government from overstepping its bounds. In the words of Jefferson, it was to provide that check on government which no other institution could provide.[2]

That this is not the end of the story is evident at once if we reflect on the reasonable limitations of a free press. We observed at the outset in describing the concept of a free press that there is no such thing as absolute or unconditional freedom. There are limitations and restrictions that affect even the freest imaginable press in the freest, most morally responsible society.

Conflicts of moral responsibility are resolved by give-and-take compromises in which certain kinds of freedoms are relaxed for the sake of securing other more important values that would otherwise be sacrificed. Partial and limited censorship is one of the kinds of compromise we sometimes require of a qualifiedly free press in order to avoid significantly greater evils, which it may also be among a free society's moral responsibilities to prevent. The extreme and consequently easy cases to decide include

---

[2]Siebert, Peterson, and Schramm, *Four Theories of the Press*, p. 51. See also Trager and Dickerson, *Freedom of Expression in the 21st Century*, pp. 201–202: "Rarely does an individual contest his or her right to attend a trial or to have access to information about pending litigation. Consequently, the free press v. fair trial issue is for the most part confined to a battle between the court system and the press. As individuals, we do not have time to attend trials, review court records, talk to prisoners, or attend parole hearings. We depend on the media to do that job and inform us of what is happening so that we know whether elected officials are doing their jobs and that laws are being enforced. Although the U.S. Constitution does not guarantee a right of access to information, courts and legislatures have recognized the important link between freedom of expression and right of access. If citizens are to discuss and debate public issues, go to the polls and vote on important matters, and be actively engaged in public affairs, they need to do so knowledgeably. Citizens need information, whether it comes directly from government or whether it comes from the mass media. Without the ability to access information, the content of our expression will have less value."

publishing photographs of child pornography or releasing sensitive military secrets that could jeopardize a society's security. If a news reporter obtains such images or information, we must more critically ask, does not the fundamental moral obligation of professional journalistic ethics require that they be published?

CENSORSHIP AND PRIORITIZED JOURNALISTIC OBLIGATIONS

Philosophers who write about the problems of applied ethics answer these kinds of questions in a number of different ways. One possibility is to say that there is no obligation to publish dangerous or highly morally objectionable images or information because a professional journalist's moral obligation to convey all relevant truths does not extend to absolutely any and every kind of information. Another possibility is to say that there is in fact an obligation to publish even the most dangerous or inflammatory materials, but that the obligation is overridden by other contrary or conflicting obligations in a prioritization of obligations that impinge on journalists hierarchically, not only in their journalistic capacity as purveyors of information, but as citizens of a free and open society.

Censorship in some form exists in either case. The exact explanation and philosophical justification for censorship can nevertheless make an important difference in application. A proper theory of censorship can be crucial in deciding about more difficult grey area cases where it is not immediately clear whether or not censorship is justified. It can be instrumental in curbing the abuse of censorship and preventing those who are charged with censoring the news from taking society down a slippery slope leading to more and more censorship, less and less freedom of the press, and finally to the subversion and co-option of a free press for purposes of political, religious, or big business propaganda.[3] Although there may be advantages and disadvantages to both models of censorship, there are good reasons to prefer the second account. Strange as it may at first seem, we shall argue that journalists do in fact have a blanket moral obligation to make all relevant information available to news consumers, but that their obligation is in

---

[3]Wortman, *A Treatise Concerning Political Enquiry and the Liberty of the Press* (1801), quoted in Knowlton and Parsons, ed., *The Journalist's Moral Compass*, p. 65: "The licentiousness of the press has of late become a theme of fashionable invective: but those who have been most clamorous in their philippics, have in general been most hostile to its liberty. The press is undoubtedly a powerful instrument; and, when left to itself, its natural direction will be towards truth and virtue. . . . Under arbitrary government it is a practice to prohibit every publication that has not been previously perused and sanctioned by some of its officers. By this means every writing, which is friendly to the spirit of freedom, is suppressed; and nothing can appear but what is on the side of government. By such regulations it is obvious that the press, instead of being a guardian of public liberty, is rendered a dangerous and servile slave to despotism."

certain cases trumped by other social concerns and by other obligations to which individuals who happen to be journalists must meet as responsible citizens.

We all wear several different hats in life, as son or daughter, father or mother, club member, professional or laborer, student, teacher, householder, taxpayer, soldier, civilian, and so on. Different roles in a society carry with them different moral obligations. Most of these, fortunately, as a general rule are perfectly compatible. Others in some instances can sometimes collide. An example is that in which I have an obligation as a father to protect my children from unpleasant experiences, but also an obligation as a policeman to arrest persons who have committed crimes. Thus, a conflict with respect to my moral obligations can arise if one of my children commits a crime and I am called upon to make the arrest, since I know in advance that the act will involve my child in a very unpleasant experience. As a biology teacher, to take another relatively clear-cut case, I might have an obligation to explain the scientific principles of evolution to my students. As a follower of a fundamentalist religion, however, I might have a conflicting obligation not to participate in what on the present hypothesis I sincerely believe to be sacrilegious falsehoods that do a disservice to God's creation of life in the universe. I have two moral obligations in this situation, and as it happens I cannot fulfill both.

Moral conflicts can sometimes be resolved in practice as well as theory. We can do so if we are able to prioritize our obligations so that one conflicting obligation outweighs or otherwise wins out over the other. If I decide it is more important or valuable, and hence more morally obligatory, to maintain my role as science teacher educating the young, then, despite my personal reservations of conscience, I may continue to teach evolution as a scientific account of the origin of life, even though I do not personally believe that the account is true. If I decide the opposite and give an alternative ordering of my moral commitments, then I might conscientiously refuse to teach evolution, possibly suffering the loss of my job as a casualty of my moral conviction. Alternatively, I might choose to buck the system and try to gain an exception for my reluctance to teach a scientific theory that I believe is out of step with my religious faith. If I am a policeman and the father or mother of a son or daughter for whom a warrant for arrest has been issued, I may decide that my obligations as a parent outweigh those of my profession as a law enforcement officer and help my child to escape. Or I might choose the opposite and decide that the law is the law no matter who is affected, that if my child has done wrong then it would be a misjudgment on my part to help him or her elude capture, and I would offer my usual assistance in the arrest just as though the accused were a perfect stranger.

What I would not want to say in any such case, however, is that in prioritizing my conflicting obligations that the relatively less highly prioritized obligation is not actually or is no longer an obligation. I still have an obligation to protect my children from unpleasant experiences. I may nevertheless come to regard that obligation as overridden by a higher, more pressing or important moral obligation. I continue also, presumably, in the second example, to have an obligation to teach science if I am a science teacher, even if I decide that the professional obligation to teach is outweighed or overridden by a superordinate religious or moral obligation. Similarly if I prioritize any of these conflicting obligations in the opposite way. Of course, we cannot simply reorder our obligations in any way we like to suit our fancy or to avoid moral dilemmas. We can only try to do so on the basis of moral principles that tell us, for example, that protection of family is more valuable than observing the law, or the opposite; or that science teaching is more important than personal religious conviction, or, again, the opposite.

MORAL RATIONALE FOR JOURNALISTIC CENSORSHIP

The prioritization of conflicting moral obligations provides a useful model also for understanding the ethics of censoring an otherwise free press. We need not say that a journalist suddenly loses or relaxes the moral obligation to report relevant information to the public, but only that in special circumstances the obligation, while not disappearing from the ethical horizon, is outweighed by a more highly prioritized obligation not to contribute to the exploitation of children in child pornography or to protect society at large from potential military defeat at the hands of its enemies by exposing vital military secrets. The moral obligation to disseminate information remains intact, and may even be highly prioritized, while still receiving only second priority to the need to protect children in the first example and to safeguard society as a whole from its most dangerous foes in the second. This trend in censorship, particularly during military actions of the United States, is noted in a recent critical survey:

> Whenever America goes to war, the press recognizes that it has a crucial responsibility to tell the public as much as it can—accurately and responsibly— about the conflict and the fate of its armed forces. As in the past, the needs of the press and the military will inevitably come in conflict. Reporting a war requires a degree of cooperation from the military. In recent conflicts—in Grenada in 1983, Panama in 1989, and the Gulf War in 1990–1991—different administrations have reduced the access of reporters to the battle zones and placed obstacles in the path of timely, independent reporting.
>
> In the current war on terrorism, press restraints have so far been even stricter than in the past.[4]

[4]Hachten and Scotton, *The World News Prism*, p. 21.

The trouble with extreme scenarios in applied professional ethics is not only that they do not represent the tricky controversial cases. Extreme scenarios, like child pornography and military secrets as classic examples of justified censorship of an otherwise free press, provide a useful starting place, because their implications are so clear-cut. The problem is that the forcefulness of extreme cases invoked to justify journalistic censorship can also constitute the thin edge of the wedge opening the way to less and less extreme instances that are increasingly morally objectionable.

Where freedom of the press and censorship are concerned, extreme cases like child pornography and national security break the precedent or absolute principle of non-censorship, making it difficult potentially thereafter to impose any limit to censorship whatsoever. This in another guise is the previously mentioned problem of the slippery slope eroding freedom of the press. The reasoning on the part of persons who want to see greater censorship of the press is that if it is legitimate to impose censorship in the cases of child pornography and national security, then why not also for the depiction of any nudity in art or for the facts concerning national assets? Information about any of a nation's resources can after all be used strategically against a free society by its enemies and could therefore imaginably constitute a national security risk. Adult nudity and sexual themes, to return to the first example, even in classical art, could eventually lead to a general breakdown of the moral fabric of society through a general atmosphere of heightened sexuality promoted by the media. Or so it might be argued. If these further abrasions of the free press are accepted, in turn, then what is the limit? Perhaps any information about our national leaders should not be publicized unless it is approved by a governmental office to make sure that the content cannot be misused by the society's domestic and foreign enemies. Perhaps no information about sex and no representation of the human body should ever be publicized, since to do so might lead to the sort of moral permissiveness that could endanger a society's values. How can we ever bring a halt to the censorship of the media and restore a strong measure of freedom to the reporting of news if these kinds of inferences are allowed to hold sway?

Case Study 14

Tomlinson's Efforts to Control Public Broadcasting

The following report was prepared by the National Coalition Against Censorship (NCAC), a watchdog organization that monitors and raises awareness about censorship of the press, artistic freedom, and other forms of expression:

"Public Broadcasting Caught in the Culture War—Summer 2005

The Public Broadcasting Act of 1967, creating the Corporation for Public Broadcasting [CPB], was enacted by Congress to establish an alternative to commercial television to inform, enlighten, and enrich the public and reflect America's common values and cultural diversity. As the overseer and fiscal catalyst for National Public Radio (NPR) and the Public Broadcasting Service (PBS), a significant mandate of the agency is to protect their independence and insulate programming from partisan politics.

Kenneth Tomlinson, Chairman of the CPB, one of five Republicans appointed by the White House to the nine-person Board, has put a new spin on its role. He wants to replace what he considers a liberal (and anti-Israel) bias in PBS news and public affairs programming with a conservative bias. To that end, and without informing his Board, he hired a consultant to monitor Bill Moyers' show Now for 'anti-Bush' and 'anti-business' biases and intends to monitor Middle East coverage on NPR news programs. The balance has already been tipped: at CPB's urging, PBS added two new programs that present only conservative views—Paul Gigot with The Journal Editorial Report, and talk-show commentator Tucker Carlson, who has since left. Additionally, CPB has appointed ombudsmen—one presumably liberal and the other conservative, to 'bring balance' to public broadcasting. However, a survey by CPB showed that listeners and viewers do not believe the programming is biased.

And now Congress wants to cut funding.

In a speech to the National Conference on Media Reform on May 15, Bill Moyers, who has recently retired from Now, called some of the charges by Tomlinson and CPB 'disturbing, and even dangerous.' Moyers described the basis for Now's creation. It was a time, he said, when research on public television found that political discussion on public affairs programs offered a narrow range of perspectives on current issues and debates. 'Economic news,' according to Moyers, 'was almost entirely refracted through the views of business people, investors and business journalists. . . . Nonprofessional workers, labor representatives, consumer advocates and the general public were rarely heard.' Now's mission was to include a diversity of opinions from all sides of the political spectrum. 'That,' said Moyers, 'created a political backlash . . . we were telling stories that partisans in power didn't want told and we were getting it right, not rightwing. . . . I've always thought the American eagle needed a left wing and a right wing. The right wing would see to it that economic interests had their legitimate concerns addressed. The left wing would see to it that ordinary people were included in the bargain. And both would keep the great bird on course. But with two right wings or two left wings, it's no longer an eagle, and it's going to crash.'

Whether it is public affairs programs or kids' shows like Postcards From Buster that are censored, public broadcasting won't flourish as a political football. No matter which party is in power, the independence of public broadcasting is essential to serving the public interest in a free society."

QUESTIONS

1. Why does the author of the above report sense that Kenneth Tomlinson wants to censure NPR and PBS? What, if anything, is the evidence for this charge? Is it correct, judging by the contents of the report?

2. If you were a reporter, writer, or editor for NPR or PBS, what would be your reaction to the Tomlinson initiatives? Suppose that funding were threatened if you did not comply with respect to providing news items considered to be friendlier to the American administration in the White House or toward Israel, as the complaint alleges? Would you, should you, resist such efforts at censorship? How, from a practical point of view, could and would you try to do so?

3. What sort of actions described might be considered as taking public broadcast journalism down a slippery slope to increasing censorship?

4. What makes governmentally supported journalism especially prone to censure and control? How are efforts to censure the press achieved and enforced? What role does money play in exerting pressure on news organizations to offer analysis and editorial opinion that some politicians might prefer in place of what journalists choose to report?

5. Does the government have a legitimate interest in keeping track of the contents of news stories and editorial features in the news when the government is footing at least a large part of the bill for news investigation and programming production costs? Why or why not? What are the limits within which governmental agencies should limit their interference in public broadcasting in order to avoid censorship of a free press within the First Amendment to the American Constitution? Can there be any justification for such practices on general grounds as opposed to brief or specific censorship during times of crisis?

THREE PRINCIPLES FOR CONTROLLING CENSORSHIP

There are three things we need in order to put the brakes on the slippery slope of censorship. If we are concerned about the possibility of rampant curtailments of a free press in a free society, then we should take advantage of the following: (1) A reminder of the moral justification for a free press; (2) An affirmation of the moral obligation of journalists to publish whatever information might be relevant to their readers or audience—an obligation, as we have urged, that is unqualified in and of itself even though it might sometimes be overridden; and (3) The basis for a principled distinction between morally justified and morally unjustified censorship of an otherwise unrestrainedly free press. The third and final safeguard is to require a good reason for allowing some cases of censorship that does not constitute a blank check for censors to restrict news reports without providing a sound justification. The point is to avoid censorship's gaining a permanent foothold or setting a bad precedent that cannot be restrained or turned back later once it is set in motion. We have already covered the rudiments of items (1) and (2), which we rehearse now only briefly in outline to provide a foundation for a more thorough discussion of item (3).

INTERDEPENDENCE OF A FREE SOCIETY AND A FREE PRESS—PRINCIPLE 1

Let us briefly recall the primary moral justification for a free press. The argument is that political and personal freedom is an intrinsically morally valuable state for the members of any society and that a free society can only be properly instituted and preserved against erosion of its freedoms generally by a free press.

The further justification for a free press as a prerequisite for a free society is that its members depend on the free flow of relevant information for purposes of self-government. A society can only remain free if a free press acts as a vigilant fourth estate, exposing and rallying the public interest against abuses of power. By publicizing what the government does, a free people monitors all aspects of its leadership and provides a check on occurrences that might otherwise undermine its liberty and independence. The only truly free people are a freely informed people, and the only way for a society to be freely informed is for its press and all media to be free. This means, as we have argued, among other things, that the press must be, to whatever extent possible, uncensored in its ability to report the news. Journalists, accordingly, who collectively have a moral obligation to serve the public by truth telling, are by implication obligated also to resist efforts at controlling the content of news and editorials by individuals within and especially by those outside the profession. A reporter cannot properly do his or her job in reporting the news, and by implication cannot fulfill the fundamental principle of journalistic ethics to provide relevant truth telling in the public interest, if the facts they need and want to be able to report are subject to regular censorship. If we think of the analogy we have sometimes stressed between journalists and scientists each gathering and making public certain kinds of facts, then we should easily be able to see that the same is true for scientists. If a scientist is similarly hampered in the free investigation of natural phenomena, then we cannot reasonably expect important scientific discoveries to be made.

The inference thus proceeds from the intrinsic moral value of a free society to its requirements for information. The moral justification for a free press is thus predicated on the importance of living in a free society and its constant need for truth about the facts of the world. Truth in turn requires a free press and free sources of information, for it is only when inquiry and the reporting of information is free that the discovery and disclosure of facts can be optimized. History is replete with examples of inquiry conducted under the burdens of censorship that did not lead to the truth or, no thanks to which, the emergence of important truths was hampered and delayed. It is always possible for truth to arise accidentally even under conditions of severe control, but we cannot expect truth finding to be maximized when inquiry is not free and unrestrained.

Where censorship exists there are always enforcement methods that range from the subtle to the brutal. These serve and are intended to serve as incentives for journalists to limit their news reporting in approved ways. The dangers for journalists in this regard soon become dangers for society as a whole, as these enforcement methods restrict the lifeline of vital information societies require in order to function effectively. We have already seen in discussing the concept of a free press that this freedom means several things. There must be an absence of any censorship to whatever extent possible in keeping with a society's other obligations, open-ended investigations of news events by journalists, the possibility of competition among truth seekers, and cross-checking of news stories, among other practical measures.

To whatever extent we limit freedom of the press, to that exact extent we limit the optimization of truth available to the members of a free society. We may in certain instances impose censorship for the sake of satisfying a morally greater obligation. The question then is always how, under such circumstances, the regulation and limitation of free inquiry by a free press is morally and most properly to be managed so as to be consistent with the moral obligations generally impinging on a society's members. A free society is morally obligated to maintain and preserve its freedom as something intrinsically morally valuable. A free press and the free flow of information it helps to sustain is one of the most important ways in which a free society safeguards its freedoms. It is not the only way, however, and there are circumstances under which the publication of certain kinds of information is more of a threat than a benefit to the maintenance of a society's freedom.

OBLIGATION TO MAXIMIZE RELEVANT TRUTH TELLING—PRINCIPLE 2

This, as we have suggested, is how the slippery slope of increasing censorship gets started. The question is how it might best be prevented from running away with the freedoms we hold precious and undoing the important work of an ideally free press.

We have expressed a preference for a particular philosophical model of the ethics of censorship. The model does not whittle away at the moral obligation of journalists to discover and publish absolutely all relevant truths at their disposal. It permits journalists in principle to publish even the most inflammatory and dangerous kinds of information that might be hurtful to a free society's interests or ultimately to its continuing freedom. While we acknowledge the unqualified moral right and even moral obligation on the part of professional journalists to publish all facts that might be potentially relevant to its readers or audience, we acknowledge that this moral obligation to maximally relevant truth telling can sometimes be outweighed and overridden by other conflicting moral obligations that have priority in the public interest.

The moral obligation for journalists to report the news remains even when the prioritization of moral obligations requires it to take a backseat to more urgent obligations. When this happens, journalists cannot in practice fulfill all of their moral obligations. In particular, they may then need to modify their pursuit of the primary moral imperative of journalistic ethics to discover and report the truth. Such a situation is not especially new or unprecedented. It can happen to any one of us we fall under conflicting obligations that are resolved by rank-ordering the demands they make on our actions. We saw this already in the case of the policeman-father and biology-teacher-religious-fundamentalist. The adjudication of conflicting moral obligations occurs also in many other situations, given the complexities of our moral lives and the logical implications of the multiple, sometimes mutually incompatible, moral obligations to which we may owe differing degrees of allegiance.

Refusing to relax or rescind the moral obligation of journalists always to tell the truth about absolutely everything without exception while permitting the obligation to be outweighed or overridden under exceptional circumstances helps hold the line against incursions of a free press. Although many social factors can threaten the possibility of more and more occasions in which the prerogatives of a free press are outweighed or overridden by conflicting obligations, there is something important about not acknowledging in such cases that journalists have simply lost their obligation to tell the truth. Instead, we recognize the need in some cases not to satisfy a particular professional obligation for the sake of a greater obligation in another capacity, such as that of being a citizen, soldier, or the like.

The same is true with respect to censorship. If it turns out to be true that in some cases journalists are morally obligated not to publicize certain facts they have discovered because of conflicting more highly prioritized obligations, news reporters should nevertheless not become complacent about their fundamental responsibility. They should not consider that their obligation is eliminated or neutralized even when circumstances require that it be overridden by other more pressing obligations. Thus, instead of concluding that journalists have no moral obligation to publish child pornography or their country's strategically sensitive military secrets, we hold that reporters do have an obligation to make such disclosures, but that they ought not to fulfill the obligation for the sake of more important contrary obligations reflecting more highly prioritized social values. We emphasize in that case that relevant truth telling is only obligatory for professional journalists in a given instance when it is in the public interest for them to do so.

Can Information be Harmful?

If it seems outrageous to suppose that journalists are morally obligated to publish the kinds of hurtful or dangerous information we have mentioned, we should remember two things.

First, information is only information. We should not suppose that the truth about anything whatsoever in the long run can ever be harmful. In the short term, on the other hand, it is obvious that significant damage can be done when the wrong information ends up in the wrong hands. This, remarkably, is potentially true of virtually any of the information published by the media; yet we do not want to bring all of journalism to a screeching halt by censoring the publication of any information whatsoever.

Second, we should also recall that although journalists are morally obligated to publish all relevant newsworthy information in their possession, we are speaking of information that by hypothesis they are more strongly or compellingly morally obligated not to release. We agree all along that journalists should not publish pictures of child pornography or instructions for making a pipe bomb, even if it happens that the pictures and instructions are part of the evidence seized in a police raid on child pornographers or a terrorist's explosives workshop and, hence, a legitimate part of a news report on these events.

The philosophical challenge has not been to debate these values, but in the spirit of free inquiry to determine exactly what concepts and principles enable us to decide that publishing sufficiently dangerous or reprehensible things is not in the public interest. We must now explain more concretely what we mean by the public interest, what truth telling in the public interest should be taken to include, and what it should be taken to exclude. If we can further decide what is "sufficiently" dangerous or reprehensible to warrant censorship or voluntary withholding of information from publication or broadcast, then we may finally be in a position to consider some practical suggestions about how to set progressive limits for press censorship and how to stem the tide against incursions of censorship directed at an ideally optimally free press.

Is there any point, then, in insisting that journalists have a moral obligation to tell the truth about matters concerning which we know in advance for other reasons they should not actually publish? We have already indicated one powerful motive for preserving the moral obligation to maximize relevant truth telling while sometimes allowing this professional obligation to be overridden by more pressing conflicting obligations. The distinction provides a brake, partly psychological and partly precedent-avoiding, against the slippery slope that otherwise threatens to undermine the freedom of the press. We do not want to say that the moral obligation to maximize truth telling on the part of journalists is something that can never be taken away, even if it must sometimes under extreme circumstances be set aside for the sake of other higher moral values.

Paradox of Censorship Exceptions for Censors

There are other peculiar aspects of censorship in a free society. Consider the fact that if there is censorship of any sort of any type of material, then some persons will need to examine the texts and images in question in order to decide that they are unsuitable for other persons to read or view.

There is something inherently undemocratic about censorship. We find ourselves nevertheless asking: If certain information is harmful to the general public, why is it not harmful in the hands of the censor, who must also ingest its content? Why suppose that some persons who alone are morally qualified to be censors are so secure in their values and willpower that they can confront censorable material without ill effects, while the general population would be so damaged by the exposure to warrant their being protected by censorship? We may think back to the fifteenth century and the Inquisition, which established an index of forbidden writings. None of these were permitted to be published, but they were collected in private and ecclesiastical libraries for higher members of the clergy to consult.

The arrogance of such an attitude is what has led many persons since the Enlightenment to resist the idea of censorship in any form. Why should certain writings on science, for example, be available only to a privileged elite? Why should only the members of a religious institution be deemed responsible enough to read such materials, while the other members of a society are kept in ignorance of new discoveries about the nature of the world that would broaden their outlook and perhaps provide them with vital information to use in living better lives?

The answer offered by church officials at the time is much the same that one encounters whenever censorship is approved. It is that the dissemination of certain kinds of information threatens the very foundations or survival of the society. This is a powerful argument. In retrospect, however, we can always wonder later whether such a society deserves to be preserved if it has no better respect for the truth than to institute permanent censorship. The trouble is that persons in power often see many types of useful information as potentially damaging to their individual interests. For their own benefit they may then try to parade these personal risks as greater threats to society at large. Thus, the newly emerging science of Galileo, Bacon, Descartes, Leibniz, and others was perceived by church authorities in the seventeenth century as threatening the religious foundations of the European societies where their congregations lived. In totalitarian governments and dictatorships like Nazi Germany, Stalinist Soviet Union, and North Korea, to name three of the most conspicuous recent examples among many others, the flow of any governmentally unregulated information is regarded as a potential threat to the regime. Virtually any information in that sense can be construed as a danger to the preservation of society, to the very fabric and foundations of the society in which heavy censorship is exercised, in the emotionally laden but nebulous phrase that is often invoked in defense of restricting information. A totalitarian government is first and foremost a regime that takes control of every aspect of the news media. The repeated lessons of history are that censorship is usually more damaging to the real foundations of society than any of the perceived threats it may be intended to remedy, with or without good intentions.

Case Study 15

Censorship of the Press in Iraq

The following paragraphs are excerpted from Robert Fisk, "Censorship of the Press—A Familiar Story for Iraqis," in the London *Independent*, June 11, 2003:

> "Paul Bremer has ordered his legal department in Baghdad to draw up rules for press censorship. A joke, I concluded, when one of the newly styled Coalition Provisional Authority officials tipped me off last week. But no, it really is true. Two months after 'liberating' Iraq, the Anglo-American authorities and their boss Paul Bremer—whose habit of wearing combat boots with a black suit continues to amaze his colleagues—have decided to control the new and free Iraqi press.
>
> Newspapers that publish 'wild stories,' material deemed provocative or capable of inciting ethnic violence, will be threatened or shut down. It's for the good of the Iraqi people, you understand. A controlled press is a responsible press—which is exactly what Saddam Hussein used to say about the trashy newspapers his regime produced. It must seem all too familiar to the people of Baghdad. Now let's be fair. Many stories in the emerging newspapers of Baghdad are untrue. There is no tradition of checking reports, of giving opponents the opportunity to be heard. There

are constant articles about the behavior of American troops. One paper has claimed that U.S. soldiers distributed postcards of naked women to schoolgirls—they even published the pictures, with Japanese script on the cards. Even the most cynical Westerner can see how this kind of lie can stir up sentiment against Iraq's new foreign occupiers.

What the Iraqis need, of course, is journalistic help rather than censorship, courses in reporting—by experienced journalists from real democracies (rather than the version Mr. Bremer seems set on creating)—rather than a colonial-style suppression of free speech.

But we're now hearing that imams in the mosques may be censored if they provoke unrest—this would obviously include the imam of the Rashid Street mosque in Baghdad, outside of which I heard him preaching last week. The Americans must leave, he said. Immediately. Subversive stuff. Definitely likely to provoke violence. So goodbye in due course, I suppose to the Rashid Street imam. And of course, we all know how the first pro-American Iraqi government of 'New Iraq' will treat the laws. It will enthusiastically adopt the Western censorship law, just as former colonies almost always take over the repressive legislation of their former imperial masters."

QUESTIONS

1. Are there any circumstances under which it is morally justified to impose censorship? What, according to Fisk, are the likely effects of censuring the new Iraqi press?

2. When a society is relatively stable and well-established, there are always remedies for libel and inaccuracies in reportage. A society in crisis, like Iraq during the American occupation after the Second Gulf War, does not have such mechanisms in place. Do these facts provide the basis for a reasonable defense of the decision to censure the press?

3. Can censorship be morally justified in a society if there is widespread disrespect for the truth and none of the usual editorial oversight to prevent the publication of falsehoods? We have been thinking of censorship as the suppression of dangerous to inconvenient or politically embarrassing truths on the part of a self-serving government. Censorship can nevertheless also involve a more socially benevolent effort to suppress falsehoods from being published. Does this seem to be what has happened with the newspapers and other news outlets in Iraq?

4. Suppose that censorship in Iraq is morally justified as an emergency measure. How long should it remain in place? What would be the signs that censorship is no longer needed and should now be phased out? What are the long-term effects of censorship likely to be on the future of a free press in Iraq?

5. Who if anyone is morally qualified to serve as censor? What skills and personal qualities must someone have to censor the news? To what additional authority or oversight should a censor be further answerable? What sort of accountability should we require of someone entrusted to censor the news?

Reconsidering Hard Cases in Favor of Censorship

Still, are there not sound reasons on some occasions to withhold information from the public? Is there not a difference between persons who are qualified and in whom a society places its trust to consider materials for their suitability to be published and made available to anyone and everyone? Do we want to see child pornography on the front pages of the *New York Times* or *USA Today* or any of the other newspapers in wide circulation throughout the world? Do we really want terrorists to be provided with blueprints to military installations and instructions for making weapons of mass destruction, along with information about where to find materials and experts to help design and build them? Do we really want the names and addresses of rape victims and covert operatives on whom the defense of our society and its freedom depends published for all to read or watch on television?

We should not simply assume that the answer to these questions is no. An argument might be made for the absolute prohibition of any sort of censorship and the supreme priority of the journalist's fundamental moral obligation to maximize truth telling. The considerations raised in support of censorship often confuse what is truly a danger to a society with what we may be uncomfortable seeing or knowing about, what we might find extraordinarily repellent, distasteful, or repugnant. These are nevertheless subjective judgements that do not necessarily imply any sort of meaningful threat to the health of society, let alone to its "very foundations." As terrible as the sexual exploitation of children is, for example, and as morally objectionable, as great an effort as we as a society should exert to prevent these things from occurring and to shut down and criminally prosecute whoever is engaged in such activities, we might step back for just a moment and ask what real harm would be done by publishing pictures of child pornography. The suggestion is not that journalists should themselves engage in the production of such materials, which we are assuming is a morally forbidden practice for anyone. Rather, we ask whether in the course of informing their readers or viewers there is any adequate reason to censor publishing photographs confiscated from illegal pornographers.

If we look to the consequences of decisions in terms of bringing about a worse or better state of affairs, in this case, for exploited children, can we say in advance with any confidence that we know it would be worse rather than better for children affected by such crimes if the photographs are published? Perhaps if the public came face to face with the degradation involved in the practice, they would be more strongly motivated to take action against child pornographers and bring the practice more quickly and decisively to an end. What real harm would be done? To what extent would the harm that might occur not be mitigated by the greater good that might also occur if the relevant information were published? Perhaps it would lead to the recovery of exploited children whose whereabouts had previously been unknown. We cannot imagine in any case that every issue of the *New York Times* day after day and year after year would feature such material, because journalists are under an obligation to maximize the publication of relevant information. Images of child pornography must compete with all the other comparatively more interesting and important information that news writers are also morally obligated to report. Furthermore, although some persons might be affected by such images and be led to commit wrongful acts as a result, it is unlikely that there will be much sustained interest or demand for pictures of child pornography to appear in the media. Many people will predictably and rightly be so offended by it that they will protest, refusing to patronize the respective news agencies or threatening to do so, so that market forces in a free society will also exert an influence counteracting any long-term practice of graphically publicizing exactly how reprehensibly children are abused in the pornography industry.

Notice that we have not in any way been advocating either the production of child pornography or its publication by a morally responsible media once it has been produced. We have only been asking in an open-minded way whether, and if so how much actual harm would be caused by such images being published and whether it is at least conceivable that a greater social good might come about as a result. We do not for one minute suggest that if child pornography were to be published by the popular media that it do so exclusively for purposes of informing the public about just what it is that pornographers do and the effect it is having on exploited children. We are not in particular considering the possibility that the popular press become an outlet for child pornography or other salacious material. We are only inquiring whether the media might be used to bring to citizens important information about how children are treated by this illegal and highly immoral business. The catchphrase that is sometimes used in such contexts is that nothing sanitizes like sunlight—the idea is that openness and public awareness helps a society to remove its dark and dirty secrets and thereby to improve the moral climate for all.

News Coverage of Capital Punishment

We might ask the same about publicizing criminal executions in those places where capital punishment is still practiced. There are undoubtedly some persons who would derive morbid pleasure from watching criminals being put to death, just as they did in times past when executions were conducted publicly in the village square or before the prison walls. This would not necessarily be a positive thing, and opponents of the death penalty have repeatedly argued that public executions and publishing information in reports of executions do not serve as a deterrent to capital offenses. The argument has frequently been made that public executions are statistically correlated with increasing numbers of capital offenses in societies, including the United States, that still practice capital punishment.

The subject again raises complicated issues. As in the example of publicizing the products of child pornography, however, it is at least imaginable that despite these negative effects, more positive results might occur to outweigh the negative consequences. Publicizing executions could make citizens aware of precisely what happens when a prisoner is put to death and thereby equip them more fully with the information they need as citizens to decide whether the death penalty is a punishment that ought to be maintained or prohibited. It is also frequently remarked by opponents of capital punishment that if only more persons could see how the death penalty is administered they would be more likely to outlaw the practice by voting it down. By extension, the same might be said of publishing the names of rape victims. It is all too easy to treat the victims of sexual assault as anonymous when we do not know anything specific about their personalities or lives. If the information were publicized, perhaps, we might think, the positive consequences would outweigh the negative. We shall later see that, with few exceptions, there are stronger social reasons connected with the right of privacy for not publishing the results of child pornography or the names of victims of crimes such as rape and sexual assault. Whether this constitutes a justification for at least some kinds of censorship of an otherwise free press remains to be seen.

Strategically Sensitive Military Information

Can similar remarks be made concerning the proliferation of details about how to build bombs or the layout of military installations and similarly sensitive information? How can the public possibly benefit from knowing such things that would only assist a society's enemies in planning and executing attacks against its interests?

Here even more clearly than in previous cases we encounter what appear to be solid reasons for withholding information from the public, and we expect that classified documents pertaining to matters of national security and a society's vital interests should not be published if they can in any way compromise a nation's defense. There is a level of information that citizens should probably be provided with in order to make informed choices about the military that are within their competence and essential to self-government in a free society. These facts, however, do not ordinarily need to include specific details that could be used to the society's military disadvantage and threaten its ability to protect its citizens' lives.

Even in these cases, if we exercise our imaginations, we might identify reasons to suppose that it would actually make a society militarily stronger to publicize its defensive and offensive assets. If it were generally known what weapons and resources a nation had, perhaps there would be less temptation for it to use its military force or for its enemies to act against it, which might improve worldwide prospects for peace. These expectations are no doubt utopian and idealistic in the pejorative sense of being unrealistic. From a practical point of view, a responsible free society cannot permit certain kinds of information about its military preparedness to be publicized, and journalists generally recognize the need to subordinate their desire to acquire and distribute information to be limited in these special cases. Where journalists do not voluntarily withhold sensitive military information, they can expect external censorship from government agencies.

It may nevertheless be instructive to ask whether the same would be true if all other societies were free and adhered to an uncensored free press that allowed military information to be published. In that event, would there still be a justification for withholding military information from the press, or is the only justification for a free society to do so the fact that other nations will not play along by openly revealing all of their assets?

Balancing a Free Press with the Need for Censorship

We can say in general with respect to all of these examples that the only justification for censoring an otherwise free press is in order to satisfy moral obligations that are in conflict with the moral requirements of maximal journalistic truth telling. We may disagree about whether or not this or that social consideration, concerning child pornography, military secrets, or executions for capital crimes, to repeat the standard list, should or should not invoke voluntarily withholding information on the part of journalists or, failing that, external censorship by governmental authorities. The general principle should nevertheless be clear enough. We accept censorship of an otherwise free press only when it is in the greater social interest to withhold than to publish certain kinds of information. The exceptions to an uncensored free press must be extraordinary or expressly limited both in scope and duration.

When two or more incompatible moral obligations impinge on any morally responsible individual and when the obligations can be prioritized on morally defensible grounds, then the agent, while morally obligated at least to some degree by all the conflicting obligations considered together, is above all morally obligated to actually follow and act in accord with only the top-ranked moral obligation, the most important obligation to which the agent is subject. Where conflicting moral obligations in news reporting are concerned, the same thesis applies. There we expect that if the fundamental moral obligation of journalists to maximize relevant truth telling runs into conflict with other more highly prioritized moral obligations, such as those preventing sensitive military information from falling into the hands of a society's enemies, then news reporters at a higher level of moral obligation are morally obligated to observe the most highly prioritized moral obligation to which they are subject as citizens rather than professional journalists. An ideal in which a satisfactory compromise between the advantages of an unrestricted free press and voluntary censorship of the press by its own self-appointed regulators was described in Tunis Wortman's nineteenth-century analysis of the concept of a free press, *A Treatise Concerning Political Enquiry and the Liberty of the Press*, first published in 1801:

> The press is undeniably possessed of extensive influence upon government, manners, and morals. Every exertion should, therefore, be employed to render it subservient to liberty, truth, and virtue. While society is furnished with so powerful a vehicle of political information, the conduct of administration will be more cautious and deliberate: it will be inspired with respect towards a censor whose influence is universal . . .
>
> It cannot be denied that the Press maintains a powerful influence over manners and morals. Argument is the most salutary and rational mean [*sic*] of correcting our prejudices, and establishing the empire of truth. There is no vehicle better adapted for the circulation of reasoning, or the communication of sentiment, than the press.
>
> An instrument which is capable of becoming prostituted to so much mischief, as well as rendering such important and extensive benefits (it will naturally be alleged), "should be carefully confined within the bounds of rectitude and virtue. While we assiduously cultivate and cherish the valuable plant, let us at the same time diligently prune its luxuriant and irregular excrescences." It would, doubtless, be desirable to control the licentiousness of the press, if any means could be pursued for that purpose without endangering its liberty.[5]

In the kinds of cases we have been describing, this can mean that journalists ought to exercise self-censorship by voluntarily withholding information or that other government agencies are morally obligated to act in such a way as to exert involuntary censorship on news reporters to prevent such information from being published.

The same is true if it is deemed of higher moral priority to withhold from publication other kinds of information, including extant images of child pornography, names and addresses of rape victims, and anything else for which a sound argument can be made that there is a higher moral priority to protect the values that would be jeopardized if information of a certain sort were to be released. Obviously, there can often be legitimate disputes about whether in fact any of these putative conflicting moral obligations should actually be considered to have higher priority over the

---

[5]Wortman, *A Treatise Concerning Political Enquiry and the Liberty of the Press* (1801), quoted in Knowlton and Parsons, ed., *The Journalist's Moral Compass*, p. 63.

journalist's fundamental moral obligation to maximize relevant truth telling in reporting the news, as we have also indicated. It is a matter of public debate in a free society as to whether any information should be censored and, if so, in what categories and for what reasons and for what periods of time.

Recovering a Free Press After Emergency Censorship

We should finally expect there must always be a definite endpoint to any involuntary censorship of news. There are typically specific times at which it is morally preferable not to release certain kinds of information. When enough time has expired, then in many instances it should be reasonable again to suppose that the information can safely be made available to the public. The point is not merely to satisfy curiosity about facts that had previously been suppressed, but to bring important data into the information mill by which a free society continues to govern itself. Even today, as a result, it is worthwhile for information connected with previous war efforts to be released now that the danger posed by at least much of what once needed to be kept secret has passed. Knowing what a society's prior military posture has been can help all members of the society contribute freely to the decision-making process whereby future military decisions are made.

DISTINGUISHING MORALLY JUSTIFIED CENSORSHIP—PRINCIPLE 3

We have examined a few extreme cases representing exceptions for restricting a free press through voluntary or involuntary censorship. The expectation accordingly is that as a rule in all but the most important situations involving conflicting moral obligations the media is to be free in the strongest possible sense, uncensored in all its news reporting in accord with the fundamental moral obligation of journalists to maximize relevant truth telling—as this and the previous chapter have emphasized—*in the public interest.*

Turning then to principle (3), we consider its role in stemming the slippery slope from censorship in extreme cases to censorship in less extreme cases and finally to censorship in many, if not most, cases. This is the danger we perceive when we open the door to censorship in the first place. It is the thin edge of the wedge, as we have described it, that can lead to the breakdown of a free press, which we have urged is indispensable to the survival of a free society. We have argued, indeed, that in some ways preserving a free press is at least as if not more vital to a society's welfare than protecting its military secrets. What we need is a principled way to block the descent down a slippery slope from censorship of a free press as an extreme exception to increasingly more and more censorship, exercised finally on the basis of mere pretext. The groundwork for the identification of such a principled limitation to censorship is already in sight. If we admit that journalists have an unqualified moral obligation always to maximize relevant truth telling in reporting the news and that their obligation as such can only be justifiably outweighed or overridden by a conflicting more highly prioritized moral obligation in the social interest, then we can hope to forestall the incremental erosion of a free press leading to full-scale censorship by identifying a well-grounded distinction between morally justified and morally unjustified censorship.

This is a strong requirement in theory and practice. It is also one that, like any other basis for moral decision-making, needs to be guarded against abuse. We require that an exception to the unrestricted freedom of the press can only be morally justified if there is a sufficiently powerful argument to support the proposition that there is a greater moral obligation to suppress a news item or a category of news items than to freely publish the information it contains. Although we have not attempted to advance a convincing proof one way or another with respect to any specific proposal to censor the news, we have already seen that it is not that easy to make a case for restricting the free expression of journalists in a free society and that the least controversial case may yet be that of the protection of vital military secrets. Even here we have learned that the task of mounting a strong enough reason to justify censorship is not as cut-and-dried as many have assumed. None of this is to say that advocates of censorship will not claim to be able to make decisive moral arguments in support of many kinds of censorship or of censorship affecting many different kinds of news reporting. That is the way in which dialectic about any matter of public concern takes shape in a free society. Defenders of a free press must then challenge those arguments as failing to make a strong enough case to justify censorship and not succumb to every consideration that might be raised to motivate censoring the news. The philosophical requirement for permitting exceptions to an absolutely free and uncensored press in an optimally free society is nevertheless the stringent demand that it be demonstrated on the basis of the highest standards of rigorous argument that there exists a moral obligation that outweighs and overrides the fundamental moral requirement of journalists to maximize relevant truth telling in and for the benefit of the members of a free society, without which a society in the long run cannot hope to remain free.

Public discourse about what is or is not an overriding moral obligation to justify any censorship of the media can proceed along many lines. The fact that disputes on these topics occur indicates the extent to which it is at least implicitly recognized that a very strong reason must always be given in order to violate the freedom of the press. We put the brakes to any slippery slope leading to increasing censorship on more and more issues with less and less ground by requiring that exceptions to unlimited free journalistic expression be justified only by the availability of correct arguments to establish that there exists a greater moral obligation to suppress the free collection and dissemination of information by an otherwise free and independent press. The same kinds of considerations also apply to other forms of censorship in the arts and in popular, scholarly, scientific, and religious writing.

VOLUNTARY AND INVOLUNTARY CENSORSHIP

If we agree that there can sometimes be adequate justification for censoring the news, then we must inquire more thoroughly into the nature of censorship and its implications for moral responsibility in the media. There are two broad kinds of censorship, as we have already indicated: voluntary and involuntary or coercive, internal self-censorship versus external censorship.

Self-censorship occurs every minute of every day in actual journalistic practice. News reporters and editors decide whether or not to run a story and, if so, what words to use and whether or not to accompany a news items with images and, if so, with what images. These are all in a sense censorings of whatever decisions might otherwise have been made and of ideas about what to include in or exclude from the news. Because such choices are made by journalists themselves, without outside pressure beyond the usual market forces, self-censorship is typically not coercive and as such represents no violation of free speech or the freedom of the press. The same is true if news reporters, editors, or publishers freely censor their reporting by voluntarily refusing to publish information about military secrets, names of rape victims, or the like. To the extent that news makers recognize an overriding moral obligation to withhold the optimal presentation of information and voluntarily choose to censor themselves, there is no violation of the freedom of the press, and journalists who take such actions in suppressing information are acting fully within the scope of the fundamental moral obligation to maximize relevant truth telling in the public interest.

What happens, however, when there is a compellingly sound argument establishing the existence of an overriding moral obligation to withhold information from the public, and news reporters, editors, or publishers are unwilling voluntarily to comply? In that case, journalistic ethics, as we have developed its precepts, implies that the news makers in question are acting wrongly. They are violating their professional ethics in that instance and exposing themselves to whatever sanctions are available under the law to punish their behavior. These penalties are generally through the imposition of fines or by incarceration, withdrawal of licenses, and the like, as well as disapprobation by the public and other members of the journalistic community. In such cases, it is morally justified for journalists to be forced to comply with involuntary censorship on the grounds that they have exceeded their mission to publish information when the obligation to do so is outweighed or overridden by a conflicting more highly prioritized moral obligation to suppress certain news items or categories of information from public disclosure.

Since it is generally in the interests of journalists not to be forcibly censored or to be punished by the law for failing to meet the obligations to suppress information, professional organizations of journalists usually set voluntary standards for the kinds of news reporting in which they will or will not engage. In this regard, journalists act reasonably and in a morally responsible way to regulate their own profession and their own individual conduct within the profession as a vital part of professional journalistic ethics. This is not to say that any particular occurrence of self-censorship on the part of news agencies in the national interest will not be greeted with skepticism and criticism as bowing to governmental pressures at the expense of the duty of reporters to collect and package whatever information might be relevant to the public they serve. We see this in the following controversy surrounding voluntary withholding of information concerning the activities of terrorists and the efforts of terrorists to use a free media to communicate their own propaganda.

Case Study 16

"Censoring" Terrorists by Official Request in a Free Society

The following passage is from *The World News Prism: Global Media in an Era of Terrorism*, sixth edition, by William A. Hachten and James F. Scotton:

> "In October [2001], the White House requested that broadcast network executives not air in full the prerecorded statements of Osama bin Laden carried on Al-Jazeera, the Arab television network. The White House expressed concern about giving the terrorists unchecked outlets for their propaganda; the White House also feared that such appearances might contain coded messages for bin Laden operatives around the world. The six major television news organizations agreed jointly to abridge future video-taped statements. But some in the press criticized this action, arguing that the American people should have unfettered access to the terrorist leader and his views.
>
> Conservative press critics also criticized the news media for being too neutral or 'balanced' in reporting and not sufficiently patriotic and outspokenly antiterrorist. But the problem for the news business was to make the public and its critics understand that the press expresses its patriotism by aggressively defending the public's right to know what's going on. That's the job of a free press, even in wartime."[6]

[6]Hachten and Scotton, *The World News Prism*, p. 22.

QUESTIONS

1. Do the likely risks of broadcasting terrorists' messages justify censorship?

2. Can censorship be controlled once it is allowed to degrade the open exchange of information guaranteed by a free press in a free society? Does the bad precedent of allowing censorship in any case automatically imply the end of a truly free press, or can censorship be properly contained while permitting the remainder of a free press to flourish?

3. Are there better ways of combating the potential effect of allowing terrorists to reach an audience with their message of hate and possibly with coded instructions to their operatives than to simply deny them media exposure? If so, what are these methods, and how can they help provide for society's legitimate interests in protecting itself from hostilities?

4. Imagine that you are a reporter or news editor and must decide whether or not to comply with a governmental restraining order censoring the publication of particular information by terrorists. What decision-making process would you enter into in response to the demand? What would you as a practicing journalist be willing to do in order to stand up for a free press and defy any effort at censorship? What should journalists do in reacting to such a situation, and why?

5. The above report indicates only that the White House "requested" that American media not broadcast prerecorded statements of Osama bin Laden carried on the Arab news network Al-Jazeera. Making such a request is logically compatible with preserving a free press, and the authors note that while controversy about the request was stirred, all six major American news agencies agreed to meet the request. What is the moral status of such "requests"? Is it possible that a request to withhold information from the public could constitute a first step on the slippery slope to outright censorship? What kinds of limits can be set for such requests and the weakening of a fully free press that they seem to imply? What sorts of pressures can governments use to supplement their requests for cooperation with news agencies concerning what is or is not reported as news? How can conscientious journalists who recognize the value of a free press resist such pressures when they do not agree that withholding newsworthy information voluntarily is in fact in the greater public interest or for the greater public good?

Summary

When we think about the voluntary decisions that journalists make to control their presentation of the news, we see that they have many opportunities to both meet their fundamental moral obligation to maximize relevant truth telling in the news and to do so in a way that still does not violate other possibly more highly prioritized moral obligations that would justify the imposition of involuntary external censorship.

In the child pornography case, for example, the standard practice that professional journalists for the most part have voluntarily adopted with respect to this painful issue is to report on the practice, to include information about arrests, prosecutions, and in general the battle against child pornography as a major effort in the war on crime, while not including as part of the reportage any salacious images of child pornography produced by offenders. Journalists can effectively convey all the essential information of the battle against child pornography without illustrating their findings with offensive pictures.

Much the same is true of many other areas of news reporting that would otherwise lead to involuntary external censorship. By voluntarily selecting information and ways of presenting it, it is possible in most if not all instances for journalists to meet their professional obligation to tell the truth about important news events without violating other more highly prioritized moral obligations to protect a society's vital interests. In the case of sensitive military information, and in whatever other areas censorship might in principle be justified, news reporters can usually inform the public about what they believe in their professional judgment is essential to their decision-making without in other ways violating the obligations that citizens have to the society whose freedoms they enjoy. In *Nicomachean Ethics* (Book 8, section 1), Aristotle argues that if all the members of a society were friends, there would be no need for justice and, hence, presumably, no need for courts of law. We can similarly say, sounding again our theme of the distinction between abstract moral ideals and workaday realities in journalistic ethics, that if all the members of the profession acted in accord with the moral obligations and the prioritization of moral obligations impinging on journalists, as journalists and citizens of their society or as moral agents generally, then there would be no need for external involuntary censorship. If all journalists were friends, in Aristotle's sense, with all other citizens of the world, if they accepted all the same moral principles and agreed on the facts governing their application, then there would never be an occasion for sanctions and censorship to be imposed on journalistic practices. Free information would reign and would never be put to dangerous use.

We know, however, that there are rogue journalists, and we know that all of the freedoms extended for proper use to the members of a society are subject to abuse. Pornographers and purveyors of hate literature shelter under the freedom of the press as well as legitimate journalists pursuing the trail of truth for the sake of providing important information in the public interest. The right to bear arms, freedom of religion, freedom of assembly, and other rights and freedoms, by virtue of having wide latitude, are always subject to exploitation by weak and unethical persons for their own aims. These abuses obviously fall outside the purposes for which the rights and freedoms were originally established. Rogue journalists, as a further implication of professional journalistic ethics, need to be properly restrained and sanctioned when they violate the moral obligation of journalists to provide relevant truth telling in the public interest. If not all journalists are virtuous friends in Aristotle's sense, then we, together with the worldwide community of journalists, have no choice but to bring offenders before the law and to impose other kinds of restrictions on and corrections to their actions. We must not shrink from such enforcement of moral obligations, while still preserving the freedom of the press to the greatest extent possible. If we value a free press and a free society, then we must recognize that every moral infraction of journalistic responsibility degrades the public conception of the profession and threatens by association to bring down coercive censorship on the profession as a whole. Self-censorship and self-regulation as a goal of journalistic ethics is a preemptive way to avoid coercive external censorship and external regulation. If properly managed, even these apparently counter-progressive measures can help proactively to preserve the freedom of the press and with it the liberty of a free and open society.

If our reasoning is correct, then, as a general rule, censorship of the press is to be strenuously resisted as incompatible with the need for a free flow of information in a free society. The professional moral obligation of journalists to maximize the discovery and publication of relevant truths for the public good is indefeasible. This means that the obligation itself never disappears or ceases to hold true, even though in extraordinary circumstances it can temporarily be outweighed or overridden by more highly prioritized moral obligations impinging on all members of a society rather than on particular individuals in their professional capacity as journalists. Searching out the real reasons for withholding information from the public reveals that it may be more difficult to justify even the kinds of censorship that have traditionally been judged morally permissible if not obligatory. The criterion is that there must be sound arguments in support of the higher prioritization of suppressing rather than publishing information in order for any proposal to censor the news to override the primary moral imperative of journalists to maximize relevant truth telling.

The slippery slope that threatens to erode the freedom of the press begins with cases that are supposed to be obviously justified instances of censorship. These can nevertheless carry the potential for nibbling away at the freedom of journalists to gather and report the news by setting bad precedents. We need not respond to these incursions by dismissing out of hand the possibility of there being any justifiable cases of censorship. We have considered three principles for limiting the pernicious effects of censorship when it is rightly shown to be absolutely necessary to protect greater social interests. These include: (1) a reminder of the reasons why the freedom of the press is to be cherished and protected in a free society; (2) an affirmation of the indefeasibility of the professional journalistic moral obligation to maximize relevant truth telling; and (3) the advancement of a plausible distinction between morally justified and unjustified kinds of or reasons for censorship. In cases where censorship is morally approved, it should be accompanied with provisions for a definite endpoint or discontinuation and, in some instances, with stipulations as to when circumstantially suppressed information might again be published; generally, such a statute of limitations should expire immediately after its full disclosure can reasonably be assumed to be no longer sufficiently harmful to justify its continuing to be withheld.

The preferability of voluntary or internal self-censorship over and above involuntary or coercive external censorship can be regarded as an extension of the ordinary exercise of intelligent choices about what news events to cover and in what way that are made by news reporters and editors in meeting their professional responsibilities every day. The decision as to when voluntary censorship should be exercised, as a final note, should always be made on the basis of sound moral judgment with good reasons for withholding information or presenting it in a certain way. This may sound reassuring, but it remains an open question in every particular situation as to what constitutes sound moral judgment and what constitutes a sufficiently good reason for voluntary censorship of the news. These controversies are a focus for never-ending debate about the legitimacy of censorship of any kind, and it would be unrealistic to expect a set of simple criteria for deciding when voluntary or involuntary censorship is morally justified. The guidelines that have been suggested for prioritizing conflicting obligations to report or withhold information indicate how extreme cases are reasonably adjudicated, but they are not watertight. We must accordingly be prepared for disputes and disagreements when conflicts arise, as they are certain to do, between the public's right to know and its right to be protected by its social institutions. Voluntary or self-censorship in any event should always proceed on the basis of what are sincerely accepted as good reasons for withholding information in the greater public good and not out of fear that if the material is not voluntarily censored then it may be subject to coercive involuntary or external censorship. The reason for this qualification is clear when we reflect that to act otherwise, out of concern for the possibility that external censorship will be imposed if voluntary censorship is not enacted, is incompatible with the fundamental requirements for a meaningfully free press.

chapter six

Protection of
Confidential Sources

The argument in support of protecting confidential sources derives from an application of the fundamental moral principle of journalistic ethics. News reporters have an obligation to provide relevant truth telling in the public interest. This responsibility attaches by implication to anything required in practice in order to discover and transmit newsworthy information to news consumers. The problems connected with confidential sources are particularly interesting in this regard. Here we explore the ethics of using and protecting anonymous news information sources. The issues are more complex than may at first appear, but in the end we shall conclude that the use and protection of confidential sources is both a moral right and responsibility for professional journalists.

CONFIDENTIALITY

The reality of journalistic investigation is that privileged information sources are often needed to discover the truth about events that are not immediately accessible to casual observation. Privileged sources provide essential information to news reporters in fulfilling their fundamental moral obligation to maximize relevant truth telling.

Insiders with special knowledge of subjects are often the only persons who are in a position to give reporters the information they need in order to transact their journalistic responsibilities. Often these sources are confidential in the sense that their jobs or other interests are vulnerable if it should become known that they have provided information to a journalist. Privileged sources accordingly have typically been treated as inviolate, not subject to revelation by journalists who rely on their information except under roughly the same extreme sorts of circumstances that are invoked to justify violations of the freedom of the press in external acts of censorship.

We now turn to the moral implications of privileged sources in news reporting. We examine the basis for their confidentiality in journalistic ethics and the question of whether and under what conditions there can be morally justified exceptions to the protection of privileged sources. There are moral dilemmas arising from the desire to preserve the anonymity of journalistic informants. We must accordingly try to determine the implications for journalistic ethics of the use of privileged sources in reporting the news.

PRIVILEGED SOURCES OF NEWS INFORMATION

The truth is out there, but not everyone has access to the facts. News reporters are obligated to seek out the truth about matters of interest to the public they serve in whatever way they can, consistent with other relatively prioritized moral obligations. Although not all news stories require the use of privileged sources, there are many instances in which they do. Let us consider a typical situation in which privileged sources need to be consulted in order to gather the vital facts of an important story.

Here is a composite scenario. Suppose that a chemical company is secretly and illegally dumping dangerous chemicals in a watershed. The only person who knows what is happening and is willing to talk about it is a bookkeeper who cannot afford to lose her job in a troubled economy and is worried about further retributions against her family. As a result, she is prepared to share the information with a news reporter only under conditions of absolute anonymity. The bookkeeper thereby becomes a privileged source of news information. The reporter, by informing the public about the corporate wrongdoing, can provide a valuable service to everyone affected by the illegal dumping. The information can only be obtained by assuring the bookkeeper that her identity will never be revealed. This, other things being equal, is a reasonable condition under the circumstances; by hypothesis it is the only possibility for the reporter to find out what needs to be known.

We can easily imagine the situation. A reporter receives a telephone call saying that someone has important information about an environmental hazard perpetrated by a local company. The reporter wants details and proof. The caller, whom only we know as the bookkeeper, is willing to provide the information, but only if the reporter promises to protect her anonymity. The reporter pledges to do so and begins to collect the data and write and produce the story. The story is published, the public is outraged, action is taken, and the company is fined and prohibited from continuing its illegal dumping of chemicals. The environment is protected, the reporter wins a Pulitzer Prize, the bookkeeper keeps her job, and all is as it should be.

A complication arises, however, if we take the example in a further direction. What might happen if the government decides that in addition to stopping the company from dumping its chemicals it also wants to prosecute the company and its officials in court? In preparing its case, the prosecutors for the government contact the reporter and demand to know how he first learned about the company's malfeasance. The reporter refuses to divulge his sources because of the strength of the promise he made to the bookkeeper. We then ask, from the standpoint not only of fundamental principles of journalistic ethics to provide relevant truth telling in reporting the news, but also of the overall interests of society within the larger framework of moral obligations to which reporters as responsible members of a society are subject, what should happen. Should the reporter be required under the law to divulge his sources? If he is so required, should he refuse and suffer the penalties, including fines, imprisonment, loss of his job or license, and the like, to stand his ground against efforts to force his compliance? Or should the reporter, from a moral point of view, simply turn over the information concerning his information source, as he is asked to do?

MORAL AND PRUDENTIAL REASONING

There are many issues at play in this example. It is important first of all to distinguish as theoretical ethical philosophers do between *moral* and *prudential considerations*. Roughly speaking, prudential considerations are reasons for what it is smart to do, given our interests and the things of value we want to protect, while moral considerations are reasons for what it is right to do.

The two categories do not always go together, although sometimes they do. Thus, I might choose to pay my taxes because I believe it is the morally correct thing to contribute my fair share to the maintenance of services in the society from whose protection I benefit, because I believe that I have a moral obligation to do so. Alternatively, I might believe that I should pay my taxes because I want to avoid the penalties of failing to pay, which could include heavy fines, confiscation of property, and even jail time. In the latter case, if those are my only motivations for paying my taxes, then I do not do so because I believe it is right to contribute financially to the common good, but because I believe it is smart to avoid the penalties for failing to comply.

While it is true that much of the motivation for human action involves prudential considerations, persons acting in their self-interests to secure gain or avoid pain, purely moral considerations, acting from a sense of what it is morally right to do, are also important factors in understanding human behavior. Sometimes persons do what they believe it is morally obligatory for them to do regardless of the consequences they may personally suffer when doing what they consider to be right does not happen to coincide with what is in their self-interests.

We are primarily concerned with journalistic ethics and the morality of decision-making having to do with privileged sources. Thus, we focus on moral reasons for whether the journalist should comply with or resist attempts to make him divulge his confidential sources. We nevertheless continue to recognize the fact that human agents are often disposed to act on prudential rather than moral considerations when the two do not happen to coincide. We are, therefore, not asking what it would be smart or prudent for the reporter to do, but what it would be morally right or morally obligatory for him to do when the government demands that he identify the confidential source of his information about the company's toxic dumping.

LEGAL PRESSURE AGAINST JOURNALISTS
TO REVEAL SOURCES

With this background in place, what conclusions should we begin to draw concerning the morally proper choices facing a reporter when a prosecutor tries to force him to divulge his confidential sources by yielding the name of his informant? We can ask more pointedly what any of us think we would or should do in such a situation, and then, more pointedly, ask why we think we would or should make one choice rather than another.

As we consider the journalistic ethics of privileged sources, we recognize that there are individual and more general professional implications to take into account. For the individual reporter, disclosing the name of a confidential informant is not only a breach of promise to the person who has provided information under the cover of anonymity, but has potentially further repercussions. If it becomes known that the reporter did not respect the informant's confidentiality, it is reasonable to expect that in the future informants who for one reason or another need to remain in secret will be reluctant to come forward to divulge what they know. This reduction in information flow for important news stories can obviously have a serious deleterious effect on the reporter's ability to meet his professional moral obligation to maximize relevant truth telling. There will then be stories he will be unable to cover because of the resulting dampening effect on his ability to get leads on interesting and important news events, for we are supposing that these by their very nature are generally not available without special inside information that only privileged sources can provide.

More importantly, by being the indirect cause of privileged sources withholding information, the reporter acts contrary to the fundamental moral obligation of all professional journalists and, indeed, of the journalistic profession. By indirectly causing potential valuable sources of news information to withhold what they alone know, the reporter does something that limits the amount and quality of journalistic truth telling on the part of any and all news investigators. To disclose privileged sources as such constitutes a clear violation of the fundamental principle of journalistic ethics. The disclosure of privileged sources by any single reporter can predictably have a chilling effect on the willingness of any and all potential confidential informants to provide leads and tell other reporters what they know and what would otherwise remain unreported and unavailable as useful information to the public. The result of bending to the will of prosecutors or others to reveal the identity of confidential news informants amounts to a betrayal of the trust on which all journalists everywhere frequently depend in order to fulfill their professional ethical obligation to inform the public.

It is a betrayal, moreover, that can inhibit not only their own personal individual ability to do their jobs, but something that can have a ripple effect that by precedent and loss of faith in the community limits truth telling for the profession as a whole. This likelihood makes it morally objectionable for journalists ever to disclose their privileged sources, regardless of the consequences, for the sake and especially for the moral health of professional journalism. To do otherwise is potentially to dry up a valuable fountain of information that the public has a right to know and that journalists have a primary professional moral responsibility to report. As an analogy, reporters who violate the trust of privileged sources who have the confidence to tell reporters what they know are like physicians with an obligation to prevent disease and heal the sick, who cripple their ability to meet these obligations by irreparably damaging their diagnostic equipment.

STANDING FIRM AGAINST COERCION FOR A FREE PRESS

What, then, in the scenario we have described, is the morally right thing to do for the reporter who has published the story on the chemical dumping and is now confronted with a demand by law to reveal his privileged information source? If the reasoning we have outlined above is correct, then it seems the only morally justified course of action for the reporter, at least from the standpoint of the responsibilities of professional journalistic ethics, is to refuse categorically to divulge the identity of his confidential informant and face the legal consequences.

An additional argument for this conclusion is found in the suspicion that the prosecutor could have an ulterior motive for demanding to know the reporter's source. The identity of the source might be sought not merely for the sake of more competently prosecuting the case against the chemical company, but possibly through a conflict of interest to discover who is responsible for the leaked information in order to exact retribution. A morally upright prosecutor would presumably never do so; but, unremarkably, not all prosecutors are morally upright, and a defending attorney for the chemical company might equally make such demands on the reporter. This could be done in order to weaken the prosecutor's case, to cast doubt on the reliability of the reporter's information in lieu of being able to question the informant directly in open court, or, acting again on behalf of the company, in order to facilitate its retribution against the informant, known in such circles as a whistle-blower, through employment sanctions, discrimination for promotion and pay increases, personal intimidation, or even more morally reprehensible and illegal acts of silencing and revenge, including acts of violence.

Under any of these imaginable outcomes, news reporters have a professional moral obligation to protect their confidential informants and privileged information sources. It is an obligation, moreover, that extends not only to the informants who rely on such protection if they are to offer information without risk of retaliation, but also the public whose interests journalists serve as information conduits from whatever information sources they may responsibly consult. We know that acting on such high professional journalistic moral principles many news reporters in the past have incurred legal and financial penalties. They have stood in contempt of court, paid fines, spent time in jail, and suffered other kinds of personal losses for the sake of upholding the protection of confidential journalistic sources. We can now understand such decisions philosophically from the standpoint of the recognition on the part of reporters that to do otherwise is to violate their primary moral mandate as journalists to report relevant truths in the public interest. To violate the trust of confidential informants would be a betrayal of their obligation to report the truth as best as they reasonably can. We should accordingly regard such morally courageous actions of news reporters as undertaken in defense of a free press. Without the continued trust of confidential sources in the preservation of their anonymity, the practical implication is that news reporting is likely to be systematically undermined.

Case Study 17

Journalistic Shield Law in American History

Richard F. Hixson, professor of journalism in the department of journalism and mass media at Rutgers University School of Communication, Information and Library Studies, writes the following in the *New York Times*, September 16, 1984, in the Late City Final Edition, New Jersey Weekly Desk, Section 11 NJ, p. 28:

> "New Jersey, where the country's second-oldest press shield law was enacted in 1933 (Maryland was first, in 1896), is among the more progressive states in recognizing this privilege.
>
> What is at issue is the journalist's right to protect the identity of sources who wish to be anonymous, as well as information contained in unpublished notes, tapes and photographs. It is comparable to the long-established privileges of lawyers, physicians, clergymen and spouses: All depend on confidentiality in their daily transactions. (This also extends to the principle that litigants should not interfere with a reporter's job by using reporters as a ready source of information in a lawsuit.)
>
> Since Peter Zenger was jailed for publishing anti-British articles in 1735 and a reward was offered to anyone who would reveal the source of Zenger's information, American journalists have fought against the forced disclosure of sources and confidential information. They argue that such disclosure would limit their access to news of public importance, and they consider source protection a part of the First Amendment.
>
> What may have been the first test of this principle in New Jersey came in 1779, when the upper house of the State Legislature registered a complaint against a satirical article that Isaac Collins had published in his *New-Jersey Gazette*.

Upset over what amounted to an anonymous attack by 'Cincinnatus' on Gov. William Livingston and the College of New Jersey (now Princeton University), the upper house demanded of Collins the true name of the author. It professed the belief that the 'Freedom of the Press ought to be tolerated as far as it is consistent with the Good of the People, and the Security of the Government established under their Authority.' "

There is more to the story, and the reader is recommended to read Hixson's article in its entirety. We fast-forward to this interesting later development:

"Late in 1981, a Superior Court judge ruled that neither the state shield law nor New Jersey's Constitution protected a newspaper from disclosing preliminary drafts of an allegedly libelous article during pretrial discovery. Nor would they protect the reporter from answering deposition questions about his or her knowledge and use of government reports that might have exonerated the plaintiff of the charges mentioned in the article.

Judge Robert T. Quackenboss held: ' The "shield law" was not intended to protect the editorial process as revealed by material selection decisions and preliminary drafts of a newspaper article.'

It wasn't long before the State Supreme Court, in *Maressa v. New Jersey Monthly* (May 1982), extended the shield to include the entire editorial process. The court held that the law 'establishes an absolute privilege in libel action not to disclose sources, editorial processes and other confidential information involved in publication of an alleged libel. The notes, memoranda, rough drafts, editorial comments, sources and other information . . . are included in the shield law's protection.'

This interpretation makes the shield law an absolute privilege in civil actions for libel, while in criminal actions the press has a qualified privilege that protects confidentiality if the four-part test is met and the Sixth Amendment is not deemed more important than the First.

'New Jersey is the state in which to be,' said Katharine P. Darrow, general counsel of the *New York Times*, following the Maressa decision.

New Jersey has moved to the front of the class in protecting the press from the disclosure of sources and other editorial decisions.

The author reminds us explicitly in other unquoted parts of his essay that currently every state in the United States sets its own standards for protecting the press and that no federal law, let alone international shield laws, exist to safeguard a reporter's papers and records. Journalists and their supporters who regard shield laws as an important item for legislative agendas and judicial endorsement both at home and globally can work to help publicize the importance of helping to sustain and enhance the liberties of a free press to whatever extent is consistent with the society's other legitimate interests, as the 1799 upper house of the State Legislature of New Jersey rightly put it (their application of the principle being something else again): 'Freedom of the Press ought to be tolerated as far as it is consistent with the Good of the People, and the Security of the Government established under their Authority.' "

QUESTIONS

1. Consider the slogan in the final quotation above. If this is what the upper house of the New Jersey State Legislature in 1799 believed, then why would they demand of Collins the name of the author of the satirical article signed only as "Cincinnatus"? Did they truly believe that using the instruments of law to force Collins to disclose his confidential source was justified as otherwise inconsistent with the "Good of the People, and the Security of the Government established under their Authority"?

2. Could the author of a newspaper satire ever reasonably be regarded as such a threat to the good of the people—in this case, it appears, to only a few powerful people offended by the satire—or the security of the government? What are some of the deeper lessons of the 1799 New Jersey resolution?

3. Do these surrounding facts in any way detract from the value of the slogan itself? Do we not approach a resonant concept of shield law if we guarantee to protect the press from any incursion especially into its confidential sources except when the good of the people or the security of the government is truly at stake?

4. If the answer is yes, then how do we as journalists decide and how do or should we expect government officials to decide what is or is not a legitimate threat to the good of the people or the security of the government? If the answer is no, then what do you think might be an alternative formulation of a shield law concept or principle?

5. If you think that a shield law needs to be more specific, try to spell out what a good statement of the law should include. We have assumed that a shield law ought minimally to extend legal protection to a journalist's confidential sources except in extreme circumstances where to respect their confidentiality would not be in the public interest, however this concept is applied. The application is what is at issue. What would be an appropriate set of guidelines for journalists who wanted to protect their confidential sources to the maximum extent possible while still observing their obligations to report news in the public interest? When does refusing to disclose a confidential source cross over into violation of what is in the public interest? Who should decide this and with what moral precepts and standards in mind?

SHIELD LAWS AND EXCEPTIONS TO PROTECTION OF CONFIDENTIAL SOURCES

In the United States, on the whole, the courts have supported and respected the rights of journalists to privileged sources and have not required them to disclose the identities of confidential informants except under the most extreme circumstances. Legislation protecting privileged sources in both journalism and law enforcement, we have seen, are generally designated by the self-explanatory name as *shield laws.*[1]

Interestingly, the circumstances typically cited as providing exceptions to shield laws fall roughly into the same categories of the overwhelmingly greater interests of society in terms of national security or the like that are invoked in those exceptional cases that have sometimes been thought to justify involuntary censorship. Some of the most famous privileged sources in the history of modern journalism have remained anonymous, their confidentiality protected even after many years. The insider source that first leaked information leading to the Watergate scandal investigations of illegal wiretapping and cover-ups by Richard M. Nixon's White House staff, known only by the code name "Deep Throat," has only recently been revealed after many decades as W. Mark Felt, a former number-two official at the FBI. That is the kind of moral respect for confidentiality that inspires whistle-blowers and privileged sources to continue to contact journalists with inside information that would otherwise never be reported, or at least not in the most timely fashion when its publication can do the most good.

MORAL COMPLICATIONS IN OBSERVING CONFIDENTIALITY

There is nevertheless another side to the journalistic ethics of privileged sources; indeed, there are several sides of the problem that we have yet to explore. First, we should note that prosecutors, defense attorneys, judges, magistrates, and other persons in authority have moral obligations and responsibilities that also need to be taken into consideration where the ethics of privileged journalistic sources is concerned.

Non-journalists as citizens of a free society also have moral obligations toward journalists and the practice of journalism. The reason, as we have seen, is that journalism serves the interests of a free society that all its members have a moral obligation to respect. Such obligations more particularly include not obstructing free interactions between journalists and privileged information sources. Members of a free society are morally obligated as a consequence not to demand, except perhaps under the most extraordinary circumstances, to know the identities of confidential informants and not to impose penalties or use the coercive machinery of the law to try to force journalists to disclose their secret sources of information. The issue of how journalists should respond if legal or

---

[1]The existence of so-called "shield laws" for the protection of privileged sources and confidential informants in journalism have largely followed the lead of similar legislation designed to protect informants in criminal proceedings. Surprisingly little has been written on the special problems of confidential information sources for the press, although much of the relevant literature can be applied from a larger body of discussion in police investigations. See Madingen, *Confidential Informant.*

other sorts of pressures are exerted to make them reveal their sources remains an important topic for the applied ethics of professional journalism. The reality once again is that all persons in a society do not always live up to their moral obligations toward journalists, so that journalists need to consider how from a moral point of view they believe they should respond to such demands.[2]

However, another important aspect of the moral responsibility of journalists that arises in connection with the problem of privileged sources concerns the question of how journalists might use the confidentiality privileges of journalistic sources as a shield behind which both they and their informants might sometimes shelter in order to avoid accountability for the contents of their news reports. To pursue the conversation on this note, let us begin with yet another extreme kind of fictional case in order to illustrate the kinds of abuses of privileged sources that might be made.

Suppose that a rogue reporter, interested in gaining fame or notoriety, decides to make up a story involving non-facts and nonevents that never happened, but that make for excellent reading or viewing. There is no hard evidence for the claims made in the story, which, let us further suppose for the sake of having a concrete example before us, concerns a politician having accepted a bribe from a foreign government to vote for a piece of legislation favoring that nation's trade agreements. The news reporter issues the story that is printed or airs and attracts an enormous amount of attention. When questioned about her grounds for making the assertion of bribery, the reporter claims privileged sources and argues that she cannot reveal the identity of the confidential informant, perhaps repeating some of the arguments we offered in the previous case to justify the sanctity of journalistic privilege.

Thus far, it is already clear that the journalist has violated the moral obligation of professional journalistic ethics to tell the truth, since by hypothesis the bribery allegation is a complete fabrication. The question is whether privileged journalistic sources ought generally to be off-limits to public scrutiny, given that the assertion that there exists an anonymous confidential informant who has disclosed the information provides cover for rogue journalists who are simply making things up and, potentially, very damaging things at that. If journalistic privilege is inviolable, then there is no way to prevent unethical journalists from exploiting its protections for their own unscrupulous behavior. Let us therefore consider instead a very real and recent case

---

[2]Recent controversies surrounding the use of confidential sources in journalism and refusals on the part of journalists to reveal informants' identities under legal pressure and while being held in contempt of court are dramatized by the recent case of Vanessa Leggett. See the cover story of the electronic *Montana Journalism Review*, 31, 2002, titled "Vanessa Leggett: Defying Court Subpoenas in the Name of the First Amendment." Similar stories have appeared in the *American Journalism Review* and civil rights publications concerning a potentially precedent-setting situation of interest to all professional journalists. The moral philosophical principles we have articulated in this chapter justify resistance even at great personal cost for journalists who are determined to uphold the right of withholding the identities of informants who prefer to remain confidential.

involving a reporter being jailed for refusing to reveal a confidential source that was involved in investigating a news report.

Case Study 18

Judith Miller and the CIA Leak

Here is a dramatic real-life case study involving prosecutorial efforts to force former *New York Times* reporter Judith Miller to reveal her confidential sources concerning the outing of a CIA operative. The situation involves many intertwined moral issues. The basic facts are these.

Valerie Plame was identified as a CIA operative in a news column written by Robert Novak, a CNN contributor and former "Crossfire" program co-host, which appeared in *The Washington Post* in July 2003. Plame is the wife of an outspoken critic of the George W. Bush administration's policy in Iraq. Novak cited two unidentified senior Bush administration officials as his sources. Special prosecutor Patrick Fitzgerald was later assigned to oversee the federal investigation into who leaked the identity of undercover CIA officer Plame. Coincidentally or more sinisterly, Novak's column was published shortly after Plame's husband, former U.S. Ambassador Joseph C. Wilson, disputed the White House's claim that Saddam Hussein's government in Iraq had sought to obtain uranium in Africa in an effort to develop a nuclear weapons program.

Matthew Cooper, a reporter for *Time* magazine, wrote an article for *Time* naming Plame as a CIA agent, for which Judith Miller at the *New York Times* collected research although she did not write about the incident herself. Miller joined the *New York Times* in 1977 and was part of a news investigative team that won a Pulitzer Prize in 2002 for its coverage of global terrorism. Plame's husband Wilson in turn wrote a July 6, 2003 article in the *New York Times*, claiming that his wife's name had been leaked as retribution for his criticism of the White House. Miller was eventually subpoenaed and ordered to testify about how she obtained her information, which she refused to do, maintaining journalistic privilege in the use of confidential sources.

On October 26, 2005, U.S. Federal District Judge Thomas Hogan ordered Miller jailed in contempt of court for refusing to testify to a federal grand jury investigating the leak of a CIA operative's name. In particular, Wilson refused to tell a grand jury about conversations about Plame she had with I. Lewis Libby, who was then chief of staff to American vice president Dick Cheney. Libby has since been charged in the incident with five indictments: one count of obstruction of justice, two counts of perjury, and two counts of making false statements.

He immediately resigned his position with the administration on October 28, 2005. Miller could have spent as much as four months in jail, until the grand jury's term expired. She was released on September 29, 2005, after eighty-five days, only when her confidential source absolved her of her promise of confidentiality; she then regarded herself as free to testify in the matter. Matthew Cooper at *Time* magazine was similarly charged, but avoided jail time by agreeing to testify, on the grounds that his source had immediately released him from his prior promise of confidentiality.

Arthur Sulzberger, Jr., publisher and chairman of the *New York Times* Company, originally announced that the company "will do all that we can to ensure Judy's safety and continue to fight for the principles that led her to make a most difficult and honorable choice." He urged Congress to "move forward on federal shield legislation, so that other journalists will not have to face imprisonment for doing their jobs." Floyd Abrams, a lawyer for Miller and the newspaper, declared that the reporter "should be honored" for serving jail time to protect a confidential source.

The paper, indeed, was initially supportive of Miller, and engaged in a long and costly legal battle on her behalf after her imprisonment. Eventually, however, it began to distance itself from her cause and criticized certain aspects of her reporting in the past. Miller, aged fifty-seven at the time, resigned her position at the *New York Times* in November 2005. In her letter of resignation, Miller did not cite disappointment over the *Times* waning support, but explained: "I have chosen to resign because over the last few months, I have become the news, something a *New York Times* reporter never wants to be."

As a further but no doubt not the final twist in this complicated and, at the time of this writing, still ongoing case, Robert Novak, who began the furor with his report concerning Plame, has declined to say whether he testified before the grand jury. He has nevertheless avoided contempt charges. In the meantime, *Washington Post* reporter Bob Woodward, who, along with his colleague Carl Bernstein, published the Watergate exposé that led to Richard Nixon's resignation on August 8, 1974, admitted on November 21, 2005 that he had kept a conversation with a Bush administration official about the identity of a CIA operative a secret for over two years and expressed regret about not having confided in his editor, Leonard Downie, Jr. Woodward did not reveal his information or its source until Libby was indicted. His source also released him from his promise of confidentiality. Woodward maintained that he had kept quiet because he "was trying to avoid being subpoenaed." He reported to CNN on November 22, 2005: "To get what's in the bottom of the barrel, you have to establish relationships of confidentiality with people at all levels of government. You have to establish relationships of trust."

QUESTIONS

1. Was Judith Miller right to refuse to testify to the grand jury until her confidential source released her from her promise not to reveal her source? Why or why not?

2. What justification might be given for journalists who risk incarceration for the sake of preserving the confidentiality of news sources? What general principles are involved, and how can they best be understood?

3. Does Robert Novak bear any moral responsibility for what happened to Miller? What about Matthew Cooper or Bob Woodward? It is easy to construe this case as one in which some reporters allowed a colleague to face penalties for the stories that they wrote or on which they reported. Does this seem to be what happened? What impact can such complications have from the standpoint of professional journalistic ethics? Who is really responsible for Miller going to jail? What should have been done, and what should have happened instead?

4. Did Special Prosecutor Thomas Hogan act properly by requiring Miller to reveal her confidential sources and then sentencing her to jail for contempt of court when she refused? What might and what should he have done instead? A representative of the judiciary in the United States has a moral and legal obligation to uphold the Constitution. Could his actions in this case be properly construed as failing to meet this requirement by trying to force a journalist to reveal her confidential sources? Hogan, in reaching his decision argued that (not quoted above): "We have to follow the law. If Miller were given a pass today, then the next person could say as a matter of principle, 'I will not obey the law because of the abortion issue' or the election of a president or whatever. They could claim the moral high ground, and then we could descend into anarchy." Is this a reasonable, morally well-justified argument, or did the judge overstep his legal authority in this matter? Does the argument that "we could descend into anarchy"—clearly a slippery slope objection— ring true, or does it sound like an exaggeration in the tug of war between prosecution and defendant by which journalists are sometimes coerced into violating their moral obligation to provide truth telling in the public interest?

5. How far would and should you be willing to go in order to protect a confidential source in reporting on politically volatile events? Should any reporter be prepared to spend time in jail in order to uphold the privilege of using confidential sources? Or should journalists capitulate to government demands that they reveal information whenever it happens to be in the government's interests for them to do so? What would such surrendering of journalistic prerogative entail in the long run for the value of a free and independent press as the fourth estate in a free society?

GUIDELINES FOR APPEALS TO CONFIDENTIALITY

One of the problems encountered by legal provisions to protect journalistic confidentiality affects all rights in a free society. How can we ensure the innocent and proper exercise of rights without thereby encouraging and lending aid and comfort to persons who are determined to abuse responsibilities and violate the rights of others? How can we defend the rights of journalists to make use of privileged sources without having to disclose their identities, while at the same time preventing rogue journalists unlimited license to abuse the right at the expense of truth telling?

Fortunately, there are practical guidelines that can help to set limits on the use and potential abuse of privileged sources. Following are a few suggestions with commentary:

1. Privileged sources should be used only sparingly; they should not become a mainstay of information for journalistic reporting.

It is the exception rather than the rule that a news story be broken by the revelations of an anonymous confidential informant. If a news reporter repeatedly makes use of mysterious sources and pleads that they are privileged as confidential, it is a warning sign of possible abuse. Journalists in such situations should be alert to the possibility that a colleague might be engaging in morally questionable reporting.

2. When privileged sources are used, they should, whenever and to whatever extent possible, be backed up and supplemented by nonconfidential publicly available information sources as an external check on their truth and reliability.

The ideal situation involving the use of journalistic privileged sources is one in which confidential informants only provide leads to newsworthy stories. This occurs when an informant tips off a news reporter to a fact or event that the reporter would otherwise not have known about or had any prior reason to investigate. The reporter then normally goes beyond the privileged source to gather publicly available information and evidence in support of the assertions to be included in the story.

In the case of the chemical dumping scenario, the informant might provide a lead or hint to the reporter that the dumping is occurring. After being informed, the reporter takes it upon himself to research the matter in conventional ways to gather the data needed to support the assertions to be made in reporting on the incident. In that case, the reporter does not rely entirely or even particularly strongly on the confidential informant alone. The reporter instead takes it merely as a clue that there is a story to be investigated of which he or she would otherwise have been unaware.

The advantage to such a preferred limited application of confidential sources is that the journalist need never indicate that anonymous information was used in the first place. The only basis for the reporter's story that need surface to public notice is then the publicly available information to which no privileged access is required and, hence, no need to invoke the right of journalistic privilege. If called upon to testify in court, however, the journalist might then be required to explain where the original information leading to the discovery of facts came from in the first place. Then there may be no choice under penalty of perjury except to admit that there was a confidential informant, and we are more or less back where we started. When there is no need for a journalist to indicate that a story was the result of receiving confidential information, the demand to disclose a confidential informant can sometimes be averted. It may not always be prudent or morally obligatory for a reporter to mention the fact that a confidential informant played a role in the investigative process, if the informant's information is used only to point the reporter in the right direction, after which the reporter independently gathers the necessary evidence. In other situations, on the contrary:

3. When journalists have only the information provided by a confidential informant to go by in reporting a news item, they should indicate the fact explicitly as part of the story and qualify the content of the report as only an unsubstantiated allegation made by an alternatively reliable informant or an informant of unknown reliability, depending on the circumstances.

By being forthcoming about the nature of the evidence supporting a news report, journalists avoid misleading their readers or viewers as to the limited verification a story carries and, perhaps, the limited extent to which they should lend credence to its content. An allegation made by a privileged source without further substantiation does not deserve to be considered a fact, and no one should be led to think otherwise by the way in which a news report is presented.

Readers or viewers should be alerted to the fact that the news they are about to ingest is nothing more than the allegation of a confidential informant. They should be apprised that the informant's identity is not going to be revealed and that the informant's veracity as a consequence has no way of being confirmed or disconfirmed unless or until further independent support is provided. In general, consumers of the news should not be misled concerning the limited extent to which a news report is intended as conveying substantiated fact or merely an allegation that the reporter has learned from a confidential source but has no other reason for believing to be true. The general principle here is that if readers are made aware of the limited evidential basis for a news report supported only by an unidentified privileged source, then they can make up their own minds as to what extent they choose to lend credence to its content.

What this means in practice for conscientious journalists is that privileged sources should only be used with great discretion. As a general rule, confidential informants should be consulted only in those situations where failure to report the information of a reliable confidential informant would be a worse disservice to their journalistic obligations than to simply withhold any information about the story unless or until independent confirmation of the allegations can be made. The upshot is that confidential sources should be offered as the basis for a news report only in rare circumstances where it would be a lapse of journalistic responsibility to say nothing at all about a matter that is of sufficient public importance rather than to say only that the reporter has been confidentially made aware of the facts. The appeal to privileged sources is not to be trivialized, but its use on the basis of these moral considerations is understood to be justified only by circumstances of utmost urgency.

The guideline should prevent the problem case we considered previously concerning a rogue reporter who tries to shelter behind journalistic privilege in order to perpetrate falsehoods. At most, reporters should be allowed by editorial and professional peer oversight to allege that such events have occurred as an otherwise independently unsupported allegation offered by a confidential informant, rather than as a reliably established fact.

More importantly, if the profession were to accept and abide by the proposed guideline, then the bribery story would not make it into the news in the first place. The only exception, contrary to what we have been supposing, is when, as we have said, it is so urgent to bring the information to the public's attention that it would be a greater infraction of journalistic principles to withhold the story unless or until it can be independently substantiated. The story in that case ought not to be published on the strength of being supported by nothing more than what is supposed to be the word of a confidential informant. If the story is published under these circumstances, then the persons who are editorially responsible for it should be subject to professional censure and appropriate penalties. According to the present proposal, they will then have acted unethically.

4. Journalists who suspect other journalists of abusing journalistic privilege should consider investigating and censuring their colleagues for the good of the profession.

As a chapter in the profession's self-regulation, journalists might be thought to have a further moral obligation to police themselves with respect to the irresponsible appeal to privileged sources. The difficulty of course is catching clever rogue journalists in the act, so that appropriate action can be taken. By reacting to abuses of confidential informants, the profession can only try to repair damage that has already been done. As with respect to all dangers, prevention is generally better than cure. We expect that the continued vigilant investigation and sanctioning of rogue journalists who abuse journalistic privilege to serve as a meaningful deterrent to journalists who might otherwise be tempted to take the easy road by falsely invoking the protection of privileged sources.

5. Questionable use of privileged sources should also be monitored within the profession by requiring individual reporters to share and check on one another's confidential informants.

Journalistic privilege protects confidential sources from public disclosure as well as disclosure to governmental agencies, courts and lawyers, executive agents, legislators, and other interested non-journalists. This, however, is not to say that responsible journalists within the profession cannot be alerted to one another's confidential sources for the sake of checking up on and verifying the reliability of the information provided by anonymous informants.

INTERNAL PROFESSIONAL OVERSIGHT FOR CONFIDENTIAL SOURCES

The precedent for such a practice is found in the confidentiality of physicians. We ordinarily expect that whatever we say to our doctor, or whatever a doctor learns about us through physical examinations and testing, is to be held in strictest confidence. To such an extent is this level of confidentiality maintained that most physicians will not even relate facts about the health of a patient to the patient's spouse, making exceptions only for incompetent patients under the administration of a caretaker.

We most definitely would not accept a physician's publicizing our health condition or personal facts about our circumstances to the general public or, say, to our friends or employers. This is not to say that physicians cannot responsibly share information about a patient's condition on a consultative basis with other responsible physicians for the sake of the patient's health. If your physician is a general practitioner and there is something about your recent examination that needs to be checked by an expert on internal medicine or respiratory diseases, then it is no violation of your right to privacy within the medical professional for your physician to consult about your case with another physician.

Can the same thing be said within the professional community of news reporters concerning the use of confidential informants? It need not constitute a violation of confidentiality for one journalist who has relied on the information provided by an anonymous source to reveal the identity of the informant, say, to an editor, for the sake of verifying at least that the informant exists and has provided sufficiently reliable information in the past to warrant publication with disclaimers of an anonymously reported news item. In practice, this is generally what happens in responsible news agencies. Most professional journalists do not want to stick their necks out in publishing a story on the basis of a confidential informant without independent confirmation that the informant exists and is in a position to offer credible information. The reputation of a news reporter is on the line with every report he or she makes. It is not only morally permissible but prudentially advisable for reporters to have at least some independent intra-professional approval of their use of confidential informants.

The recommendation here is somewhat stronger. The suggestion is to require reporters as a matter of professional ethics to have the identity of their unnamed sources shared with other journalists in a supervisory capacity when their appeal to confidential informants raises red flags that may indicate unsupported allegations or an abuse of journalistic privilege. The idea is that for a reporter to include a questionable use of information from a confidential informant in a published report the information should be cleared by an editor or senior colleague by having the reporter share enough information about the informant for the supervisor to determine that the source is real and credible. In many instances internal source-checking of confidential informants can occur without the reporter actually disclosing the informant's name or making a full disclosure of identity; in other cases the informant will need to be fully identified in order for the use of an anonymous source to be approved.

Is there a risk in such practice? It is always conceivable that an editor or another professional colleague of a journalist could reveal limited information about a privileged source with others outside the profession, with the public at large, or with prosecutors or governmental authorities who have demanded to know the informant's identity. The danger is ever-present in the sense that informants risk disclosure by any individual reporter in whom the informant confides. A news agency and the profession of journalism as a whole builds and protects its good will among potential confidential informants over a long period of time by not betraying their trust. They recognize that it is clearly in the interests of everyone involved in producing the news not to spoil the working relationships that may exist between informants and reporters, nor to handicap colleagues investigating stories for the same news agency. We should probably conclude that there is no greater problem of exposure in having other responsible journalists check on a colleague's use of confidential informants in questionable cases than having physicians share information on a consultative basis about what is otherwise strictly confidential information about a patient's personal medical history. It would nevertheless be unwise not to recognize that the more persons even among professional journalists who know the identity of a confidential informant, the more likely it is in principle for the informant's identity eventually to be revealed.

The same considerations hold with respect to all other challenges to an informant's confidentiality. There are many contexts in which news sources need to be protected from reprisals by criminals or by persons with political power, or merely from the bad feelings that result in revealing newsworthy information to the press about a friend, family member, or religious leader, to mention but a few of the most obvious categories.

Censorship and Disclosure of Privileged Sources

There is a parallelism between the circumstances under which privileged sources can be required to be disclosed and the circumstances under which it is morally permissible or even obligatory to coercively censor news reporting. This makes the protection of privileged sources in some ways the mirror image of censorship.

When do we think it is morally justified to censor the news? Typically, we argue, the only time it may be morally right to impose limitations on a journalist's freedom to investigate and publish information is when there is a more highly prioritized moral obligation to withhold specific information or types of information in specific circumstances that outweighs or overrides the journalist's fundamental moral obligation to maximize relevant truth telling. Such situations invoke the clause that truth telling must always be done in the public interest, however this is understood. The same is true, we shall now try to show, with respect to the circumstances under which it may be morally obligatory for journalists to reveal their privileged sources to legal or other governmental authorities. Here, too, we say that it is morally obligatory for journalists to reveal their sources when, but only when, a greater more highly prioritized moral value is served by revealing rather than concealing the identity of a confidential informant.

Case Study 19

Confidential Information about an Impending Medical Emergency

It is not hard to describe situations in which it might be morally obligatory for a journalist to disclose an informant's identity. Suppose that there is an impending disaster about to take place affecting a large number of persons who are certain to die if the authorities cannot uncover crucial information about the outbreak of a fatal and highly infectious disease. A health organization has been covering up the facts in order to conceal their incompetence in having accidentally released a virus on which they had been experimenting to find a cure.

The conspiracy need not take place with the knowledge of the administrators. It might be the result of an irresponsible laboratory director, one of whose assistants is aware of the facts and has gone to the press as a whistle-blower, but has demanded confidentiality for fear of reprisal and has not revealed all that he knows. In particular, we may suppose, the lab assistant has told the reporter that the deadly virus has been released, but has not included additional facts that would be essential to containing the virus, such as the specific strain of virus, the exact date of its accidental release, and the exact location where the outbreak occurred.

The reporter publishes the story, and the public is appropriately alarmed. The authorities want to take action, but they do not know what to do in order to prevent an epidemic. The reporter contacts the informant again, but he does not want to disclose these further facts because he thinks that then the laboratory director will be able to deduce that it was he who alerted the press about the accident. Under these circumstances, it is easy to make a convincing case that the reporter has an overriding moral obligation to disclose the informant's identity to the authorities so that they can question him more effectively with all the resources of the law in order to discover as quickly as possible what they need to know to forestall a biohazard catastrophe.

QUESTIONS

1. Would the medical emergency described warrant disclosing the identity of a confidential informant? Why or why not?
2. What criteria might reasonably be applied in order to decide what kind or what scope of potential emergency justifies disclosing a confidential informant's identity? How can we prevent the acknowledgment of such possibilities from degenerating into a slippery slope, the outcome of which is to undermine the use of any and all confidential informants?
3. Should confidential informants acknowledge their moral responsibility to risk having their identities revealed in order to avert disasters? What can or should journalists say to confidential informants with respect to the limits within which they are willing to protect their anonymity? Would confidential informants be likely to continue to provide information under these circumstances and with such qualifications?
4. Describe a unique case study of your own in which it would be morally ambiguous as to whether the identity of a confidential informant should or should not be revealed. What are the issues involved in trying to decide whether or not to disclose the informant's identity to the public or to government officials? Where should we try to draw the line between protection of confidential informants for the sake of good journalistic practice and situations that demand disclosure in the greater public interest?
5. Decision-making about the unconditional protection or disclosure of confidential informants is sometimes referred to as making a judgment call. Is there anything wrong with making such judgments by practicing journalists? Can journalists avoid engaging in sound practical moral judgments in this and other situations? Is there any way to help assure that journalists will make morally acceptable judgments in dilemmas involving the protection or disclosure of the identities of confidential informants?

BALANCING PROTECTION OF SOURCES AND THE GREATER PUBLIC GOOD

With a little imagination, we can expand the list of situations in which the moral obligation to protect privileged sources can be rescinded for the sake of a greater social good. As in the case of censorship, we need to consider

the problem of a slippery slope in which an incremental erosion of the protection of the identity of confidential informants in the case of emergency
situations, like a plague outbreak, terrorist threats, or nuclear meltdown,
leads to less and less extreme cases, through a series of increasingly bad
precedents, until finally there is no protection left at all for the identities of
confidential informants.

The solution for the problem of protecting privileged sources is much
the same as for the slippery slope leading from uncontroversial extreme cases
to total censorship of any and all news. It is necessary in both cases above all
to establish a principled basis for distinguishing between morally permissible
and morally impermissible applications of whatever kinds of controls are
envisioned. We can put the brakes on what is otherwise an unstoppable
descent down a slippery slope by advancing a plausible reason for allowing
some morally necessary exceptions to what is otherwise an unassailable
moral right to free and uncensored news reporting and whatever is reasonably entailed by the journalistic imperative. In the present case, the general
protection of the identity of confidential informants and privileged journalistic sources needs to be safeguarded by identifying a sound basis for deciding
when it is and when it is not in the vital public interest to require journalists to
reveal what would otherwise be their confidential sources. Protection of confidential sources is not unconditional, but, where reporters recognize the
moral imperative for truth telling in the public interest, depends on the larger
social circumstances in which the information is conveyed.

What principle is required in the case of anonymous sources to allow
some morally justifiable exceptions without giving away the store? We can
say in abstract terms as before that journalists are morally obligated to reveal
the identity of their confidential sources when, but only when, the obligation
to protect sources is outweighed or overridden by a more highly prioritized
moral obligation that applies not specifically to journalists but to any morally
responsible person as a member of society. We may wonder and debate about
precisely what moral obligations override the default journalistic moral
obligation to protect privileged sources. There are bound to be disputes and
disagreements about what situations if any warrant the suspension of the
maximal truth telling justification to protect privileged journalistic sources.
The epidemic, terrorist, and nuclear disaster scenarios are obvious and hopefully uncontroversial examples, but where does such disclosure stop?
How can we draw the line beyond which journalists would be fully within
their moral rights to refuse any attempt to make them disclose their confidential sources?

The general principle as before is that there must be a sound philosophical argument establishing that a moral responsibility for a journalist to
reveal the identity of an anonymous informant outweighs the moral obligation always to maximize relevant truth telling, given the role that protecting
confidential sources plays in gathering all the news the public needs. This

we say sets a robust requirement that does not permit the pell-mell slide down a slippery slope from uncontroversial cases in which the moral obligation for journalists is to protect confidential informants from identity disclosure to the opposite extreme at which it is morally obligatory or at least morally permissible to reveal the names of any and all privileged sources.

Summary

Can we not, however, say something more concrete about exactly where the distinction between permissible and impermissible disclosures of sources is to be found? The answer depends on the interests of society in preserving both confidentiality and whatever values might circumstantially be in conflict with the freedom of the press.

There is more at stake in the erosion of trust among potential whistle-blowers in a society than merely whatever harm they might personally suffer as individuals if their identities are revealed after leaking newsworthy information to journalists. If that were the only calculation that needed to be made, then we could simply add up the disadvantages to be suffered by the informant if the informant's identity were to be revealed against the disadvantages to be suffered by other persons in the community if the informant's identity were not to be revealed. In that case, if, for example, the informant is likely to be killed if his or her identity is disclosed, while at least two other persons are likely to be killed if the informant's identity is not disclosed, then according to moral principles that decide ethical questions on the basis of the total resulting pain or pleasure resulting from an action or a rule governing actions of this type, it should be clear that the informant's identity ought to be revealed.

Things are not this simple, fortunately or unfortunately, for a number of philosophically interesting reasons. The disclosure of confidential sources, as we have seen, through its chilling effect on the willingness of other potential informants to provide newsworthy information, can have a much broader and indeterminately expansive negative effect on society's welfare. As a practical matter, we cannot know in advance how many other lives might be saved if only potential informants were confident about the trustworthiness of journalists to put the information they can provide to good use for the public's benefit without revealing their identities if they do not choose to become known. It might indirectly cost a society an incalculable amount of pain and suffering unnecessarily to reveal the name of even one confidential informant. On the other hand, it seems reasonable to suppose that if the reasons for disclosing the identity of what had been a confidential informant are sufficiently well justified under the circumstances to a large part of the members of a society, then it is unlikely that revealing an informant's name will have much of an inhibitory effect on the willingness of other persons who prefer to remain anonymous from coming forward with valuable information they may want to contribute.

Although some informants undoubtedly provide information for the sake of receiving some kind of material reward, most do so because they feel morally compelled to prevent an injury or injustice from occurring. They will, as a rule, at least be similarly morally motivated to communicate with news reporters, while preferring to remain anonymous, on the assumption that their confidentiality will not be broken except under the most extreme and probably unforeseen conditions. We have been assuming all along that the reasons that would morally justify disclosing a confidential informant's identity would be accepted by a large percentage of the morally responsible members of the society, which is likely also to include future confidential informants. We suppose that the informant is morally responsible enough to want to alert a news reporter to a situation in which something morally wrong would otherwise occur, even if extreme circumstances morally compel a reporter to reveal a given informant's identity.

We should find it reasonable, then, to suppose that most morally responsible confidential informants will also recognize that extreme circumstances might require abandoning their protective veil of anonymity and that in most such cases they will be satisfied to comply with the request for further details about what they know. In many instances, a governmental agency that needs to further question a confidential journalistic source should be able to do so without further revealing the informant's identity to the public at large. Even if an informant is personally not persuaded by moral considerations that qualify their right to remain confidential when it is superseded by greater moral obligations involving a society's vital interests, the reasoning by which their confidentiality is overridden is likely still to hold sway with many if not most or even all other potential informants. The result is that morally responsible informants for the most part will probably not be deterred by an occasional well-justified disclosure of the identities of other informants. As a rule, such persons should generally continue to have good reasons to expect that except in the most extraordinary extreme circumstances their preference to remain anonymous will be respected by the community of journalists, thus mitigating any deterrence to their coming forward.

It is an important part of professional journalistic ethics, as a result, for all morally responsible news reporters to sustain such expectations by protecting their confidential information sources as completely and with as few exceptions as possible. They should nevertheless recognize and be prepared to act on the possibility that under uncommon circumstances their professional obligations to protect an informant's identity might be outweighed or overridden by more highly prioritized moral obligations to which they are also subject as members of a society acting as journalists in the greater social interest and for the greater social good.

chapter seven

Journalistic Respect for Privacy

In this chapter we consider another controversial aspect of journalistic responsibility in the public interest. News reporters gather information about many things that some persons would prefer to keep private. What are the limits of individual privacy as they relate to the journalistic mandate to provide maximum truth telling? When do journalists cross the line between legitimately newsworthy information and intruding on other individuals' rights not to have certain facts about themselves known? We shall establish practical criteria for respecting the privacy of figures in the news within the framework of professional journalistic ethics.

PRIVACY IN A PUBLIC WORLD

The zeal to discover and publish interesting facts can lead to certain kinds of moral abuses, even when the public's legitimate interests are served by a journalist's activity. There seems to be an ethical conflict once again for news reporters working to fulfill their primary moral obligation to maximize information delivery. If the public is interested in the private lives of political, sports, and entertainment celebrities or, indeed, of anyone at all, and if there are profits to be made in invasive types of news coverage, should journalists extend their investigations to the most intimate details of people's daily activities, of what such persons do when they think they are alone and unobserved?

CONSTITUTIONAL BASIS FOR THE RIGHT TO PRIVACY

There is often said to be a right to privacy, although different cultures at different times have had very different ideas about whether privacy is an important value. Some societies seem not to possess anything like the modern concept of privacy. The U.S. Constitution does not include the right to privacy explicitly as such in the Bill of Rights, but it has generally been interpolated as implied by the other rights considered collectively to be extended to citizens.

To such extent is this true that it was by reference to the right to privacy that the U.S. Supreme Court in its 1973 *Roe v. Wade* decision acknowledged a woman's right to abortion in the first trimester of pregnancy on grounds of a constitutional protection of privacy. Justice Harry Blackmun explained in the majority opinion report that the principle involved is an application of the Fourth and Fourteenth Amendments to the Constitution, interpreted as conferring a fundamental right to privacy.[1] The Fourteenth Amendment in particular provides for due process under the law. The Fourth Amendment guarantees that: "The right of the people to be secure in their persons, houses, papers, and effects, against unreasonable searches and seizures, shall not be violated, and no Warrants shall issue, but upon probable cause, supported by Oath or affirmation, and particularly describing the place to be searched, and the persons or things to be seized."

As information technology becomes increasingly sophisticated, the ability of ordinary citizens to conceal facts about their personal lives from public knowledge becomes more and more difficult. If there is a higher moral as well as American constitutional right to privacy, then we must try to understand its philosophical foundation and ask what relation professional journalism should take with respect to an individual's right to privacy when all facts of the person's life might potentially be newsworthy.

MORAL VALUE AND THE RIGHT TO PRIVACY

Why do many people value privacy? What, psychological reasons aside, is the moral justification, if any, for recognizing a moral right to privacy? There are several categories of arguments that might be considered in support of the ethical protection of individual privacy from various kinds of intrusion. We do not pretend to offer an exhaustive consideration of justifications for privacy, but only some of the most important reasons that might be mentioned in connection with journalistic ethics in three categories. We shall argue that the right to privacy is morally justified as: (1) the foundation and protection of individual freedom; (2) a presupposition of respect for persons as morally valuable ends in themselves; and (3) a requirement for personal happiness and avoidance of anxiety and discomfort.

(1) Foundation and protection of individual freedom

Let us consider each of these justifications in turn. The first argument indicated in item (1) holds that we ought to recognize a moral right to privacy because it is the ultimate foundation of individual freedom through which we protect political freedoms generally.

The reasoning here is straightforward. If we have no moral right to privacy, then individual freedoms cannot be protected because they cannot be effectively exercised. Consider the effect of having every aspect of our lives subject to public scrutiny. Suppose that we are interested in engaging in political activity. To do so we need to be able to meet with like-minded

[1]410 US 113 (United States Code, 1973).

persons to formulate plans as to what we may propose to do, communicate, rally support for a cause, compose and print leaflets or news releases, organize meetings, and many other things besides. If there is no privacy for our actions, then there can in principle be no place of retreat in which to undertake the kinds of actions that are necessary for meaningfully free political action. What freedom, indeed, can any person have if privacy is not first protected as a basic moral right? We, perhaps like the original members of the Constitutional Congress, may think of freedom as including the ability to take a stand against what we may perceive as abuses of power. Such freedom, in the form of an ability to protest and in other ways oppose objectionable practices, especially by the government but in principle by any powerful body, cannot realistically be exercised if every citizen's movements and actions are open to unlimited invasive search and seizure.

Acting freely presupposes being able when necessary to act lawfully against powerful forces in a society. To do this, in turn, we must be able, at least at certain times, to conceal information from those in power who would otherwise use the knowledge they have gained to control and limit every citizen's ability to challenge authority and counteract what they consider to be morally questionable applications of power. It is precisely for this reason that the founders of a free society represented by the American Constitution wrote into the ground rules for the new nation the right of a free press, free assembly, and the right to petition the government for redress of grievances. These rights, as a counterpoise to the possibility of abusive institutional power, cannot be vouchsafed if the government legally has the right to pry into all areas of citizens' lives to discover everything they are thinking and doing. It is only by preserving a private corner of our lives that we can preserve the possibility of counteracting corruption within society. To be free and able to do so requires protection from the collection of information that could otherwise thwart attempts to maintain the healthy checks, balances, and occasional challenges to authority that are essential to maintaining a free society's freedom.

The protection of the rights of American citizens "to be secure in their persons, houses, papers, and effects, against unreasonable searches and seizures," under the Bill of Rights' Fourth Amendment, recognizes the right to privacy as a matter of personal security. The government, according to the amendment, forbids unwarranted intrusions into private dwellings and belongings, especially personal papers, records, and related possessions, provides for protection of the private sphere in which persons live and prepare for actions, notably including their writings and such personal items as diaries, journals, letters, and other forms of communication. It is only if and when a specific charge against a person for the commission of a crime has been made, where there is probable cause for the search and seizure of specific related evidence, that such invasions of personal space are permitted under the law in the United States and in nations that have adopted similar protections of rights. There is a place of privacy protected by the right of persons against unwarranted search and seizure, a private area in the life of each law-abiding member of a society that society has no right to penetrate, concerning which the society has no business asking questions or poking about merely to satisfy its curiosity about what might or might not be hidden or happening there.

We have suggested that the right to privacy is an essential assumption of freedom, in the sense that without privacy there can be no other meaningful freedoms. Privacy in this regard is an individual's freedom to conduct at least a certain part of his or her life outside of the public eye. If, as we assume and as we have maintained throughout these discussions of journalistic ethics, we treasure individual freedom as intrinsically morally valuable, to such an extent that its moral status requires no argument, then anything that contributes to sustain freedom is itself morally justified by implication or extension as presupposed by other acknowledged freedoms. This, as we have now further concluded, is especially true of personal privacy. Information about ourselves, including whatever might be contained in our papers and other personal effects, in which we might record our thoughts or experiment with ideas, can sometimes be among our most important personal possessions. It would accordingly be an abuse of a government's power, contrary to whatever inherent moral rights the citizens of a free society can expect to have protected, for such things to be taken away without due cause or legal redress in case of infraction. It is by this argument that we uphold the moral justification to privacy as a precondition for other civil liberties and as a way of helping to assure their continuation in practice.

(2) Presupposition of respect for persons as morally valuable ends in themselves

We also say that a right to privacy is essential to the moral respect properly due to all persons as ends in themselves. Ethicists standardly distinguish between *intrinsic* and *instrumental value*. The distinction marks a difference between things that are valuable in and of themselves, regardless of their consequences, and things that are valuable only as a means to another end.

We generally suppose on the basis of this distinction that all persons are morally intrinsically valuable and not merely valuable as instruments to be used in accomplishing other ends. Another way to put the point is to say that persons and things that are intrinsically valuable generally are irreplaceable. In contrast, things that are only instrumentally valuable are replaceable. They have value for us only insofar as they contribute to the fulfillment of a given purpose, like tools or raw materials, for which any functionally equivalent counterpart will be just as good and just as valuable. If we agree that persons are intrinsically rather than merely instrumentally valuable, then we might come to regard the recognition of their right to privacy as part of what is entailed in the moral respect they are owed as ends in themselves. In failing to honor another person's privacy, we fail to show them the proper moral respect as intrinsically valuable ends in themselves. If we violate their privacy, we treat them instead merely as having instrumental value like tools or raw materials. In recognizing the proper moral respect due to other persons and their interests, we acknowledge a moral right to privacy.

It should be a matter for each person to decide whether or to what extent the intimate personal facts of his or her life are to be made known to other persons. Some individuals might choose to reveal everything about themselves, which they are obviously free to do. They may write a tell-all autobiography or invite videographers into their home to record every moment of every day of their lives, if that is what they want, or set up a webcam in their bedroom or bath. The point is that the decision is theirs to make. If we take it upon ourselves to discover and disclose facts involving how others live at home, the contents of their papers and effects, and what they do every waking or sleeping moment of every day, then we fail to show them adequate moral respect as persons who should be entitled to have control over such aspects of their lives by limiting at their discretion what other people can come to know.

If we wrest that level of personal decision-making away from other persons by prying into their existences, leaving them no corner of privacy free for themselves, then we are treating them merely as we do inanimate objects and nonhuman animals. For we ordinarily believe that we can investigate such things with full moral impunity to our heart's content. We believe ourselves morally entitled, for example, to study all the details of the lives of animals, their nesting and mating patterns and everything else about them, just as we think there is nothing morally objectionable about investigating and making use of inanimate objects in our possession that have no rights to withhold anything from our scrutiny. Where other law-abiding people are concerned, on the contrary, we generally assume that they have the right as individuals to reveal or conceal whatever and as much as they choose about themselves, according to their own purposes and preferences and without having to answer to others for their choice. If we do not acknowledge such a right to privacy on the part of other individuals, then we indicate by our actions that we do not consider them to be autonomous, self-ruling, or self-governing persons, capable and entitled by moral right to make decisions for themselves affecting what strangers in the outside world should be allowed to learn about them.

(3) Personal happiness and avoidance of anxiety and discomfort

Finally, a third moral justification for respecting another person's right to privacy revolves around the psychological fact that most people to a large extent and virtually all people to at least some extent seem to want to preserve some measure of privacy about themselves. They need and want to have time for themselves in which they are not accountable to others, when they can freely be themselves without worrying about how they are perceived and what other people are thinking about them.

We need not delve into amateur psychology to try to figure out why this is so. It is enough for present purposes simply to acknowledge the fact and ask what sorts of moral implications people wanting privacy in their lives may have for journalistic ethics. Many people for whatever reason are made uncomfortable, and may suffer psychological and even physical distress, when they are denied whatever level of privacy they seem to require. If we intrude on such persons' privacy, then we are depriving them of something that is of value to them, even if it is not something that we ourselves would value. It is just as though in that case we were to steal something that belonged to them from inside their homes or backyards, something in particular that is of very personal importance and signifying the most personal kind of value there could possibly be.

Ordinarily, we do not imagine that we are morally permitted to take away another person's possessions. We recognize that they have a moral right to enjoy and control the use of whatever personal assets they have legitimately come to acquire. This can be interpreted as including whatever private time they may reasonably choose to set aside for themselves, consistent with their other obligations. It can therefore include especially personal information concerning whatever it is they do during their use of private time. There is a sense in which time is all any of us really has to dispose of as we choose. We can only divide up what little time we have between work and the marketplace and family and friends and ourselves. If someone else dictates the use of our time by intruding into whatever private space and time remains, seeking to extract information about our private lives and private activities, then they are stealing something of great value that cannot be replaced.[2]

Nor should we as individuals be required to take desperate measures to escape from prying eyes and ears who want to learn things about us that we consider to be none of their business. This too causes undue trauma and anxiety for many persons and, as such, represents a kind of psychological pain. It can be an extremely unpleasant experience, from which every person has a right, except under extenuating circumstances, to be protected. It is normally morally objectionable to cause persons pain or psychological distress unless it is necessary to do so for the sake of fulfilling a more highly prioritized moral

---

[2]Difficulties in obtaining redress for violations of privacy are nevertheless not always straightforward. These hindrances raise questions concerning the extent to which the law is fully in harmony with moral expectations. See, for example, Trager and Dickerson, *Freedom of Expression in the 21st Century*, p. 208: "When freedom of expression runs up against someone else's interests such as reputation, privacy, or even the right to a fair trial, the court system generally provides a process whereby those differences can be worked out. In cases of libel and privacy, the injured person can sue. In the process of such suits, the courts will apply a myriad of rules, definitions and defenses to assist in balancing the right of expression against the other person's interests. In the United States, the courts have recognized that defendants need certain protections against frivolous suits to ensure that their expression is not chilled. Consequently, it is more difficult for people in the public spotlight to win libel cases. Privacy cases are not that easy to win either. In fact, some states do not even recognize the right to sue for certain types of privacy infringement."

obligation. This might include discovering information needed to save lives or avoid a catastrophe, although each case must be carefully considered to avoid setting bad social policy precedents. Just as I do not have a moral right to cause another person physical pain by punching them without provocation in the nose, so, similarly, I presumably do not have a moral right to cause another person psychological pain by such acts as invading their privacy.

Hence, it is morally objectionable to intrude on other persons' privacy if to do so knowingly causes them pain or psychological distress. It is also morally objectionable, we might add, if it costs them time, trouble, money, or other resources to prevent other people from snooping into their personal affairs. If we believe, as we should, that it is wrong to cause other persons unnecessary suffering, especially for the sake of our own gain or to satisfy our curiosity, and if we believe that to deliberately invade another individual's privacy against their will can cause them unnecessary suffering, then logically we must conclude that it is morally wrong without adequate justification to deliberately invade another person's privacy. It is morally wrong in that case, more particularly, to collect or publish information about what a person does in his or her private time, if to do so on the present thesis is likely to cause them undue psychological pain, discomfort, or distress, or if it costs them any personal asset with which they would otherwise not choose to part.

Case Study 20

Magazine Publication of Private Celebrity Wedding Photographs

The following selection is from a news story appearing in *The Guardian* (London), Final Edition, for May 19, 2005 concerning the unauthorized publication in the British magazine *Hello!* of private photographs from the wedding of film star celebrities Catherine Zeta-Jones and Michael Douglas. The article is written by Clare Dyer, legal editor for *The Guardian*.

> "*OK!* magazine must pay back more than £1m in damages won from its rival *Hello!* over 'spoiler' wedding pictures of Catherine Zeta-Jones and Michael Douglas, three appeal [court justices] ruled yesterday.
>
> In a judgment which media lawyers said would make it impossible for newspapers and magazines to protect their scoops, the court overturned the 2003 high court judgment in *OK!*'s favor.
>
> The judges ruled that *Hello!* had no liability to *OK!* for interfering with its exclusive by publishing snatched photographs by a paparazzo who infiltrated the celebrity couple's top-security wedding in November 2000.

The landmark judgment will also aid celebrities seeking injunctions to protect their privacy. . .

The original high court judgment against *Hello!* came after a six-week hearing in 2003 at which Ms. Zeta-Jones told how she felt 'devastated, shocked and appalled' when she realized unauthorized photographers had gatecrashed her wedding at New York's Plaza Hotel . . .

The appeal court judges, headed by the master of the rolls, Lord Phillips, held that the Douglases had a right to keep private those details of their wedding which did not feature in the photographs chosen by them for publication.

But it was the Douglases, and not *OK!*, who had the right to protect this privacy, he said.

It was not property which could be transferred to someone else, and so the high court ruling which concluded that *Hello!* was liable to *OK!* as well as to the Douglases was wrong."

QUESTIONS

1. What are the legal issues involved in this interesting case? How, if at all, do they relate to the morality of respect for privacy by journalists?

2. Originally, *OK!* magazine had exclusive legal rights to publish the Douglases wedding photographs, which *Hello!* magazine violated by taking their own clandestine photographs at the wedding. The court in England first ruled that *Hello!* owed a substantial penalty to *OK!* for infringing upon its agreement with the Douglases for exclusive publication rights and for which it had naturally made substantial payment. What does it mean from the standpoint of journalistic ethics for a higher court to have afterward ruled that *OK!* must repay the penalty to *Hello!*? What does it mean from the standpoint of the judicial protection of the right to privacy in the UK?

3. Do you agree with the *OK!* solicitors' position that the second decision in this case deprives journalists of protection for their prior agreements to exclusive publication rights? What is the exact legal principle by which the court reached its judgment, as reflected in *The Guardian* report? Can it be justified on grounds of professional journalistic ethics? If so, how? If not, why not?

4. Since the Douglases were prepared to have pictures of their wedding published in one particular magazine, on what grounds if any could they later object that unauthorized photographs appeared in another magazine? Do individuals give up their moral right to privacy if they permit any intrusion, or should they be entitled to maintain control over how, where, when, and what particular information about themselves is published?

5. Is the real issue in this case a matter of privacy or money? The Douglases accepted payment from *OK!* to have exclusive publication rights for their wedding photographs, and *OK!* sued *Hello!* for infringing upon that right. When the higher court reversed the lower court's penalty fine against *Hello!*, they argued that only the Douglases had the right to protect their own privacy through legal award, while at the same time acknowledging that *Hello!* did in fact violate their privacy by publishing unauthorized photographs of

their wedding. Do private individuals have the right in every case to determine which journalists or news sources are permitted to publish information
about them? Does this amount to a kind of censorship of the press? If so, is it
morally acceptable? Why or why not? If it is not morally acceptable, what
protections from invasions of privacy by the media remain to individuals?

JOURNALISTIC OBLIGATIONS TO RESPECT PRIVACY

Under any of the three theories for the moral justification of a right to privacy
that we have discussed there is an implication for the respect for individual's
privacy as a principle of journalistic ethics. Journalists are in a special situation
with respect to the general moral injunction against violating the rights of other
persons to privacy, because journalists are professionally charged with the job of
investigating, collecting, and publishing all types of newsworthy information.

The application of these general considerations concerning the concept
of privacy and the moral right to privacy has naturally attracted the attention
of philosophers writing about the problems of privacy and the protection of
privacy from journalistic investigation. Thus, Steven R. Knowlton writes in
this connection:

> There is no area in contemporary journalism that bothers students, and probably
> most other readers as well, as much as the journalist's apparent willingness to
> invade other people's privacy. Many believe that they see in journalists a cavalier
> attitude toward the sensibilities of those they write about, an indifference to—or
> even real pleasure in—the embarrassment and pain they cause with their probing
> questions, their intrusive microphones and harsh lights, their willingness to print
> and broadcast names and addresses and all manner of intimate details of people's
> lives. The question of privacy, therefore, is well worth exploring at some length.[3]

As a result, there are bound to be collisions and infractions of the right to
privacy in which journalists deliberately or inadvertently step across the fine
line between the information about individuals they are obligated to collect
and the information concerning individuals in their private lives that they
prefer to preserve from prying eyes and ears. The issue therefore arises
whether journalists despite their fundamental charge to report all facts in the
public interest are morally obligated not to collect or publish. The task for a
sound approach to journalistic ethics in this field is accordingly to establish
firm reasonable guidelines that will help to reinforce the exact distinction
between what is and what is not legitimate information to gather in news
reporting that will be fully respectful of an individual's moral right to privacy.

---

[3]Knowlton, *Moral Reasoning for Journalists*, p. 50. An interesting discussion of problems related
to freedom of the press among other encroachments on the right to privacy is found in *Protection
from Personal Intrusion and Privacy Protection Act of 1998: Hearings Before the Commitee on the
Judiciary, House of Representatives, One Hundred Fiftieth Congress, Second Session on H.R. 2448 and
H.R. 3224.* May 21, 1998. United States Congress. House Committee on the Judiciary.

INVESTIGATIVE JOURNALISM AND THE RIGHT TO PRIVACY

How, in the first place, shall we try to demarcate the distinction between legitimate news and violations of privacy? Exactly how far does an individual's right to privacy extend and how is it determined?

We can begin to make progress in this difficult area by eliminating some obviously inadequate answers and seeing in what more plausible directions they may point. It will not do first of all to allow news reporters to intrude into any aspect of a randomly chosen person's life merely on the grounds that there exists a readership or viewership that could or would have an interest in consuming whatever information might come to light. Market forces alone, presumably, should not be allowed to determine the distinction between what is private and what is fair game for journalists to investigate.

Nor will it do to permit the persons targeted for investigation to determine entirely for themselves what facts about their lives are to be considered off-limits to journalists. The reason why the latter basis will not serve is that it would permit individuals arbitrarily to block reporters from what could in principle be important information of public concern. If an example is wanted, we might cite the case of a politician who is involved in espionage, delivering military secrets to a foreign government, trying to shield himself or herself from legitimate journalistic investigation on the grounds that whatever dealings the politician may have had with members of another government are a sacrosanct part of his or her private life.

Somewhere between these extremes, of allowing journalists free determination of what is or is not private and of allowing individual persons to determine for themselves what is or is not private, the answer must lie. Where is the proper balance to be found? One clue is probably in the exact statement of the fundamental moral obligation of journalistic ethics for news investigators to maximize the total amount of *relevant* information they collect and report for the benefit of the public. Not all information that might be desired or for which a market exists can or should be regarded as relevant to the public interest or justified by considerations of contributing to the public good. Decisions here must reflect a fine appreciation of the exact sense in which information may be needed, for we do not want censorship to be rationalized as a restriction of information that is paternalistically judged not to be strictly relevant for or needed by the public.

We must in the first place develop professional standards for journalists to follow in choosing what kinds of stories they will investigate or take a hands-off attitude toward because they would infringe on a person's reasonable right to privacy. Thus, it does not seem intuitively to be warranted to try to discover precisely how and with whom an ordinary citizen has a personal conversation in a restaurant, even if it is a very interesting conversation, if there is no more important social issue at stake. Here we would say that such information, other things being equal, would not ordinarily be relevant to news consumers and, hence, would not fall under the journalistic obligation to maximize the investigation and reporting of all relevant information in the public interest. Similarly, it is presumably irrelevant to the general public to know what the health condition of any randomly selected person on the street is or what their sex life is like, however interesting it might be to read about or see such facts televised on the evening news. On the other hand, it is intuitively newsworthy, and hence something that falls under the journalist's moral obligation to maximize relevant truth telling, to learn about a conversation between a politician and a foreign agent to whom military secrets are being given or about the health condition of an important public figure.

VOLUNTARY DISCLOSURE VERSUS INVOLUNTARILY OBTAINED INFORMATION

As I write these words, CNN is reporting that American Secretary of State Colin Powell has been diagnosed with prostate cancer and will be undergoing surgery. Is it an invasion of Secretary Powell's right to privacy to have this information broadcast? A person's health, and in particular the condition of a gland indirectly associated with sexual performance, seems a rather personal matter.

Does society have a legitimate interest in knowing that this government official is believed to have this type of illness? There are several factors to consider. Although the story I heard did not include such facts, it is reasonable to suppose that the information was voluntarily provided by Powell or his press representative, probably in the recognition that the nation as a whole has a vital interest in knowing the health of a major government official. Let us imagine, however, for the sake of argument, that Powell or his press team did not willingly provide the information, but that a resourceful news reporter somehow discovered the fact. If its truth can be verified, does the reporter have the moral permission or even the moral obligation to report that the secretary has this type of cancer and will be undergoing surgery?

We can foresee strong arguments on both sides of the issue. For present purposes, we shall venture to suggest that the reporter does indeed have a moral obligation and hence the moral right and permission to publicize the fact that a visible public official on whom so much of the nation's business devolves and who is so close in the prescribed line of succession to being the chief executive will be having such surgery. The secretary of state, according to the U.S. Constitution, is fourth in line to the succession of the presidency. Article II, Section 1, Clause 6 of the Constitution authorizes Congress to establish a line of succession to the presidency in the event of simultaneous vacancies in the offices of president and vice president. In 1947, Congress adopted a law that places the following persons in the line of succession after the vice president: speaker of the house, president *pro tempore* of the Senate, members of the former president's cabinet in the order in which their departments were created. This makes the secretary of state fourth in line of succession to the presidency in the event of the death, disability, or resignation of those before the secretary. American citizens arguably then have a right to know if someone in this chain of succession to the highest office in the nation might be undergoing a serious medical procedure. The fact also serves the public interest in another way. By mentioning the circumstance under which a respected public figure has been diagnosed with a dangerous but treatable disease, the health condition of high-profile officials can inspire other persons to have themselves medically checked.

Where, then, should journalists try to draw the line between what is and what is not legitimate to report concerning the personal facts of a public figure like (now former) Secretary Powell or any other person in the public eye? We can immediately say, to begin, that any facts a person chooses to reveal, as is undoubtedly the case here, are legitimate for reporters to communicate if they deem them sufficiently newsworthy to interest their readers, listeners, or viewers. The problem of publishing involuntary, even if legally obtained, information about the subjects of a news story raises a deeper and more difficult issue for journalistic ethics. Journalists must try to assess the public interest, not merely in the psychological sense of what a certain percentage of the news audience might be willing to spend time reading or watching, what might hold their attention, but in the sense of what is in its legitimate interests. What kinds of information do members of a society need in order to conduct their business as self-governing citizens in a free society?

This is the true meaning of "relevance" in the statement we have formulated of the fundamental moral obligation of journalistic ethics, aimed always at the greater public good. In this sense, it is arguably relevant to the interests of a news-following public, and hence newsworthy in the appropriate meaning of the word in the present context, to learn that Secretary Powell has prostate cancer and will be treated surgically for the disease. It would then follow that even if Powell had not volunteered the information, a journalist who discovered and could lawfully verify the facts would not only be morally permitted but morally obligated to report the event as news. If an average citizen whose medical welfare is of no particular concern to the public at large were to be afflicted with precisely the same condition as the secretary, on the contrary, it would presumably be of no journalistic value by virtue of falling outside the legitimate sphere of public interest.

In that case, the facts would not fall under the requirement of journalists to contribute to relevant truth telling, because this information would not be relevant to their participation in political life. Even if it were interesting in the ordinary psychological sense of capturing and holding an audience's attention to follow the daily events in every aspect of a randomly chosen person's daily affairs, it would not be morally justified to investigate and report on such information if it is not judged to be in the public interests of a readership or audience to know these things for the sake of their participation in their own individual or political decision-making. The privacy of ordinary persons should therefore be respected by journalists and not infringed upon unnecessarily even when there happens to be a market for such information.

SLIPPERY SLOPE PROBLEMS IN PRIVACY DETERMINATIONS

If we consider once again the fallacy of bad precedent reasoning as it pertains to the problem of privacy in journalistic ethics, we begin to see that there are slippery slopes running in several different directions. Each of these poses risks for journalists that might lead them into professionally unethical conduct if they cannot establish a principled way to distinguish between justified and unjustified cases of news investigation and reporting.

Allowing reporters to investigate the health of a secretary of state sets a precedent for doing so also in the case of the secretary of transportation. If such intrusions into the private lives and personal circumstances of these officials is permitted, why not of the secretary of the secretary of transportation? Why not, then, also, of matters other than serious health issues, but of sexual preferences, intimate family details, favorite music, books checked out of the library or on-line web browsing habits, and just about anything else?

We might also consider what happens if we pursue slippery slope reasoning here in the opposite direction. If we morally forbid reporters from investigating the health of a randomly chosen person on the street, why should such a person have a greater right to privacy than a secretary of the secretary of transportation? If not of that person, then why not of the secretary of transportation, and why not of the secretary of state, and why not of politicians at the highest levels of government as they hypothetically meet and accept bribes for turning over state secrets to a foreign agent or anything else that persons involved in public affairs might do or say, as subject to the same protections of privacy as ordinary citizens?

Case Study 21

Investigating the Private Lives of the Families of Public Officials

Let us pursue a trajectory down one of these slippery slopes by asking about the families of officials. Here is a context for discussing the problem, provided by Louis Alvin Day in his book *Ethics in Media Communications*, when he writes, p. 135:

> "Privacy concerns can be particularly thorny in news coverage of the families, friends, or associates of public figures. The media have a credible record on this score, usually crossing the line only when news judgments require

further scrutiny. For example, reporters generally respected President Clinton's desire to shield daughter Chelsea from the glare of publicity. Conversely, when President George W. Bush's daughter, Jenna, pleaded 'no contest' to a charge of underage drinking, reporters played it down. But when she got into a second alcohol-related scrape just a few weeks later, the media could no longer let it pass. It would be difficult to argue with the story's news value, since it involved a violation of law. 'Like all presidential kids they're entitled to a zone of privacy, and the press is not out there stalking them,' observed Tom DeFrank, the *New York Daily News*'s Washington bureau chief. 'But as long as these girls keep doing things that give their father headaches, they're making news and we've got to cover it.'"

The example Day offers is interesting for several reasons. It is worth reflecting, first, on the fact that Day resorts to examples rather than offering a general principle. This method of argument may turn out to be a limitation of practical thinking in journalistic ethics where privacy is concerned. We have already offered a sketch of a principle, but its application in actual cases is difficult. It is bound to raise controversies that cannot be settled by any straightforward appeal to further abstract rules or guidelines. Perhaps the best we can do is to try to cultivate a sense for the practical application of the principle that the only personal information reporters can investigate with respect to individuals is information relevant to the public interest and not merely whatever the public may happen to be interested in.

QUESTIONS

1. Is there any justification for journalists reporting on the illegal behavior of elected officials? How, if at all, is it supposed to help the public to participate in self-government in a free society to learn that a president's daughter has been charged with violating a drinking law?

2. Can there be other moral justifications for reporting on such facts? If so, what are they? Are there limits to the kinds of information journalists should be allowed to publish concerning public figures or their families?

3. Are journalists morally obligated to respect the privacy of persons who willingly enter public life as politicians or celebrities? If so, why? If not, does this license to pry into their lives extend also to the members of their families? What limits, if any, for the privacy of individuals related to news figures should a journalist observe?

4. Would establishing categories of hands-off respect for privacy by withholding certain kinds of information from the public, and enforcing them coercively through legal sanctions, amount to censorship of the press?

5. Does Day get things right in arguing that the press has a legitimate interest in reporting on the daughter of an American president breaking the law by doing only what many other underage persons do in the United States every day?

CHOICE OF PUBLIC LIFE AS A DISAVOWAL OF PRIVACY

The commonplace refrain one frequently hears uttered with respect to such persons is that they choose to live in the limelight, and therefore they open themselves to this kind of celebrity hunting. If they wanted to live a private life, they should not have publicity agents and attract attention to themselves in the ways they do.

The moral issue for journalists in connection with celebrities, including persons like the president of the United States, is not whether news reporters are morally obligated to report on what celebrities do, but whether they are morally permitted to do so when there is no justification for what might be construed as an invasion of personal privacy being relevant in serving the public good. Let us take note of several facts about the above case study involving Bush's daughters and their fake IDs.

First, Bush's daughters have not chosen to be celebrities but are in the public eye only because of their father's choice to enter a public career. News consumers in the United States must evidently take an interest in much of what the president does if they are to participate fully in the decision-making of the society in which they live. Why, however, should this interest extend to the immediate members of the president's family? It may appear morally unfair and insupportable for reporters to intrude into the private lives of members of the president's family on the grounds that the president has chosen a public rather than the private life of an ordinary citizen, if his family members from their point of view in their own private lives do not consider themselves to be included in the bargain. The interest at issue seems to be something much more like journalistic voyeurism, poking into the facts surrounding the lives of the president's family for titillation value, in the same way that fans like to know all about the personal lives of other kinds of famous celebrities, like film, music, and sports stars. There is a huge industry that has grown up around the collecting of information about celebrities. The kinds of information that are reported include such things as where the celebrities go to vacation, the restaurants they patronize, who they sleep with, whether or not they use drugs, what they wear, and unlimitedly many other details. It is hard to imagine how personal information of the kind concerning an American president's family could possibly be put to practical use by ordinary citizens.

Second, and more importantly, breaking the law removes anyone, regardless of their parentage, from the realm of morally protected private behavior and makes the action one in which the public in principle has an interest. If the president's daughters had wanted to maintain their privacy, it might be said, then they should not have violated the law. They cannot have it both ways—choosing to risk getting caught drinking underage and having their privacy respected—since breaking the law is inherently not a private action. We as citizens should not want to permit illegal behavior to go unnoticed in the press simply because the individuals involved are family members of an elected official.

The question nevertheless remains whether the press has a right to nationalize and even internationalize the news that the president's daughters on several occasions broke the drinking law. We might imagine that only a local press would report the information, as would be the case for almost anyone other than family members of a public figure or celebrity. What, if anything, justifies the publishing of Bush's daughters' names and faces with the details of their minor misdemeanors in so many newspapers and on national and international television? Is this a reasonable price for them to pay from a moral point of view for the fact that their father chose to enter politics?

Granted, the Bush daughters pled no contest to breaking the law. Their violations, accordingly, should be reported in the press, as they would in the case of any other offender. Still, we should ask, does everyone in the world need to know about it? How are the public's interests served by making this information available? Again, what use are persons around the world supposed to make of such facts? Are they supposed to conclude, for example, that Bush does not deserve to be reelected as president because he was not able to prevent his daughters from drinking before they had attained legal age? That seems absurd, whatever we may think of any particular politician's performance in office. Or is it supposed to come as a revelation that Bush like any father might have difficulty disciplining his adolescent children, who in a stage of rebellion do not always act as their parents would prefer? That is also hardly newsworthy. What then, if anything, could possibly justify the worldwide dissemination of such personal information that would at most be locally reported in the case of ordinary citizens, given, once again, that Bush's daughters did not choose to be celebrities by virtue of being family members of someone who ran for political office?

The only conceivable answer is that the daughters' law-breaking constitutes a public rather than a private event; once they had done something that could reasonably be publicized in any venue, the fact that they are *de facto* public figures by virtue of their family relationship to the president makes the public facts of whatever they do outside of their private lives newsworthy to a much larger audience or readership. This may especially be true in this particular case because Bush has himself made a point of admitting his own past problems with substance abuse, which he claims to have overcome.

Does any of this constitute an adequate professional ethical justification for publishing worldwide the arrests of Bush's daughters for using fake IDs to purchase alcohol? Offhand, it would certainly not appear to be. While breaking the law means that the Bush daughters' actions should be reported in the news in some form, there seems no justification for the facts to be published outside local newspapers, just as if they did not happen to be members of the president's family. Possibly, then, the newspapers in Washington, DC or Crawford, Texas should carry the story, but not all newspapers nationwide or television programs that would not otherwise ordinarily publish the names of those who commit such relatively minor offenses. Further, just as we would not expect to see such facts meriting broadcast time on radio or television in the case of an average offender for such a misdemeanor, so there appears to be no good reason to do so in the case of a president's relatives. (This is also not the appropriate forum to address the justification for discriminating against persons who are legally adults by prohibiting them by law from obtaining alcohol entirely on the basis of age in place of cultural or institutional education that might lead to responsible drinking on the part of persons who are old enough to vote, get married without their parents' permission, and serve in the military.)

Violations of privacy admit of degree. In the above case, professional journalistic obligations to maximize relevant truth telling might be obviated by the irrelevance of the information as a national or international news item. It need not be in the greater public interest to devote newspaper columns and airtime to such trivial occurrences when so many other vitally more important events are under-investigated. Journalists who report on the story might further be charged with violating the Bush daughters' right to privacy to a greater extent than the significance of the fact of their law-breaking could reasonably justify. The situation would be very different in the event of a more egregious act of law-breaking, if, for example, the sisters had committed murder, or had engaged in espionage on behalf of a foreign government, or were distributors for an international drug cartel.

As it is, it seems difficult if not impossible to rationalize the decision on the part of journalists to make a national and international news item out of the underage drinking of the president's daughters using fake IDs, even if it is something they have done repeatedly. There is no moral justification for treating these two persons any differently than any other two young people anywhere in the United States who break the law by underage drinking. What they did was against the law, and they should be appropriately punished according to the law as it applies to anyone else. It nevertheless seems an excessive violation of their and their family's right to privacy for everyone in the country and even the world to learn about their behavior, despite being the president's daughters, if the information cannot be morally justified as having practical application in the public interest.[4]

---

[4]The potential damage to a person's reputation through widespread press coverage of alleged crimes and other kinds of wrongdoing in the media may be impossible to estimate or undo and, hence, impossible to adequately compensate. See Postman and Powers, *How to Watch TV News*, pp. 115–127; on television in the courtroom, pp. 129–143. They write, p. 142: "As for the courtroom being a semipublic space, that's exactly what it should be. The procedures are not perfect but they are designed to give everyone a fair shake, and there is no good reason to alter them. And keep this in mind: reading about a trial and seeing it on television are two quite different experiences. A man who is found not guilty ordinarily may resume his life. A man who is found not guilty but who has been seen on television during his trial may find it impossible to resume his life. Audiences may even forget if he was found guilty or not. In any case, he becomes notorious in one way or another, which is to say, he is tried twice—once in the courts, and a second time in the court of public exposure."

CELEBRITYHOOD AND JOURNALISTIC VIOLATIONS OF PRIVACY

Let us return, before we proceed, to the question of whether individuals who freely choose a public life thereby sacrifice the sort of ordinary protections of privacy that ordinary persons who do not happen to be celebrities are entitled to enjoy. Why, in the first place, from a moral standpoint, should there be any price to pay for being a celebrity? Becoming a celebrity is not an act of moral wrongdoing, and so should not obviously have any kind of penalty attached. While it is true that some celebrities at first crave publicity and then do not know how to shut it out of certain parts of their lives, this does not mean that journalists have a moral right to intrude on any aspect of such individuals' personal activities, depriving them of privacy in virtually everything they do. The principle that is appropriate here is the same that we have invoked elsewhere in considering limitations to the freedom of the press. It is the proposition that the press is to be considered free to investigate any matter that does not involve violating a more highly prioritized moral obligation.

We can see, moreover, that there is an argument to the effect that preserving privacy as a presupposition and precondition of freedom in a free society might be judged as more fundamental and hence a principle to be more highly prioritized than allowing a completely unrestricted free press to intrude upon the private lives of citizens. The basis for such prioritization is that a completely free press, as important as it is to a free society, is important only as facilitating self-government and the preservation of freedom; whereas without privacy, as we have argued, there is no freedom for a society to preserve or free self-government to be managed through the free flow of information.

Some commentators on the rights and obligations of a free press with reference to the problem of privacy have argued that the press has entertainment as well as information value. This is undoubtedly true. We need only consider the fact that most newspapers from the very beginning have included humor and gossip columns, cartoons and jokes, reviews of plays and books, art sections, and the like, that do not simply serve the austere interests of the public from the standpoint of supplying readers and viewers with the kinds of information they need to vote in elections and participate intelligently in the social issues of the day. There are entire magazines and news broadcasts and even television channels devoted entirely to entertainment kinds of news, including information about celebrities in the entertainment industry.

It nevertheless strains belief to argue that a news reporter could be morally justified in invading the privacy of another person purely for the sake of providing readers, radio listeners, or television viewers with entertainment value, to fill the moments of an otherwise dull hour with delicious tidbits about persons who are living glamorous lives as pop stars of one sort or another. Journalists are morally permitted to include items of entertainment value in their publications, but, we should insist, not at the expense of violating more highly prioritized moral obligations. One such more highly prioritized moral obligation is that of not violating the moral rights of others, including the right to privacy, in the process of gathering or presenting the news. This, we should further say, is especially true when we recall that there has yet to be established any moral obligation for journalists to cover purely entertainment news items.

If it is not relevant to the public interest for persons to know whether or not the pop singer Madonna is thinking of having plastic surgery, then there is certainly no moral obligation for reporters to cover such a story. If to do so, finally, would constitute a violation of the singer's right to privacy, if this is something she would rather not have people know, then there is a moral obligation for reporters not to publicize the fact, no matter how public a personage the celebrity in question has deliberately made herself to be or how eagerly a readership or audience might drink up such facts.

Relinquishing Privacy by Acting in a Public Place

There is a related principle that is sometimes mentioned as justifying news reporting on anything that is done in a public place or space. This, too, is an interesting basis for distinguishing between what is public and legitimately private. We consider this principle next as an alternative basis for drawing the line between legitimate and illegitimate exercise of the freedom of the press and its uncensored practice with respect to the personal lives of newsworthy individuals. Day, quoted above, now maintains:

> [T]he law of privacy has accorded substantial latitude for news gathering in public places. The general rule is that anything that takes place in public view can be reported on. The idea is that activities that transpire in public are, by definition, not private. But even in public we sometimes covet some degree of solitude. Take, for example, lovers seated on a park bench. From a legal standpoint photographers might be within their rights to capture this moment on film and publish it as an item of human interest. A sense of ethics would suggest, however, that they obtain permission from the couple for two reasons: (1) common decency requires permission before intruding into this private moment, and (2) minor inconvenience may turn to acute embarrassment if these two lovers are married, but not to each other.[5]

The proposal, unfortunately, is unsatisfactory in several ways. For one thing, it speaks vaguely of "substantial latitude" being accorded journalists with respect to reporting on events occurring in public places. We do not know from this whether or not news reporters are simply free or not free in reporting on what people do in public places. There is a circularity that

[5]Day, *Ethics in Media Communications*, p. 136.

threatens the account unless we are already in command of a firm distinction between what is public and what is private, since otherwise we will not be in a position to distinguish, as we must in applying Day's suggestion, between what is a public place and what is a private place.

Day's example is somewhat helpful, since it is relatively uncontroversial whether what we call a public park and a bench in a public park is a public place. We cannot expect in every case to draw the necessary distinction on the basis of colloquial language usage and popular terminology. Letting such considerations pass, we face a still greater problem in connection with Day's discussion of the lovers on the public bench example. Day admits that according to the principle the lovers are fair game for photographers to take their picture, since they are out there in the open, like the trees and the squirrels and the flowers on the lawn, subject to public scrutiny. If they truly want privacy, as the popular saying goes, they should get a room. There is a difference, of course, between not minding if people see that you are smooching with a lover and having them take photographs of the fact or write about it in the newspaper or broadcast it on television. We are surely not giving our implicit assent to all such forms of publicity every time we step out of the house.

Having acknowledged that, legally, photographers are free to snap away at the park bench lovers, Day then further qualifies the remark by adding that a "sense of ethics" would "suggest" that a reporter obtain permission from the couple to do so. More directly, he claims that the photographer might have such an obligation if, for example, the photograph were deemed sufficiently newsworthy for publication in a paper as a human-interest item. True enough, journalists are often desperate to fill column inches and airtime, but it is hard to see what the human interest of such an item could be. It seems to belong to the category of such little additions that punctuate the real news with captions, like "Spring is here" or "Love is in the air," that make many readers or viewers smile and feel gooey inside for a while before turning to news of the war or devastation of the South American rain forests. We may suppose for the sake of argument that there is a legitimate journalistic interest in such images and that, whatever Day means by a "sense of ethics," he is right that it would be morally preferable if not obligatory for the photographer to seek permission of the couple before publishing the photograph.

The reasons Day provides for this conclusion are nevertheless rather puzzling. He maintains, first, that "common decency," again, whatever that is supposed to mean, from an ethical standpoint, "requires permission before intruding into this private moment." If this is true, however, then it flatly contradicts the proposal that public places are fair game and open season for journalists to cover whatever events occur therein, including a good old-fashioned smoochfest. It is a "private moment" in an obvious sense, as are all such intimate encounters between persons, even if it takes place in a public location. In that case, it is not just the geography but the chronology of events that make a difference, not merely where they occur but whether they are in any sense transpiring in private time. The inference is then that space and time are not after all crucial to the concept of privacy, but that what counts as privacy and a private occurrence is something more abstract than purely spatiotemporal. What this could be remains to be seen. Second, we are advised, perhaps as a humorous note, that taking a photograph of the park bench lovers might constitute a "minor inconvenience," if, for example, either person turned out to be married or otherwise committed to someone else. Day's pronouncement, under those circumstances, could turn out to be an unfortunate understatement, and the publication of the photograph more than a minor inconvenience, if the couple's romantic embrace were to appear in a public source. Let us also leave these kinds of considerations aside, since, as we have said, perhaps the persons should have simply followed the voice of prudence and found a more private place for their tryst.

There is another philosophically more interesting question at issue. It has to do with whether such factors as inconvenience have moral implications of the sort that should restrain a news reporter or photographer from recording and publishing the event. Note that Day says a photographer should request permission "before" intruding into a private moment. From a practical point of view, however, if we try to put ourselves in the position of the lovers on the bench, once permission is granted there can then be no intrusion of privacy, although the photograph will probably lack the charm of a candid shot that the photographer presumably seeks. That, of course, will simply be too bad for the photographer, whom we are supposing has no intrinsic right to take the picture unless the subjects have given their permission. More importantly, we cannot always decide whether an event is public or private. Even when we correctly judge that an event is private, we cannot always confidently say whether or not journalists should or should not be allowed to intrude on another person's privacy merely to avoid embarrassing or inconveniencing them. For in that case, a reporter's hands would also be tried with respect to morally justified invasions of privacy for the sake of the greater social good and in the service of the imperative to maximize relevant truth telling in the public interest, when, as in the case of the public official divulging state secrets, there is no other way to gather the necessary information.

The example is misguided from the outset, as we have already hinted. The mere fact that an event is occurring in public space is by itself no guarantee that the event is public and therefore available to journalistic information gathering. We should consider extending the notion of privacy to include at least some private moments in public space. An obvious example is the tragedy of a car accident in which a child is run down and killed. The family on the scene is weeping uncontrollably and experiencing in a public place what should intuitively be a private moment of spontaneous grief and sorrowful suffering. Should photographers be allowed to capture these moments on film and use them in news stories in print and television? Opinions may differ, and certainly journalists in the past have included such images in their reporting. We, however, are not asking what journalists actually do or what they think they might need to do in order to remain competitive in their market sector, but whether what journalists do in such cases is morally justified and, if so, how and by what principles. If we believe that it is an offense, a moral indecency, to publicize what should be intimate moments of private grief, even if they occur in a public place, then we cannot justifiably distinguish between what is and what is not a morally objectionable invasion of privacy simply on the basis of whether or not the event in question occurs in what is commonly recognized as a public place, nor on the basis of whether or not to do so would constitute an inconvenience.

Notice, finally, another aspect of Day's example of the park bench lovers. For the photographer to dare interrupt the couple by asking permission to take their photograph, the photographer by that very act has already intruded upon their privacy, whether or not the picture is taken and whether or not it is taken with permission. If the moment is truly private, as Day acknowledges, then the couple should be unmolested altogether by persons interested in respecting the privacy of others and neither photographed nor interrupted by potentially obnoxious unwelcome questions. Is it such a difficult thing when they are minding their own business to simply leave people alone?

According to the principle that justifies journalistic investigation and reportage of relevant news information in the public interest, despite what we have been saying, there is in principle no corner of a person's life, no matter how private or personal, that is necessarily exempt from journalistic invasion. The issue in every instance depends on the circumstances and, more particularly, on whether or not to do so would be in the public interest, whether the information is truly needed in order for citizens to conduct the business of self-government, and whether in the end it really serves the public good. In this regard, it is hard to imagine any moral justification for photographing or in any other way interrupting the couple on the park bench. Leave them alone, we might say, give them some privacy, adapting a version of the so-called Golden Rule, just as you would prefer to be left alone by other persons if you were having a private and personal discussion or enjoying a little tongue hockey, even if you are doing so in a public place.

How do we know the circumstances whereby a couple might require a moment by themselves without the luxury of retreating to a private location? Perhaps they have just received some extraordinarily good news or extraordinarily bad news and they need to commune together right then wherever they happen to be. Perhaps they cannot afford a room or have only limited opportunities to share each other's company, and this, as the photographer sidles up, is one of those rare occasions. It is none of our business, and, if we have any common let alone moral sense, we should be able to read such a situation from a good distance away and not interfere in any way as persons, let alone as journalists or photographers, in whatever is taking place between the persons on Day's imaginary bench.

Most of the examples that philosophers and journalists have discussed as violations of privacy are more serious than the photographer's intrusion on the park bench lovers. The general principle may nevertheless be much the same, and the case is instructive in its own way. We shall continue to bear these instances in mind as we consider two further categories of privacy in relation to news reporting, concerning the accounting of suicides and the activities of paparazzi or ambush photographers who try to surprise celebrities in public and private places in order to take pictures, usually on a freelance basis, for newspapers and magazines.

Case Study 22

Reporting on Suicide as a Cause of Death

Let us turn first to the problem of news reporting of deaths by suicide. Day, again, raises the problem in an insightful way, when he maintains:

> "Suicides present a ticklish problem for reporters and editors. When the suicide is that of a public figure or when it occurs in public view, it should probably be reported. But even here journalists should approach such stories with a sense of compassion for the family and friends of the victim. And where suicides or suicide attempts are captured on videotape, a likely occurrence in today's electronic age, TV stations should use such footage with caution. Competitive pressures and the excitement of such dramatic footage can lead to a moral lapse on the part of some producers and news directors. Not only is the respect for persons an important value in the ethical decision-making process under such circumstances, matters of taste, especially where the suicide is graphic or gruesome, require that the moral agent be sensitive to the viewing audience as well."[6]

QUESTIONS

1. Is it morally objectionable for journalists to report cause of death as suicide when that is the truth of the matter?
2. Should we consider cause of death to be protected by considerations of privacy from journalistic reportage?
3. Does the public have a legitimate interest in knowing the cause of death of any given person? Is it important especially for persons outside of a suicide's immediate family to know that the person died in this way at his or her own hand? Why or why not?
4. If we prevent journalists from reporting on suicide as a cause of death in the case of ordinary individuals, do we thereby enter onto a slippery slope

[6]Ibid., p. 144.

        leading to the censorship of legitimate news items under the guise of protecting the privacy of the members of a society? What principle might be invoked to distinguish the legitimate from the illegitimate application of privacy as a basis for permitting or forbidding newsworthy information?

5.   Suppose that there were a pattern of suicides in a given community or across a broader spectrum of the world community. Would this make a difference with respect to the morality of reporting suicide as a cause of death? What if journalists were to uncover evidence of an Internet suicide pact among many different persons? Beginning with ordinary suicides by distressed persons and advancing by degrees to the scenario just described, under what circumstances would it finally be morally obligatory for journalists to report suicides by naming individuals as reporting newsworthy information in the public interest? Could or would such a point ever be reached? Why or why not?

        We may wonder why some people find information about the manner of an individual's death, whether by suicide or in another way, especially newsworthy. Other than morbid curiosity, it is not obvious why it should make any difference to a reading or viewing public how someone has died.

        Equally, however, it is not clear why anyone should be squeamish about the fact that an individual has chosen death by suicide. There are social, religious, and psychological taboos of various sorts pertaining to suicide, and we need not enter into the whys and wherefores of the "embarrassment" that a suicide in the family causes some people in order to accept it as sociological data that many individuals are troubled by the idea of publicizing the fact that someone close to them has died as the result of suicide. Why, we may wonder, is there a social stigma of any sort about persons choosing to end their own lives? What could be more natural or reasonable for some persons in difficult circumstances to commit suicide?

        The more pressing question is whether, for individuals who consider it a private matter when a loved one has committed suicide, the fact should be freely available for reporters to inform the public about or whether instead the information should be kept private in the sense of not being publicized in any of the media. There is obviously no question of violating the privacy of the dead in this case, even if the dead have interests that extend beyond the termination of their lives. It is a problem at most of respecting the privacy of the survivors of the deceased, who by hypothesis will suffer pain, discomfort, and distress at the public dissemination of the fact that the person has committed suicide. Day, at the end of his comment, also mentions the fact that some suicides are particularly "graphic or gruesome", and that this makes especially photojournalistic reportage of suicides a potential source of insensitivity that should ban their representation in the news.

        Whatever the merits of Day's other conclusions in this section, the issue of the graphic nature of some suicides is surely immaterial. Many deaths, car accidents, farming and industrial mishaps, murder and death in wartime, are as likely to be distasteful especially to immediate family members, and journalists have as a rule very properly refrained from publishing such images as accompaniments to news coverage of deaths and obituaries. We should also note that many suicides, by carbon monoxide poisoning, sleeping pills, self-suffocation, and other methods, are not as a matter of fact especially grisly and would not necessarily make for morally questionable photojournalism on those grounds alone.

The deciding factor should rather be whether the public interest is genuinely served by publishing the fact that a certain person has died as the result of an act of suicide rather than accidentally, through the violence of another person, or of natural causes. The mere fact that for such information to be disclosed can cause distress to certain family members, in particular if they associate a sense of shame with the fact that someone they know has chosen to end his or her own life, should at least be enough to give journalists pause in reporting on the fact. They should ask in every case whether there is a real need for the public to know that the death was by suicide rather than in some other manner or through some other cause.

We should acknowledge at the outset that we have reason to expect that in some cases the answer will be yes and in others no. It will largely depend on the circumstances, on who the person is, and many other things besides. If a controversy arises as to whether a person has committed suicide but tried to make it seem like an accident for the sake of not depriving the beneficiaries of his life insurance policy of the indemnity, as is typically the case under the law with respect to most policies, then it might well be of general public interest for a journalist to report that an autopsy and the official ruling of the coroner has determined that the death in question, despite initial appearances of accident, was actually a suicide. If it is suspected that a person may have died in an accident for which other persons would then be held legally liable or as a result of a disease that may have affected others who had contact with the individual prior to her decease, then again it might be relevantly newsworthy for a newspaper or television program to inform the public that the cause of death was none of these other occurrences but was instead the result of an act of suicide.

It should not merely be a matter, as Day avers as part of a conclusion he does not try to defend by argument, of whether or not the person who has committed suicide is a public figure or committed suicide in a public place. It is hard to see why either of these considerations should matter at all. The mere fact that someone is a public figure does not subtract in any way from the pain and psychological distress that might be caused to the surviving family when the information is revealed publicly to anyone with the price of a newspaper or access to a television set. Celebrity status, once again, should not be twisted and distorted into journalistic license to reveal any and all facts about persons who happen to have led public as well as private lives. If there is any sense of journalistic decency surrounding the concealment of death by suicide, we might easily conclude instead that persons especially who have led public lives of service deserve more respect than having the secret of their deliberate choice of time and manner of death revealed to all the curious. Although some incidents of suicide have been captured on film as "dramatic footage," we do not imagine under current standards of good taste and relevance in news reporting that such materials will be publicized any more than we expect equally dramatic footage of any other kinds of death to be made a public spectacle for the entertainment of persons with a morbid desire to witness a moment of death, regardless of whether or not the death is self-inflicted.

Day has somewhat more interesting things to say in summarizing his treatment of the problem of privacy in news reporting, when he proposes a general principle that seems correct as far as it goes. He continues:

> [I]n making decisions that may offend or intrude into the private lives of others, moral agents should strive for a *minimization of harm*. This value is closely related to that of *respect for persons*. When invasions of privacy are inevitable, as they sometimes are when journalists report on matters of public interest, the goal should be confined to the coverage of those details that are essential to the newsworthiness of the event. The failure to heed this admonition, for example, is at the heart of many of the complaints about the news media's treatment of the victims of crime and other tragedies.[7]

We note that the principle Day invokes here is compatible with and supplemental to the three categories of moral justification we have considered for projecting a moral right to privacy. Privacy on any of these grounds is a personal possession to be protected at least in certain cases from journalistic intrusion as a tenet of journalistic ethics and as a qualification of the fundamental moral obligation of news reporters to maximize relevant truth telling in the public interest.

That we ought to minimize harm in maximizing the reportage of relevant information in the public interest is a useful way of formulating the criterion for morally responsible journalism. We have previously considered a similar statement invoking morally responsible journalists to maximize relevant truth telling in the news only insofar as doing so is compatible with the fulfillment of other more highly prioritized moral obligations, including the obligation not to cause unnecessary harm to others. This is how we have interpreted the requirement that news reporting not only be truthful but undertaken in the public interest. Day's way of putting things, though related in spirit, leaves us with the further problems of deciding what constitutes harm and of specifying the factors against which the minimization of harm is to be gauged. What he offers nevertheless clearly seems to be on the right track in emphasizing the avoidance of unnecessary pain and suffering for those affected by the reporting of certain kinds of news items or by reporting them in certain kinds of ways. It represents a tangible sign of moral respect for the intrinsic value of persons.

[7]Ibid., p. 149.

Case Study 23

Paparazzi in the Princess Diana and Dodi Al Fayed Tragedy

We now consider the behavior of paparazzi. These are photographers who stalk celebrities and photograph them for the sake of their pictures. These images cater to the starstruck fascination of a certain segment of the population who flock to newspapers, generally of the tabloid sort, that feature ambush pictures of the stars, often doctored by computer graphics.

There are Web sites that promise to pay anonymous photographers large sums of money for providing photographs of particular celebrities, thus encouraging the enterprise of intruding on another person's privacy purely for the sake of profit. When we speak of paparazzi, we are as a result inevitably referring to a practice of obtaining photographs that is inherently intrusive, violating the privacy of celebrities primarily if not exclusively for financial reasons. The term "paparazzi" is a pluralization of the fictional Italian family name of a surprise photographer, Paparazzo, in Federico Fellini's 1959 movie, *La Dolce Vita*.

The most notorious recent case of morally questionable behavior on the part of paparazzi is that involving Princess Diana of the United Kingdom, who, as the wife of Prince Charles, was by title Princess of Wales. On August 31, 1997, Princess Diana, in the company of her friend Dodi Al Fayed, entered her Mercedes Benz automobile after leaving the Hotel Ritz in Paris, France, trying to elude paparazzi who were in pursuit on motorbikes and attempting to photograph the couple together. As the ensuing events were later reconstructed, it is believed that the cars sped through the tunnels beneath the Place de l'Alma in the city center, whereupon the car driven by Diana's chauffeur, Henri Paul, whom testing later revealed to have been under the influence of drugs and alcohol, careened into divider walls within the tunnel, spun out of control, and crashed, killing both Diana and Dodi. The paparazzi continued on through the tunnel and did not stop to lend assistance to the accident victims. We find a useful statement of the situation in a recent source dealing with the problem of privacy in the media as a topic of journalistic ethics by Robert Trager and Donna L. Dickerson, in their book, *Freedom of Expression in the 21st Century*, who remark:

> "Probably no event in recent history has had more to say about privacy and private lives than the death of Princess Diana. Although the direct cause of the car accident that killed her is yet unknown, it is clear in the public's mind that an indirect cause of her death was the incessant invasion of her private space by paparazzi and tabloid journalists. Many

argue that Diana not only sought publicity, but by virtue of her position, the media had no obligation to respect what little private life she had. Nevertheless, every human, no matter what his or her station in life and public obligations, requires some degree of privacy."[8]

The Diana case is complicated in several ways. Experts are still divided about even the most basic facts of what occurred that night and who is really to blame for the tragedy that resulted. We can say without risk of contradiction, however, that to the extent that the alleged pursuit by paparazzi contributed to reckless driving in an effort to escape from their intrusion on the privacy of Diana and Dodi, the paparazzi are at least partially causally responsible for the accident that killed two people and seriously injured another.

The accident is not simply the paparazzi's fault. Even in trying to elude persons that are stalking individuals in a driver's care, the driver remains responsible for doing so safely. If the accident happened because of excessive speed or loss of control of the vehicle, partly perhaps as a result of the driver reportedly having ingested drugs and alcohol, that too is the driver's fault. A contributing factor, as the event has usually been portrayed, is nevertheless the sense of anxiety created by the constant pressure of the paparazzi trying to catch the couple in a photograph. Many persons have since interpreted the accident that occurred as the kind of thing that a prudent person could have expected eventually to happen, given the extent to which paparazzi intrude on the privacy of celebrities and cause a level of frustration, anger, and impatience under which many individuals cannot be expected to function with the necessary amount of caution by which the probability of accidents is reduced. It is only human nature to expect that by placing excessive stress on celebrities and their staff in the way that the persistent tactics of paparazzi inevitably do there will likely continue to be such terrible incidents as befell Diana and Dodi.

Paparazzi as a result for several reasons are on morally questionable turf. They deliberately intrude on what they themselves recognize to be the privacy of celebrities, not for the sake of bringing useful socially relevant information to the public, but rather for the sake of monetary reward. There is no moral justification according to the principles of journalistic ethics that we have been considering for the actions of paparazzi as obligatory efforts to maximize relevant truth telling in the public interest. As entertainment value, moreover, there is equally no moral justification for regarding the behavior of paparazzi as morally permissible exercises in gathering information and images for the public. We consider the work of paparazzi, their methods of obtaining photographs by ambushing unwilling subjects, as invading celebrities' privacy in such a way as to violate

[8]Trager and Dickerson, *Freedom of Expression in the 21st Century*, pp. 194–195.

more highly prioritized moral obligations to respect the rights of others. Finally, paparazzi in effect steal something of value from celebrities, many of whom consider their image and likeness to be part of what they have developed as a commodity for the entertainment industry and which they do not wish to give away without appropriate compensation. For paparazzi to jump up out of the bushes with a camera and take a picture of a celebrity without permission is comparable to stealing copyrighted material, lifting information from someone's personal papers, voicemail messages, computer files, or the like. Moreover, the unauthorized photographing of celebrities over which the celebrities or their publicity agents have no control risks the distribution of unflattering or in other ways personally compromising images that can also directly affect the income-earning potential of celebrities in certain circumstances and, as such, is arguably as morally objectionable as any other form of theft.[9]

QUESTIONS

1. What do you think happened to cause the car accident involving Princess Diana and Dodi Al Fayed? To what extent does it seem reasonable to attribute the tragedy to the paparazzi?

2. Should paparazzi be tolerated, or should they be punished by the law and denounced by professional journalistic organizations? Is there a legitimate journalistic justification for the practices of paparazzi? We may think of some paparazzi as unscrupulous exploitation artists, but what is the real difference between the kinds of photographs they take and the circumstances under which they try to take them and the practices of legitimate photojournalists?

3. What kinds of journalistic guidelines should be established for celebrity photographers? How can such principles be justified within the framework of rules we have considered for journalistic ethics?

4. Leaving aside the potential danger of paparazzi photography, what should we conclude about their activities with respect to the protection of the right to privacy on the part of their unwilling subjects? Do paparazzi by definition or as a feature of their standard operating procedures necessarily violate the privacy of the celebrities they photograph? Is there a legitimate morally justified purpose for paparazzi in the journalistic quest for relevant truth telling in the public interest? Is it reasonable to characterize paparazzi as fulfilling either the requirement to tell truths relevant to a news audience or as acting in the public interest?

5. Are paparazzi in any sense journalists? Why or why not? If paparazzi are engaged in some other superficially similar but ultimately non-journalistic activity, what is it that they are doing instead? How is their work related or

[9]See Foerstel, *From Watergate to Monicagate*, chapter 6, "The Paparazzi: Feeding the Public's Appetite for Celebrities," and Stevens, *Sensationalism and the New York Press*. For a distinguished journalist's perspective on the press's role in the impeachment proceedings against President Bill Clinton, see especially Kalb, *One Scandalous Story*. Also of interest is Kalb's prior book, *The Rise of the "New" News*.

similar to journalism, and is it different from the work of regular journalists? What should be the moral attitude of professional journalists toward paparazzi? What policies, if any, should professional journalists adopt toward paparazzi?

Summary

In this chapter we have investigated problems of journalistic integrity as it relates to personal privacy. Privacy is something that is psychologically needed and wanted even by individuals who in other aspects of their lives crave publicity. We considered the extent to which our analysis of journalistic ethics in terms of the requirement to provide relevant truth telling in the public interest might sometimes require reporters to intrude on a person's privacy. Alternative efforts to justify the protection of privacy do not stand up to criticism, as we tried to show.

The concept of privacy is nevertheless not absolute. We noted that in many instances it is difficult to establish standards of privacy that would serve as fixed guides for practicing journalists. Extreme cases are easy to identify, but they do not always help in trying to decide the best course of judgment or action where grey areas are concerned. These grey areas have to do primarily with situations in which there seems to be some justification for a reporter's intruding on the privacy of an individual for the sake of investigative reporting in the public interest. The criterion we propose implies that violations of personal privacy are permitted with respect to any individual in private or public life if, but only if, doing so is likely to result in a sufficiently important news story that is truly in the public interest. We considered a number of specific situations and case studies, all involving potential violations of privacy, and we inquired into the ethics of journalists reporting on persons and events in ways that violate or at least appear to violate the right to privacy. Finally, we considered paparazzi as extreme instances of intrusive "journalism" or related journalistic-like activities that can be dangerous, even tragic, in their effects, but that more importantly stand as clear-cut examples of the exploitation of celebrities for financial gain that seems to be inconsistent with the moral objectives of professional journalism.

We conclude that one useful way of orienting journalistic ethics toward the ideals of respect for privacy is to follow the Golden Rule. We ask whether we as individuals would want to have our privacy intruded upon in this or that way under specific circumstances if doing so does not obviously contribute to the purpose of producing relevant news information in the legitimate public interest. By emphasizing relevance and what is or is not actually news reporting in the public interest, we can arrive at a sufficiently useful morally justifiable set of guidelines for deciding when it is and when it is not morally justified to pursue a news story without overriding considerations of normal respect for another person's privacy.

chapter eight

Objectivity, Perspective, and Bias

We return in this chapter to consider advanced topics in the problem of truth telling in the media. If it is true that journalists are professionally obligated to tell the truth about newsworthy events, then we must consider whether they bear an additional responsibility to recognize and overcome psychological obstacles to discovering and reporting the facts. Such impediments fall in particular under the categories of maintaining objectivity in light of subjective perspective and bias. We single out for special discussion the problem of journalists becoming "part of the story," breaking down the invisible barrier between the subject of reporting and the necessary objective distance from the facts to be reported in order to remain faithful to the truth. We suggest that while every news reporter has a perspective and some may even have a personal political, religious, or other type of bias, their reporting need not for that reason be biased in the negative sense of the word. It is possible for journalists to surmount their individual standpoints on issues in news reporting by becoming aware of and trying in their professional work to mitigate to the best of their abilities the potentially detrimental effects of perspective and bias in the search for truth.

AN IDEAL OF OBJECTIVITY

It is a point of pride among many journalists to maintain distance, objectivity, and noninterference in reporting the news. The general principle is one of reporters not "becoming part of the story" that they are trying to cover. We recall that Judith Miller, mentioned in Chapter Six, CASE STUDY 18, resigned her position at the *New York Times* for this very reason, maintaining that she had become part of the story about the CIA leak after serving jail time for refusing to reveal a confidential source. An ideal of objectivity in news reporting is presented, again by Siebert, Peterson, and Schramm, in *Four Theories of the Press*, when they explain:

> The spread of objective reporting throughout American journalism was accelerated by the decline in political partnership in the press and by the change of the newspaper from opinion journal to news medium. The growth of advertising and the drive to increase circulations also contributed to the general

acceptance of the ideal of objectivity. Newspaper reporters thought that their job required an attitude of aloofness. They became spectators rather than participants in the controversies of the day. They carefully avoided any appearance of partisanship or evaluation. News was a raw account; opinions were to be sharply separated from it and in most American newspapers relegated to the editorial page. The theory of objective reporting became a matter of professional pride among American journalists, who held that reporting the "facts of the day" was their only duty. In many countries professing libertarian principles, the theory failed to find general acceptance, and in countries where the press was tied to political parties the ideal of objectivity failed to flourish.[1]

The challenge of sustaining journalistic independence and objectivity, sticking as closely as possible to the facts in news reporting, is an essential adjunct to the primary moral obligation of professional journalists to maximize relevant truth telling in the public interest. Without maintaining high standards of objectivity, we cannot expect journalists to deliver the quality of news content that informed decision-making may require. Reporters should accordingly be aware of the ways in which critical distance and objectivity in reporting the news can be jeopardized, their need not to interfere in or become part of the stories on which they report, and to take practical precautions against challenges to epistemic independence and integrity that can unknowingly undermine their journalistic objectivity.

We shall consider some philosophical questions associated with this standard of journalistic ethics in three specific areas of news reporting, concerning: (1) The lure of physical on-the-scene involvement by modern electronic photojournalists providing a viewership with real-time video feeds from ongoing news events; (2) Criminal trial reporting that can influence judge and jury deliberations, potentially affecting and hence interfering in the outcome in a variety of ways; and (3) Embedding of journalists with the military during wartime operations, recently exemplified during the Second Gulf War or Operation Iraqi Freedom in 2003, when news reporters traveled with soldiers into the field of battle. Our focus throughout is on the problem of maintaining distance from and objectivity concerning the truth about the facts of news events and resisting the urge to report from the standpoint of personal perspective and bias.

NONINVOLVEMENT IN NEWS REPORTING

Let us first examine the topic of whether it is true that journalists are in breach of professional ethics if and when they "become part of the story" on which they are reporting. Like most matters of practical reasoning, the issues are not cut-and-dried, and the maxims and slogans that are often invoked

---

[1]Siebert, Peterson, and Schramm, *Four Theories of the Press*, pp. 60–61.

in such connections cannot be applied in the strict sense in which they are usually intended.

It may be impossible for reporters who are on the scene where dramatic events, such as those taking place during a war, are unfolding not to become a part of the action. They are unavoidably a part of what is happening simply by virtue of being there, and their presence in reporting on the facts of an ongoing action necessarily becomes one of the facts about whatever it is that is happening. When seasoned journalists maintain that they do not want to become part of the story, they nevertheless mean something different. What they are hoping to avoid is a situation in which other reporters find it important to be reporting on them, for then their very presence at a news scene will have become newsworthy in and of itself. The reason this is perceived as a problem for journalists is that they can then no longer personally continue to cover the story, since they can hardly continue for any length of time to report objectively about so personal a matter as themselves.

The situation poses interesting problems in understanding the importance of new media technologies. The existence of livecam reporting offers an almost irresistible incentive for journalists to place themselves on the ground of news occurrences in order to send back immediate photostreams and commentary. The most recent electronic photojournalistic technologies provide a special motivation for reporters, despite their principled reluctance and avowed ethical stance against direct involvement, to physically become part of the most dramatic ongoing news stories in order to provide instant coverage.

We begin to address these difficult topics by approaching them from the standpoint of more general considerations about the requirements for reliable reporting. Is it true, in the first place, that reporters can ever maintain absolute objectivity in the sense of not becoming a part of the events they are covering? The parody of journalistic interference, sometimes depicted in comedy sketches, is for a newspaper writer or editor on a slow news day to lean out the window and shoot a random passerby with a pistol, turning to the cub reporter and saying: "Print this: Sniper on the loose; city in a panic." This is the epitome of what journalists are *not* to do, of course, and of what noninterference by members of the press in the stories they are covering is supposed to entail. Reporters are emphatically not supposed to create the news in order to have something to report on and especially not by doing something that is intrinsically morally wrong. There are nevertheless many less obvious and less morally objectionable ways in which journalists are professionally concerned about the ethics of becoming involved in the events on which they report.

Can news reporters avoid contaminating the events they cover by the very fact of their presence? We see that persons under observation often behave differently than they would otherwise do; so to speak, they put on a different face for the camera when they know they are being observed.

Similarly, when individuals know that they are the subjects of news reporting, they frequently act differently than they would if they were not in the public eye. These facts suggest another sense in which reporters inevitably become part of the stories they are covering, interfering in a way in the course of events that would otherwise occur simply by being there to gather the news.

Nor are these the only ways in which newscasters can become involved in news stories being reported. As reporters turn in and publish or air their stories, the persons involved in the reports may read or see a program about themselves and adjust their future behavior in ways that would not occur if the reporting had not been made public or if they had not seen or read it. The fact that a reporter has reported on ongoing events in a certain way can thus have a direct and sometimes dramatic effect on current and future events.

As an example, consider the potential effect of a news report on a law enforcement investigation in which it is explained that the attorney general is about to issue an arrest warrant. Suppose that, as a direct result, the subject of investigation, who is watching the report on television, flees the country to avoid prosecution. In that case, at least the immediate arrest of the suspect is precluded, and hence the future course of events is altered as a result of a news report. Reporters can also become part of the story they are covering if they get caught up involuntarily in the events as they transpire. This can happen, in extreme cases, if they are reporting on terrorists or other criminals and are themselves injured, killed, or taken hostage. In other instances, they can accidentally affect the stories on which they are reporting if their mere presence unexpectedly gives away another activity in process, such as a military maneuver, a police raid, or even a celebrity surprise birthday party.

Observing and reporting, if we are being sticklers for exact meaning in application, inevitably change the facts. This is even true, we are told, in quantum physics, where the position and momentum of a quantum particle cannot be simultaneously determined. In quantum studies, according to the Heisenberg uncertainty principle, establishing either factor—position or momentum—requires physically interacting with a particle, typically by bouncing another particle off of it. When this is done, it disturbs the object in a way that changes the exact value of the other factor, so that we can never know both at once. The same is true at a macroscopic scale of information gathering in journalistic observation and reporting. If journalists regard it as morally desirable to limit as much as possible the extent to which they interfere with the stories they are covering, it is important to try to understand why so many find this an appropriate ideal. Then we can trace the cognitive and moral implications of the principle for professional journalists to see what we can learn about the proper stance for journalists to take when they are on the scene. What is supposed to be wrong in the first place with a reporter becoming part of the story?

We can understand the reluctance of news reporters to get mixed up in the events they are supposed to cover on the grounds that doing so violates the requirements of objectivity. This is, in turn, as we have amply seen, a prerequisite of truth telling. To be truly objective, an observer, and certainly a reporter, must maintain a certain distance from the events taking place in order to judge them properly. Can I preserve my professionalism and give an objective journalistic account of events surrounding the activities of a terrorist group if I have been personally threatened by its members? What if I have become so sympathetic to their cause that I can no longer appreciate the ruthlessness of their methods? Can I objectively report on a political demonstration that has taken place if I am swept up in the movement of persons down the street, maced by the police, fingerprinted and jailed, before being released? It might seem obvious that in such cases I cannot and that no one should be trusted to report objectively on the occurrences, because our observations will inevitably be colored and unduly influenced by our personal experiences.

The situation will be much the same as that affecting the level of objectivity needed to provide the right sort of report on the prospects of a corporation in which I hold large amounts of stock. If my interests are at stake, including my emotional interests as a result of direct or immediate participation in events, then as a journalist I might be psychologically or in other ways precluded from reporting objectively on the kinds of news stories I am asked to cover. If I cannot be expected to report objectively, then my truth telling capabilities in the matter unavoidably come into question. This is undoubtedly at least a major part of the reason why journalists have an aversion to and moral conviction about the need to avoid participation in the events on which they are supposed to collect information and to minimize as much as possible becoming part of the story for the sake of meeting their professional obligation to report the truth.

The tradeoff is that in many instances it is not physically possible for journalists to have the firsthand information essential for some news reporting unless, to a considerable extent, they become part of the stories on which they are reporting. They are often unable to offer as insightful an account of events if they do not personally become a part of the facts surrounding a story by virtue of their presence. My impressions of the demonstration I am supposed to cover might be less objective than if I had stayed on the sidelines and simply observed what was happening as though I were only a human camera and tape recorder. On the other hand, if I am hosed, maced, arrested, fingerprinted, and jailed, then as a journalist I will have had an unique perspective that I can bring to help an audience understand the events in my report that I could not possibly have if I were not so personally involved. Here, then, is another kind of dilemma for journalistic ethics. It involves a conflict between the imperative to maximize relevant truth telling, to gather as much useful information as possible, and to preserve objectivity by not becoming part of the reported story. The dilemma is that the information required by the principle to maximize relevant truth telling can both be enhanced by immediate personal experience and obstructed through lack of objectivity if and when the journalist becomes part of the story.

The problem is noteworthy when we turn to consider the coverage of major events, such as those involving a nation's participation in a war. There, as we have remarked, a journalist's instincts and personal and professional loyalties might be divided in precisely the ways described. Journalists, on the one hand, need to maintain their objectivity and independence from the interests of the participants in events on which they report if they are going to tell the truth. Yet journalists are also bound to be deeply personally involved when the events in question are matters as crucial as their own nation's being at war. It is unreasonable to expect that they can fully report on certain kinds of events unless they are physically on the scene and hence potentially at risk of becoming part of the story. This is a practical rather than deeply logical dilemma. As with most practical dilemmas, the solution can only be found in commonsense judgment that takes the purpose of the activity properly into account. The rule of thumb should be that reporters, if at all and to whatever extent possible, are to get as close to the action as they can to gather the facts without becoming direct participants. It is primarily for this reason that reporters are professionally forbidden from carrying weapons even when they are covering news events in dangerous conditions of war. They must not carry arms lest they be mistaken for combatants and lest they be tempted to use their weapons, transforming them immediately into active participants rather than mere objective observers. It is a fine line, nonetheless, between these two extremes of total nonparticipation and becoming not just a part of the story but the news story itself, that professional journalists must learn to manage. They do so to the best of their abilities by exercising practical wisdom and steering the best course under the circumstances that will enable them to collect as much useful information as possible without becoming so closely associated with the events as to alter their course or become a focus of reporting for other journalists.

We should expect that reporters as fallible human beings will sometimes make honest mistakes in such a difficult endeavor. Their purpose, however, should remain steadfast. They are professionally obligated to achieve a balanced compromise between being so totally removed from events that they cannot learn enough about them to provide needed information, and being so totally and directly involved that they cannot report on them with sufficient psychological distance and objectivity to produce a true account of the facts. We find these aims stretched to the breaking point, as already suggested, when news reporters are engaged as war correspondents. Warren P. Strobel, in his book, *Late-Breaking Foreign Policy: The News Media's Influence on Peace Operations*, published by the United States Institute of Peace, identifies the problem of objectivity for journalists covering wartime atrocities. He cites in particular the war in Bosnia following the breakup of the former Yugoslavia in the early 1990s:

> Within the journalistic community, the war in Bosnia opened deep fissures over the most sensitive issues for a reporter—objectivity. Reporters' professional ethos of objectivity, and the roles they sometimes take that are at odds with that self-view, were articulated by Bernard Cohen in his study of the press and foreign policy. Virtually all the journalists I spoke to who were involved in covering Bosnia acknowledged that the savagery of the fighting there and the outside world's competing views of the conflict forced a sometimes painful examination of their own role and conduct. This sentiment is crucial to an examination of the news media and peace operations because horrific ethnic fighting, atrocities, and even genocide form the backdrop for many peace operations, and this is very likely to continue to be true in the future. The debate over Bosnia was repeated, albeit in a more muted form, in another case Rwanda. The key issue here is that of *atrocities*. While news media portrayals of atrocities do not automatically cause a significant change in U.S. foreign policy, the charge that the news media have misportrayed the conflict to policymakers and the public is a serious one.[2]

Strobel is not concerned about the possibility of a news reporter getting caught up in actual fighting. The risk is that journalists could sacrifice their professional duty to remain objective observers, standing outside the events on which they are supposed to report, by being drawn in psychologically in such a way as to impair their proper judgment of the facts. We can easily imagine that this possibility poses an even greater threat to a news reporter's impartiality than direct physical involvement, when they are firsthand witnesses to events that so drastically conflict with their own or their culture's values.

What we are to imagine is that reporters in Bosnia and Rwanda, experiencing monstrous cruelties enacted by the belligerents on one side of a military conflict, become so repulsed by what they see and hear that they can no longer avoid taking sides morally and intellectually as they try to gather information and report the facts. It is not at all hard to conceive of such things happening. Strobel draws on the personal testimony of reporters in such situations who found, perhaps to their own surprise, that their objectivity began to disappear after each new encounter with the horrors of war. The implication is that journalists concerned about the professional ethics of their trade need to be on the alert for many different kinds of ways in which objectivity and effectiveness in truth telling can be compromised and for subtle ways in which reporters can become part of the story by getting caught up in the events at a moral psychological level, even if they never lift a finger to participate in other ways.

---

[2]Strobel, *Late-Breaking Foreign Policy*, p. 103.

To the extent that modern communications make it possible for reporters to document such occurrences immediately upon the scene and to the extent that the existence of technology creates a demand for reporters and camera and sound recording personnel to involve themselves in on-the-scene photojournalism, the collection of pictures and video by itself represents an unavoidable breakdown of journalistic noninvolvement. For others participating in the process of preparing news stories, those who, in effect, become virtual eyewitnesses to dramatic and often disturbing events while viewing and editing materials for presentation, the result is much the same. How could it be otherwise, we might ask, if the point of exploiting such technologies for the sake of producing more dramatic news programming is to make these events more vivid for the viewer at home? How can it be otherwise if journalists are bound by professional ethical standards to maximize their discovery and reportage of relevant news events in the public interest? If we cannot always avoid having reporters interfere in ongoing events if we are going to be properly informed about them and if new information technologies progressively undermine the distinction between journalistic distance and interference with newsworthy occurrences, we can all at least try to become more aware of the ideal to which journalists ought to aspire and the extent to which the devices of the electronic age are able to change, shape, and potentially distort the information by which we try to understand current events.

Case Study 24

Canadian Broadcasting Corporation (CBC) on Terry Milewski

The following passages are excerpted from a news release of March 23, 1999 by the Canadian Broadcasting Corporation titled "Upon the release of report by Marcel Pépin, Ombudsman, French Services, in answer to Mr. Peter Donolo's complaint concerning coverage of events surrounding the APEC summit by the CBC and its reporter Terry Milewski."

"It is important to clarify that the CBC, in its earlier responses to Mr. Donolo's complaint, did not conclude that a perceived bias did, in fact, exist, nor did it state that a breach of ethics had, in fact, occurred.

The CBC took the action it did in order to avoid a situation which could reasonably give rise to perceptions of partiality. The Ombudsman's Report confirms that this is consistent with the CBC's Journalistic Standards and Practices. Moreover, the Ombudsman agrees with the CBC that the circumstances 'might indeed have given rise, among some people of good faith' to such a perception.

We believe that the Canadian public expects no less than the highest possible journalistic standards from the CBC, and those are the standards which we applied in this case.

It should be noted that Terry Milewski was removed from APEC coverage three days before the initial letter of complaint was received from the Prime Minister's Office, because the CBC's own internal review concluded that he had become part of the story."

QUESTIONS

1. What is the significance of the fact that Milewski was removed from covering a story in which he was perceived as having become too directly involved?
2. Do some investigative reporting of your own to discover exactly what Milewski did to justify his being removed from covering the APEC story after complaints by Donolo. Did he deserve to be removed? Was the CBC being too cautious, too eager to address the complaint lodged against Milewski, or was there a legitimate issue of journalistic ethics involved?
3. How exactly did Milewski become "part of the story" in the CBC's judgment?
4. If you had been Milewski's editor, what advice would you have given him to avoid the action of being removed from covering the APEC story? Could this outcome have been prevented?
5. Should reporters have a sense themselves concerning the advisability of discontinuing coverage of a news story to which they have become too closely associated?

EMBEDDING JOURNALISTS WITH THE MILITARY

We turn finally to the issue of distance and objectivity of news reporters in wartime. We have already considered the impact of photojournalism and on-the-scene real-time electronic videography on public policy and the motivation for news reporters to become part of the story by appearing with their equipment on the ground during live coverage of events. Now we direct our attention to the involvement of journalists in military actions in connection with the recent decision of the U.S. military to "embed" journalists in troop movements for purposes of covering war events from a soldier's perspective. This is new terminology for a practice that has existed at least since the American Civil War. It nevertheless raises many moral issues, pro and con, and we shall need to examine the arguments on many sides of the proposal to integrate fighting forces with reporters in the front lines of battlefield engagements.

Case Study 25

Pentagon Directive for "EMBEDS" in the Second Gulf (Iraq) War

To begin a detailed examination of the issues surrounding the journalistic ethics of embedding news reporters with troops, we shall repro-
duce excerpts from an unclassified document from the American
Pentagon concerning the decision reached in February 2003 to include
embedded reporters with armed servicemen and women in what was
then the upcoming Iraq war. The document is remarkable in and of
itself as paper testimony to the extent to which the military considers its
obligations to a free press and its own interests in conducting warfare
as they relate to the presence of journalists on the scene. The important
section of the document states:

"SUBJECT: PUBLIC AFFAIRS GUIDANCE (PAG) ON EMBEDDING MEDIA
DURING POSSIBLE FUTURE OPERATIONS/DEPLOYMENTS IN THE U.S.
CENTRAL COMMANDS (CENTCOM) AREA OF RESPONSIBILITY (AOR).

REFERENCES: REF. A. SECDEF MSG, DTG 172200Z JAN 03, SUBJ: PUBLIC
AFFAIRS GUIDANCE (PAG) FOR MOVEMENT OF FORCES INTO THE
CENTCOM AOR FOR POSSIBLE FUTURE OPERATIONS.

1. PURPOSE.

THIS MESSAGE PROVIDES GUIDANCE, POLICIES AND PROCEDURES ON
EMBEDDING NEWS MEDIA DURING POSSIBLE FUTURE OPERATIONS/
DEPLOYMENTS IN THE CENTCOM AOR. IT CAN BE ADAPTED FOR USE
IN OTHER UNIFIED COMMAND AORS AS NECESSARY.

2. POLICY.

2.A. THE DEPARTMENT OF DEFENSE (DOD) POLICY ON MEDIA COVERAGE
OF FUTURE MILITARY OPERATIONS IS THAT MEDIA WILL HAVE LONG-
TERM, MINIMALLY RESTRICTIVE ACCESS TO U.S. AIR, GROUND AND
NAVAL FORCES THROUGH EMBEDDING. MEDIA COVERAGE OF ANY
FUTURE OPERATION WILL, TO A LARGE EXTENT, SHAPE PUBLIC
PERCEPTION OF THE NATIONAL SECURITY ENVIRONMENT NOW
AND IN THE YEARS AHEAD.

THIS HOLDS TRUE FOR THE U.S. PUBLIC; THE PUBLIC IN ALLIED
COUNTRIES WHOSE OPINION CAN AFFECT THE DURABILITY OF OUR

COALITION; AND PUBLICS IN COUNTRIES WHERE WE CONDUCT OPERATIONS, WHOSE PERCEPTIONS OF US CAN AFFECT THE COST AND DURATION OF OUR INVOLVEMENT. OUR ULTIMATE STRATEGIC SUCCESS IN BRINGING PEACE AND SECURITY TO THIS REGION WILL COME IN OUR LONG-TERM COMMITMENT TO SUPPORTING OUR DEMOCRATIC IDEALS. WE NEED TO TELL THE FACTUAL STORY GOOD OR BAD BEFORE OTHERS SEED THE MEDIA WITH DISINFORMATION AND DISTORTIONS, AS THEY MOST CERTAINLY WILL CONTINUE TO DO. OUR PEOPLE IN THE FIELD NEED TO TELL OUR STORY. ONLY COMMANDERS CAN ENSURE THE MEDIA GET TO THE STORY ALONGSIDE THE TROOPS. WE MUST ORGANIZE FOR AND FACILITATE ACCESS OF NATIONAL AND INTERNATIONAL MEDIA TO OUR FORCES, INCLUDING THOSE FORCES ENGAGED IN GROUND OPERATIONS, WITH THE GOAL OF DOING SO RIGHT FROM THE START. TO ACCOMPLISH THIS, WE WILL EMBED MEDIA WITH OUR UNITS. THESE EMBEDDED MEDIA WILL LIVE, WORK AND TRAVEL AS PART OF THE UNITS WITH WHICH THEY ARE EMBEDDED TO FACILITATE MAXIMUM, IN-DEPTH COVERAGE OF U.S. FORCES IN COMBAT AND RELATED OPERATIONS. COMMANDERS AND PUBLIC AFFAIRS OFFICERS MUST WORK TOGETHER TO BALANCE THE NEED FOR MEDIA ACCESS WITH THE NEED FOR OPERATIONAL SECURITY.

2.B. MEDIA WILL BE EMBEDDED WITH UNIT PERSONNEL AT AIR AND GROUND FORCES BASES AND AFLOAT TO ENSURE A FULL UNDER-STANDING OF ALL OPERATIONS. MEDIA WILL BE GIVEN ACCESS TO OPERATIONAL COMBAT MISSIONS, INCLUDING MISSION PREPARATION AND DEBRIEFING, WHENEVER POSSIBLE.

2.C. A MEDIA EMBED IS DEFINED AS A MEDIA REPRESENTATIVE REMAINING WITH A UNIT ON AN EXTENDED BASIS—PERHAPS A PERIOD OF WEEKS OR EVEN MONTHS. COMMANDERS WILL PROVIDE BILLETING, RATIONS AND MEDICAL ATTENTION, IF NEEDED, TO THE EMBEDDED MEDIA COMMENSURATE WITH THAT PROVIDED TO MEMBERS OF THE UNIT, AS WELL AS ACCESS TO MILITARY TRANSPORTATION AND ASSISTANCE WITH COMMUNICATIONS FILING/TRANSMITTING MEDIA PRODUCTS, IF REQUIRED.

2.C.1. EMBEDDED MEDIA ARE NOT AUTHORIZED USE OF THEIR OWN VEHICLES WHILE TRAVELING IN AN EMBEDDED STATUS.

2.C.4. NO COMMUNICATIONS EQUIPMENT FOR USE BY MEDIA IN THE CONDUCT OF THEIR DUTIES WILL BE SPECIFICALLY PROHIBITED. HOW-EVER, UNIT COMMANDERS MAY IMPOSE TEMPORARY RESTRICTIONS ON ELECTRONIC TRANSMISSIONS FOR OPERATIONAL SECURITY REASONS. MEDIA WILL SEEK APPROVAL TO USE ELECTRONIC DEVICES IN A COMBAT/HOSTILE ENVIRONMENT, UNLESS OTHERWISE DIRECTED BY

THE UNIT COMMANDER OR HIS/HER DESIGNATED REPRESENTATIVE.
THE USE OF COMMUNICATIONS EQUIPMENT WILL BE DISCUSSED IN
FULL WHEN THE MEDIA ARRIVE AT THEIR ASSIGNED UNIT."[3]

QUESTIONS

1. What does the Pentagon directive authorize journalists to do?
2. What kinds of restrictions does the Pentagon directive place on journalists
    embedded with the military? Does this amount to military censorship of
    the news? If so, is it justified? If not, why not?
3. Is there a potential in the Pentagon directive for embedded journalists to be
    more easily made part of a propaganda machine for the military? What
    should journalists think about the opportunity of being embedded with
    military units engaged in active combat?
4. Does the military have a legitimate purpose in working with journalists to
    try to "SHAPE PUBLIC PERCEPTION OF THE NATIONAL SECURITY
    ENVIRONMENT NOW AND IN THE YEARS AHEAD"? What would that
    purpose be? Should journalists automatically cooperate with such a pur-
    pose for the sake of having firsthand access to military movements and
    combat situations?
5. Are journalistic "embeds" automatically or necessarily "part of the story"
    they are trying to cover? Is this objectionable from the standpoint of jour-
    nalistic ethics? How should professional journalists try to balance the
    opportunities and risks to professional standards of objectivity involved in
    being embedded with the military as reporters?

WARTIME REPORTAGE

The Pentagon document offers a fascinating glimpse into the most recent
attitude of the American military with respect to journalistic reporting on
ongoing events during wartime. Although we have not reproduced every
word of the directive, the excerpts convey a rather exact impression of
the extent to which military planners have sought to anticipate factors relevant to the decision to embed reporters with soldiers fighting in the field.

What we discover in the proposal is at least an ostensible effort to
reconcile the interests of a free press with those of a military charged with
special responsibilities of its own. The embedded reporters, known within
the military and henceforth in the press corps as "embeds", eventually num-
bered seven hundred during the Second Gulf War in Iraq. The rationale
offered by the military for choosing to introduce embeds in its operations is

---

[3]Memorandum 101900Z February 2003 from the secretary of defense (OASD-PA), Washington,
DC, on ground rules for journalists embedded with the military, to numerous undersecretaries,
the White House strategy room, and other governmental agencies. The reader is encouraged to
review the complete document.

revealing. The principal argument is that by bringing reporters to the sites of active battles, the military declares that it hopes to achieve "LONG-TERM MINIMALLY RESTRICTIVE ACCESS" for journalists to military events and personnel, together with a level of "IMMEDIACY" that is intended to enable journalists to provide a "FACTUAL ACCOUNT," described also as "OUR STORY GOOD OR BAD" of wartime events, in the service of democratic ideals.

All this sounds noble enough. We need not become unduly cynical about the military's purposes in embedding journalists with troops in order to wonder whether, like most matters of practical affairs, there are underlying moral ambiguities and conflicts of interest, or even moral dilemmas, associated with the policy. Security factors are prominent and equally in evidence in the planners' concerns for the policy. They are naturally interested as always in time of war in journalists releasing the wrong kinds of information that could be injurious to the military's ability to conduct its operations effectively and with a minimum of casualties. There are also some surprising technical provisions against the use of artificial photographic lighting in certain circumstances. These are arguably necessary in order to avoid disclosing troop positions or size and strength to a watchful enemy. Journalists cannot simply do whatever they like when they accept the opportunity to be embedded with armed forces engaged in conflict. They must follow certain rationally justified rules for their own safety and for the security of military personnel. They are also required to have specific immunizations, to dress in certain ways (as noncombatants with protective equipment), not to carry firearms, and the like. As with other aspects of the professional journalistic guideline not to become part of the story, not only by avoiding certain kinds of physical actions in company with soldiers, preserving their status as noncombatants, but by withholding certain kinds of information from publication that could affect the course of military operations and change, especially for the worse, what would otherwise be the outcome of events. The situation with respect to reporters being embedded with the military is thus not that different in principle from the responsibilities of reporters covering an ongoing criminal trial. We are dealing throughout with roughly the same set of underlying journalistic ethical ideals and their practical application.

The experience of reporters who were embedded in the Iraq war seems on the whole to have been positive from a journalistic viewpoint. The newscasters involved in the program reported an unprecedented degree of firsthand knowledge in moving with troops engaged in battle, offering them previously unimagined insight into what it is like for soldiers to be involved in combat. They were able to convey this experience in turn in some form to their readers and viewers to help them understand the progress of the war and to follow events within the usual restrictions in a direct and personally meaningful way. A free and democratic society naturally sees it as in its self-interests to keep the public as well-informed as possible about such monumental events as the conduct of its soldiers in a war. The public has a definite right to know, within limitations, what is happening on the ground and whether or not its military is living up to the nation's values. The official explanation for why embedding was chosen for reporters in the Iraq war clearly seeks to fulfill these high-minded political objectives.

It has frequently been remarked by professional journalists since the recent embedding policy began that the decision has changed the future of war coverage forever. Whether it has done so for good or ill is likely to remain a topic of controversy. This will be especially true as subsequent conflicts in which embedding is practiced involve more and different kinds of experiences in more and different kinds of battlefield situations.

It was unquestionably remarkable, however, for viewers at home to witness, as they were able to in the spring of 2003, live coverage of battlefront engagements between American and coalition forces and forces loyal to the regime of Saddam Hussein in Iraq that was being toppled. Often the video feeds were choppy and highly digitalized, offering something like a view of the desert war through an insect's compound eye. The real-time videography nevertheless made for dramatic news, enabling viewers to see what things looked like from the standpoint of a soldier traveling by tank or armored personnel carrier across the desert at high speed from one location of engagement to another. The bounciness and breakup of mosaic video from the field and the sound and percussion of artillery, only added to the sense of realism and immediacy that was achieved there for the first time to such an extent in the history of warfare and journalism.

We do not need to reflect on such occurrences long or hard in order to worry about the moral implications of embedded news war reporting. Will it glorify war, make it seem something like a video game, hence trivial and less real, transforming the horrors of war into entertainment or infotainment, as it has come to be called? Or will embedded war reporting instead make war so real, immediate, and disgusting that a free citizenry will begin to withdraw its moral and political support from a nation's engagement in military conflict? In either case, will such a result be a morally good, bad, or neutral and indifferent thing? What should we think about such new opportunities and challenges for journalists reporting from a war front? We shall simply have to wait and see what the full implications of such a policy will finally be. We can nevertheless agree in advance that insofar as the goals of professional journalism are to maximize the amount of relevant truth telling in reporting on important news events, and insofar as embedding contributes to that goal, it is a new tool and new method for communicating the facts of military encounters that better enables journalists reporting on a war to meet their professional objectives and satisfy the fundamental moral requirement of journalistic ethics to tell as much of the truth as they possibly can about newsworthy events in the public interest, consistent with their other values and more highly prioritized moral obligations. To be there on the scene, traveling with the troops, seeing what they see, and living as the troops live, coming under fire and being there when fire is returned, can in obvious ways help the members of a free society to be better informed about its nation's military actions.

CONTROL, CENSORSHIP, AND PROPAGANDA POTENTIAL FOR EMBEDDING

Is there not, however, also a downside to journalistic embedding? Are there not ways in which embedding can be used to co-opt and control the content of journalism during times of war that can actually restrict the free flow of information that is otherwise available to journalists trying to cover the facts?

The verdict is not yet in on the journalistic ethics of embedding. From the objections and questions that have been raised about the policy and its practice, we can nevertheless foresee some of the likely difficulties and the rough outline of future debates, disputes, and controversies surrounding the use of embeds as sources of wartime news reporting. The idea of protecting journalists by keeping them with the military during conflicts seems to be positively motivated, but it also carries the possibility of abuse.

In the period from January 1992 through September 2003, 569 journalists died in the line of duty trying to cover the news worldwide, often in particularly dangerous circumstances. Of these, 275 died in war zones; 46 journalists were similarly killed reporting the news more particularly during the time of the Iraq war, between January 2002 and April 2003. In Iraq alone, 14 journalists were killed in 2003, 24 in 2004, and, in the final weeks of 2005, thus far, a total of 22. Such losses are not only a personal tragedy, but they represent the sacrifice of an extremely valuable social resource, the knowledge, training, and experience that professional journalists put to use for the sake of conveying information to the public. To the extent that embedding can help to save some lives of journalists there is a defensible moral justification for the practice. The question is whether in the process journalists are giving up too much of their journalistic independence and integrity for the sake of safety and the immediacy of experience moving with troops actively engaged in hostilities.

As an indication of the potential problems, we should cite a variety of complaints raised by some critics that embedding provides the military with an easy way to control what journalists see and hear and, therefore, on what they can or cannot report. For one thing, in the Iraq war of 2003, embedding was primarily permitted only for U.S. and British journalists, but not for journalists hailing from countries that did not support the coalition war effort. In particular, journalists from Germany, France, and Russia were denied access to the same level of information as American and British news reporters. Whether this is in fact morally objectionable or a fact of life that most nations should expect with respect to the reciprocal treatment of their journalists based on their involvement or lack thereof in a particular military action is as yet unclear. It is a phenomenon that might equally occur with respect to British or American reporters hoping to report on a military engagement by another country to which British and American governments did not contribute. Perhaps the restriction of journalistic permission during the war is only the usual diplomatic tit-for-tat that happens at various levels of foreign policy interactions. It also remains to be seen whether other nations will also begin to adopt a policy of journalistic embedding and offer embedding only to reporters from certain countries. The limiting of embed positions to favored nations nevertheless remains an aspect of the first implementation of the policy in the Iraq war to which journalists from other neutral nations have naturally objected. The exclusion of journalists of certain nationalities from embedding privileges when that is where the best story is to be found reflects a disturbing lack of cooperation between governments over the free and unfettered gathering of news. It is only intensified over concerns about the discovery and disclosure of sensitive military information when journalists from many nations want to report on wartime events by accompanying a particular country's armed forces into battle.

While in some ways embedding seems to offer journalists a more complete picture of a conflict than they might otherwise attain, there are also drawbacks. Embedded journalists for the most part go only where the military takes them and therefore see and hear only what the military permits. The provisions for embeds listed above make it clear that they are not to have access to their own transportation, but are required to travel with the military. It is reasonable to say that such requirements are intended for their safety, and perhaps for the sake of secrecy, but it is also a restriction that under wrongful implementation of the policy can easily be imagined to control the facts journalists are able to gather and on which they are able to report. As such, it amounts to a kind of directed censorship, and even propaganda for a war effort, rather than the objective impartial news reporting that journalists are professionally required to provide.

Other moral reservations concern the content of war reporting by embeds. These factors depend again on the extraordinary communications technology and photojournalistic capabilities available to contemporary news reporters, many of whom are now be able broadcast ongoing events immediately from the battlefield. What will happen, some journalists and critics have wondered, and what should we think about it if it happens, when a battlefield death occurs for the first time on live television? What will be the effect and what will be the proper professional journalistic ethical response if viewers at home watching television witness their own sons or daughters caught in real-time battle, wounded before their eyes as they watch, or even captured or killed? Will such occurrences, if they are permitted to take place, have a chilling effect on a free nation's ability to conduct war, on the standards of journalistic practice and journalistic ethics, or on the extent to which the military is willing to permit embedded journalists in the field to report freely and in real time on what they witness as they move forward with troops engaging in deadly interaction with an enemy? If the military decides that such live coverage needs to be delayed, scrutinized, and in some instances edited by military authorities on the basis of military criteria for content, will that represent a legitimate restriction of information during wartime or a morally objectionable form of journalistic censorship?[4]

What, finally, shall we conclude about the embedding of news reporters in the military during armed conflicts and the professional journalistic ethical principle of distance, objectivity, and the rule for journalists not to become part of the story? Journalists, generally, are supposed to maintain their objectivity as a precondition for maximum truth telling in reporting the news. They are supposed to avoid becoming part of the story insofar as doing so might tend to degrade a journalist's ability to report objectively on the facts.

There is an epistemic tradeoff in the embedding of reporters with soldiers. A certain element of objectivity is lost in the process, because news reporters tend to bond with the military personnel with whom they move in the embedding model, with whom they spend long periods of time under difficult conditions, and on whom they directly depend on a daily basis for their security in moving through a war zone. It is conceivable that in the course of the embedding experience at least some journalists might identify so strongly with the soldiers in their group that they begin to lose their ability to observe their actions critically and objectively and, hence, at a certain cost in terms of the maximum relevant truth telling to which journalists are professionally morally obligated. The threat to the quality of news reporting resulting from the embedding of reporters with troops therefore need not be that the military will keep too cautious an eye over where journalists go and what they see and are able to report during time of war, but rather that the journalists through too close fraternization with soldiers may begin to see things too closely from a soldier's point of view to be able effectively to critically judge what the military is doing.

This is a sense in which embedded journalists might become part of the story they are supposed to report that might adversely affect their ability to see things as they otherwise would if they were not so closely related to the soldiers with whom they are embedded. It may be a small price to pay for the opportunity to get close to the action and report on what soldiers experience in the field. For professional journalists aware of the risks and prepared to exercise vigilance to maintain their critical objective judgment, it may be possible to be embedded without becoming so much a part of the

[4]A variety of different perspectives, positive and critical, on the embedding of reporters with troops in the Iraqi war is offered by Katorsky and Carlson, *Embedded*, and Atkinson, *In the Company of Soldiers*. Additional sources on the war from journalists include the compilation from Reuters Correspondents, *Under Fire*; Editors of Time Magazine, *21 Days to Baghdad*; and NBC Enterprises, *Operation Iraqi Freedom*.

story that they can no longer critically evaluate and objectively report on the events of which they have in fact and for better or worse become physically a part. When embedded journalists are themselves wounded, killed, or captured, they do not necessarily become a part of the story they are trying to report, but of another story that will remain for other journalists to cover.

A recent deplorable example that illustrates the constant physical danger to which news reporters in politically volatile situations are subject was the capture and cold-blooded execution of thirty-eight-year-old *Wall Street Journal* reporter Daniel Pearl. Pearl was covering radical Islamic groups in Karachi, Pakistan and was lured to what was supposed to be an interview with a Muslim fundamentalist on January 23, 2002, when he was kidnapped and later reported killed about a month later on February 22.[5]

It is a hazardous occupation, and journalists in the line of fire need to take all sensible precautions when gathering the news. The desire to avoid becoming part of the story is always a concern, but it should not prevent journalists from pursuing their profession. The values of distance, independence, and objectivity in news reporting extend at most to the stories on which a journalist is reporting, not the larger story of the contemporary human adventure in which all persons, journalists not excluded, are involved, and in the general whirl of events in which any of us, including news reporters reporting on the events, might be caught up. When such things happen to a journalist who survives the ordeal, the journalist becomes an expert source of information for a story at least partly about the journalist for other journalists to report.[6]

---

[5]For an account of the facts surrounding Pearl's murder by a popular contemporary French philosopher, see Levy, *Who Killed Daniel Pearl?*

[6]Another example involving a fortunate rather than tragic outcome occurred during the aftermath of the Iraq war in the spring of 2003 when CNN medical news reporter Sanjay Gupta was sent to the battlefront to observe and report on medical facilities and treatment for both American and Iraqi soldiers injured in combat. Gupta, who, in addition to being a journalist, is first and foremost a talented neurosurgeon, was called upon to perform a number of delicate brain operations in the field under the MASH tent. Does this situation represent a morally objectionable case of a journalist becoming part of the story? Surely not, since Gupta as an individual was acting in different capacities as a news reporter who just happens also to be a surgeon. Later, he reported on his impressions of what it was like to be a physician operating in the desert during the war. Given his expertise and the urgency of his assisting the medics, Gupta would have been remiss as a surgeon with the necessary skills and experience not to have lent his abilities as needed by the wounded on both sides of the conflict on the grounds that as a reporter he could not get involved at the risk of damaging his journalistic objectivity. The same reasoning avoids objections concerning the journalistic ethos to avoid becoming part of the story for reporters who happen to witness a crime or preventable disaster about to take place. They are morally obligated to interfere and intervene in the events, not as journalists and because of their professional training and obligations as reporters, but as citizens or moral agents with more highly prioritized responsibilities that outweigh and override their obligations to maintain distance from and mere observer status concerning the events on which they are supposed to report. It remains then in theory for another journalist to report instead in their place on events in which they might accidentally have become involved in order to assure journalistic objectivity.

PERSPECTIVE AND ORIENTATION IN NEWS REPORTING

We turn now to another aspect of journalistic objectivity. In many cases, reporters, like any other epistemic agents, like ourselves when we are exercising our ordinary cognitive abilities, can simply see and hear the facts that they are reporting. They can look to see whether snow is white, or in reading a report, talking to physicians and other persons on the scene, verify to their own satisfaction whether or not in fact the president as rumored has fallen in the bathtub.

These matters are relatively unchallenging. There are nevertheless other cases whose difficulty increases with the complexity of the subject matter concerned. These often involve the motives and intentions of reporters in situations where potentially conflicting interests can skew the reportage of facts. Journalists need especially to be on guard against these factors as contributing to inadvertent falsehoods entering into their reports. *Perspective* and *bias* are two such potential obstacles to truth telling in journalism. Even if truth itself is not subjective but, as we previously suggested, an objective matter of positive correspondence between propositions and the states of affairs they are meant to express, subjective judgments about the facts opens the door to many problems of subjectivity in truth telling.

Consider perspective. There are several different senses of perspective that are relevant to truth telling generally and to journalistic reporting in particular. We can think of *perceptual perspective* as a matter of the difference in spatiotemporal location of different perceivers that can make a difference in how they perceive and hence how they judge the same event or state of affairs. If A observes a car accident from one street corner and hence from one point of view and at one angle and B observes the same accident from another place, perhaps from a fourth-floor window with a full view of the movement of traffic on the street and the drivers' and passengers' reactions in the cars, then A and B, given the difference in their locations and vantage points, might arrive at very different judgments about such matters as which car was moving faster, whether the drivers were paying attention to conditions, whether one tried to stop, whether both drivers were following the law, and so on, and, finally, in the final analysis, which if either of the drivers is most likely responsible for the accident.

We may assume for simplicity sake that both of the observers are comparably cognitively equipped to make good perceptual evaluations of the situation. The issue becomes more complicated as soon as we more realistically take into account such additional factors as difference in eyesight, whether one observer has 20–20 vision and the other 20–200, whether either or both are color-blind in the same or different ways or have what is otherwise referred to as normal color vision, whether there is smoke or other full or partial barriers to visual perception affecting one of the perceivers but not the other, whether one is suffering from a severe headache or is intoxicated while the other is clearheaded, and so on. All of these differences among perceiving subjects can make an enormous difference in what it is they perceive and what they are in a position to report as the content of their perceptions, even when they are making a sincere and honest effort to communicate only the truth about the facts of an event they witnessed as they believe it to have actually occurred.

POLITICAL AND OTHER FORMS OF PERSONAL BIAS

News reporting is subject not only to the unnoticed limitations of epistemic perspective deriving from spatiotemporal location and cultural and subcultural predispositions of journalists, but also to what is commonly called *journalistic bias*. Bias is a tendency to interpret and report on things in a particular way that favors a position with which a reporter is in sympathy or that disfavors a position with which a reporter is out of sympathy.

As with other kinds of perspective, bias can be either deliberate or subconscious. We see television reports of political figures, for example, which are clearly slanted in support of one political party or another, even if the news agency as a whole repeatedly makes a point of informing its viewers that its reportage is balanced and fair. All the subtleties of biased news reporting can be found in journalism of this kind, again either deliberately or because the reporters are not themselves aware of the extent to which they are biased toward one way of thinking about things or another. The ways in which journalistic bias manifests itself include but are by no means limited to the choice of topics to cover or avoid, the selection of flattering or unflattering photo images, the look on reporters' faces as they describe events about which they are biased, smiling widely for things they approve and being dismissive even of the successes of persons or political parties or movements with which they disagree, the preference for accompanying music that can have a subliminal effect on viewers in the case of radio or television journalism, and many other devices that can subconsciously sway the opinions of viewers in the direction of a reporter's bias.

Bias in news reporting is morally objectionable from the standpoint of professional journalistic ethics to the extent that it detracts from truth telling. Telling the truth is not simply a matter of getting facts right, but also of communicating them *as* facts without excessive opinionizing of a verbal or nonverbal sort about the value of the facts. To do so may carry another message that is not necessarily consistent with a journalist's obligation to provide maximally relevant truth telling in the public interest. By reporting facts whose truth is not in dispute in a biased way, a heavily slanted value-laden presentation of the news goes beyond and potentially conflicts with journalism's primary mission to report the facts.

Case Study 26

Allegations of Liberal Versus Conservative Bias in American Journalism

An effort to expose at least the sociological basis for certain kinds of bias in the media, expressive of a certain bias of its own, is found in the following, by now somewhat dated, report by Bernard Goldberg, republished in his recent book, *Bias: A CBS Insider Exposes How the Media Distort the News*:

"In 1985 the *Los Angeles Times* conducted a nationwide survey of about three thousand journalists and the same number of people in the general public to see how each group felt about the major issues of the day:

- 23 percent of the public said they were liberal; 55 percent of the journalists described themselves as liberal.
- 56 percent of the public favored Ronald Reagan; 30 percent of the journalists favored Reagan.
- 49 percent of the public was for a woman's right to have an abortion; 82 percent of the journalists were pro-choice.
- 74 percent of the public was for prayer in public schools; 25 percent of the journalists surveyed were for prayer in the public schools.
- 56 percent of the nonjournalists were for affirmative action; 81 percent of the journalists were for affirmative action.
- 75 percent of the public was for the death penalty in murder cases; 47 percent of the journalists were for the death penalty.
- Half the public was for stricter handgun controls; 78 percent of the journalists were for tougher gun controls.

A more recent study, released in March 2000, also came to the conclusion that journalists are different from most of the people they cover. Peter Brown, an editor at the *Orlando Sentinel* in Florida, did a mini-census of 3,400 journalists and found that they are less likely to get married and have children, less likely to do volunteer community service, less likely to own homes, and less likely to go to church than others who live in the communities where they work."[7]

QUESTIONS

1. What conclusions should a good news reporter draw from the above list of statistics?

[7]Goldberg, *Bias*, p. 126. A comprehensive treatment of cultural bias in the media is offered by Rivers, *Slick Spins and Fractured Facts*, especially chapters 2 and 3.

2. Does Goldberg make a strong case for the claim that there exists or has existed a liberal bias in the American news media? Why or why not?

3. Suppose that Goldberg is right that a liberal bias is prevalent in American journalism. Would that fact, if true, represent a threat to the requirement of journalists to maximize relevant truth telling in the public interest?

4. Is it possible that Goldberg has a bias of his own? Looking at his book as a whole, as you are encouraged to do, does Goldberg have a particular reason for investigating a liberal bias in the media? Does he make efforts to identify other kinds of bias in American journalism? Is he concerned about the possibility of a conservative bias? Should he be equally concerned about one if he is concerned about the other? Does it matter if it is true that a liberal bias outnumbers a conservative bias? Is journalistic bias acceptable as long as it is in the minority?

5. What would a critic like Goldberg need to show in order to demonstrate that a liberal or any other type of bias has had a negative effect on the quality of news reporting? What would it take to prove that political bias is inimical to truth telling in the public interest?

To evaluate Goldberg's statistics properly, we would need, among other things, to compare the percentages of unmarried journalists with or without children, likely or unlikely to engage in volunteer community service, and the like, with those of members of other specifically identified professions, of educated as opposed to uneducated persons, and with reference to many other kinds of potentially relevant factors. We need not deny, on the other hand, that many different kinds of bias exist within journalism, just as they do in any other walk of life.

The difference that intentional or unintentional bias makes with respect to truth telling can be illustrated in this way. If I report the fact that a member of a certain political party has been questioned by the police, then I am communicating potentially valuable information. If, however, in doing so, I roll my eyes or turn my head ever so slightly in disbelief or disapproval or indicate in other ways that I believe the person is probably in legal trouble, then I am communicating something more than the information represented by the facts of the news. I am communicating additionally in that case that I, and perhaps viewers who identify with me as an authoritative source of information, think the person is probably guilty. This, we should say, particularly in a society whose legal values include the principle that an accused person is innocent until proven guilty, is morally objectionable. It is an infraction of journalistic truth telling, even if it should turn out that the person being questioned by the police turns out later in fact to be guilty—something to be legitimately reported only if and when those facts come to be known.

If a particular news reporter or service repeatedly does this kind of thing in its reporting, involving many different reporters, especially toward a particular point of view, political party, religious affiliation, racial group, or any other social subdivision, ideology, or moral outlook concerning the facts of the news, then the news service as a whole is in violation of professional journalistic ethical standards and ought either to reform its practice, make a more deliberate effort to avoid embellishing its reporting with expressions of bias, or be penalized in an appropriate way by professional journalistic oversight. Since reporters are not always aware of their own biases, they can be a difficult matter to avoid or root out where they exist, even by news reporters who are conscientious about the obligations of relevant truth telling in journalism. If, on the other hand, there are news reporters or entire agencies with an agenda that favor one social faction against another and if their bias is regularly reflected in their journalistic practices, then they should be professionally censured, which is not to say censored, for their breach of the fundamental moral requirement of journalistic truth telling.

Does this mean that news reporters are morally obligated to have no political or other factional commitments of their own? Not exactly. There are several ways in which bias when recognized by journalists can be corrected. We expect every person in a society, especially those sufficiently involved in current affairs to be journalists, to have their own opinions and to favor one side of social issues over another. We cannot avoid bias in our thinking, journalists included, because to be biased at a certain level means only to have reached judgments or to have an outlook or perspective on questions of vital interest to the society in which one lives. The question is rather what to do about it. The news reporting of a reporter with a bias need not itself be biased, in the sense that facts are falsely or misleadingly reported. Reporters can make principled decisions to avoid any indication of personal bias in their news reporting: first, by becoming aware of the potential for a problem and, second, by adjusting the content of their reporting to avoid expressions of bias. It is one thing to have an opinion and quite another to express one's views. We do not expect reporters to be absolutely without bias, but we do expect them to be aware of their particular slant toward one side of an issue or the other and to make a conscious effort to prevent their bias from resulting in biased reporting.

We require news reporters to investigate events involving other cultures that are strange to us and often to the reporters themselves. If such occurrences in foreign cultures were not strange but familiar in all their details, then there would be no need to gather information about them for we would already have all the relevant information in hand. Journalists to the best of their abilities are supposed to discover and communicate relevant truths about things which they are not always properly prepared or culturally situated to understand. All we can justifiably ask of them is that they make a concerted, energetic, and sincere effort to try to report the facts as best they comprehend them and as they believe we will be able to understand them. It is nevertheless an interesting fact about the moral dilemmas facing journalists that they are expected to do something that in the nature of things is highly difficult and professionally demanding. If the moral obligation of a news reporter was actually always to tell the truth rather than always to try honestly to tell the truth, we might again find ourselves in the untenable position of positing something that journalists ought to do that they cannot practically speaking be expected to do.

INTERPRETATION BY NEWS REPORTERS AND CONSUMERS

It is worthwhile in this connection to say something about the epistemic problems of *interpretation* as they affect both the work of reporters and its reception by news consumers. To understand what is happening, it is often not enough simply to observe and remember what we have seen. We must also try to put it into a framework of ideas we already possess, to relate the facts of a new experience to other facts, including facts about ourselves.

If we try to sketch out all the essential elements of the process of news reporting in a philosophical model, we should probably need to include the facts that: (1) News reporters have a complexly internested set of perceptual, personal, and cultural perspectives from which standpoint they collect information, (2) which they must then try to communicate to a readership or audience in a particular choice of texts and images, (3) for persons whose background and presuppositions they may likely have some grasp of, but which will also include persons of very diverse perceptual, personal, and cultural perspectives. From this standpoint they must in turn try to digest the news information with which they are presented, to put to use in their own lives, notably including participation in private and social political affairs. We see that in this dynamic there are many opportunities for things to go slightly or significantly wrong, for truth telling to be inadvertently misplaced or overlooked.

Reporters, like their news clients, must not only perceive but interpret what they see. They must do so, in the first instance, to try to understand for themselves what it is they are witnessing or that concerning which they are collecting information. They must offer an interpretation of the facts for easy consumption by their readers or viewers in the media. The background and preparation of news consumers to follow the complex events and detailed explanations that are sometimes required in order to fully understand what is happening cannot always be presupposed. Journalists as a result in rendering interpretations must often simplify their reportage, round off the difficult corners in their accounts, use analogies with which their readers and audience are likely to be familiar, and, most importantly, interpret the meaning and significance of the events on which they are reporting, trying to put them in perspective against a certain choice of beliefs, expectations, hopes, fears, and desires, as best they can anticipate them, of those persons for whom they are offering their interpretations of occurrences in the news. Then, when their reports have been transmitted, the readers and viewers of the news must also interpret what they have been presented, participating actively in assimilating news information. They must engage in a cognitive process in which they see and hear things through their own individual and overlapping cultural filters representing a variety of different perspectives, assessing the importance and deeper meaning not only of the events being reported but of the reports themselves. The medium is not always the whole message, contrary to Marshall McLuhan's attention-getting but somewhat exaggerated slogan, but for any sophisticated consumer of news, it is always at least a part and often an important part of the message.

In this three-tiered process, there is interpretation as well as perception of facts taking place at every stage. Indeed, it seems only reasonable to recognize that perception as opposed to immediate sensation is generally an activity in which memory and interpretation play an essential role, for it is only in this way that thought has facts available for consideration in the first place. We open our eyes and take in light rays or direct our ears or other senses toward sound waves or other information sources. We do not have purported facts or information to accept or reject unless or until we have interpreted the data of sensation, categorized and conceptualized what is seen or heard or felt or tasted or smelled, committed at least some of it to memory, and related it to other information already assimilated. The same is true whether we are reporters on the scene trying to collect the facts, exercising sensation and judgment, interpreting what we see and hear, or whether we are news consumers, readers and viewers at home, exercising sensation and judgment both about the content of what a reporter is reporting and facts about the report itself in its mode and manner of presentation. Interpretation pervades and conditions perception and, hence, the gathering, expression, and communication of news events. What are we to make of this fact from a philosophical standpoint that bears on the problems of journalistic ethics?

SKEPTICISM, RELATIVISM, AND POSTMODERN DISREGARD FOR TRUTH

It has become a trademark of certain strains of contemporary philosophy, mostly originating in Europe after World War II, and more particularly, as it happens, in France, to argue that all efforts to discover and share truth are doomed to failure because of the layering of interpretations between perception and judgment. Such a point of view now has adherents worldwide whose skepticism poses a special challenge for journalistic truth telling.

There are no facts as such, according to this form of epistemic relativism. Instead, there are only interpretations, only a clatter of texts, broadly construed, each interpreting the other and competing for attention and loyalty by a public following, who, for rhetorical, polemical, or other reasons unrelated of necessity to matters of truth telling, will gravitate toward one way of looking at things rather than another as an intellectual culture takes shape.

As with most extreme points of view, this so-called postmodern assault on objectivity and truth is based on something reasonable that is then taken too far in one direction. It is true, first of all, as we have already acknowledged, that perception involves sensation and judgment, and that judgment is generally a matter of interpretation. Why, however, take the further apparently unwarranted step by concluding that therefore all interpretations are epistemically on a par, that there is no basis for distinguishing some interpretations as true and others as false, or that there are degrees of truth and falsehood in interpretations in perception, expression, and communication, such that it makes no sense despite the facts of interpretation to expect a meaningful distinction between truth and falsehood in journalism as in all other related cognitive activities?

The level of skepticism about the search for objective journalistic truth is reflected in the observations of journalists commenting on their understanding of the realistic expectations for the conduct of news investigation and reporting. Thus, we read:

> Most journalists today do not believe that there is such a thing as perfectly objective Truth. Carolyn Lee, the former picture editor and now assistant managing editor at the *New York Times*, represents much responsible mainstream thought in saying, "You are never going to get a purely objective look at anything." Reality, she said, "is always in the eye of the beholder." Two reporters "can take the same set of facts and write two very different stories." Similarly, she said, two photographers will approach an assignment "with different eyes" and will come back with quite different pictures.[8]

The recognition that objectivity may be unattainable remains coupled with a commitment to the effort by journalists to project the search for truth as an ideal. The commentator above, drawing on her editorial experience in the newspaper industry, contrasts objective truth as something that might be regarded as entirely mechanical and impersonal with the need for sound journalistic judgment in deciding what events should be covered and how they should be presented in the media:

> Still, it is important to add quickly that this clearly does not mean that journalists quit trying to find that elusive ultimate truth. "Of course, we try to," Lee said, while still recognizing that it is impossible. That is where judgment is involved, she said, from both the reporter and the editor. The reporter makes choices, deciding which facts to include in the story and in what order to put

[8]Knowlton, *Moral Reasoning for Journalists*, p. 40.

them. The assigning editor also makes choices, not only about which stories to cover and which to ignore, but which reporters to send to which assignments. In making such decisions, Lee said, the journalist has to think: "Do I see this story as a feature or do I see it as hard news?" The selection of the writer assigned to a story will have a great deal to do with the eventual story that gets into the paper. "You're not going to tell me I am *wrong* if I see it as something humorous that needs a certain kind of writing," Lee said.[9]

How are we to understand the truth and falsehood of interpretations of information that admittedly pervade all aspects of cognition in general and of journalistic judgment in particular? We have already said that truth and falsehood is a matter of positive correspondence or lack of positive correspondence between what is presented as an interpretation or judgment, or in some cases a news report, and the state of affairs that actually prevail.

The sort of checks on accuracy of information, reliability of witnesses and other data sources, cross-correlation of facts, and careful formulation of what a journalist can responsibly be said to know or not know, are well-established criteria in the profession. There is no need for new ethical standards or innovations in the search for objective journalistic truth. It is enough for journalists to receive occasional reminders about and enforcement of existing principles that have guided news reporting since its beginnings. It is sound practical judgment by experienced journalists themselves once again that provides the only reasonable measure of what it is relevant to report, whether a report is truthful and accurate, and how a news story should be presented. As always, we must work from clear-cut cases to establish a practical ideal and finesse the more difficult examples with goodwill and sincere effort to the best of our abilities. The same point is made by the media commentator Walter Lippmann in his classic (1922) book, *Public Opinion*, in distinguishing between news and the truth in a larger sense:

> The hypothesis, which seems to me the most fertile, is that news and truth are not the same thing, and must be clearly distinguished. The function of news is to signalize an event, the function of truth is to bring to light the hidden facts, to set them into relation with each other, and make a picture of reality on which men can act. Only at those points, where social conditions take recognizable and measurable shape, do the body of truth and the body of news coincide. That is a comparatively small part of the whole part of the whole field of human interest. In this sector, and only in this sector, the tests of the news are sufficiently exact to make the charges of perversion or suppression more than a partisan judgment. There is no defense, no extenuation, no excuse whatever, for stating six times that Lenin is dead, when the only information the paper possesses is a report that he is dead from the source repeatedly shown to be unreliable. The news, in that instance, is not "Lenin Dead" but "Helsingfors

[9]Ibid.

Says Lenin is Dead." And a newspaper can be asked to take the responsibility of not making Lenin more dead than the source of the news is reliable; if there is one subject on which editors are most responsible it is in their judgment of the reliability of the source. But when it comes to dealing, for example, with stories of what the Russian people want, no such test exists.[10]

There is no philosophical reason to despair of truth in journalistic interpretation or journalistic reportage generally. Similarly, there is no convincing argument to relax the moral requirement that journalists should always try to the best of their abilities to tell the truth about the events on which they report.

As a practical activity limited to correspondences of expressions of belief with states of affairs as perceived and interpreted in practice by sincere and clear-minded cognitive agents, journalism does not need to resolve every imaginable philosophical basis for questioning the absolute truth or certainty of knowledge. That would set too high a standard for journalism, as it would in other practical activities such as medicine and the law for which applied ethics must also consider professional criteria of moral conduct. Interpretation and the dangers of misinterpretation are a real concern for journalists insofar as they are morally required to try to the best of their abilities to report the news truthfully in the sense of corresponding to the facts and existent states of affairs that can generally be discerned by other perceivers, but this does not obviate the moral obligation of journalists to maximize relevant truth telling. The very fact that we can speak intelligibly in such contexts of interpretation as opposed to misinterpretation testifies to the fact that there is a real distinction somehow to be drawn between interpreting truly or correctly and interpreting falsely or incorrectly. We suppose interpretation in news reporting to be done on the basis of correctly or incorrectly interpreted judgments of what is perceived within the community of cognitive agents capable of examining and considering a news report. This is all we need to say with respect to the fact that news reporting and news consuming are not inherently opposed to objective journalistic truth telling.

CONJECTURE AND SPECULATION IN THE NEWS

There is yet another aspect of journalistic interpretation to be investigated. It has become a popular part of presenting the news to conjecture not only about the meaning or significance of events as they occur, but to do so in the context of speculating, sometimes rather wildly and some critics might say irresponsibly, about the facts of future upcoming events concerning which there is as yet no hard information.

---

[10]Quoted in Knowlton and Parsons, ed., *The Journalist's Moral Compass*, p. 108.

Case Study 27

2000 American Presidential Election Coverage

Let us consider a particularly instructive example. In the 2000 American presidential elections, many of the major networks reporting on the outcome of the election projected Al Gore as the winner and announced this as their interpretation of exit poll information, early election results, and other indicators that in the past have been highly reliable ways of determining how an election will turn out.

Their interpretation was not entirely irresponsible, although in retrospect it certainly seems to have been premature and imprudent to announce a winner before all the relevant facts were available. The fact is, nevertheless, and there is no reason to hesitate in calling it a fact rather than a mere interpretation, that although Gore gained a significant majority of the popular vote, he did not have enough electoral college votes to win the election under the American Constitution and so did not in fact win the election. Here is what Day, as one commentator, has to say about the incident and those responsible for it in the media:

> "While most reporters embrace accurate reporting as a first principle of ethical journalism, time and competitive pressures sometimes compromise the accuracy of news coverage. The biggest blunder in recent memory occurred when the four major broadcast networks, CNN, the Associated Press, and many of the nation's leading newspapers incorrectly named Democrat Al Gore as the winner in the 2000 presidential contest. The surreal nature of the coverage continued throughout the evening as the networks, realizing their mistake, retracted their Gore 'call,' named Republican George W. Bush as the winner, and then retracted their Bush projection, declaring the presidential race in limbo. 'It's Gore! It's Bush! It's a mess!,' lamented *Broadcasting & Cable* magazine in a headline that captured the frustration of media insiders."[11]

The networks were accordingly faced with the embarrassing fiasco of having falsely interpreted the situation and falsely reporting an event that did not actually take place. There is no doubt that they simply got things wrong and issued a false report based on a mistaken interpretation of the facts. When this became clear, they had no choice, of course, except to withdraw their prediction and correct the false report, which, much to their chagrin, they all subsequently did.

---

[11]Day, *Ethics in Media Communications*, p. 84. See Bezanson, *How Free Can the Press Be?*

This is a particularly conspicuous example, one which news corporations themselves have closely analyzed in an attempt to learn from their mistakes and avoid such errors in the future. The fact, and let us again not hesitate to call it a fact, that they recognize the problem as not merely a matter of interpretation in an area where different subjective judgments could arrive at different conclusions, powerfully indicates the recognition that there is such a thing as a difference between true and false interpretations of facts, between accurate and inaccurate or appropriate and inappropriate judgments of their meaning and significance, of what the facts in fact are, and that these objective differences in judgment come to roost in the true or false beliefs and propositions at which thinkers, including journalists, arrive.

A final lesson of the 2000 American presidential election coverage debacle has to do with the ethics of cost cutting by news networks. At one time, individual news companies hired their own pollsters and conducted their own exit interviews at election polls, drawing their own conclusions from the data they personally collected. Prior to 2000, most television news programs and networks began to rely on a single polling agency to do this work for them. Where in the past a single mistake by a single newspaper or network would have been a professional embarrassment for the reporters involved, today almost all news sources are getting their polling predictions from the same resource. When it makes a mistake, the mistake is more widely disseminated than in the past through virtually all news outlets.

QUESTIONS

1. As an exercise, keep track during an hour's news programming of all the conjecture and speculation as opposed to reporting of facts that is done in your favorite news source. What do you conclude about the percentage of news reporting currently being given over to conjecture?

2. Can conjecture and speculation in news reporting conflict with the fundamental principle of journalistic ethics to provide maximally relevant truth telling in the public interest? Is there any truth content to speculation or conjecture when it is offered, or is the justification for making educated guesses about the future outcome of world events based on something other than the moral right and responsibility of professional journalists to report newsworthy facts?

3. What sort of practical safeguards can journalists establish to help avoid disasters like the 2000 American presidential election forecast? What would you have done in an editorial capacity to prevent hasty and unsubstantiated conjecture from being published as news?

4. By going beyond the facts, do journalists in asserting conjectures about what will happen in the future make themselves "part of the story"? If so,

is this objectionable from the standpoint of journalistic ethics? Why? If not, why not?

5. Does speculation and conjecture as a part of news reporting help a readership or audience better understand and interpret the facts of news events? Why or why not? Can speculation and conjecture be justified as part of entertainment or as an effort to provide cultural context for the dry facts of the news?

UNSCIENTIFIC POLLS AND UNSUBSTANTIATED OPINIONS

We might suppose that journalists as a rule would see their business as one of reporting only on things that have already happened. Increasingly in the popular press and television, news reporters have taken to venturing predictions and projecting where the course of events on which they are reporting are likely to lead next.

This kind of reporting can sometimes help to put current events in perspective and help readers and viewers understand the outcome of ongoing occurrences. Unfortunately, in many cases there is a tendency, of which many media commentators have themselves complained, to substitute sheer guesswork for investigative journalism that presents only the facts as best the reporters have been able to discover them. Such reporting sometimes interprets the meaning of events contextually from a historical and contemporary standpoint, but this is a rather different proposition than conjecturing what the future may or may not hold. A free press, needless to say, is free to do such things, but we as critics of the free press are also free to criticize the practice if it seems professionally questionable.

Viewers of the recently popular round-the-clock news programs are often invited to participate in such efforts. They are asked to use toll-free telephone numbers or online computer connections through Web sites or e-mail to contact the news stations to offer their generally unqualified opinions about a wide range of subjects. Salient examples of this kind of thing include polls taken by news agencies asking viewers to offer their views on the whereabouts of the former Saudi terrorist Osama bin Laden. The news anchor on one occasion asked viewers to indicate whether they thought he was alive or dead and, if alive, whether he was in Afghanistan, Pakistan, or somewhere else. This is a troubling trend in news that needs to be evaluated by journalists as part of their internal self-regulation. For, obviously, there is no way for the average viewer of a news program to have any idea except sheer gut instinct as to whether bin Laden is alive or dead or where he might be hiding. What is more, there is nothing worthwhile to do with such information once it is collected, except to note that a certain percentage of viewers with no basis whatsoever for their judgments believe one thing or another about the terrorist's present circumstances.

The potentially pernicious thing about such unsubstantiated opinion polls is that they encourage a culture of unfounded speculation as a legitimate basis for news reporting. Who cares, we may be tempted in frustration at such pointless exercises to ask, what a random selection of people uninformed about the relevant facts simply happen to believe for no particular reason about a matter of fact? Who cares, generally, when turning to the news, what might or might not happen, as opposed to receiving a more penetrating analysis of what is known actually to have happened and how recent events are related to other events that have actually happened and from whose interrelation further interesting facts might be inferred? The practice of speculating on future events as a part of news reporting not only threatens to displace genuine news and news backgrounding and analysis as worthwhile journalism; insofar as it takes away from the energy of news reporters to ferret out and report on important facts, it represents a clear violation of the fundamental professional moral obligation of journalists to maximize relevant truth telling in the public interest.

There is a fine line between interpreting current news items by placing them in temporal context, both with respect to their historical background and likely future implications, on the one hand, and simply guessing what might or might not happen in the future. Parading as news, the problem is magnified when predictions are offered in the same tone of voice and with the same serious mode of presentation as that with which the facts of a news day concerning events that have actually happened are reported. It is speculation that has recently begun to supplant the proper business of news reporting, especially on television. It is tempting to wonder whether this has come about because twenty-four-hour news services simply have no better way given staffing limitations to fill so much time with something intriguing to say. Another likely hypothesis is that by involving viewers in polls, news networks hope to get viewers to stay tuned to see the results, to learn how other people feel and, hence, to boost ratings. Major network news, in the meantime, which is broadcast only for a few hours at specific times, seem to have felt a need to follow suit in order to remain competitive and offer viewers what they have by now been conditioned to expect in viewing television news reports. It is, for the reasons we have mentioned and regardless of its underlying economic motivations, a deplorable trend that should be resisted, tempered, and, to whatever extent possible, reversed, as conflicting with the obligation to concentrate on relevant truth telling in journalism. Speculation and prediction is not journalism, no more than consulting Tarot cards or a Ouija board, and should not be presented as such or even in the same forum wherever the distinction is likely to be confused.

Needless to say, the journalistic calamity in reporting the outcome of the 2000 American presidential election would never have occurred if news reporters were to confine their coverage to existent facts in evidence and did not venture into the dangerous waters of anticipating occurrences that have not as yet occurred. Many of the news sources implicated in the episode have since turned their attention to ways of improving their ability to project election winners more accurately. The real moral lesson of the 2000 election might still be eluding them, insofar as they remain insensitive to the implication that journalists, as professionals charged with the task of communicating facts in reporting the news, may have no business in the first place trying to forecast what might or might not happen in the future, concerning what might or might not turn out to be true.

Summary

In this chapter we have considered at length and in some detail what journalists can and should do to counteract the effects of subjective and cultural perspective, interpretation, bias, and judgments of relevance in covering a news story. Journalists have a fundamental moral right and responsibility to tell the truth to the best of their ability, but they are not necessarily morally obligated in every instance to get everything right the first time.

We have noted that there is often a tradeoff in journalistic practice between the value of having rapid news collection, assessment, and communication, on the one hand, and the sort of more leisurely investigation of facts that researchers in history and science usually have to verify their facts and check and recheck what they have to say before they commit themselves to saying what they believe to be the truth. The result is that journalists sometimes, hopefully infrequently, make mistakes in their reporting by accidentally presenting false information. What we generally expect and morally require journalists to do in such circumstances is to report their errors publicly to the same intended readership or audience to which the false information was inadvertently addressed. All of the news sources involved in the 2000 American presidential election did an admirable job of correcting their mistake once they discovered it. This is not quite as good as avoiding the mistake in the first place, and we have indicated some of the ways in which they might try to do so in the future, but it is the very next best thing.

If you follow news events in newspapers or over radio or television for a long enough period of time, you will sooner or later encounter this practice on the part of conscientious journalists. When necessary, they may indicate that on a certain date they reported that such and such happened, and then they add that they have since learned that the report has turned out to be false, that the facts to the best of their understanding are now something different. Sometimes news broadcasters undertake the further courtesy of apologizing for their mistakes to their audience. This is a nice civil gesture, but one that does not seem to be morally obligatory when an honest mistake has been made. It is enough to acknowledge the mistake and set the record straight. It is morally obligatory, on the other hand, from the standpoint of professional journalistic ethics, for journalists to do their best to correct their mistakes by issuing appropriate retractions and reporting what they afterward believe to be the actual facts.

Like other persons engaged as fallible agents in complicated cognitive transactions, journalists should be prepared to acknowledge their mistakes and do their best to correct them. This is also a part of the general obligation to maximize truth telling. If, practically speaking, it cannot always be done when taking a first stab in reporting an event, then the responsibility should be met as quickly as it is reasonable to do so in reporting the news over subsequent days, weeks, months, or years. Anyone can make a mistake in trying to report on complicated events. Journalists have a special professional obligation when they discover themselves to have made a mistake to do whatever is reasonable to correct the misinformation they have released and to try to undo the false impressions it may have created. What must be avoided at all costs, if journalists are to meet their professional responsibilities to maximize relevant truth telling in the public interest, is not to engage in epistemic cynicism or lapse into apathetic complacence about the possibility of arriving at the truth in news reporting because of the problems of perspective, interpretation, bias, or subjective judgments of relevance. These are all factors that professional journalists are morally responsible for learning about, becoming more aware of, and doing their utmost to counteract as potential obstacles to truthful news reporting. They draw the wrong conclusions to these facts if they decide that therefore there is no point in trying to arrive at the truth, that truth is somehow impossible, and that as a result they are free as journalists to say more or less whatever they want.

The tenets we have cited are not new moral obligations that we are suddenly extracting from thin air. They are rather immediate implications of the fundamental moral requirement of professional journalists to maximize the reporting of true relevant information in the public interest and for the public good. There are at least two broad categories of journalists who do not live up to the moral ideal of maximal relevant truth telling. Rogue journalists, generally and hopefully few in number and far between, deliberately set out to misrepresent the facts as they believe them to be, or they make up things to say and present them as news without undertaking the necessary research to discover and verify their content as facts. For these journalists we have little to say except that they are deserving of the highest moral censure by the professional journalistic community, with all the penalties that can reasonably be attached to their actions. This is journalistic malpractice at its worst, and the effects for persons who accept their fabrications as truth and try to act on such misinformation can potentially be as devastating in their effects on others as that of wrongdoers professionally engaged in deliberate medical or legal malpractice. The other category of journalists who do not live up to the moral ideal of maximizing truth telling in news reporting, as we have mentioned, are those who sincerely try to tell only the relevant truth relative to the implicit purpose of the stories they are supposed to cover, but who accidentally make honest mistakes. Journalists who unwittingly communicate falsehoods, provided they are not complacent, cynical about the problems of discovering truths, lazy, or unwilling to work hard to determine and communicate relevant facts, are not deserving of moral censure, providing that they then engage in responsible efforts to correct their mistakes and mitigate whatever damage might have occurred through the unintended transmission of misinformation.

Beyond this, professional journalists have moral obligations to become aware of the potential for the distortions of perspective, interpretation, bias, and subjective relevance judgments and to take decisive actions to counteract their effects. These, as we have indicated, can include a variety of measures. Journalists may need to submit their work to peer review and editorial scrutiny to minimize the effects of perspective; to avoid bias by limiting opinion, in the form of innuendo, body language, and other signs of approval or disapproval, and in editorial or opinion columns or reports, op-ed or opinion-editorial pieces, as they are called, to make sure that a variety of different sources from different perspectives are represented when sensitive issues are discussed in news stories; and to clearly signal to their readers or viewers when they are offering opinions as opposed to reporting facts, when they are offering a personal perspective as opposed to purporting to convey objective truths.

Professional journalists should learn in journalism school to mitigate the misleading effects of their own perspective and bias. They need at some early stage of their careers to acquire such sensitivity and training under the mentorship of a senior reporter or experienced editor from whom they learn the ropes during a period of on-the-job apprenticeship. Journalists are morally obligated to check one another's reporting for truth and accuracy, to regulate themselves and their colleagues with respect to the effects of perspective, interpretation, bias, and subjective assessments of relevance on the goal that should govern all news reporting of maximally relevant truth telling. They can do so in part by encouraging truth and avoidance of whatever detracts from effective discovery and presentation of truthful useful information. These efforts can and should be further supported through personal interaction, awards and other acknowledgments and incentives, and discouraging the opposite through criticism and in extreme cases fines, penalties, public censure, and loss of employment. The fact that these structures are in place in virtually all responsible news agencies, like the fact that responsible news agencies occasionally issue corrections of unintended mistakes in their reporting, testifies to the recognition that they have a moral obligation to maximize relevant truth telling in the presentation of information to benefit news consumers. All mechanisms for encouraging relevant truth telling and discouraging deliberate or inadvertent falsehoods in news reporting are derivatively morally obligatory by virtue of serving the ultimate moral ground of professional journalistic ethics in the requirement to maximize relevant truth telling in the discovery and communication of useful information about current events.

chapter nine

Editorial License and Obligations

We pursue the topic of journalistic perspective in this chapter by considering the ethics of editorial license. Opinion columns in newspapers and the equivalent in broadcast media offer journalists the opportunity not only to report facts but to express opinions and interpretations of news events. Here political outlook and explicit bias have their proper place, provided they are openly acknowledged as such and not confused with news facts. A news editor's special journalistic rights and responsibilities are compared with those of news reporters, as we situate the problems of editorial license and its obligations within the general framework of journalistic ethics.

EDITORIAL OPINION

In previous chapters we discussed the importance of journalists observing professional standards of accurate reporting. As a further requirement of communicating facts in the public interest, we further argued that reporters need within practical limits to remain objective and as independent as possible and to maintain a critical distance from the events being investigated, while to the best of their ability avoiding bias and mitigating the potentially truth-diminishing effects of perspective, interpretation, and subjective relevance judgments. There is nevertheless, on top of these professional obligations, an appropriate place within journalism for the free expression of opinion in newspaper editorial columns, pages, and editorial pieces in radio and television newscasts, just as we previously noted that there is an appropriate place for entertainment in the news.

We should not expect a free press to be hampered in its expression of opinion. The judgments of respected journalists make a valuable contribution to our understanding of current events that can assist us in forming our own opinions and reaching our own decisions about important events of the day. Journalists have as much right as other citizens in a free society to voice their opinions, to praise or criticize whatever they believe is worthy of praise or criticism, in addition to reporting on the facts of current interest. That journalists occupy a special position of authority as truth seekers and conveyors of information nevertheless imposes special obligations on editorial opinion as an accompaniment to reporting the news. We shall explore some of the most important of these obligations as a continuation of the topics in journalistic ethics we have already examined. Editorial opinion is an essential part of journalism, but one that is seldom discussed in any depth in standard expositions of journalistic ethics. Among other questions, we must ask: What are the responsibilities of editorial license? What moral guidelines ought to be observed in expressing opinions and offering judgments and evaluations of events alongside the reportage of facts?

Case Study 28

Ethics of Editorializing in a Free Press

The following description of the relation between a free press and the distinction between news reporting and editorializing is offered by Onora O'Neill, philosopher and Principal of Newnham College, Cambridge, as presented, appropriately enough, in the opinion column of *The Irish Times*, February 22, 2005, p. 16:

> "Press freedom should be matched with obligations to achieve standards, such as a duty to inform rather than mislead, writes Onora O'Neill.
>
> One of [playwright] Tom Stoppard's characters explained to another: 'I'm with you on the free press. It's the newspapers I can't stand.'
>
> It is a thought many of us have had. Is a free press to set aside good journalistic and editorial standards, to specialise in gossip and rumour, or to marginalise straightforward reporting?
>
> If we want press freedom do we have to accept whatever we get even if some of it is offensive, deplorable or trivialising?
>
> Contrary to many assertions, the answers to these questions are not obvious.
>
> Free press must (at least) be free from state regulation of content. If public authorities can determine what shall and what shall not be reported, the press is not free. This is non-negotiable in liberal democratic societies; no required publication of state propaganda, no state (or church!) censorship. However, not all regulation is content regulation, and not all regulation is state regulation.
>
> Press freedom is never unconditional freedom. For example, press freedom is typically limited by legislation against defamation and incitement,

by standards for advertising and for certain sorts of reporting, and by many other measures.

The European Convention on Human Rights sets out a range of legitimate reasons for qualifying press freedom (Article 10, ii), and includes a right to privacy (Article 8) . . .

Press freedom is badly configured where readers cannot readily distinguish reporting from commentary, or information from entertainment (hybrid genres such as 'infotainment' and 'advertorials' are suspect). It is misused if newspapers do not aim for accuracy, check their facts and correct mistakes.

It is abused if the public is not safeguarded from 'news management' that covertly pursues or protects the interests of owners, editors and journalists (especially when reporting on financial, planning and political issues).

It is endangered if the interests of owners, editors and journalists and conflicts of interest are hidden from the public, leaving those with an interest free to promote it under the guise of reporting or offering independent commentary . . . "

QUESTIONS

1. How does the author propose to relate the freedom of the press to the journalistic responsibility not to mislead readers or viewers as to the distinction between "reporting" and "commentary"?

2. What is the difference between these two journalistic functions? Can any news report ever be entirely uncontaminated by editorial opinion or commentary? How can readers and viewers learn to recognize the differences between the two? What can happen if the distinction is progressively blurred?

3. To what extent, if any, is an editorialist responsible for distinguishing editorial content from news information? To what extent, if any, is a reader or viewer responsible for identifying and applying the distinction to what is read and heard or viewed?

4. Explain what the author means by ways in which "news management" can pursue or protect the interests of owners, editors, and journalists in disguised form as news reporting. Can such efforts typically involve editorials masquerading as news? Identify, describe, and criticize a case study of your own from recent editorial pages of a newspaper or news program in which a vested interest seems to take the form of news reporting. Why is such a thing objectionable from the standpoint of journalistic ethics?

5. O'Neill extols the virtues of self-regulation on the part of journalists in the interests of preserving a free press. How should a free press try to regulate itself in particular to avoid the abuse of editorial prerogative? What, if anything, should happen if the press fails to regulate itself adequately? Is censorship and coercive restraint of journalistic freedom the only alternative?

DISTINGUISHING NEWS FROM COMMENTARY

The first principle of editorial responsibility is that editorial opinions should be explicitly distinguished from statements of fact. Journalists primarily report on occurrences that are presented as answers to the traditional five journalistic "wh-questions" of who, what, when, why, and where. That is their bread and butter, and how they are generally known to the public, as purveyors of important or merely interesting facts.

When journalists go beyond the facts, it seems reasonable that their readers and audience should be clearly signposted of the difference, so that it is clear at this stage that they are not simply reporting events but offering value judgments. There are a number of devices by which this distinction is indicated for the alert reader or viewer of the news. Newspapers standardly contain editorial columns that are explicitly captioned as such, marked as editorial expressions of opinions, and often containing such phrases as, "I believe," "in my opinion," "in this commentator's view," "as I see things," and the like. All of these kinds of devices serve to distinguish the expression of a pundit's editorial opinion from news reports of facts.

The point is to avoid confusion so that the public does not misunderstand or fail to recognize the division between what is meant to be presented as fact and what is meant to be presented as opinion about and evaluation of the facts. Similar graphic techniques are used on television, where the editorial spot is often graphically highlighted on screen by means of a vivid label calling attention to the fact that what is now being offered is an "Editorial," "Opinion of the Management," or "Analysis and Evaluation." The idea is to keep separate the domains of news reporting of the facts and what journalists working for the news agency or its owners or managers might think about the meaning and value of the facts. The explicit earmarking of the distinction between fact and opinion about the facts and the institution of the editorial column or its equivalent on radio and television news observes an important principle of journalistic ethics to maximize relevant truth telling by not misleading the public as to what a reporter believes is fact and what is only editorial opinion, evaluation, and expression of value.[1]

It is because we have already identified maximally relevant truth telling as the primary duty of journalists that we now argue that explicitly distinguishing between reportage of facts and expression of editorial opinion is entailed as a further requirement of professional journalistic ethics. The reason is that not to make the distinction between fact and opinion clear potentially conflicts with a journalist's responsibility to inform news

---

[1]For a comprehensive account of the combined role of news reporting, analysis, and editorial commentary, see Merritt, *Public Journalism and Public Life*.

consumers in the public interest and for the public good. What happens if the distinction between fact and opinion is not sufficiently respected? Among the most obvious implications of failing to mark the difference carefully enough for readers and viewers is that they might come away from reading a newspaper or watching a television news program with the mistaken impression that it is simply a fact, for example, that a foreign government is acting rightly or wrongly, that abortion is morally permissible or morally impermissible, that a certain bill currently being debated before the legislature should or should not be passed—when these value judgments are only the editorial opinions of the columnist or media moguls. There are facts, on the one hand, as news reporters investigate and report on them, and then there are opinions, interpretation, and analysis of the meaning and value of the facts. In the interest of maximally relevant truth telling, the two should never be confused.

Editorial opinions consequently should not be conveyed indistinguishably along with the other facts of the news as though they were also items of information. Professional journalists are obligated by their responsibility to maximize relevant truth telling in the public interest not to encourage readers and viewers to confuse such facts as the proposition that a foreign government has acted in this or that way, that abortions are being performed or are not being performed, or that a certain bill is currently being debated before the legislature with editorial attitudes toward the value or larger implications of the facts for society. A journalist misleads the public in a way that is incompatible with the fundamental moral obligation of professional journalistic ethics to provide relevant truth telling insofar as he or she condones the expression of opinion or the analysis and evaluation of events as though the contents of such opinions were themselves a straightforward matter of fact. Again, journalists have every right, though not necessarily the professional moral obligation, to express personal and managerial opinions about the meaning and importance of interesting developments in the news. If they choose to use a news forum, newspaper or radio or television program, to present opinions and value judgments about the news, then they are obligated to do so in a way that does not lend itself to confusion with the facts, which they have a more urgent fundamental responsibility to discover and communicate to the public.

FACT-VALUE GAP AND THE NATURALISTIC FALLACY

The distinction between fact and value, news and opinion or evaluation about the facts reported in the news, is a pervasive division that is widely recognized in moral philosophy. The distinction is sometimes known as the *fact-value gap*, and the effort to bridge the fact-value gap or blur the distinction between facts and values, is referred to somewhat misleadingly as the *naturalistic fallacy*.

The fact-value gap marks a distinction whereby values supposedly cannot be validly derived from facts or states of value from statements of fact. As an example, consider the fact that a war has occurred or a debt has been repaid. We can imagine different persons having different opinions about the morality of such actions, some believing war to be inherently wrong, others accepting the concept of a just war and regarding the war in question as just and therefore morally defensible or even praiseworthy. Some persons might believe that repaying debts is always a good thing, while others want to look more closely into the circumstances of the debt and its repayment. They may wonder, for example, whether the debt upon being repaid allows a person to commit a malicious act that otherwise could not have been undertaken for lack of funds or whether in paying the debt the debtors are impoverished to such an extent that innocent persons suffer unnecessarily for an amount of money that is insignificant to the lender.

The Cambridge University moral philosopher G. E. Moore, in his influential 1905 book, *Principia Ethica*, argues that the fact-value gap is established by what he calls the "open question" argument. The idea of an open question is that it remains undecided or indeterminate whether a fact, no matter how completely described, is good or bad. If it remains an open question whether the occurrence of a war or repayment of a debt or any other occurrence is good or bad, then we cannot suppose that the facts of the case considered in themselves are either good or bad, either morally right or morally wrong, morally praiseworthy or morally blameworthy. If this is true, then the moral evaluation of a set of facts must always be something superadded to any statement of facts being evaluated.[2]

Thus, as we have seen also in the newsroom, there are, on the one hand, the facts of the day's news, and then, on the other hand, there is the entirely different question of whether the events that have occurred are good, bad, or indifferent, whether they should or should not have occurred, and of what should or should not happen next as a consequence. We consider the topic at some length because of its general interest in moral philosophy and its special application to the distinction in applied journalistic ethics between reporting the news as fact and offering editorial opinions, analysis, and evaluations of the facts reported in the news.

The naturalistic fallacy is supposed to categorize a mistake of reasoning in which, according to Moore, an attempt is made to define an indefinable concept. Moore introduced this terminology to highlight the problem of trying to analyze the concept of good in terms of a natural property, especially a natural psychological property like happiness or pleasure, as we find among so-called eudaemonistic or hedonic moral egoists and consequentialists, including utilitarians, such as Jeremy Bentham, James Mill, John Stuart Mill, Henry Sidgwick, and others. Moore criticizes ethical theories that try to explain good

[2]Moore, *Principia Ethica*, §13, pp. 66–68; also pp. 143, 178.

or goodness as anything other than itself or that presuppose that the meaning of the concept of moral goodness can be reduced to any natural property or phenomenon. Moore does not deny that pleasure and intelligence are good, in the sense of having the property of being good. They are good things, he believes; they are just not identical with the concept of good or goodness itself. Pleasure has the property of being good and so does intelligence and so, surely, do many other things besides. To predicate the property "good" of such things is only to say that pleasure and intelligence are among the great variety of good things, not that they are identical with the property good nor that the concept of moral goodness can be analyzed as the concept of pleasure, happiness, intelligence, or any other naturally occurring phenomenon. Moore regards any attempt to identify the concept of moral good with natural things, especially psychological states, not only as false as a matter of fact but a fallacy of reasoning that he dubs the naturalistic fallacy.[3]

As a founder of analytic philosophy, Moore believes that some concepts are irreducible or unanalyzable. In analyzing concepts, just as in analyzing chemical compounds, we reach a point in the analysis where we finally hit bedrock, the simplest possible concepts that by definition as a result are themselves unanalyzable. Moore points to the naturalistic fallacy, driven by the open-question argument, as proving that the concept of good in particular is unanalyzable, incapable of being further reduced to other more simple or primitive concepts. He compares the unanalyzability of the concept of good with what he takes to be the obvious unanalyzability of the concept of the color yellow, which he believes is already as simple, primitive, or atomic as any concept to be found within our conceptual scheme.[4]

Moore distinguishes between necessary associations of properties among things that are good as opposed to component properties of the concept of good by which it could be defined or in terms of which it could be analyzed. The color yellow is associated with a particular wavelength of light absorption and reflection, a certain number of Angstrom (Å) units by which it is related to but distinguished from other colors, each of which has a distinctive characteristic light wavelength. Moore is unimpressed with such facts about yellow things as providing a satisfactory definition or analysis of the concept yellow. These, he believes, are entirely different matters. By analogy, he argues that certain properties might also accompany virtually any occurrence of a good thing, such as the property of pleasure or happiness, intelligence, or the like. By themselves, such correlations would not imply that moral good can be defined or analyzed in terms of any of these things, even if they are always found together. The open question encourages us to ask of

---

[3]Ibid., pp. 12, 15, 19–21, 90–95. See also Hutchinson, *G. E. Moore's Ethical Theory;* Sylvester, *The Moral Philosophy of G. E. Moore;* and Olthuis, *Facts, Values and Ethics.*

[4]Moore, *Principia Ethica,* pp. 9, 12–16, 92.

any occurrence of pleasure, in effect, "But is it really good?" If Moore is right, then we can similarly ask of any reflected light wavelength of the appropriate band, "But is it really yellow?" Insofar as these remain open questions until we settle them independently of their association with a particular natural property, we cannot accept an analysis or definition identifying them with anything other than themselves. The way we answer the question whether something is yellow is simply by looking at it and exercising our senses. Moore proposed something similar with respect to our intuitive sense as to whether something is or is not morally good.[5]

Here is another way to think about Moore's challenge to the identification of good or goodness with natural facts. If we begin with the proposition that "I am good" in the sense of "I have the property of being good", and if someone proposes that good is to be defined as whatever produces pleasure, then careful substitution of the right kinds of terms produces evidently false propositions: "I am whatever produces pleasure" or "I have the property of being whatever produces pleasure". We should then infer that "whatever produces pleasure" is not an adequate definition of the concept of moral good. We might try to reformulate the definition of good as an analysis according to which good is the property of being productive of more pleasure than pain. Then, if it is true that I am good, it is at least logically and grammatically unobjectionable to conclude, on the basis of the same kind of substitution that Moore considers in his criterion, that I am productive of more pleasure than pain. This still might not yet be a satisfactory definition of the concept of good. If the analysis fails, however, it does not appear to do so because of the kinds of identity and word substitution problems that Moore seems to think will occur whenever we try to replace a property term by its naturalistic definition in a true proposition. If the definition of good as being productive of more pleasure than pain is incorrect, it must be criticized on the basis of its content rather than merely by reference to its supposedly logically definitionally fallacious form. Moore argues that ethics can either be based on a false definition of good that it mistakes for something complex, or it can move forward without trying to define the concept good.

In effect, then, the second alternative is to treat moral goodness as indefinable and unanalyzable, a primitive concept of our moral conceptual scheme. Moore maintains that if ethics starts with the kind of analysis of right conduct as conduct conducive to happiness, then it is but a short step to what he believes is the obviously false conclusion, assuming there are many different good things, that goodness itself is nothing other than pleasure or happiness. If this were correct, once again, however, then we could never sensibly ask, as we evidently can, whether this or that particular instance of pleasure or happiness is good. The open-question argument thus undermines any

[5]Ibid., pp. 126–129, 143–146, 154–160, 194–198. Note that Moore distinguishes between intuition of moral good and moral sense as a kind of sixth sense, the latter of which he rejects.

effort to identify moral goodness with a natural property, whereas to try to do so is to commit what Moore calls the naturalistic fallacy.

INFERENTIAL VERSION OF THE NATURALISTIC FALLACY

There is also an inferential fallacy similar to Moore's criticism of the naturalistic fallacy in David Hume's (1739–40) *A Treatise of Human Nature*. Hume had already underscored Moore's problem of trying to deduce what ought to be the case from what happens to be the case. Hume famously writes:

> In every system of morality, which I have hitherto met with, I have always remark'd, that the author proceeds for some time in the ordinary way of reasoning, and establishes the being of a God, or makes observations concerning human affairs; when of a sudden I am surpriz'd to find, that instead of the usual copulations of propositions, *is*, and *is not*, I meet with no proposition that is not connected with an *ought*, or an *ought not*. This change is imperceptible; but is, however, of the last consequence. For as this *ought*, or *ought not*, expresses some new relation or affirmation, 'tis necessary that it shou'd be observ'd and explain'd; and at the same time that a reason should be given, for what seems altogether inconceivable, how this new relation can be a deduction from others, which are entirely different from it.[6]

We know that such inferences generally cannot be correct. It does not follow logically from the assumption that a murder was committed that therefore it ought to have been committed. Nor does it necessarily follow logically that the murder ought not to have been committed, however much we may regard the choice of the word "murder" as already expressing an implicit value judgment about a wrongful killing. It does not follow logically from the assumption that minorities have been socially discriminated against that therefore they ought or ought not to be or continue to be discriminated against. Nor in particular does it follow logically that because it is a fact that a certain group of people have a certain skin color or other physical characteristic that therefore they ought or ought not to be treated in a discriminatory way.

We can say on the basis of this version of Hume's inferential naturalistic fallacy that acts of racism and bigotry, among many other moral wrongs, are not only morally objectionable but logically confused even when they are based exclusively on true facts. If facts were values, if they were simply identical to values, then we could settle many if not all moral problems and determine the right course of conduct by the methods of natural science. Of course, we do not imagine that we can do anything of the sort. If, following Moore's use of the open-question argument, we can in principle always ask

---

[6]Hume, *A Treatise of Human Nature*, p. 469.

about the value of science and if in every case we can wonder whether the practice of natural science is itself morally good, then we cannot reduce moral good to the scientific discovery of facts. As we said before, there are the facts on the one hand, and then there is on the other hand the question of the value and further meaning, including rightness or wrongness, of the facts.

Although Moore confines his discussion of the naturalistic fallacy to definitions rather than inferences, his concept is often extended to deductive arguments. In historically imprecise treatments, Moore's definitional naturalistic fallacy is often supposed to be merely another way of expressing the inferential version of a similar fallacy in Hume. The two are nevertheless importantly different. Where Moore speaks of the naturalistic fallacy, Hume refers to the fact-value or is-ought gap. Nor is this merely a terminological difference. It is reasonable to consider the two objections together in any case as calling attention to the same problem of trying to define in terms of or derive moral value exclusively from natural facts. There is a fallacy at work here that underscores the conceptual difference between matters of fact and matters of value, as between is-statements and ought-statements. We can neither define nor deduce moral good in the sense of what ought to be the case from or in terms merely of what happens to be the case. We cannot, similarly, therefore, according to this reasoning, definitionally or inferentially derive moral values from natural facts. The differences and similarities between Moore's definitional naturalistic fallacy and Hume's fact-value or is-ought gap are brought out in the following comparison:

DEFINITIONAL NATURALISTIC FALLACY (MOORE)

Good (normative value concept) = df

natural property or properties (scientific factual concept)

INFERENTIAL NATURALISTIC FALLACY IS-OUGHT GAP (HUME)

1. Scientific statement of fact (is-statement)

2. Normative statement of value (ought-statement)

If we can always ask whether any fact ought to be the case, as Moore's open-question argument assumes, then we cannot reduce what ought to be the case from what happens as a matter of fact to be the case. We can always ask of any such descriptive facts or is-statements about the world whether they or their implications ought to be the case, which indicates that the facts themselves do not determine whether or not they ought to be true. Moore asks this kind of question when he observes that we cannot define what ought or ought not to be true about the psychological facts concerning pleasure or pain or what ought to be true concerning human development from the evolutionary facts about its course and direction. The same problem applies if we try to infer truths of moral value from scientific facts. In definitional and inferential forms, the naturalistic fallacy or is-ought gap fixes alternatively an analytically or logically unbridgeable gulf between facts and values and, in particular, between natural properties and the concept of moral good.

We can now appreciate what Hume means by what has been called the fact-value or is-ought gap and what Moore means by the naturalistic fallacy. We can further see why Moore believes the fallacy to be the source of conceptual confusions and false conclusions in moral philosophy. The same difficulty is manifested in definitions, inferences, and moral reasoning generally, if Moore is right, and with respect to both attempts to identify goodness with something other than itself. They are all ultimately efforts to define value in terms of fact or value in terms of non-values that are therefore necessarily doomed to failure. The naturalistic fallacy once again tells us that we cannot define values in terms of something other than a value, so that we cannot understand good as something other than itself. It further implies that there must be simple, basic, fundamental, ultimate, primitive, irreducible, indefinable, unanalyzable value, which Moore identifies for the purposes of ethics as moral good.

Is-Ought Gap and the Distinction between News and Opinion

We are interested in Hume's and Moore's moral philosophies only insofar as their critique of so much of the past history of ethics involves a version of the fact-value or is-ought gap that helps us to understand the distinction in journalistic ethics between reporting the news and expressing an editorial opinion in which the meaning or political, religious, or other value of the news is expressed. We find the same basic distinction between factual news reports and opinion editorials or op-eds as we do generally in moral philosophers who have remarked on the separation of matters of fact from matters of value. Just as there is a firm distinction between the question of what is true and whether it ought to be true, so there is an important distinction in journalistic ethics between reporting news facts and expressing an editorial opinion about the value of the facts, whether what has happened is a good thing or not.

Moral philosophers sometimes speak of the relation between facts and values as one in which values *transcend* facts. By this they generally mean that values are something over and above the facts and are not themselves special kinds of facts or reducible to matters of fact. In such a view, values stand entirely outside the realm of facts as the goodness, beauty, further importance, or other value *of* the facts. Something paralleling this two-part division between facts and values, what is and what ought to be the case, as we have suggested, can be discerned also in the division between professionally responsible news reporting and editorial columns and opinion statements. Insofar as journalists recognize the importance of the difference between news and news evaluation they can be said to be observing at least implicitly the fact-value is-ought gap. The very fact that news organizations distinguish between these two vital aspects of news and opinion writing and broadcasting indicates that they have a sound grasp of this distinction. They do not expect the facts of the news to speak for themselves in terms of their social value, but require evaluation and commentary as something additional to the bare reportage of facts. To invoke this distinction we need not naively assume that the journalistic investigation of facts is ever completely value-free. It is only reasonable to suppose that a reporter's motivations for wanting to look into one set of events rather than another, as well as many of the choices that give shape and direction to the actual work of investigating, composing text and in some cases supplementing it with a selection of images, and, finally, presenting the package for consumption as a news report, reflects a large complex of values throughout the process.

To return for a moment to a previous composite case study, why is a journalist more interested in the closing of a shelter for the homeless than in an empty warehouse fire? Why is another journalist more interested in an empty warehouse fire than in the closing of a shelter for the homeless? Both are facts, we may suppose, and there are facts about both of these occurrences that might deserve to be reported as such on the nightly news. Why, in reporting on a story, does a journalist choose one set of facts rather than another, with this or that particular emphasis, illustrated by these kinds of photographs or video rather than others that might equally be appropriate? In these and countless other ways journalists consciously or unconsciously express their values, including moral, social, religious, and artistic or aesthetic. Working as a reporter or editorialist or news commentator, they must make their own sense of the world and of what is right and wrong. It is an inextricable part of the profession, often interwoven so deeply and indistinguishably into their reporting of the facts of the news that they may themselves often fail to recognize the fine line between facts and values in their reportage.

There is nevertheless a distinction between facts and values, even when the two appear inseparable in a news report. Moreover, there is a distinction between the values that go into the finding and reporting of facts, which are implicitly manifested in factual news reporting, and the values that are explicitly expressed in offering editorial commentary and opinion pieces about the facts that constitute the news.

If we cannot always distinguish between facts and values in the sense of identifying absolutely value-free as opposed to value-laden facts contained in news reports, we can at least distinguish theoretically between fact-free statements of value and value-laden statements of fact. This, in turn, is all we may need in order to appreciate the fact-value or is-ought gap sufficiently to explain the journalistic practice of reporting the news as value-laden facts and nonfactual statements of value concerning the facts in editorial opinions presented in op-ed newspaper columns and radio and television spots. Whereas all reporting of facts may depend on the values of reporters, editors, and others involved in producing the news, the explicit evaluation of facts reported in the news is another thing. Commenting on the greater meaning of news facts provides an opportunity for journalists to say what they think about the value of the news that they or others report. In op-ed pieces they can say not only that a shelter for the homeless has closed, but to express their editorial opinion that this should not have occurred, that it is a bad thing for the community or a good thing, and why.

Case Study 29

National Conference of Editorial Writers Foundation (NCEW)

The fact that professional journalists are aware of the importance of editorializing as a legitimate function of the press is indicated by the following report involving the National Conference of Editorial Writers (NCEW). The conference sponsors a yearly minority writers seminar "that provides editorial writing techniques to new minority journalists and editors who have been writing for two years or less." Kate Riley, editorial writer for *The Seattle Times*, offers the following description of this work in the Washington, DC publication, *The Masthead*, NCEW publication, Autumn 2004, volume 56, issue 3, p. 25:

> "Elbert Garcia is a young New Yorker, working for a small weekly community newspaper where he does everything.
> But after a tantalizing few days at the NCEW Foundation-sponsored Minority Writers Seminar, he said he felt a pull toward the opinion side of the shop.
> 'I never thought of editorial writing as being a very creative form of writing,' says Garcia, who works for the *Manhattan Times*. But it is. The best thing was going to the seminar and really focusing on crafting editorials.

'Thinking about the different ways you could do that was eye-opening.'

Garcia was among sixteen journalists who participated in the seminar April 29 to May 2 in Nashville. The annual event is one of several missions of the National Conference of Editorial Writers Foundation. The Foundation has a multi-pronged mission to support and promote editorial writing, whether it's those actively practicing the craft or those, like Garcia, considering a career.

The Foundation puts on the Minority Writers Seminar in conjunction with the Freedom Forum Diversity Institute at Vanderbilt University. Seminar participants provide only their transportation to and from the seminar, which is open to minority journalists interested in opinion writing or those who have been writing opinion for two years or less.

Former Foundation president Tommy Denton noted that about twenty-five percent of participants in the Minority Writers Seminar become editorial writers.

Established in 1981, the Foundation also supports those already practicing the craft of editorial writing, through its quarterly publication of *The Masthead* magazine, foreign travel trips, and foreign travel and State Department briefings. The NCEW Foundation board is committed to providing some financial support for regional conferences geared specifically for editorial writers . . . "

QUESTIONS

1. Why is it worthwhile for there to be an organization like the National Conference of Editorial Writers (NCEW)? What purpose do they serve in the larger journalistic community?

2. What values seem to be embodied in the work of NCEW? What does the organization want to accomplish?

3. The NCEW's work is not limited to sponsoring the minority writers seminar. What other kinds of issues should a national organization of editorial writers be concerned with? What issues of professional journalistic ethics are relevant to the mission of such an organization?

4. Compare the statements of ethics codes for professional journalists collected in the Appendixes to the present book. Try to write out a comparable code of ethics that is tailored specifically to the problems encountered by editorial writers of op-ed pieces. What principles should be most important for them? To what extent do the ethics codes of professional journalistic organizations already cover the particular responsibilities of editorialists and to what extent must they be modified or supplemented?

5. News reporters, news readers, and editorialists are all journalists, along with camera and sound personnel, editors, managers, and others. What should be the attitude of the professional journalistic community toward its editorial writers? What role and what special tasks do editorialists have within contemporary ranks of professional journalism? What special moral rights and responsibilities do editorialists face? How best can these journalistic rights and responsibilities be exercised?

EDITORIAL OPINION AS NEWS PERSPECTIVE

Editorials and op-ed items serve a valuable function. They supplement and complete the basic facts of the news, which have hopefully been relevantly selected and truthfully reported. They offer a more personal perspective on whether or not the events are a good, bad, or indifferent thing and what further implications they may have in terms of the goals and values of a community, nation, or the world community as a whole.

It is significant that although some news sources feature editorial commentary in virtually every issue or every broadcast, many prefer to limit their editorializing to special occasions. In this way they may call greater attention to the event, making it stand out as something that sets particular events apart as worthy of special commentary beyond the mere reporting of facts presented as news. Major events in world affairs, milestones of one sort or another, scientific and diplomatic breakthroughs, turning points in ongoing struggles, beginnings or conclusions of great social movements, special heroism or villainy, often deserve to be singled out by editorial comment. They can be made all the more poignant by virtue of being reserved for moments of particular importance in the newspaper columns or broadcasting schedule that are not ordinarily covered.

Editorials can nevertheless be presented at any time whenever journalists have something noteworthy to say in taking the measure of current events, explaining what they take to be the value of whatever has occurred or is expected to occur. By putting events in perspective and offering moral, aesthetic, religious, political, and other kinds of judgments about newsworthy occurrences, editorial commentary can help consumers to better understand the facts of the news. They can serve to stimulate thinking about the further meaning of events, even and especially when they disagree with the opinions expressed. They allow journalists to assess the times, to touch base with the values of their readers or audience, and to provide a voice for what is often perceived as the values of the larger community or culture, who, even if they do not need journalists to tell them what to think about the news that is reported, may find it useful to learn that there are others who feel as they do or who feel rather differently.

Finally, editorials can sometimes enable journalists to influence public opinion. This, too, is arguably a legitimate function of journalism, provided that it is carefully distinguished from the reporting of news as matters of fact, assuming that editorialists seek to direct the course of public opinion in ways that are not otherwise morally objectionable. Does the separation of news fact and editorial opinion entail that reporters as such should never try politically or in other ways to evaluate the facts? We need not insist that news reporters are morally wrong to offer editorial commentary or that newspapers, radio stations, television networks, and other news services hire different persons to report the news as opposed to allowing the same individuals to fill both roles. The same persons can perform both functions for the news, provided that their activities are made sufficiently distinct in practice. This is indeed what most news reporters do, changing hats, so to speak, as they switch from reporting on the facts of the news to presenting statements of editorial opinion and back again to reporting the news.

The kinds of devices one frequently sees are the same we have previously mentioned. They include using a special banner or title for editorials, having the news anchor speak in a different stage set or pretend to read from a paper manuscript instead of directly from the television monitor or teleprompter, or in any number of other ways that signal to the reader or audience that opinion and evaluation rather than the straight reporting of news is taking place. With a clear way of marking the distinction between reporting the news and expressing editorial opinion in evaluating the facts of current events, the same journalists acting alternatively as news reporters and editorialists can satisfy the obligations of professional journalistic ethics to provide relevant truth telling in the public interest by helping readers and viewers symbolically to understand the difference between the content of what is presented as facts and what is offered as expressions of value.

EDITORIAL LICENSE AND IDEOLOGICAL SPIN

The careful distinction between news and opinionated evaluation of the news by itself does not satisfy all moral requirements to which editorialists are subject. Editorialists do not simply have a license to spin. There are further specific professional ethical obligations for the writing and delivery of editorials.

Spinmeisters there will always be, including those who may claim to occupy a no-spin zone. We can begin to articulate the moral parameters for editorializing by remarking the commonsense restriction against inciting a readership or audience to acts of violence or as a shelter and excuse for conveying falsehoods.

These uses of the media are morally objectionable, in the first instance, because they violate more highly prioritized moral obligations that are incumbent on all citizens and all moral agents of any society. They are also guilty of contradicting the specific moral obligations of professional journalists always to maximize relevant truth telling in any news-related capacity. As before, we must try to plot a course through the thickets of ethical dilemmas for applied moral reasoning by identifying clear-cut extreme cases and establishing practical commonsense principles to cover the obvious situations and offer guidance in the more controversial mid-range cases.

Journalists are just as answerable for their moral choices in editorializing as they are in reporting the facts. What values shall they express and try to promote? What kind of moral climate should they help to create among the public they serve when expressing editorial opinion, getting this or that off their chests, usually at the end of the regular news broadcast or in a special column of a newspaper devoted to voicing attitudes about recent happenings or expectations for the future?

In an obvious sense, these questions take us beyond the limitations of professional journalistic ethics into the sphere of general theoretical ethics and the problem of what constitutes a correct moral philosophy. We might say that if we can settle these more difficult matters of deciding the right direction for ethics, whether consequentialist (aimed at the general happiness) or deontological (aimed at satisfying the requirements of moral duty regardless of consequences), conservative or liberal, or some hybrid or third alternative to these standard categories, then editorialists might be morally obligated to promote whatever values are conducive to a preferred morality. Such a higher-order moral obligation with its implications for editorializing in applied journalistic ethics can be considered to be just another sense in which journalists like other professionals are subject to more highly prioritized moral obligations that impinge on all members of a society regardless of their profession and independently of their specific vocational obligations.

Of course, not all editorialists necessarily agree about basic moral issues or, from a theoretical standpoint, about what is the correct moral philosophy to follow and try to live by. More importantly, many editorialists and journalists generally will not necessarily think about such things philosophically at all. For the most part, they will be content to act in accord with their gut instincts concerning what is right or wrong or the culture of values in which they have been raised that consequently feels most comfortable for them in meeting life's ethical challenges. This includes what many persons of practical outlook will refer to as their code of values, together with a sense of the virtues it is important for individuals and society as a whole to cultivate. In view of this fact, we should be reluctant to judge the merits of editorials on the basis of whether or not they advance the cause of what we deem philosophically to be a preferred moral theory, since philosophers are also sharply divided over the problem of which among many conflicting moral philosophies is ultimately correct. If editorialists are not morally responsible for possessing all the right answers to the most difficult problems of ethical theory, they are at least as morally responsible as anyone else to try to find the answers and to proceed on the basis of what at any given point they fairly judge to be the right morality. What, precisely, this is we shall leave to the good consciences of editorialists and the outcome of longstanding debates in general theoretical ethics.

PROFESSIONAL ETHICAL GUIDELINES FOR EDITORIALISTS

In the meantime, there remains much that we can say by way of offering professional applied ethical guidelines that may be useful to editorialists. What, positively speaking, should editorial opportunities be used to do, what values should editorialists promote, and what kinds of individual and social behavior should they help to cultivate?

We can only hint at some of the most promising possibilities. All are admirably exemplified by the best editorialists who provide a useful commentary about values on a foundation of newsworthy facts in a complete journalistic enterprise. Editorialists can help to raise environmental consciousness, lead readers and viewers to appreciate what is good and deplore what is bad, alert the public to moral wrongdoing by politicians, help an audience to understand what is at stake in a policy being decided, place current events in a larger social and historical context of values, question authority and motivate citizens to active participation through voting and other forms of social activism, and unlimitedly many other things besides.

Good editorials make us think about the facts presented in the news— even and sometimes especially when we do not agree with the values they represent. They encourage us to question what such occurrences mean to us individually, for the societies in which we live, the world at large, and even for the history and future development of our species, of civilization and all humanity.

It is not too grandiose to say such things, however rare it is for sufficiently gifted editorialists to be sufficiently inspired by events to put things in the most panoramic perspective. A properly managed editorial stance can lead many persons to right thinking and right action, while an improper irresponsible editorial license can lead people morally astray. The editorial columns and broadcasting spots in newspapers, radio, and television are an extraordinary journalistic pulpit that can be used for good or evil, precisely because they reach a large number of thinking persons and because their subject matter in essence is the evaluation and appraisal of social good and evil.

The risks entailed by editorial license within its proper moral boundaries are much the same as those we considered earlier in connection with the problems of journalistic bias, perspective, interpretation, and subjective judgments of relevance. The practical methods by which potential dangers can be counteracted are much the same for editorializing as for news reporting, in the journalistic equivalent of the fact-value or is-ought distinction.

News companies are entitled, although again not morally obligated, to develop a characteristic editorial stance, to represent a particular value outlook on the news that they report. They can become known, for example, for being conservative or liberal in the political values they espouse, to begin with a crude and ultimately unsatisfactory way of dividing up attitudes toward a government's relation to its citizens. They can be religious, agnostic, atheistic, socialist, communist, capitalist, pro-choice, pro-life, however unsatisfactory these labels may be. They can try to promote militarism, pacifism, interventionism, noninterventionism, isolationism, and, in short, the whole gamut of personal and social political outlooks and values that editorialists like other thoughtful citizens might be inclined to endorse or oppose. A newspaper or broadcasting network might seek to establish its place in the competitive journalistic marketplace by staking its claim to any of these kinds of politically oriented viewpoints, complemented by appropriate news reporting and editorializing.

The mainstream tradition of news in the United States in its journalistic history, as in many other parts of the world, is for news sources generally to have greater respect and thus to sustain more authority for the accuracy and truthfulness of its reporting, its objectivity, and its impartiality, the more it is judged to be independent of any particular sort of social or political agenda, the less it is perceived as having some sort of axe to grind. We have described a free press as a "fourth estate" of government, particularly in the United States and those nations whose constitutions are modeled on the American tripartite division of executive, legislative, and judicial branches of government. On such a conception, just as there is a tradition upheld by the Constitution of maintaining separation of church and state within the official divisions of the bureaucracy, so by extension the same kind of religious impartiality and social agenda neutrality has come to be seen as incumbent also on journalism as an unofficial part of the checks and balances that help preserve the liberal democracy in which a free press flourishes.

The reason for this is obvious when we reflect that the more strongly news reporters are associated with a given set of policy preferences or political orientation, the more likely it is that their choice of what news to cover, what facts to consider worth relating to their readers or audience, and how they are likely to present them, with what emphasis or spin, will be slanted toward its interests in shaping and affecting social and political events. How can we trust the content of the news reported by a news source that we know from its editorials and from subtle and not-so-subtle clues contained in the delivery of its reportage is heavily biased toward excessively conservative or excessively liberal political values? Why should we expect that what we are told by such a news source represents the impartial truth rather than a program of preferences dictated by values and itineraries rather than the plain facts reported as objectively as possible? Even if a news network continually chants the mantra that they report and the viewer decides what to think about the news, something no mature news viewer needs to be told anyway, there is unlikely to be much long-term respect among a broad cross-section of news consumers for such a newspaper or network. For it will be clear from all aspects of their news coverage and editorial commentary that the paper or network as a whole has a strongly biased social or political agenda.

WAYS OF PROMOTING EDITORIAL PLURALISM

Journalists who are committed to a truly pluralistic approach to editorializing as an appropriate adjunct to objective news reporting, to the independence of both the facts they report and the values they editorially represent, can meet their professional ethical obligations in a variety of ways, many of which are read or heard or seen every day in responsible news reporting and editorializing.

Some of the most obvious methods are to rotate editorial opportunities among persons representing different points of view and different types of moral, social, and political values. Something of the same effect can also be achieved by including panels of editorialists from different parts of the social and political spectrum arguing with one another and expressing different values, exposing the advantages and disadvantages of different ways of evaluating the same news events, and allowing news consumers thereby more undirected freedom of choice to decide which opinions they find more agreeable to their own way of looking at things, even as their own ways of looking at things evolves through exposure to op-eds. Guest editorials diversify a news outlet's responsibility to express values from a variety of different perspectives, shedding light on the meaning of news events and exemplifying many different moral standpoints.

If the purpose and moral justification of editorializing is to promote moral values and evaluate the news in a broader context of social and political concerns, then it might be argued that journalists have a professional obligation to encourage multiple expressions of values and to feature discussion and disputes about values from many different angles. The advantages of such an approach should be obvious when compared with that of a highly directed, dedicated or polemical editorial stance in which a single doctrinaire viewpoint or family of related viewpoints is hammered home whenever an editorial is presented. It might be equally argued, on the contrary, that journalists truly committed to a certain set of values are morally obligated to defend those values and not merely hold out a menu of values from which news readers and watchers are invited to pick and choose. If you believe in what you have to say, why would you present your ideas as just one among many possibilities that might be adopted but for which there is ultimately no better rationale than for others? Those who want to promote different values are then free to do so from behind the editorial news desks of other news sources, among which readers and viewers in turn are free to shop around until they find what they like. If the idea of journalism is to provide maximally relevant information in the public interest, however, then a case can still be made for the conclusion that newspapers and news programs are professionally morally obligated to inform a readership or audience of the range of values by which news events might be interpreted and into which larger contexts they might differently belong. We can imagine good arguments being offered on both sides of the dispute.

Case Study 30

Journalistic Ethics and the Power of Editorial Opinion

Here is testimony to the power of editorial opinion in effecting social change. We choose from unlimitedly many possibilities an example involving local water districting in California. The report is from *The Quill*, a publication of the Society of Professional Journalists, June–July 2004. The society in 2003 awarded its Sigma Delta Chi Award for Editorial Writing to Tom Philp of *The Sacramento Bee*. Philp wrote a series of newspaper editorials on "The Water Barons," exposing the "overt secrecy" of California water districting.

> "Tom Philp recognized that California water districts were a recipe for disaster—or at least incredibly poor business practices. More than 450 independent agencies operated in the state with minimal supervision and took in large sums of money from ratepayers' water bills. Philp, associate editor/editorial pages for *The Sacramento Bee*, recognized the potential disaster and created 'The Water Barons,' a series of more than 20 editorials.
>
> 'This began with one phone call from one source in one water district hearing a rumor that another had just fired its controller for raising too many questions about extra payments to management,' said Philp. 'We sent a records request to this water district to review expenses of the elected records and of the management.'
>
> As suspected, Philp found immense expense abuses.
>
> One water district has a tradition of mixing water business with ratepayer-subsidized golf (in Pebble Beach, no less). Another district welshed on a promise to a grand jury to approve all travel in public and to permanently strip directors of their district credit cards. At another, the entire staff belongs to one family.
>
> In the weeks ahead we will venture in more detail into the hidden empires of water districts and the people who run them. It should be quite a journey. These governments—often small, often mundane and usually operated with minimal scrutiny—turn out to be worth some attention, from both the public and the Legislature.
>
> 'This is about important, but obscure, governments that too often behave as if nobody is watching,' said Philp. 'And one particular water district, Sacramento Suburban, where the misbehavior was downright fraudulent—failing to report hundreds of thousands of dollars in income, for example, prompting federal indictments of two top managers and one conviction to date.'

Philp wrote the series on an off-deadline basis over the course of 2003. His research included sifting through more than 8,500 pages in requested records.

'I flagged questionable spending with Post-It notes as I reviewed the records,' Philp said. 'I ended up getting an industrial-strength three-hole puncher so I could store all the documents in three-ring, three-inch-thick notebooks, with all these Post-Its sticking up from the top.'

The change resulting from 'The Water Barons' still echoes in the day-to-day operations of California water districts.

'(The agencies) have taken steps to behave as if somebody is watching— or may be soon,' said Philp."

QUESTIONS

1. How can editorializing play a role in journalism as a force for social good?
2. What is the distinction between investigative watchdog journalism of the sort exemplified by Tom Philp's series of editorials on "The Water Barons" and editorials that express opinions about received news items without undertaking special news investigations?
3. Philp's project is sometimes classified by journalists as a "campaign," in the past less culturally sensitively as a "crusade." This is a practice of using the editorial columns of a newspaper or other media programming in order to rouse public opinion and get the police, legislature, or other regulative agencies to take action in order to correct a social wrong. What guidelines, if any, should be established to assist in editorial campaigning? Are there limits to what kinds of topics campaigning editorialists should be permitted or encouraged to pursue? If not, why not? If so, what form should they take, and how can they be justified in a context that respects the freedom of the press?
4. What positive benefits does the case study above indicate have resulted and can be expected to continue to result from Philp's investigative editorializing? If we take Philp's case as typical, what can we learn from it generally about the value and potential power for social good that occurs as a byproduct of this type of journalism?
5. Compare and contrast the advantages and disadvantages of news reporting versus editorializing in the conception of journalism as a force for social good. What can an editorial writer accomplish that an ordinary news reporter cannot achieve? What can a news reporter accomplish in this regard that is more difficult or unattainable for an editorialist? Are these simply two different ways of trying in some cases to accomplish the same purpose, or are these two journalistic functions different in the opportunities they afford? Locate Philp's original editorials and read them carefully, marking the distinction between Philp's reporting the results of his investigations, the facts of the California water districts on the one hand, and the specifically editorial component of his op-ed pieces. Does he clearly distinguish between these two functions, or can you find places where his presentation might mislead a reader?

Summary

To repeat, there is no professional moral obligation within the principles we have elaborated for journalists to editorialize in the first place. To do so, nevertheless, is certainly a natural and, properly managed, morally permissible use of newsprint and airwaves. It is their right to editorialize and, as we have emphasized throughout, with journalistic rights come journalistic responsibilities. Attention should perhaps accordingly be shifted in understanding the issues from the makers to the consumers of news reportage. What should readers and viewers of editorials do, and how should they think about what they are presented when journalists change hats and turn from reporting the facts of the news to expressing values in their editorial opinions?

For one thing, it is as important for consumers of news to make an effort to distinguish between what is offered as news versus what is offered as editorial opinion in reading, listening to, or watching the news. We as news recipients should make a point of determining whether what we are being exposed to in the work of journalists is a statement of fact or the expression of values and opinions of the significance of news events.

This requires in the first place that we be aware of and mindful of the distinction as we prepare to absorb information and values from the media. We bear a measure of responsibility ourselves not to confuse the two when they are properly presented, even if they are not always explicitly distinguished. It is up to us to know when we are being given facts and when we are being fed values. In particular, we should not assume that when a journalist with a respected reputation for accurate reporting of facts also expresses values that the values expressed necessarily carry the same weight of acceptability as the reliability of independently verifiable facts. Facts are facts, and judgments about the values of facts are not facts and should not be conflated with or misconstrued as facts. Editorialists have a responsibility not to conflate the two, but readers and viewers also bear a responsibility to keep the two categories distinct in their own thinking about journalistic content.

We should be aware of the distinction and take the time to ask ourselves which we are being presented and what sort of weight we should attach in our thinking to these different kinds of news experiences. When an editorialist expresses values, we should recognize that it is always a matter of personal judgment that we need not share even if and when we fully accept the facts and truth of the reportage of facts to which the editorial expression of values is superadded. It is up to us as individuals to determine the meaning and value of the facts that journalists present for ourselves as evaluators. We should regard editorials as offering only one way of thinking about such things that we are free to accept or reject, but that in any case we should consider merely as guiding us in our own consideration of values in assessing the import and moral right or wrong of the facts on which journalists report. The ultimate responsibility for assessing the value of the facts of the news rests with each of us as individuals, even when charismatic writers, reporters, and announcers make an attractive and compelling case for their point of view.

Moreover, we should not permit ourselves to get emotionally carried away with the statements of values conveyed by opinion editorials. Recognizing that editorials offer only a particular valuational appraisal of facts for our consideration can help us to avoid being incited precipitately to ill-considered actions. Values are partly a function of emotional reaction; yet they are equally if not more properly the result of calm rational reflection on what is good and bad, beautiful and ugly, important and unimportant, on what goals and purposes it is worthwhile to have and to pursue, and of how means and ends should best be connected for the sake of securing more ultimate values. A commitment to a value and the decision to act on the basis of such a commitment are therefore not merely matters of triggering emotional responses, but of thinking through what is in one's best interests, as well as those of others in the family, community, nation, and humanity, and even for the projected interests of the animal kingdom and inanimate environment.

As a part of the obligation not to allow ourselves to be taken in by any single editorialization of values, we may further, last of all, consider it a moral requirement as readers and viewers of news, just as we may find it necessary to cross-check important news items against reports from several different independent and unrelated news sources, also to compare and evaluate editorials concerning the same subjects from multiple sources representing different values and different social, political, and other points of view. In the process, we may find our own values taking a more firm shape. We should resist the same type of value dogmatism that we warned against on the part of editorializers, keeping an open mind and using the multiplicity of news and editorial values outlets to constantly challenge our own understanding of events and our own sense of values as responsible citizens of the world, doing what we can to learn about the facts surrounding current events, and acting effectively in accord with an enlightened moral standpoint in all our most fully informed and properly value-driven decision-making.[7]

---

[7]See Stonecipher, *Editorial and Persuasive Writing,* and Hulteng, *The Opinion Function.* A sampling of some of the best and most interesting op-ed pieces is collected by Trager, editor, *Great Events, Great Debates.*

Afterword

Journalism as a Force for Social Good

NEWS TO CHANGE THE WORLD

As I write these concluding remarks, the world seen through the eyes and ears of its journalists has witnessed an extraordinary series of events. We consider just the following three dramatic occurrences, in which news reporters played a vital role in alerting public opinion and bringing about meaningful responses leading to positive change.

London Terrorist Bombings

On July 7, 2005, four terrorist suicide bombers struck in central London, killing fifty-two people and injuring seven hundred. The coordinated attacks hit the transport system near the end of the morning rush hour. Three bombs exploded at 8:50 a.m. on underground trains just outside the Liverpool Street and Edgware Road stations and on another traveling between King's Cross and Russell Square. The final explosion occurred approximately one hour later on a double-decker bus in Tavistock Square, in the vicinity of King's Cross.

The bombers have since been identified from security videos in public transportation entrances, and their backgrounds, motivations, and support structures have been investigated. An abandoned car used by some of the bombers was discovered containing unexploded homemade bombs with nails and ball bearings for shrapnel and packed with peroxide-based explosives. As part of the ongoing investigation of the crimes, London police subsequently conducted careful examinations of the homes of the four bombers. It was learned that at least two of the bombers had recently visited Pakistan in November 2004, reportedly for religious training, where it is speculated they may have become radicalized and induced to undertake suicide bombings. All four of the young men were respectable community members, and persons who knew them were greatly surprised when informed about their acts of terrorism. Millions of persons worldwide watched on television and later followed the investigation in newspapers everywhere as the events unfolded. The riveting video and documentary content provided on television, especially by the BBC and CNN, offered detailed up-to-the-minute information, alerted Londoners to the possibility of further terrorist actions, and set up a worldwide intelligence network of individuals helping the police with information pursuant to the crimes.

Hurricane Katrina

Hurricane Katrina was the fourth hurricane and the first category 5 hurricane of the 2005 Atlantic Ocean hurricane season. It was not the most powerful hurricane of 2005, falling third behind Hurricane Wilma and Hurricane Rita in the total of eleven tropical storms that had occurred earlier during the year. It was ranked by the National Oceanographic and Atmospheric Administration (NOAA) as the sixth most powerful storm ever recorded in the Atlantic basin. It began in the Caribbean, struck land as a category 1 hurricane north of Miami, Florida, on August 25, 2005, and then, gaining momentum in the Gulf of Mexico, struck again on August 29 near Buras-Triumph, Louisiana, as a category 4 hurricane.

Eventually, the wind and water broke through the outdated levee system that was supposed to protect New Orleans from nearby Lake Pontchartrain and the Mississippi River. The levee system, which was only designed to withstand a category 3 hurricane and for which federal funding had recently been eliminated in a cost-cutting decision, gave way, flooding the city of New Orleans after it was thought the area had escaped the worst of the damage from the hurricane itself. Most of the city was inundated primarily by water from the lake. Heavy damage was also inflicted on the coastal regions of Mississippi and Alabama, making Katrina one of the most destructive and devastating natural disasters in U.S. history.

The official death toll from the hurricane was eventually set at more than 1,325, making Katrina the third deadliest hurricane in U.S. history, after the Galveston hurricane of 1900 and the Okeechobee hurricane of 1928. At the time of this writing, 6,644 other persons remain unaccounted for, 1,300 of whom are feared dead. The financial damage of the storm is estimated to be from $200 to $300 billion, which is more than twice that of the previously financially costliest Hurricane Andrew. The affected area includes more than 90,000 square miles of the United States, covering an area almost as large as the United Kingdom. On September 3, Homeland Security Secretary Michael Chertoff described the results of Hurricane Katrina, including the damage caused by the hurricane itself and the subsequent flooding of New Orleans and its priceless historic districts, as "probably the worst catastrophe, or set of catastrophes" in United States history.

The human toll in terms of loss of life, displacement, trauma, unemployment, disease and injury, including robbery, rape, assault, and murder among the survivors awaiting rescue, is a national disgrace and a testimony to the lack of planning, organization, and preparedness on the part of government officials at FEMA, the Federal Emergency Management Administration, whose politically appointed director, Michael Brown, was eventually required to step down on September 12, 2005, under public pressure. He was widely blamed for the delayed and in many ways inadequate response of the federal government to the crisis by persons who also questioned his qualifications for the position, the political nature of his appointment, and found him manageri- ally incompetent during the emergency.

What was particularly striking about news coverage of the hurricane and its aftermath was the livestream video of events taking place on the ground. Thousands of persons fled the hurricane, but those who for one rea- son or other were unable to leave were forced to resort to primitive methods of survival. In the absence of official authorities to take charge of the situa- tion, many were further exposed as victims to unscrupulous fellow citizens in what has been described as a general breakdown of society. Anyone watching the images broadcast from New Orleans or the surrounding areas of Louisiana, Mississippi, and Alabama, was struck by the pictures of Americans on rooftops or standing in lines for hours and days awaiting reception at the shelters that were hastily set up and that in turn harbored health and social dangers of their own. In Europe, where I watched the events surrounding the hurricane from afar, newscasters and commentators were astonished that the greatest nation in the world, as it is often hailed, was unprepared for the disaster and so slow in responding to the emergency that many persons were left without evacuation or resources or assistance of any kind to sustain themselves for at least three days and in many cases for several weeks.

The surge of public opinion against the American administration of the time became a second kind of hurricane. People were outraged that more was not being done and that the federal government seemed either indiffer- ent to the plight of its citizens in the affected areas or unable to help. After a time, largely due to the powerful impact of video and news reports from the scene, the government, after its initial shock, began airlifting persons, bring- ing in supplies, restoring order, working on reconnecting utilities, fighting a host of disease and health problems that resulted from the storm, and taking charge with the help of local authorities to begin the difficult process of returning persons to their homes, many of which were completely destroyed by the winds and flooding. It would be hard for anyone who lived through those times vicariously by following events in the newspapers and television not to appreciate the extent to which public outcry was a direct factor in moving the government finally to begin to take decisive action and equally hard not to credit the media with raising public awareness about the tragedy taking place in New Orleans and the surrounding area in the wake of Hurricane Katrina.

Pakistan Earthquake

Pakistan in the area around Kashmir was struck by a 7.6 Richter scale earthquake on October 8, 2005. The United States Geological Survey (USGS) issued the following Preliminary Earthquake Report from the National Earthquake Information Center at the World Data Center for Seismology in Denver, Colorado. The facts as reported by the USGS are these:

"At least 86,000 people killed, more than 69,000 injured and extensive damage in northern Pakistan. The heaviest damage occurred in the Muzaffarabad area, Kashmir where entire villages were destroyed and at Uri where 80 percent of the town was destroyed. At least 32,335 buildings collapsed in Anantnag, Baramula, Jammu and Srinagar, Kashmir. Buildings collapsed in Abbottabad, Gujranwala, Gujrat, Islamabad, Lahore and Rawalpindi, Pakistan. Maximum intensity VIII. Felt (VII) at Topi; (VI) at Islamabad, Peshawar and Rawalpindi; (V) at Faisalabad and Lahore. Felt at Chakwal, Jhang, Sargodha and as far as Quetta. At least 1,350 people killed and 6,266 injured in India. Felt (V) at Chandigarh and New Delhi; (IV) at Delhi and Gurgaon, India. Felt in Gujarat, Haryana, Himachal Pradesh, Madhya Pradesh, Punjab, Rajasthan, Uttaranchal and Uttar Pradesh, India. At least one person killed and some buildings collapsed in Afghanistan. Felt (IV) at Kabul and (III) at Bagrami, Afghanistan. An estimated 4 million people in the area left homeless. Landslides and rockfalls damaged or destroyed several mountain roads and highways cutting off access to the region for several days. Landslides occurred farther north near the towns of Gilgit and Skardu, Kashmir. Liquefaction and sandblows occurred in the western part of Vale of Kashmir and near Jammu. Landslides and rockfalls also occurred in parts of Himachal Pradesh, India. Seiches were observed in Haryana, Uttar Pradesh and West Bengal, India and many places in Bangladesh."

The toll of human suffering, loss of life and property, displacement of persons, destruction of entire villages, and the efforts of persons driven out of their homes or who have had their homes completely destroyed, has been devastating. As I write these words it is already winter in the Pakistani mountains where many of the homeless are trying to make shelter as best as they can, who have or choose no other way out. The Pakistan earthquake in its sheer magnitude vastly overwhelms the disaster in the southern U.S. Gulf Coast caused by Hurricane Katrina. The differences in economy and mechanical infrastructure of the two affected regions and the remoteness of so many of the victims in Pakistan has already affected many more people with harsher consequences in a part of the world where it seems to be immeasurably more difficult for life to rebound than in the southern United States.

Journalism can help us to better understand the scope of catastrophes by comparing facts and statistics and showing images of what is happening elsewhere in the world. On-the-scene reporters bring back video and photos that effectively give us telescopic vision. When we see what has befallen other people less fortunate than ourselves, then we may find ourselves moved by compassion to offer whatever assistance we can. Citizens of all countries who give generously to persons in need must have accurate news information about the world situation so that they can decide whether to donate and if so to what most urgent causes, however they may choose to prioritize them. They must decide who and where in the world their help might be needed most.

LESSONS FOR JOURNALISTIC ETHICS

We see in the three examples of recent major news events one of the primary ways in which journalism is expected to provide truth telling in the public interest. It has a responsibility to the general public to publish truths, the relevant facts about the world that it discovers. Journalism in particular reveals new truths when it exposes corruption, acting as an independent watchdog of the public interest, or when it reports on important historical or scientific discoveries and national and international political events, or when it mounts an editorial campaign in support of a worthwhile cause. We tend to think of the importance of journalism as a force for social good when we consider the reportage of major world events. The Watergate exposé, the Clinton scandal, the impeachment and prosecutorial procedures in the Clinton scandal, earthquakes and devastating weather events, major military operations, history-changing discoveries, of which a different selection might be made almost any news day of the year, come most frequently to mind. What these examples continue to demonstrate, no matter how often they are repeated and no matter how deeply analyzed, is that the field of journalism holds the potential for great social good.

Anyone who truly wants to help change the world should consider journalism as a way by which persons with the right talent and training can make a positive difference. That is idealism, of course. We are sometimes taught that market realities have made the ethics of journalism obsolete and that only sales, ratings, and ultimately the financial side of the news business matters. I would say to cynics about the virtues and values of good journalism that it is the height of impracticality not to invest in the ideal of contributing one's energy to any practical method that has proven itself, as journalism repeatedly has, as leading to making life better for more persons, for the betterment of the social good. Journalistic ethics is another name for quality news reporting, and it is ultimately quality news reporting that sells newspapers and news airtime. We, as members of the world community, whatever particular society we happen to belong to, discover new reasons for being grateful to news reporters every day. It is often a difficult and dangerous as well as rewarding job, and without ethically educated journalists reporting the facts, working with a sound understanding of their moral rights and responsibilities as professional journalists, our view of the world situation and many day-to-day decisions would be at the mercy of every rumor and under-informed hope or fear.

This, we recall, is what Thomas Jefferson found so indispensably valuable about a free press in the new democracy. If journalism and hence journalistic ethics was important in the eighteenth century when handwritten messages were delivered by boat, horse and coach, and then by foot, how much more so are they today, when we have such an astonishing array of media technology for collecting, editing, and delivering the news to so many receptive readers and viewers worldwide. The same is proportionately true even for the less ambitious news sources in print or electronic media aimed at a share of the total news market for persons with specialized interests. They too can avail themselves of an appropriate technology that helps give a polished appearance even to news presentations in audio, video, or printed media operating on a relatively shoestring budget. Good journalism has never been about the technology but about the questions reporters ask and their methods of seeking and then communicating the answers. An advanced technology can obviously help in this endeavor, but it is not always necessary, and it is not even always advantageous. How important is it to feature the latest gizmos on television news, divided screens with multiple participants all interacting live via monitors and on the television screen, when the moderator asks shallow uninteresting questions and does not even appear to listen to the answers?

INFORMATION HIGH TECHNOLOGY

The new technological possibilities for photojournalism raise special questions of journalistic moral rights and responsibilities and of the potential for journalism as a force for social good. The situation is similar to that by which special moral responsibilities arise from the power of other technological developments that raise previously unanticipated moral dilemmas.

Where media technology is concerned, we should not fail to take into account the fact that with these new devices more persons can be affected and in more dramatic ways by the compact size and dense data storage capacities of some of the new equipment, used in conjunction with a highly developed system of ground and satellite communications for which linkups are possible even from handheld devices. The potential for modern media to change public policy or exert an effect on an electorate, to alter opinion and thereby bring about social movements for good or bad, and to convey events as they are happening into a viewer's living room, make today's modes of journalistic communication more powerful than ever. We need look no further for examples than the three with which this Afterword begins, in the London bombings, Hurricane Katrina, and the 2005 Pakistan earthquake. Such increased power, as we have already noted, is generally accompanied by ethical judgment concerning practical affairs with proportionately amplified moral responsibilities.

The availability of miniaturized photographic equipment and powerful listening and recording devices additionally raises special issues concerning a previous chapter's topic of journalistic respect for privacy. Electronic eaves-dropping and imaging potentially make every aspect of our private lives penetrable to professional information gatherers, as much for legitimate jour-nalistic reasons as for idle curiosity. There are so many different aspects of news reporting affected by new journalistic technologies that we can only consider a limited sample. After glancing at some of the historical back-ground to the rise of photojournalism and advanced media technologies, we turn our attention first to the impact of graphic images and real-time reportage on public opinion and policy making. Then we consider questions concerning the moral responsibility for how these kinds of information sources are used. Finally, we take up the ways in which mass electronic com-munication makes possible to a greater extent than ever before the emotional manipulation of an audience and some of the moral problems presented by this unprecedented enhanced potential. We cannot afford to overlook them, because they are an essential present-day reality with an immense impact on the potential for journalism as a force for social good.

Historical Background: Twain's Congo Pamphlet

Where did such capabilities begin? What moral lessons can we draw from journalistic experience with the evolution of media technology? Historians of journalism disagree about exactly where and when photojournalism took root, but one frequently mentioned and somewhat surprising origin is the American novelist Mark Twain's photo-illustrated pamphlet *King Leopold's Soliloquy*.

Originally written in 1904 and published in 1905, Twain's sardonically written work is a fictional lament by the king of Belgium. King Leopold had vast colonial commercial enterprises in what was then the Belgian Congo in equatorial Africa. The king's wealth was based primarily on mineral exploitation in gold, diamond, and copper mining, ivory, rubber, and other commodities. These riches were extracted in mines and harvested on planta-tions that were operated as slave camps. The king was deeply involved in a lucrative slave market and human trafficking that was considered illegal in most parts of the civilized world at the time. Leopold maintained discipline at the mines and plantations through his representatives by means of torture, mutilations, and murder. The most widely practiced form of punishment in the colonies was amputation of the right hand, in which, according to Twain, brutal overseers with machetes sometimes harvested hundreds of slaves' right hands in a single day.

Twain's moral sensibilities were outraged by these occurrences. Accordingly, as he had done in some of his previous social awareness height-ening novels like *Huckleberry Finn*, *Pudd'nhead Wilson*, and *Joan of Arc*, he sought to arouse public indignation at the atrocities committed in the Congo by publishing an exposé that, some historians of journalism maintain, included for the first time photo documentation of these crimes against humanity. Twain's intention was explicitly to raise an uproar that in due course might bring such horrendous practices to an end. Twain's pamphlet not only includes remarkable photos of the victims of mutilation, children who had had their right hands amputated, it also speaks at length, in the imaginary voice of King Leopold, of what a nuisance it had become for persons to be visiting the area with the new portable cameras made by Kodak. For these, Twain has Leopold say, made it possible for the first time to collect irrefutable evidence of the mutilations that were taking place in controlling the enslaved workforce. Twain writes:

> The kodak has been a sore calamity to us. The most powerful enemy that has confronted us, indeed. In the early years we had no trouble in getting the press to "expose" the tales of mutilations as slanders, lies, inventions of the busy-body American missionaries and exasperated foreigners who found the "open door" of the Berlin-Congo charter closed against them when they innocently went out there to trade. . . . Then all of a sudden came the crash! That is to say, the incorruptible *kodak*—and all the harmony went to hell! The only witness I have encountered in my long experience that I couldn't bribe. Every Yankee missionary and every interrupted trader sent home and got one; and now—oh well, the pictures get sneaked around everywhere, in spite of all we can do to ferret them out and suppress them. Ten thousand pulpits and ten thousand presses are saying the good word for me all the time and placidly are convincingly denying the mutilations. Then that trivial little kodak, that a child can carry in its pocket, gets up, uttering never a word, and knocks them dumb![1]

The photographs included in Twain's pamphlet rejected by the original publisher that commissioned it, were deemed too violently graphic and possibly as not only offensive to delicate sensibilities but political dynamite. Of course, it was Twain's purpose to offend and outrage so that something positive might be done. The photographs make a poignant statement that shows the viewer in an undeniable way exactly what was happening in the Congo. One cannot look upon the faces of young Africans displaying the stumps of their arms where once right hands had been and not feel an

[1]Twain, *King Leopold's Soliloquy*, 2nd edition, p. 68. Useful historical and critical sources on these topics include Baldasty, *The Commercialization of News in the Nineteenth Century*. See also, Barnouw, *The Sponsor: Notes on a Modern Potentate*, and *Tube of Plenty*, 2nd ed. Further perspectives on the impact of new communications technologies on journalistic ethics are provided by Leslie, *Mass Communication Ethics*. For a flavor of the early history of journalism in the United States, see especially Barnouw, *A Tower in Babel* and the other volumes in his history of American broadcasting. Also, Meyer, *The Story of the New York Times*. Dicken-Garcia, *Journalistic Standards in Nineteenth-Century America*. Hamilton, *The Country Printer*. Nord, *Communities of Journalism*. Blenheim, *News Over the Wires*. Schwarzlose, *The Nation's Newsbrokers: The Formative Years: From Pretelegraph to 1865*. Standage, *The Victorian Internet: The Remarkable Story of the Telegraph and the Nineteenth Century's On-Line Pioneer*.

immediate sense of righteous moral anger about the misdeeds inflicted on these people at the beginning of what was supposed to be the more enlightened twentieth century.

To see is often to know and understand. Photographic images can often be worth a thousand words. They make a powerful impact on the viewer, and Twain, himself a longtime newspaperman, was well aware of their potential for influencing a world audience. He was in this sense a pioneer if not in fact absolutely the first writer to make use of the developing new technological medium of photojournalism. In Twain's era, it was the portability of the newly patented Kodak camera that made such revelations possible in journalistic communication. Today it is a wide array of miniature cameras, satellite uplinks, computer Web sites with astonishing real-time photographic capabilities, and a host of other new devices that can bring viewers almost anywhere in the world to whatever newsworthy events are occurring virtually anywhere in the world. Yet even into the early 1900s, photographs were not yet published in newspapers, but used only as the basis for drawings and etchings of what the photographs contained. This practice is in obvious ways questionable, as it brings a graphic artist in between the original photograph and the newspaper reader. Twain's pamphlet was remarkable for including photographs themselves long before this became common practice in daily newspapers.

The continuity of journalistic values against the background of an increasingly sophisticated media technology is succinctly expressed in the following account of today's international news networks, facilitated by the growth of electronic information technology. William A. Hachten and James F. Scotton, in their book *The World News Prism*, write:

> The expanded international news system is largely an outgrowth of Western news media, especially those of Britain, the United States, and, to a lesser degree, France and Germany. A world news system exists today because the peoples of Western democracies wanted world news, and the great independent newspapers, newsmagazines, news agencies, and, later, broadcast organizations have cooperated and competed to satisfy those wants and needs. Editors and correspondents, working for independent (that is to say, nongovernmental) and profit-making news organizations, have developed the traditions and patterns of providing the almost instantaneous world news upon which people everywhere have come to rely. The credibility and legitimacy that such news generally enjoys rests on its usually unofficial and independently gathered nature as well as its informational or generally objective content. The enduring ethic of Western journalism was summed up more than one hundred years ago by an editor of the *Times* of London:
>
> > The first duty of the press is to obtain the earliest and most correct intelligence of the events of the time, and instantly, by disclosing them, to make

them the common property of the nation. The duty of the journalist is to present to his readers not such things as statecraft would wish them to know but the truth as near as he can attain to it.[2]

The authors emphasize not only technological innovations, but more especially the reputation of the free press in the industrially developed world. A reputation for truthfulness is a precious commodity that is built up slowly over time, but can quickly be damaged if not adequately sustained. The point is that the basic moral values that guide the worldwide journalistic network are much the same regardless of the technology employed at any given time to gather and communicate the news. The difference, as we shall also argue, is that the new information technologies increase the potential for positive or negative effect among news consumers, additionally raising unusual problems of their own as reporters discover facts and file news stories virtually at the speed of light.

MEDIA INFLUENCING POPULAR OPINION

The impact of news reporting in the age of information technology on the shaping of foreign as well as domestic policy in a free society is attested to by Warren P. Strobel's *Late-Breaking Foreign Policy: The News Media's Influence on Peace Operations*, published, significantly, by the United States Institute of Peace. Strobel illustrates his general observations with the specific case of how opinions shifted through the effectiveness of photojournalism during the Vietnam war, brought more up to date with references to the recent war in Somalia:

> Officials, however much they might bemoan the fact, cannot conduct modern foreign policy without explaining it to, and building support among, the American public. This they do through the news media. At times, policymakers, and especially the president, through their powers of governance, can string along the news media and the American public, or deceive them about their course. But if government officials stray too far from their public mandate, the news media will sooner or later make this fact transparent, and those officials will find public opinion in open revolt, demanding, usually without

[2]Hachten and Scotton, *The World News Prism*, p. 32. The quotation continues, ibid.: "That nineteenth-century statement represents a journalistic ideal; actual practice is often much different. Some transnational media have close, compromising ties to their governments, and all independent media are subject to varying kinds of controls and influences from the corporate interests that own them. Nonetheless, the news media of Western nations have more freedom and independence to report world news, and hence more credibility, than media of other nations. And because of greater financial resources and technology, Western media have a greater capability to report world news."

great specificity, a change of policy. Thus, more than passing similarities can be found between what eventually happened in Vietnam and what happened in Somalia in the summer and fall of 1993. Somalia lacked a geostrategic rationale such as the containment of communism, which persuaded Americans to sustain costs in Vietnam long after they otherwise would have, but it had real-time television to bring the costs to the American people for evaluation much more rapidly.[3]

Strobel expresses cautious liberal optimism about the constructive role of a free press in a free society. He believes that the truth will out over attempts by the government to use the means of power at its disposal to continue a policy that when exposed by the media loses its support and can even be overwhelmingly opposed through the proper availability of information concerning an action and its effects.

The assumption is that when the public learns that something morally objectionable is being done, they will often choose the morally proper course by opposing it. To facilitate such a democratic process of oversight and checks and balances in a society, nothing provides better more effective information about the conduct of foreign policy than competent open-minded free journalistic inquiry, making use of every advantage of modern communications technology. The implication is that journalism, and especially real-time photojournalism, can be a valuable tool in foreign policy. It is in fact a two-edged sword, an instrument that cuts both ways, both for or against the government's initiatives, depending on how the media responds, how they choose to handle the presentation of facts, and the intrinsic merits of the policies on which they report. The theory is that a free press will enable a free people to reach the right decisions about what its government is doing both domestically and in its foreign policy. Journalism makes the facts available in such a compelling fashion that no government in a free pluralistic society can in the long run sustain a morally objectionable decision.

DOUBLE EFFECT OF MEDIA IMPACT ON POLICY MAKING

The implication is twofold. First, it follows that no intrinsically morally objectionable policy can be expected to remain in effect when a free press simply reports the facts. Second, the power of the press, especially in reporting on the enactment of a government's objectives, suggests, as Strobel maintains, that governments must enlist the support of journalism in order to win the popular approval for its actions that are ultimately necessary to a policy's long-term success.

Considering these inferences only reinforces the need for the press to remain free. If journalists allow themselves to be co-opted by a government

---

[3]Strobel, *Late-Breaking Foreign Policy*, p. 9.

that has become savvy to the value of positive news coverage of its activities overseas, then the freedom and independence of journalism is at risk of being undermined. On the thesis of the interdependence of a free society and a free press, the upshot threatens in turn and as a direct result also to undermine the freedom and independence of the society as a whole. As governments become increasingly aware of the impact of global photojournalism on the viability of foreign policy, there will predictably be more energetic efforts to enlist the use of the press as an instrument of the government's agenda and, hence, more pressure put on the press to surrender its critical independence.

The implication for journalistic ethics is that an additional level of responsibility belongs to everyone involved in the news industry to be vigilant against attempts to pervert the cause of journalism, news exposés, watchdog investigations, editorial evaluations, and of all information in the public interest that threatens to transform it into a vehicle for policy propaganda. The very success of photojournalism in affecting the course of American foreign policy objectives makes it a more appealing target for co-option by the power structure within a society. This, we know, is the very thing the authors of the U.S. Constitution were concerned to prevent and that they sought to counterbalance by instituting the right of a free press as a fundamental condition for the maintenance of a free society. The upshot is that the freedom of the press, especially from governmental influence, becomes even more precious and the responsibilities of journalists to preserve their independence even more urgent. This is true in light of the impressive advances in modern technological photojournalism in all areas of application, but more especially in those uses where it can either bolster or counteract a society's most important vested interests, including its involvement in foreign affairs.

IDEOLOGY IMPLICIT IN MASS COMMUNICATIONS TECHNOLOGY

An eloquent statement of the problem is offered by Neil Postman in his book *Amusing Ourselves to Death*. Postman describes the influence of popular media and recent communications technology. He emphasizes the extent to which such technology encourages if not necessitates the transformation of informative journalistic reporting and analysis, with its almost exclusive lock on viewing time and the public's imagination, into a dangerous form of entertainment. He argues that we would be naive to regard such modern media technologies as ideologically neutral:

> To be unaware that a technology comes equipped with a program for social change, to maintain that technology is neutral, to make the assumption that technology is always a friend to culture is, at this late hour, stupidity plain and simple. Moreover, we have seen enough by now to know that technological

changes in our modes of communication are even more ideology-laden than changes in our modes of transportation. Introduce the alphabet to a culture and you change its cognitive habits, its social relations, its notions of community, history and religion. Introduce the printing press with movable type, and you do the same. Introduce speed-of-light transmission of images and you make a cultural revolution. Without a vote. Without polemics. Without guerilla resistance. Here is ideology, pure if not serene. Here is ideology without words, and all the more powerful for their absence. All that is required to make it stick is a population that devoutly believes in the inevitability of progress. And in this sense, all Americans are Marxists, for we believe nothing if not that history is moving us toward some preordained paradise and that technology is the force behind that movement.[4]

The danger Postman senses, and concerning which he urges all intelligent viewers especially of televised news to be aware, is that the technology itself is not innocent. Rather, the fact that such devices and services have developed reflects a desire on the part of powerful forces in a society to have access to the beliefs and opinions of citizens. There is a reason, in other words, why particular kinds of information technologies have been funded, developed, and made available. The ominous possibility is that the technology embodies the will and effort of certain persons to reach and influence, even to manipulate, public values for their own personal political ends.

An ideal situation is one in which government, regardless of the current state of media technology, is prevented from bending a free and independent press with all the amenities of contemporary communications science at its disposal to the government's purposes. If governmental interference in news coverage is prevented, then the only domestic and foreign policy objectives a free society could realistically prosecute would be those that are acceptable to a free and well-informed electorate, which in turn are only those that a free people will rightly judge to be morally correct. If the press functions in this way, then a nation should in practice as well as principle be preserved from inflicting unjust policies on the world. It will then, as the founders of the American republic seem to have wanted, in the long run only be able to project its will upon the world in ways that are morally responsible and morally defensible.

The press can provide the necessary information to help persons of goodwill curb injustices and take a lead in helping to keep a free society's foreign policy proceeding in a morally justified direction. A free press at its best can help a nation properly guide itself, keeping it from going astray, earning the hatred and mistrust of other peoples adversely affected by a nation's actions, and degrading the moral status of the society within the global family of nations. If a free press is supposed to help prevent a free society from moral wrongdoing, then that process is thwarted and the safeguards it

[4]Postman, *Amusing Ourselves to Death*, pp. 157–158.

otherwise facilitates are undermined to whatever extent the press is made a tool of the society's propaganda effort for the sake of enlisting public support for whatever policy a society chooses to enact.

There is much work for journalists to do. Journalists will never run out of facts to report or causes to champion. The questions concerning the quality of journalism are ultimately all questions of journalistic ethics, of doing the job required of journalists in a way that reflects the time-honored values of truth and service to the public good. Every deserving person benefits when journalists perform their duties in accord with the standards of journalistic ethics, as journalists do their essential part to uphold the moral rights and responsibilities of a free press in a free society.[5]

[5] An indirect demonstration of the power of the media is found in Orson Welles's October 30, 1938 broadcast of a radio script prepared from H. G. Wells's science fiction novel, *The War of the Worlds*, for the program "The Mercury Theatre on the Air." Welles announced at the beginning of the broadcast that he was only reading a teleplay, and he repeated the same announcement forty minutes later into the program. However, in the interim between these notices, a number of listeners tuned in and had no clue that the content of the broadcast was not for real and thought that they were hearing a newscast reporting that New Jersey was actually being invaded by Martians. It is a tribute to Welles's theatrical abilities that so many people believed his storytelling was true and that the events he was describing in a more or less hysterical voice struggling to stay calm under fire were actually happening. Widespread panic and havoc were produced by the broadcast, even though in fact none of it was real. People jumped in their cars and fled for the country away from urban centers, started boarding up their houses and getting ready for an alien attack. What we can deduce from the experience is the immense capability of the media to influence the behavior of a wide range of persons when it is not handled properly and when an audience is not prepared to critically judge what it is being offered. Welles's broadcast was fiction, but it indicates how great an impact journalistic reporting over the mass media can have, whether the information is correct or incorrect, if it is irresponsibly delivered and enough people believe that it is true.

Appendix 1

Society of Professional Journalists—Code of Ethics

PREAMBLE

Members of the Society of Professional Journalists believe that public enlightenment is the forerunner of justice and the foundation of democracy. The duty of the journalist is to further those ends by seeking truth and providing a fair and comprehensive account of events and issues. Conscientious journalists from all media and specialties strive to serve the public with thoroughness and honesty. Professional integrity is the cornerstone of a journalist's credibility. Members of the Society share a dedication to ethical behavior and adopt this code to declare the Society's principles and standards of practice.

SEEK TRUTH AND REPORT IT

Journalists should be honest, fair and courageous in gathering, reporting and interpreting information.

Journalists should:

- Test the accuracy of information from all sources and exercise care to avoid inadvertent error. Deliberate distortion is never permissible.
- Diligently seek out subjects of news stories to give them the opportunity to respond to allegations of wrongdoing.
- Identify sources whenever feasible. The public is entitled to as much information as possible on sources' reliability.
- Always question sources' motives before promising anonymity. Clarify conditions attached to any promise made in exchange for information. Keep promises.
- Make certain that headlines, news teases and promotional material, photos, video, audio, graphics, sound bites and quotations do not misrepresent. They should not oversimplify or highlight incidents out of context.
- Never distort the content of news photos or video. Image enhancement for technical clarity is always permissible. Label montages and photo illustrations.
- Avoid misleading re-enactments or staged news events. If re-enactment is necessary to tell a story, label it.

- Avoid undercover or other surreptitious methods of gathering information except when traditional open methods will not yield information vital to the public. Use of such methods should be explained as part of the story.
- Never plagiarize.
- Tell the story of the diversity and magnitude of the human experience boldly, even when it is unpopular to do so.
- Examine their own cultural values and avoid imposing those values on others.
- Avoid stereotyping by race, gender, age, religion, ethnicity, geography, sexual orientation, disability, physical appearance or social status.
- Support the open exchange of views, even views they find repugnant.
- Give voice to the voiceless; official and unofficial sources of information can be equally valid.
- Distinguish between advocacy and news reporting. Analysis and commentary should be labeled and not misrepresent fact or context.
- Distinguish news from advertising and shun hybrids that blur the lines between the two.
- Recognize a special obligation to ensure that the public's business is conducted in the open and that government records are open to inspection.

MINIMIZE HARM

Ethical journalists treat sources, subjects and colleagues as human beings deserving of respect.
Journalists should:

- Show compassion for those who may be affected adversely by news coverage. Use special sensitivity when dealing with children and inexperienced sources or subjects.
- Be sensitive when seeking or using interviews or photographs of those affected by tragedy or grief.
- Recognize that gathering and reporting information may cause harm or discomfort. Pursuit of the news is not a license for arrogance.
- Recognize that private people have a greater right to control information about themselves than do public officials and others who seek power, influence or attention. Only an overriding public need can justify intrusion into anyone's privacy.
- Show good taste. Avoid pandering to lurid curiosity.
- Be cautious about identifying juvenile suspects or victims of sex crimes.
- Be judicious about naming criminal suspects before the formal filing of charges.
- Balance a criminal suspect's fair trial rights with the public's right to be informed.

ACT INDEPENDENTLY

Journalists should be free of obligation to any interest other than the public's right to know.
Journalists should:

- Avoid conflicts of interest, real or perceived.
- Remain free of associations and activities that may compromise integrity or damage credibility.

- Refuse gifts, favors, fees, free travel and special treatment, and shun secondary employment, political involvement, public office and service in community organizations if they compromise journalistic integrity.
- Disclose unavoidable conflicts.
- Be vigilant and courageous about holding those with power accountable.
- Deny favored treatment to advertisers and special interests and resist their pressure to influence news coverage.
- Be wary of sources offering information for favors or money; avoid bidding for news.

BE ACCOUNTABLE

Journalists are accountable to their readers, listeners, viewers and each other.
    Journalists should:

- Clarify and explain news coverage and invite dialogue with the public over journalistic conduct.
- Encourage the public to voice grievances against the news media.
- Admit mistakes and correct them promptly.
- Expose unethical practices of journalists and the news media.
- Abide by the same high standards to which they hold others.

The SPJ Code of Ethics is voluntarily embraced by thousands of writers, editors and other news professionals. The present version of the code was adopted by the 1996 SPJ National Convention, after months of study and debate among the Society's members.

Sigma Delta Chi's first Code of Ethics was borrowed from the American Society of Newspaper Editors in 1926. In 1973, Sigma Delta Chi wrote its own code, which was revised in 1984, 1987 and 1996.

From Society of Professional Journalists, 3909 N. Meridian St., Indianapolis, Indiana 46208, www.spj.org. Copyright © 2006 by Society of Professional Journalists. Reprinted by permission.

Appendix 2

International Federation of Journalists— Declaration of Principles on the Conduct of Journalists

DECLARATION OF PRINCIPLES ON THE CONDUCT OF JOURNALISTS

Adopted by the Second World Congress of the International Federation of Journalists at Bordeaux on April 25–28, 1954 and amended by the 18th IFJ World Congress in Helsingör on June 2–6, 1986.

This international Declaration is proclaimed as a standard of professional conduct for journalists engaged in gathering, transmitting, disseminating and commenting on news and information and in describing events.

1. Respect for truth and for the right of the public to truth is the first duty of the journalist.
2. In pursuance of this duty, the journalist shall at all times defend the principles of freedom in the honest collection and publication of news, and of the right of fair comment and criticism.
3. The journalist shall report only in accordance with facts of which he/she knows the origin. The journalist shall not suppress essential information or falsify documents.
4. The journalist shall use only fair methods to obtain news, photographs and documents.
5. The journalist shall do the utmost to rectify any published information which is found to be harmfully inaccurate.
6. The journalist shall observe professional secrecy regarding the source of information obtained in confidence.
7. The journalist shall be aware of the danger of discrimination being furthered by the media, and shall do the utmost to avoid facilitating such discrimination based on, among other things, race, sex, sexual orientation, language, religion, political or other opinions, and national or social origins.

8. The journalist shall regard as grave professional offences the following:
   - plagiarism
   - malicious misrepresentation
   - calumny, slander, libel, unfounded accusations
   - the acceptance of a bribe in any form in consideration of either publication or suppression.
9. Journalists worthy of that name shall deem in their duty to observe faithfully the principles stated above. Within the general law of each country the journalist shall recognize in professional matters the jurisdiction of colleagues only, to the exclusion of every kind of interference by governments or others.

Appendix 3
Ethics Code: Associated Press Managing Editors

CODE OF ETHICS

Revised and Adopted 1995

These principles are a model against which news and editorial staff members can measure their performance. They have been formulated in the belief that newspapers and the people who produce them should adhere to the highest standards of ethical and professional conduct.

The public's right to know about matters of importance is paramount. The newspaper has a special responsibility as surrogate of its readers to be a vigilant watchdog of their legitimate public interests.

No statement of principles can prescribe decisions governing every situation. Common sense and good judgment are required in applying ethical principles to newspaper realities. As new technologies evolve, these principles can help guide editors to insure the credibility of the news and information they provide. Individual newspapers are encouraged to augment these APME guidelines more specifically to their own situations.

RESPONSIBILITY

The good newspaper is fair, accurate, honest, responsible, independent and decent.

Truth is its guiding principle.

It avoids practices that would conflict with the ability to report and present news in a fair, accurate and unbiased manner.

The newspaper should serve as a constructive critic of all segments of society. It should reasonably reflect, in staffing and coverage, its diverse constituencies. It should vigorously expose wrongdoing, duplicity or misuse of power, public or private. Editorially, it should advocate needed reform and innovation in the public interest. News sources should be disclosed unless there is a clear reason not to do so. When it is necessary to protect the confidentiality of a source, the reason should be explained.

The newspaper should uphold the right of free speech and freedom of the press and should respect the individual's right to privacy. The newspaper should fight vigorously for public access to news of government through open meetings and records.

ACCURACY

The newspaper should guard against inaccuracies, carelessness, bias or distortion through emphasis, omission or technological manipulation.

It should acknowledge substantive errors and correct them promptly and prominently.

INTEGRITY

The newspaper should strive for impartial treatment of issues and dispassionate handling of controversial subjects. It should provide a forum for the exchange of comment and criticism, especially when such comment is opposed to its editorial positions. Editorials and expressions of personal opinion by reporters and editors should be clearly labeled. Advertising should be differentiated from news.

The newspaper should report the news without regard for its own interests, mindful of the need to disclose potential conflicts. It should not give favored news treatment to advertisers or special-interest groups.

It should report matters regarding itself or its personnel with the same vigor and candor as it would other institutions or individuals. Concern for community, business or personal interests should not cause the newspaper to distort or misrepresent the facts.

The newspaper should deal honestly with readers and newsmakers. It should keep its promises.

The newspaper should not plagiarize words or images.

INDEPENDENCE

The newspaper and its staff should be free of obligations to news sources and newsmakers. Even the appearance of obligation or conflict of interest should be avoided.

Newspapers should accept nothing of value from news sources or others outside the profession. Gifts and free or reduced-rate travel, entertainment, products and lodging should not be accepted. Expenses in connection with news reporting should be paid by the newspaper. Special favors and special treatment for members of the press should be avoided.

Journalists are encouraged to be involved in their communities, to the extent that such activities do not create conflicts of interest. Involvement in politics, demonstrations and social causes that would cause a conflict of interest, or the appearance of such conflict, should be avoided.

Work by staff members for the people or institutions they cover also should be avoided.

Financial investments by staff members or other outside business interests that could create the impression of a conflict of interest should be avoided.

Stories should not be written or edited primarily for the purpose of winning awards and prizes. Self-serving journalism contests and awards that reflect unfavorably on the newspaper or the profession should be avoided.

Ethics Code: Associated Press Managing Editors
Author: Associated Press Managing Editors
Published: January 28, 1999
Last Updated: February 17, 1999

Appendix 4

Code of Ethics and Professional Conduct of the Radio-Television News Directors Association

The Radio-Television News Directors Association, wishing to foster the highest professional standards of electronic journalism, promote public understanding of and confidence in electronic journalism, and strengthen principles of journalistic freedom to gather and disseminate information, establishes this Code of Ethics and Professional Conduct.

Adopted at RTNDA2000 in Minneapolis September 14, 2000

PREAMBLE

Professional electronic journalists should operate as trustees of the public, seek the truth, report it fairly and with integrity and independence, and stand accountable for their actions.

Public Trust: Professional electronic journalists should recognize that their first obligation is to the public.

Professional electronic journalists should:

Understand that any commitment other than service to the public undermines trust and credibility.

Recognize that service in the public interest creates an obligation to reflect the diversity of the community and guard against oversimplification of issues or events.

Provide a full range of information to enable the public to make enlightened decisions.

Fight to ensure that the public's business is conducted in public.

Truth: Professional electronic journalists should pursue truth aggressively and present the news accurately, in context, and as completely as possible.

Professional electronic journalists should:

Continuously seek the truth.
Resist distortions that obscure the importance of events.
Clearly disclose the origin of information and label all material provided by
   outsiders.

Professional electronic journalists should not:

Report anything known to be false.
Manipulate images or sounds in any way that is misleading.
Plagiarize.
Present images or sounds that are reenacted without informing the public.

Fairness: Professional electronic journalists should present the news fairly and
impartially, placing primary value on significance and relevance.
   Professional electronic journalists should:

Treat all subjects of news coverage with respect and dignity, showing
   particular compassion to victims of crime or tragedy.
Exercise special care when children are involved in a story and give children
   greater privacy protection than adults.
Seek to understand the diversity of their community and inform the public
   without bias or stereotype.
Present a diversity of expressions, opinions, and ideas in context.
Present analytical reporting based on professional perspective, not personal bias.
Respect the right to a fair trial.

Integrity: Professional electronic journalists should present the news with integrity
and decency, avoiding real or perceived conflicts of interest, and respect the dignity
and intelligence of the audience as well as the subjects of news.
   Professional electronic journalists should:

Identify sources whenever possible. Confidential sources should be used only
   when it is clearly in the public interest to gather or convey important
   information or when a person providing information might be harmed.
   Journalists should keep all commitments to protect a confidential source.
Clearly label opinion and commentary.
Guard against extended coverage of events or individuals that fails to
   significantly advance a story, place the event in context, or add to the
   public knowledge.
Refrain from contacting participants in violent situations while the situation is
   in progress.
Use technological tools with skill and thoughtfulness, avoiding techniques
   that skew facts, distort reality, or sensationalize events.
Use surreptitious newsgathering techniques, including hidden cameras or
   microphones, only if there is no other way to obtain stories of significant
   public importance and only if the technique is explained to the audience.
Disseminate the private transmissions of other news organizations only with
   permission.

Professional electronic journalists should not:

Pay news sources who have a vested interest in a story.

Accept gifts, favors, or compensation from those who might seek to influence coverage.

Engage in activities that may compromise their integrity or independence.

Independence: Professional electronic journalists should defend the independence of all journalists from those seeking influence or control over news content.

Professional electronic journalists should:

Gather and report news without fear or favor, and vigorously resist undue influence from any outside forces, including advertisers, sources, story subjects, powerful individuals, and special interest groups.

Resist those who would seek to buy or politically influence news content or who would seek to intimidate those who gather and disseminate the news.

Determine news content solely through editorial judgment and not as the result of outside influence.

Resist any self-interest or peer pressure that might erode journalistic duty and service to the public.

Recognize that sponsorship of the news will not be used in any way to determine, restrict, or manipulate content.

Refuse to allow the interests of ownership or management to influence news judgment and content inappropriately.

Defend the rights of the free press for all journalists, recognizing that any professional or government licensing of journalists is a violation of that freedom.

Accountability: Professional electronic journalists should recognize that they are accountable for their actions to the public, the profession, and themselves.

Professional electronic journalists should:

Actively encourage adherence to these standards by all journalists and their employers.

Respond to public concerns. Investigate complaints and correct errors promptly and with as much prominence as the original report.

Explain journalistic processes to the public, especially when practices spark questions or controversy.

Recognize that professional electronic journalists are duty-bound to conduct themselves ethically.

Refrain from ordering or encouraging courses of action that would force employees to commit an unethical act.

Carefully listen to employees who raise ethical objections and create environments in which such objections and discussions are encouraged.

Seek support for and provide opportunities to train employees in ethical decision-making.

In meeting its responsibility to the profession of electronic journalism, RTNDA has created this code to identify important issues, to serve as a guide for its members, to facilitate self-scrutiny, and to shape future debate.

Further Reading

Alia, Valerie, Brennan, Brian, and Hoffmaster, Barry, eds., *Deadlines and Diversity: Journalism Ethics in a Changing World*. Nova Scotia, Canada: Fernwood Publishing, 1996.

Ames, William E. *A History of the National Intelligencer*. Chapel Hill: University of North Carolina Press, 1972.

Andrews, J. Cutler. *The North Reports the Civil War*. Pittsburgh: University of Pittsburgh Press, 1955.

————. *The South Reports the Civil War*. Princeton: Princeton University Press, 1970.

Atkinson, Rick. *In the Company of Soldiers: A Chronicle of Combat*. New York: Henry Holt & Company, 2004.

Baldasty, Gerald J. *The Commercialization of News in the Nineteenth Century*. Madison: University of Wisconsin Press, 1992.

Barnhurst, Kevin G., and Nerone, John. *The Form of News: A History*. New York: Guilford Press, 2001.

Barnouw, Erik. *A Tower in Babel: A History of Broadcasting in the United States to 1933*. New York: Oxford University Press, 1966.

————. *The Golden Web: A History of Broadcasting in the United States 1933–1953*. New York: Oxford University Press, 1968.

————. *The Image Empire: History of Broadcasting in the United States from 1953*. New York: Oxford University Press, 1970.

————. *The Sponsor: Notes on a Modern Potentate*. New York: Oxford University Press, 1978.

————. *Tube of Plenty*, 2nd ed. New York: Oxford University Press, 1990.

Berger, Meyer. *The Story of the New York Times, The First 100 Years, 1851–1951*. New York: Arno Press, 1970.

Bezanson, Randall P. *How Free Can the Press Be?* Carbondale: University of Illinois Press, 2003.

Black, Jay, Steele, Bob, and Barney, Ralph. *Doing Ethics in Journalism: A Handbook with Case Studies*. Boston, MA: Allyn and Bacon, 1995.

Blenheim, Menahem. *News Over the Wires: The Telegraph and the Flow of Public Information in America, 1844–1897*. Cambridge: Harvard University Press, 1995.

Brown, Charles H. *The Correspondents' War: Journalists in the Spanish-American War*. New York: Scribner, 1967.

Christians, Clifford G., and Covert, Catherine L. *Teaching Ethics in Journalism Education*. Garrison, NY: Hastings Center, Institute for Society, Ethics and the Life Sciences, 1980.

Christians, Clifford G., Fackler, Mark, Rotzoll, Kim B., and McKee, Kathy Brittain. *Media Ethics: Cases and Moral Reasoning*, 6th ed. Boston, MA: Addison Wesley Longman, 2001.

Cohen, Elliot D., and Elliott, Deni, eds., *Journalism Ethics: A Reference Handbook*. Santa Barbara, CA: ABC-CLIO, 1997.

Cornebise, Alfred E. *Ranks and Columns: Armed Forces Newspapers in American Wars*. Westport, CT: Greenwood Press, 1993.

————. *The Stars and Stripes: Doughboy Journalism in World War I*. Westport, CT: Greenwood Press, 1981.

Crawford, Nelson Antrim. *The Ethics of Journalism*. New York: A.A. Knopf, 1924; 1969.

Crouthamel, James L. *Bennett's New York Herald and the Rise of the Popular Press.* Syracuse: Syracuse University Press, 1989.

Day, Louis Alvin. *Ethics in Media Communications: Cases and Controversies,* 4th ed. Belmont: Wadsworth Publishing, 2003.

Dewall, Gustaf von. *Press Ethics: Regulation and Editorial Practice.* Düsseldorf, Germany: European Institute for the Media, 1997.

Dicken-Garcia, Hazel. *Journalistic Standards in Nineteenth-Century America.* Madison: University of Wisconsin Press, 1989.

Dickerson, Donna Lee. *The Course of Tolerance: Freedom of the Press in Nineteenth-Century America.* Westport, CT: Greenwood Press, 1990.

Downie, Leonard Jr., and Kaiser, Robert G. *The News about the News: American Journalism in Peril, With a New Afterword.* New York: Vintage Books, 2003.

Editors of Time Magazine, *21 Days to Baghdad: Photos and Dispatches from the Battlefield.* New York: Time-Life, 2003.

Edmonds, David, and Eidinow, John. *Wittgenstein's Poker: The Story of a Ten-Minute Argument Between Two Great Philosophers.* New York: HarperCollins, Ecco Books, 2002.

Elson, Robert T. *Time Inc.: The Intimate History of a Publishing Enterprise,* edited by Duncan Norton-Taylor, 3 vols. New York: Atheneum, 1968–1986.

Fielding, Raymond. *The American Newsreel, 1911–1967.* Norman: University of Oklahoma Press, 1972.

Filler, Louis. *The Muckrakers: Crusaders for American Liberalism,* enlarged ed. University Park: Penn State University Press, 1976.

Fink, Conrad C. *Media Ethics.* Boston, MA : Allyn and Bacon, 1995.

Foerstel, Herbert N. *From Watergate to Monicagate: Ten Controversies in Modern Journalism and Media.* Westport, CT: Greenwood Press, 2001.

Franklin, Bob, ed., *Social Policy, the Media and Misrepresentation.* London, UK: Routledge, 1999.

Friedrich, Otto. *Decline and Fall: The Death Struggle of the Saturday Evening Post.* New York: Curtis Publishing, 1970.

Friendly, Fred W. *Minnesota Rag: The Dramatic Story of the Landmark Supreme Court Case That Gave New Meaning to Freedom of the Press.* New York: Vintage Press, 1981.

Fuller, Jack. *News Values: Ideas for an Information Age.* Chicago: University of Chicago Press, 1996.

Goldberg, Bernard. *Bias: A CBS Insider Exposes How the Media Distort the News.* Washington, DC : Regnery Publishing, Inc., 2002.

Gramling, Oliver. *AP: The Story of News.* Port Washington, NY: Kennikat Press, 1940.

Hachten, William A., and Scotton, James F. *The World News Prism: Global Media in an Era of Terrorism,* 6th ed. Ames: Iowa State University Press (Blackwell), 2002.

Hamilton, Milton W. *The Country Printer: New York State, 1785–1830.* Port Washington, NY: I. J. Friedman, 1964.

Hart, Jim Allee. *The Developing Views on the News: Editorial Syndrome 1500–1800.* Carbondale: Southern Illinois University Press, 1970.

Hausman, Carl. *Crisis of Conscience: Perspectives on Journalism Ethics.* New York: Harper Collins, 1992.

Hindman, Elizabeth Blanks. *Rights vs. Responsibilities: The Supreme Court and the Media.* Westport, CT: Greenwood Press, 1997.

Hohenberg, John. *Foreign Correspondence: The Great Reporters and Their Times,* 2nd ed. Syracuse: Syracuse University Press, 1995.

Hulteng, John L. *The Opinion Function: Editorial and Interpretive Writing for the News Media.* New York: Harper & Row, 1973.

Hume, David. *A Treatise of Human Nature* [1739–40]. L. A. Selby-Bigge (ed.), 2nd ed., revised by P. H. Nidditch. Oxford: Clarendon Press, 1978.

Hutchinson, Brian. *G. E. Moore's Ethical Theory: Resistance and Reconciliation*. Cambridge: Cambridge University Press, 2001.

Iggers, Jeremy. *Good News, Bad News: Journalism Ethics and the Public Interest*. Boulder, CO : Westview Press, 1998.

Jordan, William G. *Black Newspapers and America's War for Democracy, 1914–1920*. Chapel Hill: University of North Carolina Press, 2001.

Kalb, Marvin L. *The Rise of the "New" News: A Case Study of Two Root Causes of the Modern Scandal Coverage*. Joan Shorenstein Center on the Press, Politics, and Public Policy, John F. Kennedy School of Government, Harvard University, 1998.

———. *One Scandalous Story: Clinton, Lewinsky, and Thirteen Days that Tarnished American Journalism*. New York (Simon & Schuster): Free Press, 2001.

Kant, Immanuel. *Practical Philosophy*. Mary J. Gregor (ed. and trans.), Cambridge: Cambridge University Press, 1996.

Katorsky, Bill, and Carlson, Timothy. *Embedded: The Media at War in Iraq*. Guilford: Lyons Press, 2003.

Kluger, Richard. *The Paper: The Life and Death of the New York Herald Tribune*. New York: Alfred A. Knopf, 1986.

Knightley, Phillip. *The First Casualty*. New York: Harcourt Brace Jovanovich, 1975.

Knowlton, Steven R. *Moral Reasoning for Journalists: Cases and Commentary*. Westport, CT: Praeger, 1997.

Knowlton, Steven R., and Parsons, Patrick R., eds., *The Journalist's Moral Compass: Basic Principles*. Westport, CT: Praeger, 1995.

Kovach, Bill. *The Elements of Journalism: What Newspeople Should Know and the Public Should Expect*. New York (Random House): Crown Publishers, 2001.

Lambeth, Edmund B., Meyer, Philip E., and Thorson, Esther, eds., *Assessing Public Journalism*. Columbia, MO: University of Missouri Press, 1998.

Leslie, Larry Z. *Mass Communication Ethics: Decision Making in Postmodern Culture*. Boston, MA: Houghton Mifflin Co., 2000.

Levy, Bernard Henri. *Who Killed Daniel Pearl?* Hoboken: Melville House Publishing, 2003.

Lewis, Anthony. *Make No Law: The Sullivan Case and the First Amendment*. New York: Vintage Press, 1992.

Logan, Robert A., Fears, Lillie M., and Wilson, Nancy Fraser. *Social Responsibility and Science News: Four Case Studies*. Washington, DC: Media Institute, 1997.

Luxon, Norval Neil. *Nile's Weekly Register: News Magazine of the Nineteenth Century*. Baton Rouge: Louisiana State University Press, 1947.

Madingen, John. *Confidential Informant: Understanding Law Enforcement's Most Valuable Tool*. London: CRC Press, 1999.

Mander, Jerry. *Four Arguments for the Elimination of Television*. New York: Quill, 1978.

Marbut, Frederick B. *News from the Capital: The Story of Washington Reporting*. Carbondale: Southern Illinois University Press, 1971.

Merrill, John Calhoun. *Journalism Ethics: Philosophical Foundations for News Media*. New York: St. Martin's Press, 1997.

———. *The Princely Press: Machiavelli on American Journalism*. Washington, DC: University Press of America, 1998.

Merritt, Davis. *Public Journalism and Public Life: Why Telling the News is Not Enough*, 2nd ed. Mahwah, NJ: L. Erlbaum Associates, 1998.

Mill, John Stuart. *Utilitarianism* [1863]. London and New York: Longmans, Green and Co., 1907 (15th ed.).

Milton, Joyce. *The Yellow Kids: Foreign Correspondents in the Heyday of Yellow Journalism.* New York: Harper & Row, 1989.

Moore, G. E. *Principia Ethica.* Cambridge: Cambridge University Press, 1905; 2nd ed., revised, 1922; 1994.

Moore, Roy L. *Mass Communication Law and Ethics,* 2nd ed. Mahwah, NJ: L. Erlbaum Associates, 1999.

Morris, Joe Alex. *Deadline Every Minute: The Story of the United Press.* New York: Greenwood Press, 1957.

NBC Enterprises. *Operation Iraqi Freedom: The Insider Story.* Kansas City: Andrews McMeel Publishing, 2003.

Nevins, Allen. *The Evening Post, A Century of Journalism.* New York: Boni and Liveright, 1922.

Nord, David Paul. *Communities of Journalism: A History of American Newspapers and their Readers.* Urbana: University of Illinois Press, 2001.

O'Brien, Frank M. *The Story of the Sun.* New York: D. Appleton and Company, 1928.

O'Neil, Robert M. *The First Amendment and Civil Liability.* Bloomington: Indiana University Press, 2001.

Olen, Jeffrey. *Ethics in Journalism.* Englewood Cliffs, NJ: Prentice-Hall, 1988 (Occupational Ethics Series).

Olthuis, James H. *Facts, Values and Ethics: A Confrontation with Twentieth-Century British Moral Philosophy, in Particular G. E. Moore.* New York: Humanities Press, 1968.

Porter, Philip Wiley. *The Reporter and the News.* New York: D. Appleton-Century Company, Inc., 1935.

Postman, Neil. *Amusing Ourselves to Death: Public Discourse in the Age of Show Business.* Harmondsworth: Penguin Books, 1985.

Postman, Neil, and Powers, Steve. *How to Watch TV News.* Harmondsworth, UK: Penguin Books, 1992.

Powe, Lucas A., Jr. *The Fourth Estate and the Constitution.* Berkeley: University of California Press, 1991.

Pritchard, David, ed., *Holding the Media Accountable: Citizens, Ethics, and the Law.* Bloomington, IN: Indiana University Press, 2000.

Ramsey, Doug, Ellen Shaps, Dale, and Bassett, Edward P., eds., *Journalism Ethics: Why Change?* Pasadena, CA: Foundation for American Communications, 1986.

Reuters Correspondents. *Under Fire: Untold Stories from the Front Line of the Iraq War.* London: Reuters Books, 2004.

Rivers, Caryl. *Slick Spins and Fractured Facts: How Cultural Myths Distort the News.* New York: Columbia University Press, 1996.

Ruhl, Robert, and Mabel Ruhl Endowment. *Ruhl Symposium on Ethics in Journalism.* Eugene, OR: University of Oregon School of Journalism, 1986–7.

Russell, Nick. *Morals and the Media: Ethics in Canadian Journalism.* Vancouver, British Columbia, Canada: UBC Press, 1994.

Schwarzloze, Richard A. *The Nation's Newsbrokers: The Formative Years: From Pretelegraph to 1865.* Evanston: Northwestern University Press, 1989.

———. *The Nation's Newsbrokers: The Rush to Institution: From 1820 to 1920.* Evanston: Northwestern University Press, 1990.

Seib, Philip M. *Campaigns and Conscience: The Ethics of Political Journalism.* Westport, CT: Praeger, 1994.

———. *Journalism Ethics.* Orlando, FL: Harcourt Brace College Publishers, 1997.

Siebert, Fred S., Peterson, Theodore, and Schramm, Wilbur. *Four Theories of the Press: The Authoritarian, Libertarian, Social Responsibility and Soviet Communist Concepts of What the Press Should Be and Do.* Urbana and Chicago: University of Illinois Press, 1963.

Smith, Jeffery A. *Printers and Press Freedom: The Ideology of Early American Journalism.* New York: Oxford University Press, 1988.

Smith, Ron F. *Groping for Ethics in Journalism*, 4th ed. Ames, IA: Iowa State University Press, 1999.

Splichal, Slavko, and Sparks, Colin. *Journalists for the 21st Century: Tendencies of Professionalization Among First-Year Students in 22 Countries.* Norwood, NJ: Ablex Publications, 1994.

Standage, Tom. *The Victorian Internet: The Remarkable Story of the Telegraph and the Nineteenth Century's On-Line Pioneers.* New York: Berkley Books, 1998.

Sterling, Christopher, and Kittross, John. *Stay Tuned: A Concise History of American Broadcasting*, 3rd ed. Mahwah, NJ: Lawrence Earlbaum Associates, 2002.

Stevens, John D. *Sensationalism and the New York Press.* New York: Columbia University Press, 1991.

Stonecipher, Harry W. *Editorial and Persuasive Writing: Opinion Functions of the News Media.* Mamaroneck, NY: Communication Arts Books, Hastings House, 1990.

Strobel, Warren P. *Late-Breaking Foreign Policy: The News Media's Influence on Peace Operations.* Washington, DC: United States Institute of Peace, 1997.

Summers, Mark Wahlgren. *The Press Gang: Newspapers and Politics, 1865–1878.* Chapel Hill: University of North Carolina Press, 1994.

Sylvester, Robert P. *The Moral Philosophy of G. E. Moore.* Edited with an Introduction by Ray Perkins, Jr. and S. W. Sleeper. Foreword by Tom Regan. Philadelphia: Temple University Press, 1990.

Talese, Gay. *The Kingdom and the Power: The Story of the Men Who Influence the Institution That Influences the World—The New York Times.* New York: World Publishing Co., 1969.

Time Magazine Editors. *21 Days to Baghdad: Photos and Dispatches from the Battlefield.* New York: Time, 2003.

Trager, Oliver, ed., *Great Events, Great Debates: A Quarter Century of Editorial Opinion.* New York: Facts on File, 1996.

Trager, Robert, and Dickerson, Donna L. *Freedom of Expression in the 21st Century.* Thousand Oaks, CA: Pine Forge Press, 1999.

Tucher, Andie. *Froth and Scum: Truth, Beauty, Goodness and the Ax Murder in America's First Mass Medium.* Chapel Hill: University of North Carolina Press, 1994.

Twain, Mark. *Collected Tales, Sketches, Speeches, & Essays 1891–1910.* New York: The Library of America, 1992.

United States Congress, House of Representatives. *Protection from Personal Intrusion and Privacy Protection Act of 1998: Hearings Before the Committee on the Judiciary, House of Representatives, One Hundred Fiftieth Congress, Second Session on H.R. 2448 and H.R. 3224.* May 21, 1998. House Committee on the Judiciary.

Index